Studien und Texte zu Antike und Christentum
Studies and Texts in Antiquity and Christianity

Herausgeber / Editor:
CHRISTOPH MARKSCHIES (Berlin) · MARTIN WALLRAFF (Basel)
CHRISTIAN WILDBERG (Princeton)

Beirat / Advisory Board
PETER BROWN (Princeton) · SUSANNA ELM (Berkeley)
JOHANNES HAHN (Münster) · EMANUELA PRINZIVALLI (Rom)
JÖRG RÜPKE (Erfurt)

65

Charles H. Cosgrove

An Ancient Christian Hymn with Musical Notation

Papyrus Oxyrhynchus 1786:
Text and Commentary

Mohr Siebeck

CHARLES H. COSGROVE, born 1954; studied at University of Tübingen (Germany), Instituto Superior Evangelico de Estudios Teológicos (Buenos Aires, Argentina), Chicago-Kent College of Law (Chicago); M.Div. Bethel Theological Seminary; Ph.D. Princeton Theological Seminary; Professor of New Testament at Northern Seminary, Lombard, Illinois (USA) from 1984–2011; Professor of Early Christian Literature, Garrett-Evangelical Theological Seminary, Evanston, Illinois (USA), since 2011.

ISBN 978-3-16-150923-0
ISSN 1436-3003 (Studien und Texte zu Antike und Christentum)

Die Deutsche Bibliothek lists this publication in the Deutsche Nationalbibliographie; detailed bibliographic data is available on the Internet at *http://dnb.d-nb.de*.

© 2011 by Mohr Siebeck, Tübingen, Germany.

This book may not be reproduced, in whole or in part, in any form (beyond that permitted by copyright law) without the publisher's written permission. This applies particularly to reproductions, translations, microfilms and storage and processing in electronic systems.

The book was typeset by Martin Fischer in Tübingen using Garamond Premier typeface, printed by Laupp & Göbel in Nehren on non-aging paper and bound by Buchbinderei Nädele in Nehren.

Printed in Germany.

Preface

This study is a comprehensive examination of Papyrus Oxyrhynchus 1786, a fragmentary musical score of a third-century Greek Christian hymn. The fragment is housed in the collection of Oxyrhynchus papyri at the Sackler Library, one of the Bodleian libraries of Oxford University. Previous studies of the fragment – some soon after its initial publication in 1922 and others scattered over the ensuing years – have been relatively short. A number of them have made lasting contributions to our understanding of the hymn. Others are of dubious value. Specialists in ancient Greek music have provided indispensable technical studies of the text and musical notation. Students of ancient Christian thought and liturgy have offered limited and sometimes misleading discussions of the music of the text. Some areas of interest have been largely neglected or overlooked. There have been few efforts to interpret the hymn text as a theological and liturgical document of the early church.[1] Almost no consideration has been given to the social setting of the hymn in late-third-century Oxyrhynchus. Apart from a debate about whether the hymn belongs to the Greek musical tradition, there has been no detailed musical analysis of the melody.[2]

The purpose of the present study is to consolidate the gains of past scholarship and to expand on them by providing a comprehensive examination of the hymn's text, music, and social setting. An opening chapter rehearses previous research on the hymn. A second chapter is devoted to establishing the text and musical notation of the hymn, giving an account of what is visible under high magnification at points where the papyrus has been worn or damaged. Chapter three interprets the text of the hymn in the context of early Christian literature. Chapter four examines the formal and rhetorical features of the hymn. Chapter five provides a detailed musical analysis, which is undergirded

---

[1] I hasten to add that classicists have observed important parallels in the language of the hymn to the later hymns of Synesius and to hymnic and poetic motifs in other Greek literature. These are an indispensable foundation for theological and liturgical study of the hymn. The only substantial discussions of the text as a theological document are valuable comments in Wolbergs (1971, 102–11) and somewhat flawed interpretations in Meier (2004, 47–60).

[2] Mountford (1929, 176) and Winnington-Ingram (1968 [1936], 44–45) proposed interpretations of its scale type. A number of interpreters have commented on the melody's use of melisma.

by an appendix on pitch centers in ancient Greek music. Chapter six situates the hymn in the social world of third-century Oxyrhynchus.

My interest in P.Oxy. 1786 began in 1999 when I first learned that scores survive of ancient Greek music and that they include a Christian hymn. My piqued curiosity led me to study the available scholarship on this hymn, and I soon discovered that one needs a sophisticated working knowledge of ancient Greek music if one wishes to understand its melody. Acquiring that knowledge, which is largely the province of classicists, proved to be no small task. I have received personal guidance from a number of specialists who patiently answered my inquiries – Martin West (Oxford University), John Landels (formerly of the University of Reading), Andrew Barker (University of Birmingham, UK), and Stefan Hagel (Austrian Academy of the Sciences). I owe a particular debt to Hagel, with whom I have had considerable correspondence over the last decade about many aspects of ancient Greek music. His guidance has been invaluable. He also devised the Greek musical notation fonts used in this book.

I also wish to thank The Egyptian Exploration Society for permission to publish an image of P.Oxy. 1786 (and the photographic details in chapter two). I am grateful as well to the Sackler Library of Oxford University and the staff of the papyrology rooms, who made it possible for me to study the fragment there. I wish to mention in particular Daniela Colomo, curator of the collection. Other scholars have also assisted me along the way. David Martinez of the University of Chicago gave me help with questions about papyrology. Peter Parsons, for many years head of the Oxyrhynchus Papyri Project, answered my queries about Arthur Hunt's working methods.

In writing this book, I have kept in mind that its readers are likely to include both specialists and nonspecialists and that some may not be adept in one or more of the disciplines on which it draws. Hence, I have translated almost every phrase of Greek and Latin and have explained all the technical concepts of ancient Greek music (and music generally) to which I refer.

Chicago, April 1, 2011   Charles H. Cosgrove

Table of Contents

Preface V
Citations and Abbreviations XI

Chapter One: Introduction 1
Wellesz and Holleman 6
Interpretation Since Holleman 9
The Scope of the Present Study 11

Chapter Two: Text and Musical Notation 13
Transcription 14
    Key to the apparatus: 15
    Papyrus Oxyrhynchus 1786 15
    Text 15
    Notation 16
Questions Touching the Reading of the Text of P.Oxy. 1786 16
    Line 1 16
    Line 2 17
    Line 3 23
    Line 4 26
    Line 5 26
The Greek Musical Notation System 28
Questions Touching the Reading of the Notation in P.Oxy. 1786 31
    Line 1 31
    Line 2 31
    Line 3 32
    Line 4 32
    Line 5 33
The Arsis Pointing 34
The Rhythm 35

Table of Contents

Chapter Three: Interpretation of the Text 37

The Eminent Ones (line 1) 37

... Nor the Day (line 2) 38

Call for Cosmic Stillness (lines 2–3) 38
    Cosmic Stillness in the Greek Tradition 39
    The Cosmic Stillness Motif in P.Oxy. 1786 44

While We Hymn (line 3) 47

Community Hymn to the Trinity (lines 3–4) 47

The Doxological Response of the Powers (lines 4–5) 49
    Worshiping with Angels (line 4) 50
    The Doxological Formula (lines 4–5) 59

Concluding Summary 62

Chapter Four: Formal and Rhetorical Analysis 65

Genre and Form 66

The Opening of a Greek Hymn 68

Deictic Self-Referentiality 73

Deictic Self-Referentiality and the Imaginal World of the Hymn 77

Chapter Five: Musical Analysis 83

A Theoretical Introduction 84

Scales 85

Melodic Hierarchy Among Tones 89

Musical Analysis of P.Oxy. 1786 90
    The Hierarchy of Tones in P.Oxy. 1786 90
    The Unfolding of the Melody 93
    Structure and Character of the Melody 98
    Degree of Melisma 102
    Repetition and Variation 104
    Melody and Verbal Accent 108
    Use of Typical Melodic Patterns 115
    Performance 116
        Articulation 116
        Tessitura 117

Table of Contents IX

    Tempo and Phrasing 117
    Solo or Ensemble? 126
    Unison 127
    Instrumental Accompaniment 127

Chapter Six: Social Setting 129

Date of the Hymn 129

Oxyrhynchus 130
    The Size of the Christian Population 132
    Persecution of Christians in Egypt 134
    The Hymn in an Era of Sporadic Persecutions 137
    Social Status and Property of Christians at Oxyrhynchus 138
    Christian Literature 138

Greek Music Culture at Oxyrhynchus 140
    Musical Scores 141

The Purpose of P.Oxy. 1786 as a Musical Score 142

The Performance Setting of P.Oxy. 1786 146

The Greek Musical Tradition among Ancient Christians 150

Appendix: Pitch Centers and Tonal Structure in Ancient Greek Melodies 157

Pitch Centers in Monophonic Music 158

Pitch Centers in Ancient Greek Melodies 158
    Standing (Frame) Notes 159
    The Role of Mesē 160
    Dynamic (Functional) and Thetic (Positional) Note Naming 162

Applications of Greek Music Theory to the Surviving Musical Documents 164

Melodic Emphasis 167

Analysis of Greek Melodies for Pitch Centers and Tonal Organization ... 169
    Identification of Pitch Centers and Their Intervallic Relations 169
    Melodic Movement Through Pitch Centers 173
    Finals 174
    Starting Notes 176

Temporal Priority and Finality 177

Cadences 179

Conclusions 180

Tonal Analysis of Individual Scores 181
    Paean of Athenaeus, remains of 5 sections: Delphi inv. 517, 526, 494, 499 181
    Paean of Limenius, remains of 10 sections: Delphi inv. 489, 1461, 1591, 209,
    212, 226, 225, 224, 215, 214 184
    The Seikilos Inscription 186
    Invocation of the Muse 187
    Invocation of Calliope and Apollo 188
    Hymn to the Sun 189
    Hymn(s) to Nemesis 191
    P. Ber. 6870 + 14097 (1–12) 192
    P.Oxy. 1786 194

Discography 195

Works Cited 196
    Ancient Christian and Byzantine Literature 196
    Ancient Jewish Literature 199
    Other Literature of the Greco-Roman World 200
    Other Literature 202

Index of Subjects and Names 213
Index of Modern Authors 217
Index of Ancient Texts 220
Index of Greek Words 230

Citations and Abbreviations

Abbreviations for names of ancient writings are those listed in *The SBL Handbook of Style for Ancient Near Eastern, Biblical, and Early Christian Texts*, ed. Patrick H. Alexander et al. (Peabody: Hendrickson, 1999). All translations of ancient writings are the author's own unless otherwise indicated by the words, "ET by" (English translation by). The numbering of the hymns of Synesius follows the order in Gruber and Strohm (1991).

Abbreviations of series titles and other works are those listed in the *SBL Handbook*. Additional abbreviations are given below.

AAA	Acta Apostolorum Apocrypha
AKWG	Abhandlungen der Akademie der Wissenschaften in Göttingen
ANCL	Ante-Nicene Christian Library
BKA	Bibliothek der klassischen Altertumswissenschaften
BKP	Beiträge zur Klassischen Philologie
CCSA	Corpus Christianorum, Series apocryphorum
CCTC	Cambridge Classical Texts and Commentaries
CID	Corpus des Inscriptions de Delphes
CRLM	Cambridge Readings in the Literature of Music
CUF	Collection des Universités de France
DAGM	Pöhlmann and West, *Documents of Ancient Greek Music*
EH	Europäische Hochschulschriften
ET	English translation
FPCRCDCO	Fonti / Pontificia Commissione per la Redazione del Codice di Diritto Canonico Orientale
GG	Grammatici Graeci
GRM	Graeco-Roman Memoirs
LG	Lexicographie Graeci
LT	Lectio Teubneriana
MS	Mnemosyne Supplementum
OCM	Oxford Classical Monographs
PCHMTL	Publications of the Center for the History of Music Theory and Literature
PRM	Psychological Review Monographs
QSMAG	Quellen und Studien zur Musikgeschichte von der Antike bis in die Gegenwart
SAK	Studien zur Alten Kirchengeschichte
SGL	Scriptores Graeci et Latini
STAC	Studien und Texte zu Antike und Christentum
SWC	Sammlung Wissenschaftliche Commentare
WS	Wiener Studien
WS	Woodbridge Studies

CHAPTER ONE

Introduction

Upon its discovery, Papyrus Oxyrhynchus 1786 was greeted with interest by specialists in ancient Greek music, who have typically been classicists. A flurry of notices as well as substantial articles appeared immediately after its publication. Hunt, the hymn's original editor, assigned the fragment to the latter part of the third century on the grounds that its handwriting is not as late as the fourth century (*terminus a quo*) and that the grain account on the recto appears to date from the first half of the third century (*terminus ad quem*).[1] He did not supply a translation but characterized the sense of the piece as follows: "Creation at large is called upon to join in a chorus of praise to Father, Son, and Holy Spirit, and the concluding passage is the usual ascription of power and glory to the 'only giver of all good gifts'."[2]

Hunt judged the meter of the hymn to be anapaestic with a few forgivable irregularities. He interpreted the musical notation in the light of what was then known of Greek music, attending in particular to recent work on the Berlin paean by Reinach. Hunt puzzled over the use of a colon (:) in the hymn as a musical symbol and tentatively concluded that certain regularly-spaced dots were thesis-points (to mark the beginning of the thesis in the arsis-thesis scheme of Greek verse). Later studies would clarify these matters.

Wilamowitz brought Hunt's publication to the attention of German scholarship and proposed that the hymn was an adaptation of a pagan prayer into which Christians inserted, against the poetic meter, a Trinitarian formula.[3] Other scholars did not accept the suggestion that the hymnist reworked a borrowed poem, but Wilamowitz's observation that the hymn shares features with the hymnody of Mesomedes turned out to be an enduring insight. Another review of Hunt's publication came from Crönert, who noted parallels between the language of P.Oxy. 1786 and the hymns of Synesius (c. 370–c. 413), a Christian theologian and poet.[4] Further contributions to reconstructing the text and placing it in the context of Greek literature and hymnody followed in examinations of the hymn by Del Grande and Terzaghi.[5] Thanks to these

---

[1] Hunt and Jones (1922).
[2] Hunt and Jones (1922, 22).
[3] Wilamowitz-Möllendorff (1922, 317).
[4] Crönert (1922, 398).
[5] Del Grande (1923); Terzaghi (1963 [1925]).

early efforts, only reinforced by subsequent investigations, it is now apparent that the words partially preserved in line 2 express a widespread motif of cosmic stillness before an offering to a deity: σιγάτω, μηδ' ἄστρα φαεσφόρα ... ποταμῶν ῥοθίων πᾶσαι ("Let [them] be silent. Let the luminous stars not [...] of all surging rivers").

In 1922, Abert, a musicologist with training in classical philology, reviewed certain technical aspects of the hymn, commented on the musical-aesthetic quality of the song, and considered its significance for the history of church music.[6] Abert observed that scholarship in his day was becoming increasingly accustomed to thinking of ancient Jewish Temple music and its psalms as the chief source of early Christian music. The emerging view was that Greek musical influences appeared only later, when Christianity expanded into more culturally-refined circles. Abert held up P.Oxy. 1786 as counter-evidence. He then gave a sketch of Christian hymnody in Egyptian Christianity in the first four centuries, suggesting that Greek forms of Christian music may have flourished in that part of the world from an early date. In a subsequent essay,[7] Abert again joined the debate about whether ancient Christian music was Jewish *or* Greek, calling this a false opposition and insisting that in varying degrees and ways ancient Christian music was both Jewish and Greek. He emphasized once more that the music of P.Oxy. 1786 is thoroughly Greek but now characterized it as Greek music stirred by a new spirit ("das Wehen eines neuen Geistes"[8]). Abert claimed to hear a curious disquiet or agitation ("eine seltsame Unruhe"[9]) not found, he judged, in the other extant Greek musical documents. It is not altogether clear what Abert meant by this, but it sounds like an insinuation that P.Oxy. 1786 represents a special *Christian* kind of Greek music that is reaching for something more than what the pagan melodies of the other ancient scores offer.

Another 1922 essay on P.Oxy. 1786 came from the pen of Reinach, the first specialist in ancient Greek music to subject the hymn to close analysis.[10] Reinach criticized musicologists who rejected the possibility of a Hellenistic origin of church music and who posited instead a synagogue origin of ancient Christian music. The claim that the church's lost melodies developed from synagogue chants unknown to us amounted, Reinach remarked, to the old fallacy of explaining the obscure by the more obscure.[11] Like Abert, Reinach was contending with an early-twentieth century shift in scholarship away from the assumption that Christian music grew out of the Greek tradition

---

[6] Abert (1921/22).
[7] Abert (1926).
[8] Abert (1926, 287).
[9] Abert (1926, 287).
[10] Reinach (1922).
[11] Reinach (1922, 9).

to the assumption (soon to become the dominant twentieth-century view) that the Jewish musical tradition – and *not* Greek music – was the source of the church's music. According to this thesis, an unbroken musical tradition extends from synagogue chant to the liturgical chant of the Eastern and Western churches. Confident in this assumption, scholars engaged in hypothetical reconstructions of early Christian music based on the much later evidence of Jewish and Christian chant.

Reinach took P.Oxy. 1786 as an instance of ancient Greek music. He found its poetry largely unoriginal but not completely lacking in charm. He affirmed Hunt's judgment that the meter is thoroughly anapaestic, noting that the anapaestic meter was one of the most popular in the imperial period. Observing certain metrical irregularities, he also agreed with Hunt that a poet is permitted a few cola that do not quite fit the metrical scheme. Nevertheless, in an important insight, Reinach pointed out that the irregularities in the verbal metrical structure are brought into the general scheme by the music.[12] This observation would be corroborated and further refined by West. Reinach also recognized that the "points" marked the arsis ("upbeat"),[13] not the thesis as Hunt had thought; and he noted that if one follows an anapaestic interpretation of the meter, it appears that the arsis pointing gets off track beginning with the word πᾶσαι in line 4. Reinach put this down to a copyist's error.[14]

Reinach proposed his own readings of the text and notation of the hymn and presented two transcriptions, one a strict documentary version and the other a free modernizing arrangement. For the latter he supplied missing notes and words, emended the notation where he thought it suspect, and provided a piano accompaniment prepared by a conservatory-trained musician (a certain "Mlle G. R.").[15]

Not long after Reinach's contribution, Ursprung, a specialist in church music, offered comments on P.Oxy. 1786 in an article published in 1923[16] and a second in 1926.[17] Ursprung suggested that the hymn was probably sung by a solo singer and had its place at the "agape" meal or a similar setting.[18]

---

[12] Reinach (1922, 14–16).
[13] The term arsis (ἄρσις) originally referred to the lifting of the foot in dance. The thesis (θέσις) was the lowering of the foot. At some point "arsis" and "thesis" became rhythmical terms for analyzing Greek verse. For convenience, one can call them "upbeat" and "downbeat."
[14] Reinach (1922, 21–23).
[15] Reinach's two versions are reproduced side by side in Stäblein (1955, 1053–56) with conjectured bracketed notes from the second placed not in the second but in the first at the very beginning, with the notation of the second sometimes left out where it is identical with the first and sometimes included where identical, and without the piano accompaniment of the second. All of this makes a confusing impression, especially since Stäblein did not explain the different aims of the two versions.
[16] Ursprung (1923, 105–32).
[17] Ursprung (1926, 387–419).
[18] Ursprung (1923, 125–26).

The composer, he surmised, likely hailed from Alexandria and belonged to the circles of Clement and Origin.[19] Ursprung found the hymn to be Greek in character but with some novel elements. Noting that the melody piles up sequences of falling patterns, he concluded that the hymn relies heavily on stereotypical Greek solmization examples, which make it look almost like a school exercise.[20] He also contended that the hymn's melisms[21] far exceed what then-known documents of Greek music display and that its uses of "amen" sound like anticipations of Gregorian "Amen-Jubilations."[22] Moreover, the melismatic style is an "Oriental" influence that was already making itself felt to a lesser degree elsewhere in Roman-era Greek music, as evidenced by the song of Seikilos and the Berlin paean.[23] In these respects, Ursprung concluded, the hymn appears to anticipate later church song. Finally, the hymn does not adhere faithfully to its metrical scheme and fails to keep its melody anchored to the verbal accents of its text. These departures from the conventions of Greek composition are particularly evident, Ursprung suggested, in certain "ecstatic" moments in the hymn, specifically with the mention of the Holy Spirit and in the amen sequences.[24] All of this, he thought, suggested a very personal expression of praise.

Some of Ursprung's judgments require substantial modification; others do not stand up at all. With many more documents for comparison, we can now see that the melismatic style of P.Oxy. 1786 is not more pronounced than in other Greek scores from the same period. In fact, the tendency toward greater melismatic composition was a trend in Greek music of imperial times.[25] A diminishing correspondence between melody and word accents is also a feature of third-century Greek music.[26] As for the metrical problems, they stem from the inclusion of traditional Christian formulas and not from the hymnist's inability to produce lines that scan properly. Here it is important to recall Reinach's observation that the melody helps to carry the meter at those points where traditional language cannot be accommodated to the anapaestic scheme.[27]

---

[19] Ursprung (1923, 132).

[20] Ursprung (1923, 112). Ursprung found these solmization patterns in Vivell (1911, 44). Vivell, however, referred not to solmization patterns but to note-groups and tone-groups, taking his examples from the then-current collection of ancient Greek musical documents by Jan.

[21] Melisma is the setting of a single syllable to more than one note. An instance of this is a melism.

[22] Ursprung (1923, 112).

[23] Ursprung (1923, 112–13).

[24] Ursprung (1923, 113).

[25] See West (1992b, 202–4).

[26] See chapter five; also Cosgrove and Meyer (2006).

[27] West has also made this point very forcefully (West [1992a, 48]).

Chapter One: Introduction

Ursprung granted that P.Oxy. 1786 was shaped by Greek song, but he also stressed its departures from Greek music, which he associated with a spiritually bankrupt pagan world. In his view, the Christian religion arrived at just the right moment to liberate music by offering a new form – ecstatic music from the heart, inspired by the Spirit, the kind of song Paul recommends in 1 Cor 14:15 and Eph 5:18–19 (Col 3:16).[28] Ursprung was convinced that the melody of P.Oxy. 1786 surpasses in beauty all the other known Greek songs from antiquity.[29] Having worked with this hymn for some time, I agree that it presents a lovely melody. But only a highly prejudiced Christian musical imagination could hear in this hymn the *redemption* of pagan melody!

Wagner, a specialist in ancient Greek music, offered a comprehensive analysis of P.Oxy. 1786 in a 1924 article.[30] He went over much of the same terrain as Reinach, including the establishment of the vocal text and musical notation (giving his own readings after correspondence with Hunt), the influence of the Greek tonal accent on the melody, the arsis pointing, the meter of the hymn, parallels in other Greek literature to the content of the hymn, the question of the settings in which the hymn might have been sung, the mode of performance, and the musical-aesthetic qualities of the hymn. Wagner described various felicities of musical and textual construction in P.Oxy. 1786 and believed he could hear in the hymn the whole of ancient Christian faith singing down through the centuries.[31] But he judged that the piece poses technical challenges to the singer (because of the melisms) and therefore concluded that it was not a song meant for the ordinary congregation.[32] Others, having made some effort at performing the hymn, would repeat this claim about its difficulty. In my experience, however, untrained singers do not find the hymn technically difficult to sing. The melody has a compass of only an octave and none of the intervals (all diatonic) or rhythms are hard to hear or produce vocally.

Wagner found a combination of Greek and "Oriental" (Jewish, Syrian, etc.) styles in the hymn and noted points of similarity – melodic but not rhythmic – with later church melodies, explaining that these are not direct connections but common features arising from the laws of modal agreement.[33] Like Abert, he assessed the significance of the hymn for church music, stressing that it shows a close connection between ancient Christian music and the music of Greek antiquity. One feature of Wagner's analysis that caught

---

[28] Ursprung (1923, 117–20).
[29] Ursprung (1923, 114).
[30] Wagner (1924, 201–22).
[31] Wagner (1924, 211).
[32] Wagner (1924, 212). On this point Wagner was echoing Abert, who also judged that the melody of P.Oxy. 1786 is an advanced form of hymnody not meant for the "poor in spirit" (Abert [1921/22, 529]).
[33] Wagner (1924, 215n20).

special notice from other scholars was his claim that the central part of the fragment, from σιγάτω to πνεῦμα, is in dactyls. His metrical analysis has not proven persuasive.[34]

A final word from 1920s scholarship on P.Oxy. 1786 came in the form of a few very brief remarks by Mountford in a survey of ancient Greek music. Like Abert and Wagner, Mountford saw the hymn as proof that the church produced hymns in the Greek musical tradition, "making use of a type of music to which their proselytes were accustomed."[35] He went so far as to suggest that "if the early Christians at first modeled their music on Jewish Psalmody, they had abandoned it even before the more wealthy classes joined the new religion in considerable numbers."[36] This assertion hardly stands up today against all the evidence that psalmody flourished in the fourth century and was probably popular in the third century as well,[37] whether or not it was part of Christian music from the beginning.

Wellesz and Holleman

A major challenge to the original general consensus that P.Oxy. 1786 is a specimen of ancient Greek music came from Wellesz, an influential scholar in the field of Byzantine music. In a 1945 article, Wellesz gave an idiosyncratic interpretation of the rhythmical notation and claimed that the hymn was *not* a piece of Greek music at all but belonged rather to an "Oriental" musical tradition common to Jews and Syrians.[38] He suggested that the composer of the hymn probably used ancient melodic formulas that go back to the most primitive church, which, Wellesz maintained, inherited its musical tradition from Jewish psalmody.[39] He found striking melodic similarities between P.Oxy. 1786 and Byzantine hymnody, as well as Gregorian chant.[40] He even suggested that the text might be a Greek translation of a Jewish or Syrian hymn.[41] Not all church-music historians were persuaded by Wellesz's interpretation,[42] but his view has

---

[34] There is general agreement that the hymn is in anapaests throughout. See Terzaghi (1963, 670–71); Pighi (1941, 199–208); Münscher (1952); Dihle (1954, 189–90); Pöhlmann (1970, 108); West (1992a, 47–48); Pöhlmann and West (2001, 192).
[35] Mountford (1929, 178).
[36] Mountford (1929, 178).
[37] See McKinnon (1987, 7–11).
[38] Wellesz (1945); idem (1961, 152–56).
[39] Wellesz (1945, 45); cf. idem (1961, 156).
[40] Wellesz (1945, 44).
[41] Wellesz (1961, 155–56).
[42] Jammers (1962, 34–41) challenged Wellesz's interpretation of the hymn, arguing (on the basis of the earlier studies by Hunt and Wagner) that, musically and metrically, the hymn fit generally (although not fully) with what was then known of ancient Greek music.

continued to exert influence,[43] despite being rejected by specialists in ancient Greek music, including Winnington-Ingram, Pöhlmann, and West.[44]

Wellesz contended that the hymn shows metrical irregularities, if treated as Greek music, but makes perfect sense if regarded as an example of free rhythm characteristic of the "Oriental" style. In support of this argument he gave a reading of the rhythmic notation of the hymn that no specialist in Greek music has accepted. Moreover, both previous and subsequent specialists in Greek poetry have shown that the composer took care to construct the hymn in quantitative Greek meter (anapaests throughout).[45] Wellesz also pointed to the hymn's rich flow of melody in its melisms, which he regarded as uncharacteristic of Greek music but typical of the Oriental style. Although he was aware that the Berlin paean (P.Ber. 6870) shows a similar melismatic style, he discounted this evidence. Today we possess many more Greek musical documents from the imperial period, which show increasing use of melisma as a Roman-era trend. Wellesz also discovered a use of repeated melodic formulas linked by intervening melodic passages of varying length. This reminded him of the use of melodic formulas in Byzantine and Gregorian chant. This observation, too, easily gives a misleading impression. It is possible that the hymn uses formulas, which would not be surprising or necessarily un-Greek.[46] Moreover, exact and varied repetition of patterns separated by intervening material is also typical of other Greek musical documents.

The next important study of the hymn appeared in 1971. In an anthology of gnostic and early Christian psalms and hymns, Wolbergs presented a critical text of the lyrics and provided the most comprehensive discussion to that time of parallels in other ancient liturgical texts and literature (both pagan and Christian).[47] This examination led him to propose that the hymn was intended for use in the eucharistic service. As for the musical notation, Wolbergs

---

[43] The continuing influence of Wellesz can be seen in Crocker's treatment of P.Oxy. 1786 in what is otherwise an excellent study of Gregorian chant. Although Crocker observed "a few indications of verbal or musical rhythm," he made no specific mention of the rhythmic signs in the musical notation and in his transcription set up the hymn like a chant, ignoring the rhythmic notation (Crocker [2000, 71–72]). The influence of Wellesz also dominates other recent studies of the hymn: Tripp and Wheeler (1997); idem (1989); and Meier (2004, 41–67). Tripp and Wheeler overlooked West's work and relied heavily on Wellesz (1945) and Leclercq (1937). Meier was apparently also unaware of West's trenchant critique of Wellesz and concluded that the hymn shows close affinities with Gregorian chant, as opposed to ancient Greek music. He identified these Gregorian affinities as the hymn's "expressive" melodic style (melisms, rhythmic "carelessness," and intervallic leaps), use of a diatonic scale, and construction with internally-related phrases and cadences (Meier [2004, 62–63]). This is almost pure Wellesz, and all of it is misleading as an argument that the hymn's melodic character is more proto-Gregorian than Greek.

[44] The following critique of Wellesz reflects the work of Winnington-Ingram and West, whose studies of the hymn are presented in greater detail below.

[45] See the authors listed in n. 34 above.

[46] See West (1992b, 194).

[47] Wolbergs (1971, 13–14, 100–111).

deferred to Wellesz, observing that, although early studies placed the hymn in the Greek tradition, Wellesz had shown a more immediate influence from the musical culture to which Hebrew chant belongs, a musical tradition adopted by the church and leading directly to Byzantine and Gregorian chant.[48]

A year after Wolbergs' study, Holleman restated and amplified Wellesz's position on the hymn.[49] According to Holleman, the church fathers rejected Greek music, the reason being that Greek music was "beat" music. At least that was the case by Hellenistic and Roman times, Holleman explained, when the rhythm of Greek music had developed from a quantitatively-based meter to a stress-based meter with dominant beats being accented by rhythm instruments such as castanets and clappers. "It is precisely this Hellenistic element," he said, "the 'beat'-character of music all over the Roman Empire, that for centuries long was combated by ecclesiastical authorities East and West as endangering liturgical music and poisoning the Christian mind."[50] By contrast, he argued, the rhythm of early Christian music, out of which Gregorian chant developed, was neither stress-based nor quantitative. It was unstressed and free of rhythm because note values tended to be equal.[51]

Siding with Wellesz, Holleman also claimed an "Oriental" origin for P.Oxy. 1786 and cited in support a short review of Wellesz's 1945 article. The review was by Winnington-Ingram, a leading specialist in ancient Greek music.[52] Winnington-Ingram had expressed a degree of openness to Wellesz's theory in a 1954 article for *Grove's Dictionary*;[53] but he had changed his mind by the time of his subsequent review, in which he allowed that Wellesz "may be correct" but also insisted that the song "should be interpreted in the light of our other Greek evidence" and chided Wellesz for not taking seriously that the musical notation is Greek.[54] Despite the tenor of Winnington-Ingram's review, Holleman construed it as support for the possibility of a non-Greek, Syrian origin for the hymn. In a more pointed footnote in another study, Winnington-Ingram spoke more plainly:

When [Wellesz] comes to transcribing the hymn, he interprets the rhythmical notation entirely without reference to the evidence of the other fragments of Greek music. Yet this is the relevant evidence. The words are Greek, the metre is Greek, the melodic notation is Greek; so is the rhythmical notation, and it is used consistently with anapaestic interpretation of the metre.[55]

---

[48] Wolbergs (1971, 101).
[49] Holleman (1972, 1–17).
[50] Holleman (1972, 9).
[51] Holleman (1972, 13–17).
[52] Winnington-Ingram (1958, 10).
[53] Winnington-Ingram commented on P.Oxy. 1786 that "its affinities are perhaps with Asiatic rather than with Greek music" (Winnington-Ingram [1954, 780]).
[54] Winnington-Ingram (1958, 10).
[55] Winnington-Ingram (1955, 80–81n2).

Evidently, Holleman did not know this footnote and probably would not have been deterred by it because he was convinced that he had an ally in Pöhlmann, another specialist in Greek music.

Holleman adduced comments from a 1960 study in which Pöhlmann interpreted the metrical irregularities, the melismatic tendencies, and an absence of correspondence between melody and word accent in P.Oxy. 1786 as influences of Hebrew religious music on an author who used Greek models but had no ear for Greek.[56] A decade later, however, when a more seasoned Pöhlmann brought out his critical edition of Greek musical documents (a 1970 publication apparently unknown to Holleman), Pöhlmann was of a different mind. Although he repeated his view that the composer did not possess a sure-footed sense for quantitative meter or an ear for the Greek tonal accent, he no longer claimed these as evidence of un-Greek influences – probably because he now recognized them as tendencies of late Greek music.[57] Moreover, Pöhlmann observed that Winnington-Ingram had offered a secure metrical-rhythmic analysis of the hymn and had shown, against Wellesz, that the piece fits closely with the other Greek musical documents.[58]

Like Wellesz, Holleman disregarded the rhythmic notation. His transcription stripped the hymn of rhythm, making almost all note values equal in duration and dispensing with the bar lines that other transcribers of Greek music use to represent metrical-rhythmical regularity. Faced with the fact of the text's use of Greek musical notation, he argued that the hymn is "a demonstration of the inadequacy, and at least as far as rhythmical signs, of the fundamental error of using the existing Greek notation for Christian music."[59]

Holleman was not a specialist in ancient Greek music and seems to have had only a passing knowledge of it. What struck him as obvious is hardly evident when one gives the rhythmic notation its due and makes a close comparison of P.Oxy. 1786 with other ancient Greek musical documents of the imperial period. When that is done, it is hard to see how rhythmic and melodic signs that yield a perfectly good ancient Greek melody, reflective of other Greek music of the period, demonstrate that Christian song was too un-Greek to be expressed in Greek musical notation.

Interpretation Since Holleman

In the nearly forty years since Holleman's article, P.Oxy. 1786 has been largely neglected by church historians and specialists in ancient Christian music,

---

[56] Pöhlmann (1960, 47).
[57] Pöhlmann (1970, 108).
[58] Pöhlmann (1970, 109).
[59] Holleman (1972, 11).

receiving at most a short paragraph or two here and there. Quasten dealt briefly with the artifact in his erudite treatment of music in Christian and pagan antiquity. In a footnote to his comments on P.Oxy. 1786 in the second German edition of that work (1973), Quasten reported on the question whether the hymn is Greek or Jewish / Syrian, adducing a list of opinions that included those of Wellesz and Holleman along with Holleman's references to Winnington-Ingram and Pöhlmann. Although Quasten did not take a stand on the issue, his list left the impression that scholarship was leaning toward Wellesz.[60] As we have seen, by the early 1970s scholarship was divided in a peculiar fashion, with specialists in ancient Greek music regarding P.Oxy. 1786 as a piece of Greek music and historians of early Christian music holding that it is not Greek but Jewish / Syrian.

Following the original editor of P.Oxy. 1786, Quasten interpreted the text of the hymn as expressing a frequent theme of the church fathers, namely, that all creation should praise God with hymns. He was apparently unaware of the opinion, based on literary parallels and a different reconstruction of the text and syntax of lines 2 and 3, that the hymn uses a widely-attested motif of Greek literature and hymnody in calling for various cosmic elements to be *still* before an offering or divine epiphany.[61] Literary and syntactical considerations now make it almost certain that the hymn employs this cosmic stillness motif,[62] which strengthens the impression that we have a piece of Greek Christian music (and a precursor of the hymns of Synesius, some of which display the same motif[63]).

The first edition of the *New Grove Dictionary of Music and Musicians* (1980) included an article on the music of the Christian church by Hannick, who briefly surveyed scholarship on P.Oxy. 1786, finishing with Holleman's essay.[64] Hannick termed the hymn an "isolated attempt to record a melody" and concluded that even if Holleman's theory about the hymn is "exaggerated," nevertheless, "it must be admitted that this fragment does not prove that Christians in 3rd-century Egypt used Greek notation, nor [*sic*] that the melody of this hymn was typical of early Christian music."[65] Hannick's characterization of the document as an "isolated attempt to record a melody" is an unfortunate formulation. The word "attempt" echoes Holleman's misguided

---

[60] Quasten (1983 [1973], 105n59b).
[61] Pöhlmann (1970, 107); Wolbergs (1971,13–14, 106–8); Del Grande (1923, 173–9); Terzaghi (1963, 673–74); Pighi (1941, 214–15).
[62] On the literary parallels, see West (1992a, 48–50). A syntactical consideration pointed out by Wolbergs (1971, 106) is that μηδέ is not postpositive and therefore should be construed not with σιγάτω ("Let it / them be silent") but with what follows (where stars and rivers are mentioned).
[63] Synesius, *Hymn.* 1.72–85; 2.26–43.
[64] Hannick (1980, 367–68).
[65] Hannick (1980, 368).

notion of a failed experiment, and "isolated" suggests the dubious reasoning that if only one fragment of notated Christian music has been found, only one such score ever existed. We will consider this question in detail in chapter six.

McKinnon wrote the article on music in the early church for the second edition of the *New Grove Dictionary of Music and Musicians*. In a few remarks about P.Oxy. 1786, he recognized the hymn as a piece of Greek music but insisted that no implications could be drawn from it for our knowledge of ancient Christian music generally or even music in Greek Egyptian Christianity.[66] This judgment left the impression that the hymn was likely as not an isolated instance of a Christian hymn in a Greek musical style, as Hannick had suggested.

The most important treatment of the hymn after Holleman was a 1992 study by West, a specialist in ancient Greek music who in the same year published a superb history of ancient Greek music and went on to become Pöhlmann's co-editor for a revised critical edition of the ancient Greek musical documents.[67] If Winnington-Ingram had been tactfully skeptical about Wellesz's interpretation, West was direct and emphatic. He showed how the composer accommodated metrically-difficult Christian formulas in two ways.[68] First, at some points the hymnist let the music carry the meter (an observation Reinach had also made). At other points the hymnist shaped the traditional formulae to fit the meter. West also presented an array of Greek parallels to the hymn's description of cosmic silence to show that the motif has "impeccably Hellenistic credentials."[69] As for the music of the hymn, West corrected a number of Wellesz's factual misstatements and demonstrated how neatly P.Oxy. 1786 fits into the Greek music of its time and place. Having made the case that every feature of the fragment can be illustrated from the extant scores of second- and third-century Roman Egypt, West concluded that "musically speaking the hymn stands squarely in the Greek tradition."[70]

The Scope of the Present Study

Papyrus Oxyrhynchus 1786 is the only bit of ancient Christian music yet to come to light, preceding in time the earliest extant manuscripts of Gregorian chant that contain musical notation (neumes) by six centuries.[71] Hence, it

---

[66] McKinnon (2001, 805).
[67] West (1992b); Pöhlmann and West (2001).
[68] West (1992a, 47–54).
[69] West (1992a, 49).
[70] West (1992a, 54). The tendency of a past generation of early-church historians to assume that early-Christian music grew out of Jewish music and not Greek music has recently been addressed by Porter, who has also taken note of West's work on P.Oxy. 1786 (Porter [2000]).
[71] See, for example, Jeffrey (1982).

warrants a comprehensive treatment that builds on the scholarship of specialists in ancient Greek music and also considers the hymn as an important artifact of church history. Because P.Oxy. 1786 is a short fragment and derives from the end of the history of ancient Greek music as documented by surviving scores, it has not been a principal focus of students of ancient Greek music, who have naturally been more interested in reconstructing what can be known of music in the Classical era (the music of the great dramatists, the music that caused debate in Greek philosophy, the music for which the philosophers such as Aristoxenus sought to provide general theories, and so forth), in the Hellenistic era as represented by two substantial multi-sectioned scores from a cultic ceremony at Athens in 127/128 B.C.E. (the Delphic paeans), and in the Roman era as represented by the composer Mesomedes. Nevertheless, specialists in ancient Greek music have made the most important contributions to understanding the hymn. As for historians of ancient Christian liturgy and music, whose principal scholarly interests naturally include an artifact such as P.Oxy. 1786, they have treated the hymn only occasionally and often with an insufficient grasp of ancient Greek music. The challenges of mastering the technical scholarship on the subject have no doubt deterred some from exploring the hymn for themselves.

As a specialist in ancient Christianity, a musician, and one who has devoted nearly a decade to gaining a serious acquaintance with the scholarship on ancient Greek music, including familiarity with the surviving scores, I aim to provide a comprehensive examination of P.Oxy. 1786 as an expression of ancient music and early Christian faith. Hence, the present work engages the overlapping interests of classical philologists and specialists in ancient Greek music, who wish to understand the hymn as an example of Greek music from the late Roman era. It also addresses the interests of church historians, for whom the hymn provides an example of early Christian devotional piety. The study speaks to students of church music history as well, for whom the hymn presents the most ancient surviving instance of a notated Christian melody. One hopes that in further discoveries, perhaps even in the examination and publication of yet unedited papyri from past discoveries, another such hymn will come to light. Fragments of ancient Greek musical scores do continue to appear.[72] But for now, P.Oxy. 1786 is our only example of pre-Gregorian Christian music. For that reason alone it deserves a comprehensive treatment.

---

[72] Since the publication in 2001 of Pöhlmann and West's *Documents of Ancient Greek Music* (*DAGM*), which included quite a number of fragments of Greek music not known to Pöhlmann when he brought out his edition of the scores thirty years earlier (Pöhlmann [1970]), two other bits of ancient Greek music have been published: P.Louvre E 10534 (Bélis [2004]) and P.Oxy. 4710 (Yuan [2005]).

CHAPTER TWO

Text and Musical Notation

The remains of the hymn score are found on the back of an account of grain deliveries in which a number of towns of the Oxyrhynchite nome appear. The hymn text is oriented at right angles to the text of the grain account so that the left-hand border of the hymn is on the opposite side of the place where the grain account reaches the bottom border of the papyrus roll. The hymn was inscribed in this relation to the papyrus so that the scribe could write out the text parallel with the fibers. What goes before and after the hymn is an undeterminable amount of papyrus constituting the length of the roll or at least a portion of the roll cut out to accommodate the hymn and whatever text(s), if any, may have preceded or followed it.

The fragment is 29.6 × 4.8–5 cm.[1] All sides are ragged. We do not have the beginning or end of the grain account, and the length of the original roll is not known. The grain account shows its top and bottom margins, however, which tells us that the original width of the roll was just over 29.6 cm. The manuscript lines of the hymn extend across this entire width. After the double amen in line 5, there is blank space, indicating that the hymn did not continue on. The top of the fragment is damaged, making it uncertain whether ms. line 1 is the first line of the hymn.

Hunt, the hymn's first editor, was uncertain whether a single hand produced the text and the musical notation.[2] Pighi saw the same hand in both.[3] The script exhibits moments of cursive but is generally a somewhat literary hand,[4] upright with rather nicely formed letters.

In the course of preservation, bits of cellophane tape were applied at two points.[5] These are not visible in the photograph of the original edition but were present when the digital image was made. Presumably they were added, as an aid to preservation, at some point between 1922 and the early 1970s, when the

---

[1] This is Hunt's original measurement, with which my own measurement tallies. See Hunt and Jones (1922, 21).
[2] Hunt and Jones (1922, 21).
[3] Pighi (1941, 192).
[4] Hunt and Jones (1922, 21).
[5] The taping is between ποταμῶν and ῥοθίων in the middle of the fragment and in the lower left-hand corner at the beginning of ms. line 5.

papyrus was glassed.[6] The currently-available digital photographic image was made in the 1990s. Comparison of the original photograph with the current state of the papyrus shows that there has been some deterioration, particularly in the lower left-hand corner, at the beginning of ms. line 5 of the text.

Transcription

The following transcription of the text and musical notation is based on examination of the original manuscript in the papyrology rooms of the Sackler Library at Oxford. A digital photographic image of the fragment is available at a website of Oxford University devoted to the Oxyrhynchus Papyri. In preparing the transcription I have given special consideration to the judgments of Hunt and West. From what I can establish, they are the only two past commentators on the papyrus who viewed it first-hand. Hunt examined the fragment for the 1922 original publication. He looked at it again in the course of answering questions from Wagner. Wagner included Hunt's responses in a 1924 article.[7] West made a fresh examination of the fragment for *Documents of Ancient Greek Music*, which he and Pöhlmann published in 2001.[8] In preparation for the present commentary, I also studied the papyrus in Oxford in the summer of 2007. West in his examination (and I in mine) enjoyed one important technical advantage over papyrologists in Hunt's day, namely, the use of a binocular microscope.[9]

Wagner, relying only on a photograph, dissented from Hunt's readings at a number of points, even when Hunt confirmed his original readings after examining the fragment afresh in response to inquiries from Wagner. I regard these readings by Wagner as extremely dubious and therefore have not included them in the apparatus, although I discuss a number of them below.

---

[6] According to Daniela Colomo, curator of the Oxyrhynchus papyri at Oxford, R. A. Coles glassed the papyrus at the beginning of the 1970s (personal correspondence). No official record of the conservation of individual papyri exists; hence, it is unknown when the tape was applied to P.Oxy. 1786.

[7] Wagner (1924, 202n4).

[8] Pöhlmann and West (2001, 192).

[9] Microscopes of various kinds were around in Hunt's day but apparently were not then used in the study of papyri. In a private communication to me, Peter Parsons, for many years head of the Oxyrhynchus Papyri Project, gave the following account of what is known on this subject: "We have no formal account of Hunt's working methods, but I have been checking the oral tradition with my colleagues, and we agree that it's very unlikely that he used a microscope. The same was true, in the next generation, of E. Lobel (who recommended reading papyri after a snowfall, since that produced a fine white light), and I think also of my old teacher H. C. Youtie at Ann Arbor, whose magnifying glass I now own. This may be a matter of habit, but it's true also that the binocular large-field microscopes recently available are much more useful than the older types, since they allow the paleographer to see each letter in a wider comparative context."

Key to the apparatus:

DAGM (2001) = Pöhlmann and West (2001)
Hunt (1922) = Hunt and Jones (1922)
Hunt (1924) = Hunt's readings based on reexamining the fragment in response to queries by Wagner, as reported in Wagner (1924)
West (2001) = West's readings for *DAGM* (2001)
All other references are keyed to the bibliography.

Notation contained in brackets [ ] indicates a conjecture.
Small question mark (?) adjacent to slur mark indicates a conjecture.
Large question mark (?) indicates an indecipherable note symbol.
Sublinear dot indicates uncertainty.

Papyrus Oxyrhynchus 1786

```
    [                                     ][    ]⌣[                              ]
1  [    space for about 31 letters and 5 lexical spaces   ] ομου  πασαι τε θεου λογιμοι δε...?ι....?[...]

    [                                      Ι Ζ ΙΖ ΟΦ CΦ Π Φ  :Ζ Ι  Ζ  ΖΕ  Ζ  ΖΤ Ι Φ [  ]Ι
2  [       space for 28 letters           ο]υ ταν η ω   σι γατω μηδ αστρα φαεσφορα χ[..]δε–

    [                                    ] Ζ Ι :ΖΕ : Ι[Ζ]Ζ ΖΟ ΙΖ ΖΙ Π Φ :ΖΙ Φ :ΟΖ R
3  [σ]θων, [εκ]λειπ[οντων] ρ[ιπαι πνοιων, πηγαι] πο τα μων  ρο θι ων πα σαι    υμ νουντων  δη μων

   [  ]Ç C Φ CR :ΦC Φ ΦΖ :[ΖΕ]Ζ Π ΖΦ Φ  Φ?Ο  ΟΟ Ο ΟΙ Ι  Ζ:ΖΕΖ ΖΙ ΙΖ  Ζ  Ζ  ΖΟ Φ
4 [π]ατε ρα χ'υιον  χ'α γι ον  πνευμα    πα σαι δυναμεις επιφανουντων  α μην  α μην κρατος αι νος

  ??? [ ] :ΦCR Φ  C  :COΖ  ΖΙ  Ι Ο    Ζ Ç    ΖΙ ΙΖ  ΟΦ CΦ COΖ :ΖΙΖ   ΟΦ CΦ
5 [αει και δο  ξα  θε  ω  ] δ[ωτ]η[ρι]  μονω[ι] πα[ν]των αγα θων  α  μην    α μην
```

Text

1 [31 letters] Hunt (1922), West (2001) *Supplement*: [Σὲ πάτερ κόσμων, πάτερ αἰώνων, μέλπωμεν] ὁμοῦ [=32 letters + lexical spaces] Pöhlmann (1970) τε̣ Hunt (1922), West (2001) α̣ . [...] . [..]α̣ρ Hunt (1924), δε̣[.].[.]α̣ι[ ]... γ West (2001)   **2** [28 letters] Hunt (1922) *Supplements:* [ὅσα κόσμος ἔχει πρὸς ἐπουρανίων ἁγίῳ σελάων πρ]υτανήῳ Pighi (1941), [οὐ τὰν δείλαν ο]ὐ τὰν ἠῶ Reinach (1922), [οὐ νύκτα (⌣ –) ο]ὐ τὰν ἠῶ *DAGM* (2001) χ[..]δε or ζε West (2001)   **3** [σ]θων Hunt (1922), West (2001) [.] . λε̣ι?[.....]ρ[+ 13 letters] Hunt (1922), [ἐκ]λειπ[όντων] ρ[West (2001) *Supplements*: [χ'ὑψηλῶν ὀρέων κορυφαὶ μηδ' ὠκεανός καὶ τῶν] ποταμῶν ῥοθίων παγαί Reinach (1922), [ἀπο]λ̣ε̣ι[πόντω]γ ῥ[αδιναὶ προχοαί] ποταμῶν ῥοθίων πᾶσαι Pighi (1941), [ἀπ]ο̣λ̣ε̣ι̣π̣[όντων] ῥ[ιπαὶ πνοιῶν, πηγαὶ] ποταμῶν ῥοθίων πᾶσαι Pöhlmann (1970), [ἐκ]λειπ[όντων] ρ̣[ιπαὶ πνοιῶν, πηγαὶ] ποταμῶν ῥοθίων πᾶσαι *DAGM* (2001)   **5** δ̣[ωτ]ῆ[ρι] μόγῳ πάντων Hunt (1922), West (2001 [μονωι]) *Supplements* (preceding δωτῆρι): [νῦν κεὶς αἰῶνας (or δόξαν νῦν κἀεὶ) δίδομεν] Hunt (1922), [δόξ' εἰς αἰεὶ βασιλῆι θεῷ] Reinach (1922), [νῦν κ' εἰς αἰῶνας ἀμήν ἀμήν] Wagner (1924), [ἀεὶ καὶ δόξα θεῷ] Pighi (1941)

Notation

1 2 hyphens West (2001)   **2**]Ż Hunt (1922), ?̣ Ż West (2001) Ọ̄Φ̄C̄Φ̄ Hunt (1922, hyphens 1924), Ō̇Φ̄ C̄Φ̄ West (2001)   **4** C̣ Hunt (1922), Ȯ West (2001) Φ̄Ż Hunt (1922, 1924), West (2001) Ī[.] Hunt (1922), ?̣?̣ West (2001) Φ Ż Hunt (1922), Φ? West (2001) Ō̄I Ȯ Hunt (1922 with printing error), Ō̄I İ Hunt (1924, corrected), West (2001) ŻO Hunt (1922), Z̄Ȯ West (2001)   **5**] : Ç̄Ç̄ Φ̄C̄R Hunt (1922), ? R̄ [ ] : Φ̄C̄R West (2001) C̄Ȯ̇Ż Hunt (1922), : C̄Ȯ̇Ż West (2001)

Questions Touching the Reading of the Text of P.Oxy. 1786

There is general agreement that the hymn text is in anapaests,[10] and the following discussion assumes anapaests as the most workable metrical scheme.[11]

Line 1

A missing portion of the papyrus at the beginning of line 1 could have accommodated about 31 letters and 5 lexical spaces (based on line 2). It is possible that additional lines preceded line 1.

Pöhlmann suggested a possible opening by borrowing language from Clement of Alexandria's hymn at the end of *Paedagogus* (line 59) and from the fourth-century hymn writer Synesius (*Hymn*. 1.266–67): Σὲ πάτερ κόσμων, πάτερ αἰώνων, μέλπωμεν (32 letters, 5 lexical spaces).[12] It is possible that ὁμοῦ goes with what precedes, in which case Clement's μέλπωμεν ὁμοῦ works, contextually and metrically, and the language from Synesius helps complete the space with a fitting opening that satisfies metrical requirements. It should be noted, however, that the language borrowed from Clement and Synesius does not occur in the opening lines of their hymns.

ὁμοῦ πᾶσαι τε θεοῦ λόγιμοι δε

Taken together, ὁμοῦ and πᾶσαι might modify a preceding noun. In that case, θεοῦ goes with that preceding construction (because of the postpositive τε) and λόγιμοι with something that follows. Since λόγιμος was treated sometimes as a 2–1–2 adjective and sometimes as a 2–2 adjective, it could go with πᾶσαι (πᾶσαι τε θεοῦ λόγιμοι). In that case, it does not stand on its own as a substan-

---

[10] Terzaghi (1963, 670–71); Pighi (1941, 199–208); Münscher (1952, 209–13); Dihle (1954, 189–90); Pöhlmann (1970, 108); West (1992a, 47–48); Pöhlmann and West (2001, 192).

[11] A presentation of an anapaestic scanning of the hymn text compared with the rhythm of the musical notation is provided in a separate section below.

[12] Pöhlmann (1970, 106 [apparatus]).

Chapter Two: Text and Musical Notation 17

tival adjective. It is just as possible that λόγιμοι modifies a subsequent missing noun. Wagner suggested τάξεις in view of the association of this word with angelic beings.[13] But a first-hand inspection of the manuscript in magnification rules out a word beginning with τ. A visible bit of ink suggesting a flat base points to δ or ζ. What follows is very faint and the papyrus is partially damaged; stray marks are difficult to distinguish from ink. The letter is not υ (which excludes the otherwise attractive possibility of δυνάμεις) or ο (which eliminates Pighi's δοῦλαι[14]) or α (which rules out δ'ἀρχαι). West guessed δε[,[15] which might suggest δεσπότιδες, meaning "queens."[16] That word would fit the space[17] and perhaps the sense, if the very uncertain letter before the apparent iota could be tau. Filling the word out as δεσπότιδες is worth contemplating only because no other word seems to meet the requirements of the remains of ink, the grammar, and conceivable possibilities for the sense. Perhaps heavenly entities of some kind – the moon and evening stars (regarded as feminine by Ptolemy) – are referred to poetically as "eminent queens."[18] In view of the uncertainties, however, I put no confidence in this guess.

If πᾶσαι goes with a preceding substantive, then λόγιμοι could modify either a masculine or a feminine noun, or it could stand on its own as a substantival adjective.

Line 2

υ ταν ηω

Hunt proposed that these letters are a misspelling of the end of the word πρυτανείωι.[19] The word πρυτανεῖον means a chief place, such as a town hall, center, or other central or sacred locale. If the word is used metaphorically here, it might refer to some heavenly place, such as the divine throne-room.

---

[13] Wagner (1924, 216). Wagner thought he saw a trace of an alpha and pointed to a fourth-century parallel in the interpolated letters of Ignatius, which reads τὰς ἀγγελικὰς τάξεις καὶ τὰς τῶν ἀρχαγγέλων καὶ στρατιῶν ἐξαλλαγάς (*Trall.* 5; (Lightfoot [1973, 152]). The authentic Ignatian epistle to the Trallians has τὰς τοποθεσίας τὰς ἀγγελικάς. Wagner noted that elsewhere in early Christian literature, forms of τάξις and the related term στρατιαί are associated with angels / heavenly beings.
[14] Pighi (1941, 214).
[15] Pöhlmann and West (2001, 190–91 [transcription and critical apparatus]).
[16] LSJ lists δεσπότις (under δεσπότης) as a form of δέσποινα.
[17] Using the word φαεσφόρα in the line immediately below as a guide to spacing permits the reading δε[σπότ]ι[δες].
[18] On the feminine gender of the evening stars and planets, and the moon, see Ptolemy, *Tetrabiblos* 1.6 (§ 20). The word δεσπότιδες would also be attractive if the hymn gave indications of an orientation to gnostic thought, which contemplated female heavenly powers, the female "aeons." But nothing in the hymn suggests a gnostic bent.
[19] Hunt and Jones (1922, 25).

But Pöhlmann and West (also Wagner)[20] have pointed out that the spacing between the letters is lexical, not syllabic. This seems clearly to be the case with the space between υ and τ.

If we have more than one word, then Reinach's proposal, [οὐ τὰν δείλαν ο] ὐ τὰν ἠῶ, gains credibility.[21] This involves taking ταν as the Doric form of τήν. Noting that Synesius uses the terms νύξ and ἠώς (or ἀώς) for night and day, Pöhlmann and West suggested οὐ νύκτα [⏑ –], οὐ τὰν ἠῶ.[22] It is difficult to imagine what might fill the intervening space (⏑ –) as required by the meter. Both Reinach's suggestion and the modification of it by Pöhlmann and West have the further difficulty that in a negative construction joining two things, we expect the second negative particle to be οὐδέ. But poetic style no doubt permits the omission of the conjunction. In any case, if something like Reinach's solution is correct, then we have a line describing an action that does not happen, or does not cease, night and day. In view of the ensuing call for stillness on the part of natural entities (σιγάτω κ.τ.λ), I hazard the guess that the sentence ending with ο]ὐ τὰν ἠῶ refers to natural phenomena that do not cease their movements (or sound) night or day.

σιγάτω μηδ' ἄστρα φαεσφόρα χ[..]δε–

A diseme *leimma* precedes σιγάτω.[23] In the extant musical documents, diseme *leimmata* mark syntactical breaks in some songs and perhaps a lengthening of a note in others; in one place they seem to signify breaks in the middle of sense units, perhaps for dramatic effect.[24] The diseme *leimma* in line 3 of our hymn is almost certainly a rest and not a note lengthening, which would have given the second note for -ῶ a triseme value. No other notes in the fragment carry more than diseme value. Not only that, the musical phrase for οὐ τὰν ἠῶ is echoed twice at the end of the hymn, where the notation for the last (long) syllable is in each case a melism composed of two monosemes, not a monoseme and a triseme.

---

[20] Pöhlmann and West, (2001, 194); Wagner (1924, 218).

[21] Reinach (1922, 13).

[22] Pöhlmann and West (2001, 193n8 [referring to Synesius, *Hymn*. 1.345; 2.5; 3.21; 5.6]).

[23] The diseme rest after πνεῦμα in line 4 may have originally been a tetraseme rest. Taking it that way solves a problem with the arsis pointing. See Winnington-Ingram (1955, 80–81).

[24] Diseme *leimmata* marking syntactical breaks: P.Oslo 1413a lines 1–15; b–f (one in line 8 after Ἀχιλεύς and one in line 9 after προλιποῦσαι; probably after ἀόρατον in line 14); diseme *leimmata* that may indicate musical pauses in the middle of sense units: P.Oxy. 3704 frg. 1↓(in line 4 after ἐ]ξ σκοπέλων; in line 5 after Σικελῶν; in line 6 after πρηστὴρ and after ἢ τυφὼς); cf. the triseme *leimma* in P.Yale CtYBR inv. 4510 col. i (line 3) and see Pöhlmann and West (2001, 137). The use of a diseme *leimma* to lengthen a note to a triseme value occurs in Mesomedes' hymn to Nemesis (line 3) and in P.Oxy. 2436 ii (line 6).

Chapter Two: Text and Musical Notation

The preceding also argues strongly for taking σιγάτω as the beginning of a sentence, especially since the other instances of diseme rests in our hymn mark breaks before the introduction of new grammatical subjects: "we" in line 3 and "the powers" in line 4. There are also additional reasons for interpreting σιγάτω as the beginning of a new thought. The melody at σιγάτω is paralleled by the almost identical melodic figure following the rest in line 3, which marks a pause before ὑμνούντων. Both places share in common the use of acephalous ("headless") anapaests (for the metra of σιγάτω and ὑμνούντων). Hence, the two phrases are metrically and melodically parallel.

It is not immediately clear whether σιγάτω has an express subject. It may be an impersonal construction: "Let there be silence."[25] Our only extant expressions for the falling of silence in an impersonal sense use a verb of being with a noun for silence, e.g., ἦν σιωπή (Sophocles, *Oed. col.* 1623; Appian, *Lib.* 385.1) and ἐγένετο σιγή (Rev 8:1). Presumably a call for silence in this impersonal sense could be expressed as ἔστω σιωπή,[26] but no examples have come down to us. An alternative is to assume that the implied subject of σιγάτω is someone or something(s) mentioned in the lacuna before οὐ τὰν ἠῶ. We might also take the subject as either express or implied in what immediately follows. If the subject is implied, the sense would be, "Let them [natural entities] be silent; let not the shining stars [shine? move?]. If it is explicit in what follows, the words σιγάτω μηδ' ἄστρα go together to give the sense "Let the stars not be silent ..."

Evidently, Hunt's interpretation of the syntax entails this last construal (taking μηδέ with σιγάτω), for he characterizes the general sense of lines 2 and 3 as a call for "Creation at large ... to join in a chorus of praise."[27] Two considerations argue against this interpretation. First, evidence to be presented in chapter three argues strongly that the hymn's language in these lines belongs to a Greek tradition of inner-hymnic calls for the natural world to fall silent in honor of a deity (at the appearance of a god or before the offering of sacrifice or song to a god). Second, connective μηδέ is not postpositive but takes first position in a sentence or clause;[28] hence, we should construe the μηδέ here not with σιγάτω but with a verb that follows, presumably a verb lost in the partial lacuna in χ[..]δε[σ]θων.[29] Moreover, connective μηδέ is correlative, not disjunctive,[30] which argues against the interpretation, "Let them [creatures of

---

[25] West translates, "Let it be silent" (1992b, 325).
[26] Cf. εὐφημία ἔστω, εὐφημία ἔστω (Aristophanes, *Thesm.* 295–96 Henderson).
[27] Hunt and Jones (1922, 22).
[28] This point has been made by Wolbergs (1971, 106). When used as a conjunction, οὐδέ or μηδέ is invariably the first word in a clause (see Denniston [1954, 199]). It usually continues a negation expressed with μή or μηδέ (BDAG, *s.v.* μηδέ). In our passage, there is no preceding μή or μηδέ, but in context a negation (the ceasing of noise) is implied by σιγάτω.
[29] Meier (2004, 44n16) is therefore mistaken when he asserts that "der text-kritische Befund" (*sic*) speaks against the interpretation that there is a call to silence.
[30] The particle μηδέ is not disjunctive but correlative; it is a "negative correlative" (BDF § 445).

some kind mentioned in the preceding] be silent, *but* let the stars ... rushing rivers [praise, make noise]." Hence, we should interpret μηδ' ἄστρα ff. as continuing a call for stillness begun with σιγάτω. The sense is something like "Let it / them be silent; let not the shining stars ..."

It might be argued, however, that one should not put too much weight on the position of μηδέ in a metrical poem, since a poet might well sacrifice conventional syntax for the sake of meter and rhythm. That is a fair caution. Nevertheless, had our hymnist wished to negate the verb σιγάτω, he had a perfectly conventional way of doing so without disturbing his metrical and rhythmic scheme: μὴ σιγάτω ἄστρα φαεσφόρα κ.τ.λ. This phrasing is rhythmically identical to σιγάτω μηδ' ἄστρα φαεσφόρα κ.τ.λ. Hence, the fact that our hymnist wrote not μὴ σιγάτω but σιγάτω μηδ' is a further argument for the otherwise natural assumption that the conjunction μηδέ is in its regular syntactical position. That said, the judgment that the natural elements are called to silence does not depend solely on a grammatical rule regarding μηδέ. It is also based on the recognition that the specific language of lines 2 and 3 strongly suggests the presence of the cosmic stillness motif of Greek hymnody. The position of μηδέ simply reinforces the judgment that we have here the conceit of a call for cosmic quiet.

The cosmic stillness motif is presented in full detail in chapter three. Here it suffices to mention that the stock language of the motif includes the third-person imperative σιγάτω as well as reference to various natural elements – rivers, winds, birds, the sea, mountains, etc. Mesomedes begins one of his hymns with the words, "Let all heaven keep holy silence (εὐφαμείτω πᾶς αἰθήρ); let earth, and sea and winds, mountains, valley be silent (σιγάτω), and also echoes, songs of birds" (Heitsch no. 2.2, lines 1–6). Two words from our hymn (ῥοθίων and ποταμῶν) happen to be found in one of Synesius' formulations of the motif: "Cease, rushings of noisy waves, mouths of rivers (λήγετε ῥιπαὶ γυρῶν ῥοθίων, ποταμῶν προχοαί)" (*Hymn.* 1.78–80 Gruber and Strohm).

The neuter plural ἄστρα (from τὸ ἄστρον) would ordinarily take a singular verb. But a plural middle ending is suggested by θων in the papyrus (the only letters visible at the far left in line 3), which probably signals the Classical form of the third-person plural middle ending for the imperative (–σθων).[31] This impression is strongly reinforced by the fact that hymnic calls to silence / stillness are typically expressed with third-person imperatives. The use of a plural verb for a neuter plural suggests that the stars are personified and addressed as worshiping individual entities.[32]

---

[31] The Classical imperative ending is also found in ἐπιφωνούντων in line 4.
[32] See Smyth (1956, 264; § 959: "A plural verb may be used when stress is laid on the fact that a neuter plural subject is composed of persons or of several parts").

Damage to the papyrus at the end of line 2 has made it impossible to read or even offer a convincing guess about the verb that goes with ἄστρα. Hunt proposed λειπέσθων;[33] Del Grande suggested λαμπέσθων;[34] Wagner offered μηδὲ χθὼν. It should be kept in mind that, of these three scholars, only Hunt had looked at the papyrus itself. In microscopic examination of the fragment, West determined that the initial letter is most likely χ (not λ or μ) and judged that the next visible letter has a flat base, hence ζ or δ.[35] My own examination of the fragment confirms the presence of a flat base for this letter (the right-hand end of which is clearly visible under magnification). This rules out the π required for Hunt's λειπέσθων and Del Grande's λαμπέσθων.[36]

What remains of the initial letter of the damaged word is the bottom of a slanting stroke angled leftward toward the baseline and a dark coloration (clearly ink) angled rightward toward the baseline. The rightward angling stroke runs along the very edge of a hole in the papyrus. This right-hand hasta extends a bit lower than the left-hand hasta. The papyrus is missing just above the point where the two strokes come together. Hence, all that remains is a shape resembling, roughly, ∧. The thicker left side of this shape is slightly concave and its thinner right side is longer (extends lower) and takes the ragged shape of the damaged edge of the papyrus. At first sight, the remains suggest part of a χ, λ, or perhaps μ. Comparison with other instances of μ in the papyrus make it immediately evident that the presence of this letter is highly unlikely. Comparison with the two instances of χ elsewhere in the fragment – in χυιὸν and χἄγιον in line 4 – shows the same low intersection of hastas as in the letter in question and also the extension of the right hasta a bit lower than the left. Comparison with one certain instance of λ and one uncertain instance elsewhere in the fragment – in λόγιμοι in line 1 and in ἐ[κ]λειπ[όντων] in line 3 – shows that in neither case do the hastas of these lambdas join as low as in the letter under consideration. In view of this evidence, χ seems to be the most likely choice, although λ cannot be completely ruled out in view of the irregularity of the scribal hand in letter formation.

---

[33] Hunt and Jones (1922, 24).

[34] Del Grande (1923, 11–17). Del Grande's λαμπέσθων was accepted by Pighi (1941, 215) and West (1992b, 324). Del Grande changed his mind in later comments on the hymn (Del Grande [1931, 452] following Wagner). West changed his mind upon examining the papyrus himself for Pöhlmann and West (2001).

[35] "The reading presented in *Documents of Ancient Greek Music* results from my re-examination of the papyrus: it appeared to me that the first letter was chi, not lambda, and the fourth letter (after a gap of two letters) had a flat base" (West, personal correspondence, 2004, after kindly looking at the fragment one more time in response to a query).

[36] In his discussion of this portion of the hymn, Meier seems unaware of the uncertainties. In his transcription (which follows Pöhlmann and West [2001]), he represents the remains here as χ[..]ζε, but in his discussion of the word he speaks of λ[…]ε and reports that the interpretation λαμπέσθων is generally uncontested (Meier [2004, 43 and 44]).

Between χ (or λ) and ζ (or δ) is space for two or at most three letters. Then comes what looks like part of an epsilon formed with a short cross-bar that extends only to the right[37] and a somewhat angular lower segment. The epsilon in ἐπιφωνούντων looks somewhat similar, but the very straight lower segment of the letter in question does not resemble the curve of the typical epsilon. Nevertheless, it is hard to imagine what else the letter could be.

To the right of the putative epsilon is a long curved stroke which appears to be a connector meant to join this half of the word with its completion on the next line. Assuming that the epsilon is the theme vowel of an imperative, which makes sense in context, that completion, at the beginning of line 3, is probably σθων. Only ων is clearly visible following the damage to the edge of the papyrus, although part of the θ is detectable (see below under line 3). Inferring the end of the word as –εσθων would also explain the diseme value in the musical notation for the syllable containing the ε, since the conjunction of σ and θ would make that syllable long.

The stretch of letters from χ (or λ) to ζ (or δ) occupies two centimeters. Measurements of other two-centimeter stretches show that this much space can accommodate no more than five letters and that in some cases five consecutive letters take up a bit more space. This means that no more than two or three letters once stood between χ (or λ) and δ (or ζ).[38] Wagner's supplement, μηδὲ χθὼν, is too short. The η cannot fill the space between the μ (dubious in any case) and the next visible letter (the possible δ).[39] For the same reason, the conjecture χαζέσθων (middle: "retire," "shrink back") does not work; it also does not meet the metrical requirements, which call for – or ⏑ ⏑ at the beginning of the word (the first two syllables of χαζέσθων make ⏑ –).

If we read the first letter as χ and the letter after the gap as delta (hence χ[..]δεσθων), the only word listed in *LSJ* that tolerably meets the requirements of sense is χλάδω, making χλαδέσθων. The existence of the word χλάδω is inferred by *LSJ* from three instances of what is apparently the perfect form used in a present sense. These examples are all found in Pindar, where they seem to have the meaning "exult," "shout," "ring out," "swell in sound" (*Ol.* 9.2; *Pyth.* 4.179; P.Oxy. 1604 [2.10]). Assuming the existence of a present middle form, χλαδέσθων, this would give the sense, "Let not the stars ring out," which is in keeping with the cosmic stillness motif. It also makes sense in view of a long Greek tradition that stars sing, that is, make the "music of the spheres." Nevertheless, supplementing with the present-tense imperative

---

[37] The cross bars of other epsilons in P.Oxy. 1786 vary in length and position, as well as in the direction of their curves.

[38] The transcription of Pöhlmann and West suggests space for two letters between χ and the flat-base letter δ or ζ (Pöhlmann and West [2001, 190]).

[39] Wagner's supplement is not a verb because he concluded that μηδ' ἄστρα κ.τ.λ. goes with σιγάτω.

χλαδέσθων assumes the currency of a word in the Roman period that is unattested for that time and may have been outmoded in its present-tense form, required here, already in Pindar's time. Moreover, χλαδέσθων, like χαζέσθων, does not satisfy the metrical requirements.

Given the dearth of alternatives, one might contemplate the possibility that the first letter is a badly-formed κ or that we have a quasi-homophonic scribal slip of χ for κ. The present middle imperative κελαδέσθων ("sound") fits the requirements of meter and sense (in the Pythagorean view, stars make music; see also Job 38:7), as well as space. But the left hasta for κ is typically a straight line without a curve (cf. the κ in line 4).

Line 3

–[σ]θων [ἐκ]λειπ[όντων] ῥ[ιπαὶ πνοιῶν, πηγαὶ] ποταμῶν ῥοθίων πᾶσαι.

The mention of surging rivers (ποταμῶν ῥοθίων) after σιγάτω μηδ' ἄστρα suggests that we have a cosmic stillness motif applied to various natural entities: "stars ... of surging rivers." In Synesius, for example, other elements, along with rivers (streams, waters), are also summoned to stillness: the air, upper air (ether), earth, sea, winds, waves, trees, and birds (*Hymn.* 1.72–85 and 2.28–43). The remains after -[σ]θων show a gap followed by a shape resembling Λ, which could be part of λ or χ. Next are marks that could be construed as the bottom of ε with faint remains of the cross-stroke (and are difficult to interpret as some other letter). Two bits of ink consistent with the vertical stroke of an ι or left-hand side of π appear to the right, followed by a more complete vertical stroke. Looking for a word that expresses the idea of rivers quieting down, Pighi suggested ἀπολειπόντων (which can mean "cease," "fall" or "sink");[40] West suggested ἐκλειπόντων (which can also mean "cease").[41]

Since ποταμῶν ῥοθίων is in the genitive and is followed by πᾶσαι, it is almost certainly preceded by a noun that πᾶσαι modifies. A noun such as προχοαί, πηγαί, ῥιπαί, or ῥοαί is required, that is, a feminine plural term for the source or power of rivers, the noise that rivers make, or the action of a river that produces noise. This leaves a good number of possibilities. After the stars and before the mention of rivers we expect a reference to the wind or air, common terms in parallel contexts. In that case we would have the stars above, the winds / air between earth and heaven, and the rivers of the earth below – a call for the universe as a whole to be still.

---

[40] Pighi (1941, 215).
[41] West for Pöhlmann and West (2001, 191 [critical apparatus]).

The earliest effort at a complete supplement for this part of line 3 was made by Reinach. Assuming Hunt's construal of μηδέ with σιγάτω, Reinach proposed the following:[42]

σιγάτω	[_] _ _ _
μηδ' ἄστρα φαεσφόρα [χ'ὑψηλῶν	_ _ ⏑⏑ _ ⏑⏑ _ _ _
ὀρέων κορυφαὶ μηδ' ὠκεανός	⏑⏑ _ ⏑⏑ _ _ _ ⏑⏑ _
καὶ τῶν] ποταμῶν ῥοθίων παγαί	_ _ ⏑⏑ _ ⏑⏑ _ _ _

Qu'ils ne gardent pas non plus le silence, les astres porteurs de lumière, (ni les sommets des hautes montagnes, ni l'océan, ni) les sources des fleuves impétueux!

Let not the shining stars keep silence, nor the peaks of the high mountains, nor the oceans, nor the sources of the rushing rivers.

Reinach incorrectly read παγαί (Doric for πηγαί) instead of πᾶσαι. Although the word is a bit washed out, the third letter is clearly σ, not γ.

The next effort at a complete supplement came from Del Grande:[43]

λει[βέ-	_ _
σθων μὴ πηγαὶ]	_ _ _ _
ποταμῶν ῥοθίων	⏑⏑ _ ⏑⏑ _
πᾶσαι	_ _

Let not the sources of all the surging rivers pour forth.

This supplement is not long enough to fill the space.

Wagner, assuming dactyls in this part of the hymn, supplemented as follows:[44]

[πᾶσα·	_ _ ∧
ἠχούντων ἄνε-	_ _ _ ⏑⏑
μοι προχοαὶ] ποτα-	_ ⏑⏑ _ ⏑⏑
μῶν ῥοθίων πᾶσαι	_ ⏑⏑ _ _ _

... all. Let the winds sound forth (and) all the outpourings of the surging rivers.

Following Hunt, Wagner assumed that the cosmos is called to noisy praise, not silence: "Let neither the shining stars keep silence nor all the earth" (σιγάτω μηδ' ἄστρα φαεσφόρα μ[ηδ]ὲ χθὼν πᾶσα]). Then: "Let the winds sound forth ..."[45]

Some years later Pighi offered the following:[46]

---

[42] Reinach (1922, 12, 16 [readings and supplements], 13 [translation]).
[43] Del Grande (1923). This article was unavailable to me. I have relied on Pighi (1941, 196) for Del Grande's reconstruction.
[44] Wagner (1924, 208).
[45] Wagner (1924, 217 [on σιγάτω going with μηδ' ἄστρα] and 209 [for the supplements]).
[46] Pighi (1941, 215).

[ἀπο]λειπ[όντω]ν   ⏑⏑ _ _ _
ῥ[αδιναὶ προχοαί]   ⏑⏑ _ ⏑⏑ _
ποταμῶν ῥοθίων   ⏑⏑ _ ⏑⏑ _
πᾶσαι   _ _

Recedano le molli correnti dei fiumi fragorosi, tutte.
Let the soft currents of the surging rivers withdraw, all of them.

Pighi recognized that the hymn most likely contains a cosmic stillness motif, hence his suggestion that the first word is ἀπολειπόντων ("let them withdraw"). Pighi's ῥαδιναὶ προχοαί means something like "slender outpourings," which he translates "molli correnti" – "soft/weak currents"). This does not fit well with ποταμῶν ῥοθίων ("rushing/surging rivers"). The cosmic stillness motif in other Greek poetry leads us to expect adjectives describing noisiness or vigorous activity in both phrases. Moreover, Pighi's supplement was an anapaest short, requiring him to posit an additional tetraseme rest before the rest that already precedes ὑμνούντων.

Pöhlmann accepted Pighi's ἀπολειπόντων and proposed ῥιπαὶ πνοιῶν, πηγαὶ, drawing attention to ταχύπτεροι πνοαί, ποταμῶν τε πηγαί in Aeschylus (*Prom.* 88–89 Smyth) and ῥιπαῖς ἐχθίστων ἀνέμων in Sophocles (*Ant.* 137 Lloyd-Jones). He reconstructed the lines as follows:[47]

[ἀπ]ο̣λ̣ε̣ι̣π̣[όντων]   ⏑⏑ _ _ _
ῥ[ιπαὶ πνοιῶν,   _ _ _ _
πηγαὶ] ποταμῶν   _ _ ⏑⏑ _
ῥοθίων πᾶσαι   ⏑⏑ _ _ _

This can be translated, "Let rushings of winds cease (and) all sources of surging rivers."[48]

Pöhlmann and West followed Pöhlmann's original supplement with one change – the suggestion of ἐκλειπόντων instead of ἀπολειπόντων. The result is a longer series of spondees:[49]

ἐ̣[κ]λειπ[όντων]   _ _ _ _
ῥ[ιπαὶ πνοιῶν,   _ _ _ _
πηγαὶ] ποταμῶν   _ _ ⏑⏑ _
ῥοθίων πᾶσαι   ⏑⏑ _ _ _

In addition to the examples of language from Aeschylus and Sophocles, Pöhlmann and West drew attention to an especially pertinent passage in the fourth-century Christian hymn-writer Synesius, where commands for reverent silence are addressed to "heaven" (αἰθήρ), "earth" (γᾶ), "sea" (πόντος), "air" (ἀήρ), "blasts of swift winds" (πνοιαὶ βαλιῶν ἀνέμων), and "rushings of surging

---

[47] Pöhlmann (1970, 106 [apparatus]).
[48] If we construe πᾶσαι as governing both phrases, then: "Let all rushings of winds (and) sources of surging rivers cease."
[49] Pöhlmann and West (2001, 191).

waves, outpourings of rivers" (ῥιπαὶ γυρῶν ῥοθίων, ποταμῶν προχοαί) (Synesius, *Hymn*. 1.72–80 Gruber and Strohm).

ὑμνούντων δ' ἡμῶν

These words are clearly legible. The expression is almost certainly a genitive absolute, the δέ signaling a new clause and making it clear that ὑμνούντων ἡμῶν belongs syntactically with the next finite verb (the imperative ἐπιφωνούντων): "While we sing ... let the powers respond ..."

Line 4

[π]ατέρα χυἱὸν χάγιον πγεῦμα πᾶσαι δυνάμεις ἐπιφωνούντων ἀμὴν ἀμήν, κράτος αἶνος

No significant doubts touch the reading of this line. Note the Classical form of the ending on the imperative ἐπιφωνούντων.

Line 5

[ἀεὶ καὶ δόξα θεῷ] δ̣[ωτ]ῆ̣[ρι] μ̣ό̣ν̣ῳ̣[ι] [πάν]των ἀγαθῶν, ἀμὴν ἀμήν.

Hunt suggested that δωτῆρι might have stood in the space preceding μόνῳ, but he was extremely cautious: "the scanty vestiges well suit μονω, but δ[ωτ]η[ρι] is highly doubtful, though some such word is demanded by the sense."[50] What can be seen of parts of the conjectured δωτῆρι are just the upper tips of letters. A rounded mark is almost certainly the upper left hook of δ. At a later point there is a tip of a hasta. Gauging the size of δωτῆρι from the appearance of its letters elsewhere in the fragment shows that it would match the bits of visible letter tops and would fit the space with a little room to spare.[51]

The case for δωτῆρι strengthens when we consider the context. The words κράτος αἶνος at the end of line 4 and the double amen in line 5 indicate that the hymn closes with a doxology. Hence, at some point θεός must appear, presumably in the dative, to name the one to whom κράτος, αἶνος etc. are ascribed and to identify the one who dispenses "all good things." In the New Testament the following verbs are used in descriptions of God as the giver of gifts:

---

[50] Hunt and Jones (1922, 25).
[51] To make this measurement, I created a mock-up δωτῆρι composed of individual digital images for each letter in the scribe's hand from other parts of the fragment. Each image started from its left-hand edge to the beginning of the letter that follows it. In this way letter spacing was accounted for. I compared this mock-up to the remains of the letter tops and the note symbols in line 5.

δίδωμι (Matt 7:11), χαρίζομαι (Rom 8:32), and παρέχω (1 Tim 6:17). None of these words are found in New Testament doxologies (although 1 Tim 6:17 probably reflects doxological language: θεῷ τῷ παρέχοντι ἡμῖν πάντα). Of the three verbs, only δίδωμι has δ, which is one of the decipherable letters of the uncertain word, but τῷ διδόντι is too long and even without the article does not match the remains.

Also favoring δωτῆρι is West's observation that δωτῆρι μόνῳ πάντων ἀγαθῶν is a version of the Homeric formula, θεοί δωτῆρες ἐάων ("the gods, givers of good things"), which is also clearly attested in the Alexandrian tradition.[52] Callimachus applies it to Zeus (*Hymn. Jov.* 1.91); Clement of Alexandria uses it of the Christian God: ὁ τῶν ἀγαθῶν ... δοτήρ (*Str.* 7.7.43.2 Stählin, Früchtel, and Treu; see also *Str.* 7.7.36.4). These parallels, together with the requirements for a match with the visible bits of the letters, remove any significant doubt that δωτῆρι is the correct reading.

To the left of δωτῆρι, the upper tips of an omega are just discernable. Further left, only fragmentary remains of letters are visible. Judging from size and spacing in the words above (in line 4), it appears that there is room for sixteen letters (including the suspected omega) and two lexical spaces.[53] The following supplements have been proposed:

Hunt: νῦν κεῖς αἰῶνας or δόξαν νῦν κἀεὶ[54] (12 or 13 letters, 3 lexical)

Pighi: ἀεὶ καὶ δόξα θεῷ[55] (13 letters, 3 lexical spaces)

Reinach: δόξ' εἰς αἰεὶ βασιλῆι θεῷ[56] (20 letters, 4 lexical spaces)

Wagner: νῦν κ' εἰς αἰῶνας ἀμήν, ἀμήν[57] (21 letters, 5 lexical spaces)

Wagner's supplement is too long and does not account for the final omega. An argument for θεῷ is that it fits the metrical requirements implied by the musical notation, which calls for a word with the metrical pattern ⌣ _ . Reinach's conjecture adopts θεῷ, but it is also too long. Pighi's proposal is a bit on the short side but satisfies the requirements of the meter.[58] Of special significance is the fact that the -νος of αἶνος at the end of line 4 must be a short syllable (in view of the musical symbol above it). Hence, the first syllable of the first word in line 5 must be short and must begin with a vowel.

---

[52] West (1992a, 50–51).
[53] Hunt (Hunt and Jones [1922, 24]) estimated space for fifteen letters. Reinach (1922, 11) suggested space for 15–20 letters, which is too generous.
[54] Hunt and Jones (1922, 25).
[55] Pighi (1941, 215).
[56] Reinach (1922, 16).
[57] Wagner (1924, 208 and 209).
[58] Pighi's supplement for line 5 was adopted by Pöhlmann and West for *DAGM* because it is the only one that fits both the space and the rhythmic pattern of the musical notation (Pöhlmann and West [2001, 191, 193]).

Pighi's ἀεί belongs to the space occupied by πατέρα in the corresponding place in the line above. Perhaps the line was indented a bit here. A melismatic musical pattern in the notation might also have called for giving this word more space than it would otherwise have needed. In any case, it is hard to imagine a better supplement than Pighi's – one that fits the metrical requirements, musical notation, and, with a little room to spare, the space for fifteen or sixteen letters (and three lexical spaces).

The Greek Musical Notation System

The extant ancient Greek musical documents display a relatively simple method of musical notation. Letters of the Ionian alphabet, supplemented by additional signs, serve as note symbols for vocal music and are placed above the text so that they correspond to the syllables meant to be sung to them. A different set of symbols is used for instrumental music (and instrumental accompaniment).

The interpretation of the vocal and notational systems is known to scholars from a number of sources,[59] above all from Alypius, a late-Roman-era[60] authority whose Εἰσαγωγὴ μουσική ("Introduction to Music") consists, in its extant form, almost wholly of tables of notation symbols. Alypius explains these tables in some preliminary remarks, where he refers to the symbols (σημεῖα) for the fifteen τρόποι (another term for τόνοι), which he then sets forth in two sets of notation, one for text (λέξις) and the other for instrumental accompaniment (κροῦσις).[61] All manuscripts of Alypius break off before the tables are complete, but information on notation from other writers and from the musical documents themselves permits reconstruction of a more or less comprehensive picture.

The term τρόπος (= τόνος) is sometimes translated "key." In Alypius' notation tables, each note of the scale in a given key is assigned a symbol from a comprehensive set of some seventy symbols. This set (which can be abstracted from the tables) amounts to a scale of all the pitches in use (but not strictly fixed to an absolute pitch scheme) in intervals of a microtone. This abstract scale of notation symbols spans just over three and a half octaves. In his tables, Alypius begins with Lydian in the diatonic genus and presents each symbol by matching it with its corresponding scale step in that key. Hence, anyone who wanted to find the symbol for, say, *Parhypatē hypatōn* in the Ionian key

---

[59] Aristides Quintilianus, Gaudentius, Alypius, *Anonymous Bellermanni*, Martianus Capella, and Boethius (see West [1992b, 254n1]).

[60] Alypius is often assigned to the third century. Thomas Mathiesen (1999, 594) places him later, dating his treatise to somewhere between 350 and 500 C.E.

[61] Mathiesen (1999, 595).

would consult the table for Ionian and find the symbol next to the scale-step *Parhypatē hypatōn*. For modern scholars, knowledge provided in the music handbooks about the scales permits interpretation of the musical documents with the help of the tables of Alypius and others.

The notation tables presented by writers of the late-Roman era are likely to be most accurate for Roman-era music, although they seem to work for earlier musical manuscripts as well.[62] In any case, Alypius, whose complete tables for the diatonic genus survive, can be regarded as a reliable authority for the notational symbols used in P.Oxy. 1786, a manuscript that belongs to the final period of the production of Greek musical scores.[63]

P.Oxy. 1786 uses the notation symbols R Φ C O Z̆ I Z E. In the fragment, these symbols are written as follows (the relative proportions being roughly as shown):

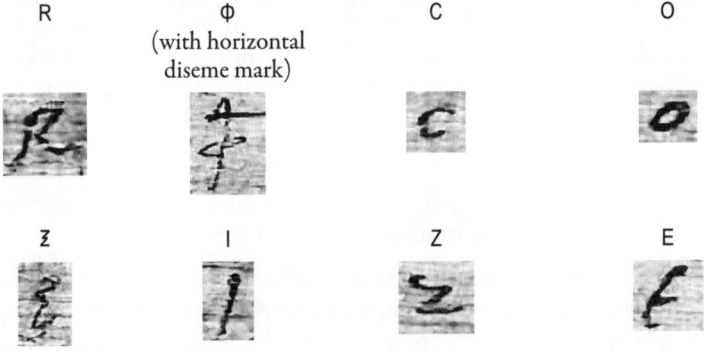

The details above, excerpted from a digital image, present the clearest and perhaps best-formed instances of the symbols in the fragment.

A system for rhythmic notation was also in use. Most pre-Roman-era vocal pieces probably had little need for rhythmic symbols. The rhythm was implied by the text, with short syllables being sung to short notes and long syllables to long notes.[64] But an instrumental piece would have required notation for its pitches and their time value. The use of rhythmic notation for vocal music

---

[62] On the whole matter, see West (1992b, 254–73).

[63] The latest musical documents are papyrus fragments dated to the third and early fourth centuries C.E. Along with P.Oxy. 1786, they are P.Oxy. 3161 recto (late third) century, P.Oxy. 3161 verso (late third century), P.Oxy. 3162 (third century), P.Oxy. 3705 (third century), P.Oxy. 4466 (third century), P.Oxy. 4467 (third century), P.Ms.Schøyen 2260 (third/fourth century), P.Oxy. 4710 (third/fourth century). Another document, P.Mich. inv. 1250, has been assigned a broad range of possible dating (first to third century).

[64] Some of the musical scores dated to the Classical period show occasional diseme marks (e.g., P.Vienna G 2315; P.Ashm. inv. 89B/29–32 frg. 16 and frg. 20). Two songs from the Hellenistic period – the paeans of Athenaeus and Limenius – make no use of rhythmic notation.

became increasingly common in Roman times, due to an increasing use of melisma, the setting of a syllable to more than one note.[65]

Presumably, tunes from the Roman or late-Roman era whose texts were not based on quantitative meter also required extensive rhythmic notation. As far as we can tell, however, all the vocal texts among the extant musical documents express quantitative meter, perhaps as a matter of tradition among professionals. This holds true even for the latest songs, those datable to the late third century. By that time, a good deal of popular song was no doubt being composed without reference to the requirements of quantitative meter. But we possess no artifacts of such music. The same goes for poetry. The surviving remains of Greek poetry show that quantitative meter continued to supply the governing scheme down through the third century, although in that century poets began to show freedom in offending against Classical norms.[66] The first poetry regulated by accents alone appears in some of the verse attributed to Gregory of Nazianzus. Whatever was going on in non-literate (or non-literary) circles, literary poets and professional musicians continued in the quantitative metrical tradition, evidently well beyond the point when quantities were distinguished in everyday speech.

P.Oxy. 1786 uses the following rhythmical signs:

∧ or ⌒   *leimma* (λεῖμμα), signifying a rest of monoseme time value; sometimes used to indicate a lengthening of a note;

—   diseme mark, a form of time symbol indicating a metrical long (and usually shown in modern transcriptions as the equivalent of a quarter note in time), placed above the notation symbol to which it applies;

‿   a hyphen, written beneath a set of notes to show that they belong together;

:   the double point or colon, placed before a group of notes to indicate that they belong together;

·   *stigmē* (στιγμή) or arsis point (sometimes formed as °), placed above the syllable of the arsis.

In the musical documents, these signs (and a few others[67]) often appear in combination, especially in post-Hellenistic compositions. For example, a diseme mark can be placed over a *leimma* ($\overline{\cap}$) to show that the *leimma* carries a

---

[65] In some Hellenistic documents a simple melism is shown by writing out the vowels of the syllable twice and placing the corresponding note symbols above the doubled vowels. This is the procedure in the Delphic paeans (Athens, 127/128 B.C.E.). With more frequent and more complicated uses of melisma, a more sophisticated form of notation was needed.

[66] See West (1982, 163–64).

[67] There are additional time signs, which show longer lengths of time.

diseme time value. The use of the diseme stroke, hyphen, and colon in combination is a way of showing melismatic subdivisions of time:

: $\overline{\Phi \underline{C} R}$ = ♪♬

The diseme mark indicates time, the colon signals a group, and the hyphen in this case shows a subdivision of time within the group.

Questions Touching the Reading of the Notation in P.Oxy. 1786

Line 1

All that is visible of notation in line 1 are two curved shapes suggesting the bottoms of adjacent hyphens, which imply a pair of melisms. In relation to the line below, these hyphens are situated above πᾶσαι.

Line 2

The tip of a time-value stroke stands above and to the left of the remains of the note symbol for υ. The height of its placement shows that it is part of a diseme symbol and not an arsis point. An arsis point probably stood above and to the left of the remains of the diseme mark where the papyrus is missing. A curved stroke to the upper left of υ (in the words below) could be the remains of a hyphen or the tail of a note symbol. The placement argues for a hyphen, as comparison with the hyphen in the next set of notation marks shows.[68] In that case we have a melism. The note symbol above υ is probably a partly worn-away $\bar{Z}$, and musical analysis supports the reading $\bar{Z}$ (parallel cadential forms at the end of the piece; see chapter five).[69]

The first note for -ω looks clearly like C. Hunt read C with confidence; West put it down as C but was uncertain, perhaps on the possibility that the open right side was a result of wear on an original O.[70] The size of the symbol argues strongly for C.[71] The cadential pattern at the end of the hymn also favors reading C here.

---

[68] West judges that the mark is a hyphen (Pöhlmann and West [2001, 190]); so also Wagner (1924, 202 and 209).

[69] The marks somewhat resemble Z, but comparison with a Z in line 3 argues against this possibility. Wagner (1924, 209) and West (Pöhlmann and West [2001, 190]) tentatively settle on $\bar{Z}$.

[70] Hunt and Jones (1922, 24); Pöhlmann and West (2001, 190).

[71] The C in this copyist's hand is generally about a third larger than the O. There is one place where, in proximity to each other, a large O is the same size as a small C (in the notation for the final amen), but generally there is a distinct difference in size.

Line 3

Notation for line 3 is preserved beginning with ποταμῶν. The symbols are clearly legible up to the first syllable of ῥοθίων, where the notation is incomplete. A colon before the note Ι above the ῥο- indicates a melism. The position of a *stigmē*, above and to the right of Ι, also suggests a pair of notes for ῥο- . The space after Ι, where we expect the second note symbol, is empty. The papyrus is very much intact here, and the notation is otherwise unfaded. A few very small marks (ink) are visible where the second note should be.[72] Since the melism must entail a division of a monoseme (in view of the meter), the interval is probably not wide. Wagner suggested Z.[73]

Line 4

The note for the second syllable of πατέρα could be C or O. Comparison with other examples of these symbols in the fragment suggests C (given the size, the forward slant, and the clear termination of the bottom of the letter).

The note for the last syllable of χἄγιον is a bit uncertain but is most likely Z.

A colon and a diseme mark appear to govern the notation for the first syllable of πνεῦμα. No *stigmē* is visible, although one belongs here.[74] The rhythmic signs suggest a melism, but the note symbols are indecipherable. Hunt guessed Ι̣?̣ and Wagner proposed Ι Z. Nothing suggests the presence of Z, and the mark Hunt took as part of Ι is probably too slanted to be that symbol. Pöhlmann and West prudently put question marks for both notes. The melody moves from Z through two notes and then touches Z again for the -μα of πνεῦμα. This favors Z E or E Z for the indecipherable notes (to give Φ Z Z E Z or Φ Z E Z Z for -ον πνεῦμα) since in the three other places where the melody moves from Z through one, two, or three notes and then back to Z, it goes up to E as soon as it leaves Z (see the notation for μηδ' ἄστρα in line 2, ποταμῶν ῥοθίων in line 3, and ἀμὴν ἀμήν in line 4).

The notation for ἐπιφωνούντων is clear. Hunt gave the notation for the final syllable (-των) as O[75] but later communicated to Wagner that this was a printing error.[76] The notation is clearly Ι with diseme time symbol and *stigmē*.

---

[72] Hunt detected signs that ῥοθίων was written over an erasure (Hunt and Jones [1922, 25]), and Wagner (1924, 203) wondered whether this erasure also took out the second note. A microscopic examination of the manuscript shows faint marks that might be ink or only discoloration.

[73] Wagner (1924, 203, 209); so also Pöhlmann and West (2001, 190).

[74] "A dot is probably to be restored above the notes on πνευ, the papyrus having been rubbed here" (Hunt and Jones, [1922, 25]).

[75] Hunt and Jones (1922, 24).

[76] Wagner (1924, 203).

Line 5

Comparing the photograph published in the original edition of P.Oxy. 1786 with the current state of the papyrus shows that there has been some deterioration in the left-hand corner of the fragment. This affects the space below [π] α of πατέρα and also the space further on where the symbol(s) for the ει of ἀεὶ in Pighi's supplement would have stood (i.e., under the letters χυ from χυἱὸν in line 4 above). A bit of cellophane tape stands as witness to an effort to keep the fragment from falling apart here. Under magnification, it is apparent that a strand of papyrus has been dislodged and shifted a bit to the left, affecting the appearance of the ink that it carries in relation to other ink on the papyrus. The middle of this strand is very thin, and this thin portion can be seen in both the original photograph and the 1990s digital image; the strand forms the bottom edge of one of the holes in the papyrus. To the left of this hole, the strand is wider and divides into a fork, open on the right so that the thin strand crossing the base of the hole is attached as the top "tine" of this fork. Both parts of the fork carry ink marks belonging to the symbol identified as R by Wagner and West. In this area the bottom edge of the dislodged strand is folded over at points, obscuring ink. Assuming a hiding of ink and not absence of ink at the points where the strand curls, the visible marks appear to be part of a straight line. This suggests a flat base and makes it more difficult to imagine R. A flat base would require Z or Δ, but the ink above shows no hint of a diagonal. Perhaps the base did not look quite so flat but somewhat curved when the fragment was in its original condition, in which case Hunt's C is credible. Imagining the strand shifted a bit to the right where it seems to belong does not help to establish a symbol.

Two years after publishing his edition of the fragment, Hunt communicated to Wagner that letters and symbols on some parts of the papyrus had faded.[77] Deterioration and shifting of parts of the fragment are evident from a comparison of the photograph in the original edition with the digital image from the 1990s. Some of the papyrus at the bottom left-hand corner is absent in the later photograph. The holes are also differently shaped, suggesting that the effort at repair changed the appearance of the papyrus. Deterioration may have eliminated some remnants of ink that were present when Hunt first examined the fragment. He also had the advantage of being able to manipulate the strands into what he regarded as their original position. In any case, looking at the papyrus in its *current* condition does not give the impression of Hunt's : CC. The reading R for the first of these note symbols is easier to understand from both the digital image and direct examination but also stands

---

[77] See Wagner reporting Hunt's observation that, due to subsequent deterioration, marks suggesting a note symbol at the beginning of line 3 were no longer as visible as they had been when Hunt initially studied the papyrus (under "V 3" in Wagner [1924, 204]).

under considerable doubt, given uncertainty about where the visible bits of ink originally stood in relation to each other.

The notation corresponding to the supplement θεῷ is C: followed by COƵ. Beneath COƵ is a hyphen and above is a diseme time symbol. Hunt and West both saw the hyphen under all three of the notes COƵ. I confirm this – a thin line that sweeps beneath the whole group. Wagner doubted that this thin line was a hyphen and added a hyphen in his transcription to join only the second and third notes.[78] Hunt interpreted the group of notes as a triplet (and it is so rendered in the modern musical transcription made by Jones);[79] Pöhlmann and West construed it as another instance of the ♪♫ rhythm, presumably because other examples of three notes to a long syllable show a hyphen linking the second and third notes.[80]

The Arsis Pointing

When used in musical notation, *stigmai* mark the arsis components of each unit of the metron. In the case of anapaests, the basic form is:

˘̇ ˘̇ _

Alternates to this form are the following:

˙_ _ and ˘̇ ˘̇ ˘ ˘

The placement of the *stigmai* in P.Oxy. 1786 makes perfect sense up until πᾶσαι in line 4; from there to the end of the hymn the *stigmai* are misplaced, falling not on the arsis where they belong but on the thesis. Reinach was the first to observe this. In reaching for an explanation, he rejected the possibility that for the rest of the hymn the composer shifted from anapaests to dactyls; instead he suspected a copyist's error.[81] Winnington-Ingram offered an explanation of how such a copyist's error might have come about. The pointing works if one treats the two-beat rest before πᾶσαι as a four-beat rest. The copyist, Winnington-Ingram proposed, mistook a tetraseme mark in his exemplar for a diseme mark.[82] The diseme, a common symbol, stands for two beats; the tetraseme, a rare symbol, stands for four beats.[83] "We can only suppose,"

---

[78] Wagner (1924, 204 and 208).
[79] Hunt and Jones (1922, 24).
[80] Pöhlmann and West (2001, 190); so also Pöhlmann (1970, 106).
[81] Reinach (1922, 22–23).
[82] Winnington-Ingram (1955, 80–81). Winnington-Ingram's solution has been accepted by Pöhlmann and West (2001, 193).
[83] The musical amalgam *Anonymous Bellermanni* gives the symbols for diseme, triseme, tetraseme, and pentaseme. The tetraseme and pentaseme symbols are not attested in the extant musical documents (see West [1992b, 266]). They are probably late signs, developed in the latter

Winnington-Ingram concluded, "that the dots were supplied mechanically by someone who did not realise what had happened at this point"[84] – that the *leimma* carried a tetraseme value and was therefore followed by an arsis syllable.

A difficulty with Winnington-Ingram's explanation is that it is hard to imagine a copyist overlooking the evidence of his exemplar, which presumably had the points in their right places, something that would have been evident to him as he inserted the notation symbols. It is possible, however, that, having misunderstood a tetraseme mark as a diseme, he aimed to *correct* his original by putting the marks in their "right" sequence. Or he added the arsis pointing only at the very end without consulting his exemplar.

The Rhythm

The following scansion and representation of the musical rhythm assumes Winnington-Ingram's interpretation of the text as anapaestic with a correction of a diseme rest to a tetraseme in line 4 after πνεῦμα.[85]

	Scansion of Text	Notated Rhythm
.........]ὁμοῦ	.........] ⌣ _	
πᾶσαι τε θεοῦ	_ _ ⌣⌣ _	
λόγιμοι δε [.....	⌣⌣ _ ? [.....	
[3 metra?]		
ο]ὐ τὰν ἠῶ	_ _ _ _	[ ]⌣⌣ ⌣⌣⌣
σιγάτω,	(diseme rest) _ _ _	(diseme rest) _ ⌣⌣_
μηδ' ἄστρα φαεσ–	_ _ ⌣⌣ _	_⌣⌣ ⌣⌣_
φόρα χ[_ _]δε[σ]θων	⌣⌣ [ ] _	⌣⌣ [? _] _
[ἐκ]λειπ[όντων]	_ _ _ _	[ ]
ῥ[ιπαὶ πνοιῶν	_ _ _ _	[ ]
πηγαὶ] ποταμῶν	_ _ ⌣⌣ _	[ ]⌣⌣⌣⌣
ῥοθίων πᾶσαι.	⌣⌣ _ _ _	⌣⌣⌣⌣ ⌣⌣⌣⌣
ὑμνούντων	(diseme rest) _ _ _	(diseme rest) _ ⌣⌣_
δ'ἡμῶν [π]ατέρα	_ _ ⌣⌣ _	⌣⌣_ ⌣⌣_
χυιὸν χἄγιον	_ _ ⌣⌣ _	_⌣⌣ ⌣⌣⌣⌣

---

part of the Roman era. The hymn of P.Oxy. 1786 is certainly late enough to have had a four-beat rest represented by a tetraseme symbol.

[84] Winnington-Ingram (1955, 81).
[85] On this, see "Arsis Pointing" above.

	Scansion of Text	*Notated Rhythm*
πγεῦμα	_ _ (tetraseme rest?)	⏑⏑_ (tetraseme rest?)
πᾶσαι δυνάμεις	_ _ ⏑⏑_	⏑⏑_ ⏑⏑_
ἐπιφωνούντων	⏑⏑_ _ _	⏑⏑_ ⏑⏑_
ἀμὴν ἀμήν,	⏑_ ⏑_ treated as _ _ _ _	_ ⏑⏑⏑ ⏑⏑⏑⏑
κράτος αἶνος [ἀεὶ	⏑⏑_ ⏑⏑_	⏑⏑⏑⏑ ⏑⏑[ ]
καὶ δόξα θεῷ]	_ _ ⏑⏑ _	[ ] ⏑⏑⏑ ⏑⏑⏑⏑
δ[οτ]ῆ[ρι] μόγῳ[ι]	_ _ ⏑⏑ _	⏑⏑_ ⏑⏑_
[πάν]των ἀγαθῶν,	_ _ ⏑⏑ _	⏑⏑⏑⏑ ⏑⏑⏑⏑
ἀμὴν ἀμήν.	⏑_ ⏑_ treated as _ _ _ _	⏑⏑⏑ ⏑⏑⏑ ⏑⏑⏑⏑

Note: In the representation of musical rhythm, small shorts (⏑⏑) are divided shorts:

_ ⏑⏑ ⏑⏑⏑⏑ =

CHAPTER THREE

Interpretation of the Text

1   ]ὁμοῦ πᾶσαι τε θεοῦ λόγιμοι δε ... ? ι ... ? [...
2   ο]ὐ τὰν ἠῶ σιγάτω, μηδ' ἄστρα φαεσφόρα χ[..]δε-
3 [σ]θων [ἐκ]λειπ[όντων] ῥ[ιπαὶ πνοιῶν, πηγαὶ] ποταμῶν ῥοθίων πᾶσαι. ὑμνούντων δ'ἡμῶν
4 [π]ατέρα χυἱὸν χἄγιον πγεῦμα πᾶσαι δυνάμεις ἐπιφωνούντων ἀμὴν ἀμήν, κράτος αἶνος
5 [ἀεὶ καὶ δόξα θεῷ] ᾷ[ωτ]ῆ[ρι] μόγῳ[ι] [πάν]των ἀγαθῶν, ἀμὴν ἀμήν.

1 ... together all the eminent ones of God ...
2 ... night] nor day (?) Let it / them be silent. Let the luminous stars not [ ],
3 ... [let the rushings of winds, the sources] of all surging rivers [cease]. While we hymn
4 Father and Son and Holy Spirit, let all the powers answer, "Amen, amen. Strength, praise
5 [and glory forever to God], the sole giver of all good things. Amen, amen."

The words of the hymn, to the extent they have been preserved, refer to three groups of participants and their actions: natural elements, which are called to be still; a "we," who sing the hymn to the Trinity; and powers, who answer the Trinitarian hymn with a doxology. There are also remnants of a preceding line and a half in ms. line 1 through the middle of line 2.

The Eminent Ones (line 1)

As noted in chapter two, the bits of text in line 1 admit taking πᾶσαι and θεοῦ with λόγιμοι or with a preceding noun. The plural adjective λόγιμοι, which can be a masculine or a feminine form, is in the nominative and therefore modifies the subject of an action or predication; or it is itself the subject (as a substantival adjective). The word λόγιμος means "eminent," "famous," "notable," but Terzaghi construes λόγιμος here as a synonym of νοερός (intellectual) in a neoplatonic sense.[1] Wolbergs follows suit, holding it more likely that λόγιμοι is

---

[1] Terzaghi (1963, 672). Cf. Pighi (1941, 219): "razionali, intellettive."

used here as a synonym for λόγικοι and that it describes angels in a way analogous to πνεύματα νοερά in the *Apostolic Constitutions* and λογικῶν πνευμάτων in one of the liturgical prayers attributed to Serapion of Thmuis.[2] The idea is that *rational* heavenly beings praise God with what Paul called λογικὴ λατρεία ("rational worship" in Rom 12:1) in contrast to the appropriate silence of the irrational entities (stars, rivers, etc.).[3] The use of λόγιμος as a synonym of λόγικος is unattested, however, and it is difficult to see why the hymn-writer would employ λόγιμος with an uncommon meaning when λόγικος was available to him.

Wolbergs also entertains the possibility that λόγιμοι is a synonym for ἔνδοξοι ("honored," "glorious"), a term applied to angels in the *Shepherd of Hermas*.[4] No doubt the common meanings of ἔνδοξος and λόγιμος overlap. In any case, there is certainly no reason why angels could not be called λόγιμοι in the sense of "eminent." The second-century (C.E.) lexicographer Julius Pollux uses this term in laying out descriptions of elite soldiers: στρατιῶται ἐπίλεκτοι ("select soldiers"), ἔκκριτοι ("chosen above all"), πρόκριτοι ("preferred"), δόκιμοι ("tested"), εὐδόκιμοι ("well-tested"), ἄριστοι ("excellent"), ἀριστεῖς ("finest"), ἀριστεύοντες ("excelling"), κρατιστεύοντες ("being the best"), λογάδες ("select"), λόγιμοι ("eminent") (Julius Pollux, *Onom.* 1.176 Bethe).

... Nor the Day (line 2)

Space for about 28 letters precedes υ ταν ηω in line 2. The discussion in chapter two showed that West's interpretation of this phrase as ο]ὺ τὰν ἠῶ ("not the day" / "nor the day"), suggesting a larger construction meaning "neither night nor day," is probably the best guess. In that case, the phrase may describe an action by God (ruling, sustaining, or the like) that does not *cease* night or day. Or the phrase might modify something done by the λόγιμοι or another subject.

Call for Cosmic Stillness (lines 2–3)

Hunt reads σιγάτω with μηδ' and construes its subject as ἄστρα φαεσφόρα. Accordingly, he surmises that the hymn calls for the cosmos "to join in a chorus

---

[2] *Apos. Con.* 7.35.3 Funk; *Sacr. Ser.* 10.1 Funk. See Wolbergs (1971, 104–5). Not mentioned by Wolbergs is the appearance of λογικὰ πνεύματα in reference to heavenly beings in Cyril of Jerusalem, *Ador. et cult.* (PG 68:325.39) and the description of angels as "intellectual fire" and "intellectual spirits" (οἱ μὲν ἄγγελοι νοερὸν πῦρ καὶ πνεύματα νοερά) in Clement of Alexandria, *Exc.* 1.12.2 (Sagnard [1970, 82]).

[3] Wolbergs (1971, 104–5).

[4] Wolbergs (1971, 104). See Herm., *Sim.* 59.4 [V.6.4]; 83.2 [IX.6.2]; 89.8 [IX.12.8].

of praise to Father, Son, and Holy Spirit."[5] He is followed in this interpretation by Reinach, Ursprung, and Wagner.[6] This construal of σιγάτω κ.τ.λ. suggests that the hymn takes up the idea of nature's praise found in the Psalms (notably Pss 19, 47, 69, 96, and 148). But Del Grande, Terzaghi, Pighi, Pöhlmann, Wolbergs, and West separate σιγάτω syntactically from μηδ' ἄστρα φαεσφόρα. According to these interpreters, the hymn employs a motif of cosmic silence found in other Greek literature, including hymns.[7] A closer examination of the motif of cosmic stillness in Greek writers supports this second interpretation. The language in P.Oxy. 1786 about the natural elements reflects a traditional idea of silence before an offering, which was well established in Greek liturgy, drama, and hymnody. This interpretation of σιγάτω κ.τ.λ. is further supported by syntactical considerations noted in chapter two.

Cosmic Stillness in the Greek Tradition

The comic stillness motif has two roots – one in ritual practice and the other in the notion that nature, like human beings, falls spontaneously still (in fear or reverence) when a deity appears. From early times, an offering (libation, animal sacrifice, ritual prayer or hymn) was preceded by a command for proper deportment. Our oldest examples, which no doubt reflect long-established practice, come from Homer. In a scene from the *Iliad*, an assembly of warriors listens "in silence ... as is fitting" (σιγῇ ... κατὰ μοῖραν) to a prayer of Agamemnon, who is about to sacrifice (*Il.* 19.255–56 Murray). In another scene, before the pouring of a libation, heralds are instructed, "Bring water for our hands and call for holy circumspection (εὐφημῆσαί τε κέλεσθε), that we might lift a prayer to Zeus, son of Cronos, that he will have mercy on us" (Homer, *Il.* 9.171 Murray). As its etymology suggests, εὐφημέω means "speak well," but in ritual contexts it acquired the further connotation of avoiding inauspicious words. Hymns had to be composed of words that qualified as εὐφημία (Plato, *Leg.* 801a1; Pindar, *Pyth.* 10.35; Euripides, *Herc. fur.* 694).[8] And when onlookers at a sacrifice were commanded to observe εὐφημία, they had to be careful not to say anything inappropriate. Hence, εὐφημία (and its related verbs) became associated with "ritual silence," and the command εὐφημεῖτε acquired the sense, "Observe holy silence!"

In Classical drama we meet a number of scenes in which calls for ritual silence are issued before an offering (hymn, libation, prayer). In *Women at the Thesmophoria* a call to holy silence introduces a hymnic prayer by a chorus

---

[5] Hunt and Jones (1922, 22).
[6] Reinach (1922, 13); Ursprung (1923, 111); Wagner (1924, 217).
[7] Del Grande (1923, 174); idem (1931, 452); Terzaghi (1963 [1925], 673–74); Pighi (1941, 214–15); Wolbergs (1971, 106–8); Pöhlmann (1970, 107, 109); West (1992a, 48–50).
[8] See Furley and Bremer (2001, 1:57n170).

of women: εὐφημία ἔστω, εὐφημία ἔστω (Aristophanes, *Thesm*. 295–96 Henderson). Likewise, in *The Bacchanals* an instruction, "let everyone dedicate a reverent mouth" (στόμα τ' εὔφημον ἅπας ἐξοσιούσθω), precedes a hymn (Euripides, *Bacch*. 69–70 Kovacs). Cries of σπονδὴ σπονδή, εὐφημεῖτε εὐφημεῖτε appear in a libation scene from *The Peace* (Aristophanes, *Pax* 433–34 Henderson). In *Hecuba*, Euripides has Neoptolemos signal that the army should be silent because a prayer is about to be offered: σημαίνει δέ μοι σιγὴν Ἀχαιῶν παντὶ κηρῦξαι στρατῶι. κἀγὼ καταστὰς εἶπον ἐν μέσοις τάδε· Σιγᾶτ', Ἀχαιοί, σῖγα πᾶς ἔστω λεώς, σῖγα σιώπα (*Hec*. 529–33 Diggle).⁹

The custom of commanding silence at the beginning of a religious rite persisted into the Roman period, being found among both Greeks and Romans. Pollux defines heralds by first describing their role as proclaimers of silence at religious events: Τὸ δὲ κηρύκων γένος ἱερὸν μὲν Ἑρμοῦ, κατεκήρυττε δ' ἡσυχίαν ἔν τ' ἀγῶσι καὶ ἱερουργίαις (*Onom*. 4.91 Bethe). He also observes that one meaning of the verb ὑποκηρύξασθαι is "proclaim silence beforehand" (τὸ προειπεῖν ἡσυχίαν; *Onom*. 4.94 Bethe).¹⁰ As far as Roman custom is concerned, ritual silence is portrayed in a graphic illustration found in a frieze from the south side of the Ara Pacis (completed in 9 B.C.E.). The frieze depicts the imperial family engaged in a ceremonial act involving a solemn procession. A veiled woman covers her lips with her forefinger, representing the protocol of silence.¹¹ The formula *favete linguis* is the Latin equivalent of εὐφημεῖτε (see, e.g., Horace, *Carm*. 3.1.2).

The expectation of holy silence was also extended to nonhuman creatures and entities in drama and hymnody. In *Women at the Thesmophoria*, Aristophanes parodies the call to silence before an offering, and for the first time in extant Greek literature not only human beings but also animals and parts of inanimate nature are commanded to observe ritual silence: "The servant comes with fire and myrtles ... All people keep holy silence (εὔφημος πᾶς ἔστω λαός)! Shut your mouth (στόμα συγκλῄσας)! For the throng of the Muses is home, making melodies under the master's roofs. Let the upper air hold still its winds. Let the gleaming swell of the sea not roar ... Sleep winged race! And wild beasts of the field, do not loose your feet" (*Thesm*. 39–48 Henderson).

---

⁹ The words εὐφημέω and σιγάω are sometimes found in combination, at least as early as Classical times. In *Acharnians*, following an initial command, εὐφημεῖτε, εὐφημεῖτε, the chorus leader adds, σῖγα πᾶς (Aristophanes, *Ach*. 237–38 Henderson). The context is Dicaeopolis' procession to make a sacrifice. In *Iphigeneia at Aulis*, when preparations are being made for the sacrifice of Iphigeneia, Talthybios commands the attending army to observe reverence and silence (εὐφημίαν ἀνεῖπε καὶ σιγὴν στρατῷ) (Euripides, *Iph. aul*. 1564 Kovacs).

¹⁰ Plutarch also mentions the custom of proclaiming εὐφημία at the beginning of processions and festivals but thinks of εὐφημία not strictly as silence but as reverence in both speech and thought (*Mor*. 378d).

¹¹ Simon (1986, 74–75).

The extension of the call to silence to natural entities appears in later hymnic texts (see below), where it merges with another tradition – the idea of the spontaneous cowed silence of nature before a divine epiphany. Our earliest depictions of the spontaneous silence of nature in response to a god's appearance are from Classical drama. In *Birds*, Aristophanes describes how various families of animals become frightened when the birds (gods of sorts,[12] soon to be joined by the heavenly Muses) start singing the praises of their feathered kingdom, and a windless sky calms the sea (κύματά τ' ἔσβεσε νήνεμος αἴθρη) (*Av.* 777–78 Henderson). Euripides takes up the idea a few years later in *Bacchae*. Having narrated how Dionysus appeared to a group of revelers, calling out from above and rebuking them for desecrating his rites, Euripides describes the response of nature at the sound of the god's voice: "The air fell silent (σίγησε δ' αἰθήρ), and the wooded glade kept its leaves in silence (σῖγα δ' ὕλιμος νάπη φύλλ' εἶχε), and you could not have heard the sound of any animal" (*Bacch.* 1084–85 Kovacs).

The motif appears later in a paean to Apollo by the musician Limenius, composed for a cultic ceremony in 128/7 B.C.E. and erected with musical notation on the south wall of the Athenian treasury at Delphi. The hymn begins with an invocation of the Muses, followed by a description of cosmic silence and the epiphany of Apollo. The text is not fully intact. West translates lines 8–12 (section 2 of the hymn) as follows: "The whole vault of heaven rejoiced (πᾶ[ς δὲ γ]άθησε πόλος οὐράνιος), the air held the tempests' swift courses in windless calm ([νη]νέμους δ' ἔσχεν αἰθὴρ ἀε[λλῶν ταχυπετ]εῖς [δρ]όμους), and Nereus' thunderous swell abated (λῆξε), and mighty Ocean that surrounds the earth with his watery embrace."[13] These words describe the traditional moment of stillness in preparation to receive the epiphany of a god, the epiphany here being the birth of Apollo.

Another hymn to Apollo, this one from the Roman era, gives an opening account of the birth of the god, accompanied by a description of stillness in nature: "The earth stood still, the air stood still (ἵστατο μὲν γᾶ, ἵστατο δ' ἀήρ), the island stiffened, the sea-swell stiffened (πάγνυτο νᾶσος, πάγνυτο κῦμα)" (Heitsch no. 51). Here the natural realm is immobilized with fearful respect when Apollo enters the world.

The spontaneous response of fearful stillness in the presence of a god and the ritualized practice of reverent, circumspect silence (or avoidance of inauspicious words) when an offering is made are not exactly the same, but both can be understood as expressions of reverence for deity. It is therefore not surprising that they became associated. In some texts the stillness of nature before a

---

[12] "Recognize us as gods and you will have us to use as your prophetic Muses ..." (*Av.* 723–24 Henderson).

[13] *Delph.* inv. 489 et al., lines 8–10 Pöhlmann and West; ET from West (1992b, 294).

divine epiphany and the ritual call to silence before an offering combine and even coalesce so as to be almost indistinguishable.

In one of Callimachus' hymns a *call* for worshipers to be silent is accompanied by a *description* of the sea falling silent as Apollo approaches his shrine:

1 How the laurel branch of Apollo trembles!
2 How the whole shrine trembles! Away, away, whoever is sinful!
3 Phoebus knocks at the doors with his beautiful foot.
...
6 Open! you bolts of doors.
7 Open your locks! The god is no longer distant.
8 You young men, get ready for song and dance!
...
16 The shell [lyre] is no longer idle.
17 Keep holy silence, listeners to the song of Apollo (εὐφημεῖτ' ἀίοντες ἐπ' Ἀπόλλωνος ἀοιδῇ).
18 The sea, too, keeps holy silence (εὐφημεῖ καὶ πόντος) ...

Hymn. Apoll. 1–18 Asper

Very different is the spirit in which the two motifs are joined in an anapaestic hymn in Lucian's satirical comedy *Podagra*. In a bit of burlesque reminiscent of *Thesm.* 39–48, Lucian depicts a call for human beings and natural elements to be reverently silent in anticipation of Gout's epiphany. "Goddess, kindly appear," declares the sufferer, "and I, together with your devotees, will begin the hymns, singing the songs of the gouty" (*Pod.* 126–28). Then the chorus starts up the hymn: "Let the air be still and windless! (Σῖγα μὲν αἰθὴρ νήνεμος ἔστω). And let every gouty man keep holy silence! (καὶ πᾶς ποδαγρῶν εὐφημείτω). Behold, the goddess ... comes" (*Pod.* 129–33 MacLeod).

A coalescence of the two motifs is also evident in one of Mesomedes' hymns to the Sun: "Let all heaven keep holy silence (εὐφαμείτω πᾶς αἰθήρ); let earth, and sea and winds, mountains, valley be silent (σιγάτω), and also echoes, songs of birds" (Heitsch no. 2.2, lines 1–4). Here, too, we have an offering (the hymn) and an epiphany. The summons to silence is not only to secure proper deportment for the singing of the hymn but also and expressly to prepare for the appearance of the god: "for there is about to step forth to us Phoebus of unshorn hair" (Heitsch no. 2.2, lines 5–6).

Commands for silence before hymnic offerings also appear in two hymns of Synesius, a Christian Neoplatonist who lived from the late-fourth century into the early-fifth:

Hymn. 1.72–85 (Gruber and Strohm):

72 Let them be silent (εὐφαμείτω),
73 heaven and earth.
74 Let the sea stand still (στάτω πόντος);
75 let the air stand still (στάτω δ' ἀήρ).

76 Cease (λήγετε), blasts
77 of swift winds.
78 Cease, rushings
79 of noisy waves,
80 mouths of rivers,
81 welling fountains.
82 Keep silent (ἐχέτω σιγὰ),
83 hollows of the world
84 during the offering
85 of holy hymns.

Hymn. 2.28–43 (Gruber and Strohm):

28 Let the earth be silent (σιγάτω)
29 at your hymns,
30 at your prayers.
31 Let it keep holy silence (εὐφαμείτω),
32 all that the world contains.
33 For they are your works, Father.
34 Let them cease (καταπαυέσθω),
35 the rushing of the winds,
36 noise of trees,
37 tumult of birds.
38 Still be the atmosphere (ἥσυχος αἰθήρ).
39 Still be the air (ἥσυχος ἀὴρ).
40 Listen to my songs.
41 Gushing of waters,
42 noiseless (ἄψοφος) now
43 stand (στάτω) throughout the land.

The fact that the cosmic stillness motif appears in Callimachus' hymn to Apollo (third century B.C.E.), Limenius' hymn to Apollo (second century B.C.E.), another hymn to Apollo (anon., Roman era), one of Lucian's satirical hymns to Gout in *Podagra* (second century C.E.), one of Mesomedes' hymns (second century C.E.), and in two of the hymns of Synesius (d. circa 414) suggests a well-established conceit of Greek hymnody. This judgment is reinforced by two other examples. A hymn preserved in the *Corpus hermeticum* uses the motif to express the importance of receptiveness to the gnostic teaching of the tractate (*Corp. herm.* 13.17–20).[14] The stillness motif also appears in a Greek magical hymn, where the command for silence is part of the incantation, an expression of its binding power.[15] The presence of the conceit in a magical

---

[14] This didactic element is also present in Synesius' second hymn, where silence is commanded not only as an expression of holy respect but also as the precondition for attentive listening. The hymn is an act of worship by the cosmos but also instruction given to the cosmos: κλυέτω μολπᾶς (*Hymn.* 2.40 Gruber and Strohm).

[15] See Preisendanz and Henrichs (1973–1974, 1:40 = *PGM* III.198–205) // Hymn 5 in 2:241–42); also idem (1973–1974, 2:14–15 = *PGM* VII.320–24). Cf. also the description of cosmic stillness and magic spinning in a poem by Theocritus (*Idyll* 2.33–34).

poem, a text that stems from circles at a considerable social remove from the world of literati such as Callimachus, Lucian, and Synesius, suggests that the motif was a familiar and widespread poetic device.

Calls for holy silence are also found in the Jewish tradition. A famous line in Hab 2:20 declares, "The LORD is in his holy temple. Be silent, all the earth, before him!" It is unlikely that this passage influenced the author of P.Oxy. 1786 since the Greek translators render the interjection הַס (Hush! Be silent!) with the verb εὐλαβείσθω, "Be fearful." Somewhat similar is Zech 2:13: "Be silent, all people, before the LORD, for he has roused himself from his holy dwelling" (NRSV; 2:17 Heb). Here, too, the Greek translators render הַס with εὐλαβείσθω (=Zech 2:17 LXX). In Isa 41:1 God commands the coastlands (most naturally interpreted as the peoples of these regions) to be silent: "Listen to me in silence, O coastlands; let the peoples renew their strength ..." (NRSV). Again, the Septuagint is different: "Restore yourselves to me, O islands (ἐγκαινίζεσθε πρός με, νῆσοι); for the rulers shall obtain strength ..." A passage from the mystical-poetic *hekhalot* literature[16] deserves mention here as well: "Be silent for me, O voice of all the creatures I have created, that I may hearken and listen to the voice of my children's prayer."[17] This passage and those just quoted from the Jewish scriptures do not belong to the specific conceptual-linguistic tradition that informs the call for silence in P.Oxy. 1786. Nevertheless, the passage from the *hekhalot* corpus contains a similar idea (a call for the created order to be silent before the prayer-offering of the people); and Hab 2:20 and Zech 2:13 show that the notion of reverent silence was part of ancient Israelite understandings of proper decorum in the face of an epiphany. We no doubt have to do with a widespread ancient Mediterranean tradition.

The Cosmic Stillness Motif in P.Oxy. 1786

In chapter two we examined the question whether the stars, rivers, and whatever other natural elements may have been named are commanded to be silent or not. In terms of the sense of the hymn as a whole, whether the natural elements are summoned to reverent stillness or to active praise, they are being cast as participants in the cosmic liturgical event described by the hymn. If the less likely alternative is correct (that nature is commanded *not* to be silent), the chief effects for interpretation would be as follows: 1) to alter a detail of the

---

[16] The term *hekhalot* means "shrines." The *hekhalot* literature is a group of Jewish writings in Hebrew dated roughly to the second through fifth centuries C.E. The corpus is preserved in medieval manuscripts (the earliest dating to the fourteenth century) and in some fragments from the Cairo Genizah. See Elior (1986–1987, 213–14).

[17] *Hekhalot Rabbati* § 173 in Schäfer (1981), as quoted and translated in Elior (1997, 257n77).

liturgical picture painted by the hymn; 2) to make irrelevant the discussion below regarding calls for silence in early Christian liturgy, with the exception of the reference to *Trad. ap.* 79.26–32 (nature pausing at midnight to quietly bless the creator), a passage that would no longer be quite as apposite but would still be relevant; and 3) to remove the foundation of the argument in chapter four about the length of the hymn (the observation that calls to silence belong to the openings of hymns).[18]

That said, the remains of lines 2 and 3 of P.Oxy. 1786 appear to contain telltale signs of a cosmic stillness conceit that was well established in ancient Greek hymnody. In the same context we find the command σιγάτω and references to natural elements ("luminous stars" and "rushing rivers"). Ordinary rules of syntax encourage us to construe the negative connector μηδ' with what follows rather than with σιγάτω. A less natural construal of the syntax lets one imagine that the hymn is voicing the biblical idea of nature's noisy praise, which is also found in early Christian writings. But even granting that the syntactical position of μηδέ might permit this interpretation,[19] the specific language in lines 2 and 3, occurring in a hymn that shows other signs of indebtedness to a literate Greek tradition of hymnody (Greek musical notation, Classical imperative forms,[20] and the Homeric δωτήρ formula in the doxology), points strongly in a different direction, namely, to the Greek conceit of cosmic stillness before an offering.[21]

It is natural to take the stillness motif in P.Oxy. 1786 as a purely poetic expression meant to evoke in the religious imagination a scene of reverence and not to suggest that stars literally stop shining or that rivers literally stop flowing. Nevertheless, it is possible that the Christians who sang the hymn took for granted that in some real sense the cosmos becomes reverent and attentive when the church joins with the heavenly powers in worship. Three versions of a passage in the *Apostolic Tradition* (third century) refer to creation pausing at

---

[18] The discussion of deictic self-referentiality in chapter four would not be affected by the alternative interpretation except in terms of the kind of action nature is summoned to perform in the hymnic self-reference in lines 2 and 3.

[19] It was pointed out in chapter two that connective μηδέ is not postpositive but takes first position in a sentence or clause. Admittedly, syntactical conventions are not always followed, especially in poetry. But one assumes that a convention has been observed unless there are countervailing reasons for thinking otherwise. In the case at hand, there are no contrary indicators. Had our hymnist wished to negate σιγάτω, he could have put μή in front of it without disturbing his metrical scheme or rhythm.

[20] The verb ἐπιφωνούντων in line 4 carries the Classical imperative ending. One guesses that the [ ]θων at the beginning of line 3 is also part of a Classical imperative ending.

[21] The telltale language led specialists in Greek hymnody to reject Hunt's original surmise and to conclude that P.Oxy. 1786 exhibits the cosmic stillness idea. As noted above, there was already a dissent from Hunt's interpretation by Del Grande in 1923. Since then, with the single exception of Wagner (1924), all classicists who have commented on the hymn have agreed with Del Grande.

midnight to honor God. The Latin version phrases this moment as follows: "For the elders who passed [it] on to us taught us thus, because at this hour all creation rests (*omnis creatura quiescit*) for a moment so that they might praise the Lord (*laudent dominum*); stars and trees and waters pause for an instant (*stare in ictu*), and the whole army of angels serves him at this hour to praise God together with the souls of the righteous" (*Trad. ap.* 79.26–32 // 41.15 Tidner). The Sahidic version says: "from that hour all creation pauses, quietly blessing God. The stars and the trees and the waters act in like manner as those who attend. And all the host of angels worship with the souls of the righteous. They sing ..." (41.15).[22] The Ethiopic has: "in this hour all creation toils to praise God. The stars, the plants, and the waters stand for an hour [or "for a while"]; and all the armies of angels, as they serve in this hour with the souls of the just, praise God" (41.15).[23] It is difficult to know how Christians imagined this. Apparently, they thought that some actual alteration in nature took place, perhaps that the dying down of the winds at nighttime and the stillness of lakes on a windless night were visible signs of a general reverent stillness of nature in the deep of night, a quietude that could be assumed for heavenly bodies as well.

A call for ritual silence is found in the instructions of the *Apostolic Constitutions* regarding deportment at the Eucharist. "And after the prayer, let some of the deacons devote themselves to the offering of the Eucharist, serving the body of the Lord with reverent fear (ὑπηρετούμενοι τῷ τοῦ κυρίου σώματι μετὰ φόβου), and let other deacons observe the people and command them to be silent (ἡσυχίαν αὐτοῖς ἐμποιείτωσαν)" (*Apos. Con.* 2.57.15 Funk). This tradition no doubt inspired the use of the silence motif in one of the later traditional hymns of the Great Entrance, "Let All Mortal Flesh Keep Silence" (Σιγησάτω πᾶσα σὰρξ βροτεία). But there is no reference in *Apos. Con.* 2.57.15 (or in "Let All Mortal Flesh Keep Silence") to nature observing silence or comporting itself reverently while the church sings.[24]

In the end, the question of how the cosmic stillness motif was understood by those who used P.Oxy. 1786 must remain open. The composer couched the

---

[22] ET from Bradshaw et al. (2002, 200).

[23] ET from Bradshaw et al. (2002, 200); Ethiopic text with German translation in Duensing (1946, 142–3).

[24] Pighi (1941, 214n1) adduces some interesting lines from a prayer preserved among the Rainer papyri and dating perhaps to the third century: ὅτε καταχέονται καὶ φένονται [read φαίνονταί] σου [αἱ] ἀκτῖνες ἐν τῇδε τῇ τῶν κτίσεων [πλ]άνῃ, τότε πρὸ σοῦ δύνουσι δυνάμεις [πᾶ]σαι καὶ ἄγγελοι καὶ διοικηταὶ τῆς ζω[ῆς] τοῦ τε οὐρανοῦ οἱ τύποι καὶ τῆς γῆς [...]ουργήματά τε καὶ κλίματα ἄσ[τρα] τε τὰ φαι[ν]όμενα καὶ αἱ τοῦ δρόμου [δυν]άμεις πάντα δύνει καὶ ἀμβλύνε[ται] τῇ τοῦ φωτός σου θέᾳ καὶ τῷ τῆς [ἀρι]στείας σου κάλλει μόνος δὲ σὺ φαίνῃ [κα]ὶ φαίνεις εἰκόνα τῆς τοῦ σοῦ πατρός... ("When your beams pour down and shine into the wandering of created things, then, before you, all powers and angels and governors of life, forms of heaven and earth, [ ] and climates, stars, and manifestations, and all powers of movement sink and become dim at the spectacle of your light and the beauty of your excellences, and you alone shine. And you shine forth

stillness motif in words borrowed from the Greek hymnic tradition, where it is metaphorical; but whatever the composer intended, interpretations of the meaning of the motif by worshipers may have varied from the poetic to the quasi-literal. We will come back to this in chapter four.

While We Hymn (line 3)

The phrase ὑμνούντων δ' ἡμῶν ("while we hymn") is a genitive absolute. The δέ suggests that the clause goes with what follows, modifying the imperative ἐπιφωνούντων. Moreover, it is common for genitive absolutes to stand first in the sentences to which they belong. The sense is as follows: "While we hymn ..., let the powers respond ..."

Although the statement is very short, it entails two interesting rhetorical elements. First, it is self-referential speech: the voice of the hymn singing about its own singing. Second, it is deictic speech, an utterance that locates the speaking in the here and now. These two – self-referentiality and deixis – often occur together in Greek poetry. A more detailed discussion of deictic self-referentiality in P.Oxy. 1786 will be given in chapter four.

Community Hymn to the Trinity (lines 3–4)

The "we" (ἡμῶν) of the Christian community hymns the triune deity, naming each member of the Trinity and linking the three names through the use of καί without any prepositional phrases. In the later third and early fourth centuries, mention of Christ and the Spirit in praise formulations was more typically done with prepositional phrases, especially in doxologies. For example, one of the most common forms of the numerous Trinitarian doxologies in books 7 and 8 of the *Apostolic Constitutions* reads as follows:

δι' οὗ σοι δόξα ἐν ἁγίῳ πνεύματι εἰς τοὺς αἰῶνας· ἀμήν ("*through* whom [your Christ] to you [God the Father] be glory *in* the Holy Spirit forever. Amen") (*Apos. Con.* 7.45.3 mss. a and h Funk).[25]

Another common form in the *Apostolic Constitutions* uses a prepositional phrase in referring to Christ but not in referring to the Spirit:

---

the image of your Father... ") (Inventory no. 19898 recto, lines 20–29, in Wessely [1906–1924, 2:447–48]). It is not clear whether the dimming of creation is to be understood as an act of homage or – as I think more likely – an effect of the overwhelming splendor of the divine light.

[25] Mss. a and h have δι'οὗ; mss, d, e, p, and v have μεθ' οὗ. Variant readings no doubt reflect the witting or unwitting tendency of scribes to conform the language to Trinitarian forms that were familiar or more congenial to them.

μεθ' οὗ σοὶ δόξα, τιμή, αἶνος, δοξολογία, εὐχαριστία καὶ τῷ ἁγίῳ πνεύματι εἰς τοὺς αἰῶνας· ἀμήν ("with whom [your Christ] to you [God the Father] be glory ... and to the Holy Spirit forever. Amen") (*Apos. Con.* 8.13.10; except ms. d Funk).[26]

In three places in the *Apostolic Constitutions* we find a Trinitarian doxology phrased exclusively with datives, for example: σοὶ πᾶσα δόξα, σέβας καὶ εὐχαριστία, τιμὴ καὶ προσκύνησις, τῷ πατρὶ καὶ τῷ υἱῷ καὶ τῷ ἁγίῳ πνεύματι ... ("to you [God] be all glory, reverence and thanksgiving, honor and worship, to the Father and to the Son and to the Holy Spirit ...") (*Apos. Con.* 8.12.50 Funk).[27]

The various doxological formulations in the *Apostolic Consitutions*, a composite work that underwent editing over time, reflect a heterogeneity of traditional liturgical forms, some no doubt older than others. No effort at standardization in doxological language was made until the late fourth century in the wake of the great conflicts over the nature of the Trinity. By the middle of the fourth century, the forms using instrumental language of Christ ("through Christ") and locative language of the Spirit ("in the Spirit"), although traditional, were regarded by some as Arian, and were interpreted by Arians as ancient evidence in support of their views (Sozomen, *H.E.* 3.20.8; Theodoret, *H.E.* 2.19; the Arian writer Philostorgius, *H.E.* 3.13). In this atmosphere, Basil of Caesarea was accused by some members of his congregation of introducing a novelty when, in a prayer, he uttered a doxology in the form "*with* the Son together *with* the Holy Spirit" and also used the more common form, "*through* Christ *in* the Holy Spirit," creating, his detractors said, a contradiction. The formulas using "with Christ" (e.g., μεθ' οὗ) and "with the Holy Spirit," instead of the usual instrumental constructions, accorded, in a very explicit way, equal praise for Father, Son, and Spirit. Evidently, Arian tendencies caused some to object to this; others may simply have found troublesome any departure from what they regarded as fixed traditional forms. In defending himself, Basil maintained that his accusers were making false distinctions;[28] and he adduced, among various historical proofs, an ἀρχαίαν τὴν φωνήν ("old formula") of the vesper service in which the people declare, probably in a hymn, Αἰνοῦμεν πατέρα καὶ υἱὸν καὶ ἅγιον πνεῦμα θεοῦ ("We praise Father, Son, and the Holy Spirit of God") (*Spir. sanct.* 29.73.42–43 Pruche).[29] The

---

[26] Ms. d has δι' and ἐν.

[27] See also 7.48.3 mss. m and v; and 8.15.9.

[28] For example, defending the view that older Trinitarian forms with prepositions express Trinitarian orthodoxy, Basil insisted that δόξα πατρὶ καὶ υἱῷ καὶ ἁγίῳ πνεύματι and δόξα πατρὶ καὶ υἱῷ σὺν τῷ ἁγίῳ πνεύματι are the same (*Spir. sanct.* 27.68.25–27 Pruche).

[29] Basil writes as follows about the origin of this vesper praise: "We cannot say who was the father of these words of lamp-lighting thanksgiving. Nevertheless, the people utter the ancient formula (ὁ μέντοι λαὸς ἀρχαίαν ἀφίησι τὴν φωνήν)" (*Spir. sanct.* 29.73.39–41 Pruche). The words quoted by Basil appear in nearly identical form in the hymn Φῶς ἱλαρόν ("Happy Light"). Hence,

language indicating the Trinity as recipients of praise in this formulation is close to that of P.Oxy. 1786: ὑμνούντων δ' ἡμῶν πατέρα χυἱὸν χἅγιον πνεῦμα.

It is likely that by the late fourth century, in the wake of the Arian controversies, the opening line of what came to be known as the Lesser Doxology (Gloria Patri) assumed a more or less standard form as praise for all three persons of the Trinity without any prepositional phrases. We find no Trinitarian praise of this form in doxologies that can be confidently dated to the first part of the fourth century or earlier,[30] unless we class the praise statements from the vesper formula in Basil and from P.Oxy. 1786 as *doxologies*. In any case, both of these praise statements appear to date from about the same time[31] and they share a similar grammatical form: verb of praise in the first-person plural followed by the names of the members of the Trinity in the accusative linked by copulatives. In this respect these formulations are different from doxologies in which praise – usually with a number of epithets – is ascribed using datives.

The Doxological Response of the Powers (lines 4–5)

While the community praises the Trinity, "all powers" (πᾶσαι δυνάμεις) respond with a doxology addressed to "God the sole giver of all good things."

It is possible that every conceivable power is meant by πᾶσαι δυνάμεις, perhaps by analogy with the cosmic worship described in Phil 2:10 ("that every knee might bow – of heavenly, earthly, and underworldly beings"). In that case, the hymn summons not only heavenly powers loyal to God but also hostile powers (demons, rebellious angels, et al.) to participate in the chorus

---

Basil is likely referring to a vesper *hymn*, either to Φῶς ἱλαρόν or to a hymn whose words were perhaps later incorporated into Φῶς ἱλαρόν.

[30] The *Apostolic Constitutions* was put together out of the *Didache* and other materials around 375 C.E. It is doubtful that the Trinitarian doxologies that do not use prepositions with reference to Christ and the Holy Spirit (*Apos. Con.* 8.12.50; 8.15.9; and mss. m and v of 7.48.3) reflect traditions that are much earlier than 375, and in any case it would be difficult to show that they do. A number of other examples of Trinitarian doxologies without prepositional phrases in reference to the Son or the Spirit may go back to the third century or earlier but cannot be dated with any confidence and are more likely later: a doxology in the longer ending of *Acts of Thomas* (170.28); a Christian interpolation at the end of the *Testament of Abraham* (14.9). A Trinitarian doxology that uses datives with Father and Son and "with" to include the Holy Spirit appears in Clement of Alexandria, who is no doubt expanding on a traditional formula: αἴνον τῷ μόνῳ πατρὶ καὶ υἱῷ, υἱῷ καὶ πατρί, παιδαγωγῷ καὶ διδασκάλῳ υἱῷ, σὺν καὶ τῷ ἁγίῳ πνεύματι ("praise to the only Father and to the Son, Son and Father, Son, instructor, and teacher, with the Holy Spirit") (*Paed.* 3.101.2 Stählin and Treu).

[31] Basil was born in 330 C.E. and was raised in a Christian household. It is difficult to say at what age he would have become acquainted with the vesper formula (or hymn) that he quotes or whether he had any knowledge, other than presumption, that it was very old. It might have been introduced into the vesper service at the end of the third century or even in the early fourth century, putting its date of composition around the time of P.Oxy. 1786.

of praise. It seems more likely, however, that the hymn has in view the angels traditionally thought of as worshiping God around the heavenly throne.

A common assumption of the patristic era is that God rules the world through a hierarchy of various heavenly beings. Using biblical language derived from the church's Jewish heritage and firmly embedded in earliest Christian tradition, second- and third-century Christian writers often referred to these beings as angels but sometimes called them by other names, including "powers" (δυνάμεις[32]). In our hymn, the choice of the term δυνάμεις instead of ἄγγελοι or some other name for heavenly servants of God owes manifestly to metrical considerations. The word δυνάμεις is a perfect half of an anapaestic metron.

Heavenly powers singing with the earthly congregation of God's people appear in one of the prayers of the *Apostolic Constitutions*, which depicts the heavenly worship carried out by various beings (seraphim, cherubim, angels, archangels, thrones, dominions, rulers, authorities, and powers) and then, gathering all these celestial worshipers under the term "powers," says, "Israel, your earthly assembly from the nations, vying with the heavenly powers (ταῖς κατ' οὐρανὸν δυνάμεσιν) night and day, sings with full heart and willing soul ..." (*Apos. Con.* 7.35.4 Funk). These words may come from a Jewish prayer, which the church adopted, applying the name "Israel" to itself.[33]

It is unlikely that the powers in P.Oxy. 1786 are *stars*. In the Bible and early Christian literature, stars are sometimes depicted as praising God,[34] but a reference to stars sounding a doxology would contradict the role of the stars in line 2, where they probably figure in a call for cosmic stillness.

Worshiping with Angels (line 4)

During the Second Jewish Commonwealth, notions of heavenly worship carried out by thousands of angelic beings, often depicted as divine warriors, flourished in the minds of Jewish authors, whose descriptions of the heavenly realm no doubt reflected widespread popular assumptions. People naturally thought about the relation between earthly worship in the Jerusalem temple and angelic worship in the heavenly temple. Our ancient Jewish sources give

---

[32] On heavenly beings – angels or other heavenly servants of God – as δυνάμεις, see Ps 148:2 LXX; Dan 3:61 LXX; *T. Ab.* 14.12 (resc. A); Philo, *Conf.* 171; 1 Pet 3:22; Justin, *Dial.* 36.4–5 quoting Ps 23:10 LXX; and *Dial.* 85.6 quoting Ps 148:2 LXX; *Mart. Pol.* 14.1; *Apos. Con.* 7.35.4; Chrysostom, *Sac.* 6.4.41–43.

[33] Various prayers found in *Apostolic Constitutions* 7 and 8 are thought to be prayers of the Hellenistic synagogue that have been reworked by Christians. On the whole subject, see Fiensy (1985); Graves (1997).

[34] The Septuagint depicts the stars praising (Ps 148:3). In the Hebrew of Job 38:7 (but not the Greek) the stars "sing." In Baruch they "rejoice" (εὐφράνθησαν, Bar 3:34 LXX); so also in the Greek version of Ps.-Ephraem Syrus, *Imit. prov.* (τὰ ἄστρα χαίρει) (Phrantzolas 1:260, line 5).

us some hints about the different ways in which this relationship was imagined but provide no comprehensive picture of the range and detail of various conceptions.

According to *Jubilees*, a book composed perhaps in the 2nd century B.C.E., two orders of angels keep the Sabbath – one order administering the Sabbath liturgy in heaven and the other order administering the earthly Sabbath worship (*Jub.* 2:18). The angels of the earthly Sabbath are joined by Israel. Moreover, the Levitical priests are to "serve in [God's] sanctuary as [like] the angels of the presence and the holy ones" and to be "like them with respect to honor and greatness and sanctification" (*Jub.* 31:14; cf. 30:18).³⁵ Hence, the author(s) of *Jubilees* saw a precise correspondence between the liturgy of the earthly temple and the liturgy of the heavenly temple³⁶ and understood that the earthly Sabbath service, conducted by both human officiants and angelic ones, was united with the worship in heaven.

The idea that earthly worship is a communion of human beings with angels may have been an assumption of the Qumran community as described by the *Community Rule*. Two passages are particularly suggestive. According to one, God "joins their assembly to the sons of heaven (סודם ועם בני שמים חבר) in order to (form) the council of the community" (1QS XI, 8 Martínez and Tigchelaar). According to the other, "the angels of holiness are [in the congrega]tion" (בעד]תם כיא מלאכי קודש)) (1QSa [1Q28a] II, 8–9 Martínez and Tigchelaar). Taken together, the evidence strongly suggests a community self-understanding in which the saints think of themselves as joined with angels in a kind of living temple for the worship of God.³⁷ This impression is strengthened when we consider that *Jubilees* was studied at Qumran and that it resonates at many points with the theology of various writings of the Qumran community. Moreover, the *Songs of the Sabbath Sacrifice* appear to be psalms of the community's Sabbath liturgy understood as a liturgy shared with the angels. For example, although the rather well-preserved song for the seventh Sabbath (4Q403 frg. 1, I, 30–46) was, presumably, performed by the community (or a choir of the community), it consists of a series of commands for the heavenly powers to praise God.³⁸

A tractate of the *Babylonian Talmud* asserts, "Moreover, the ministering angels do not begin to sing praises in heaven until Israel have sung below on

---

³⁵ Translation (based on the Ethiopic text) of Wintermute in Charlesworth (1983–1985, 2:115).

³⁶ According to *Jub.* 8:19, the Garden of Eden was the Holy of Holies, which probably implies not that the Holy of Holies was on earth but that the Garden was (still is) in heaven.

³⁷ Wolfson notes that these community self-descriptions border on the angelomorphic (Wolfson [2004, 212 with n10, 177–213]).

³⁸ Newsom, speaking of the *Songs* as a corpus, thinks that they were meant for "a type of communal mysticism, specifically a communion with angels in the act of praise" (Newsom [1997, 28]).

earth" (*Hullin* 91b).³⁹ In a similar vein, the *hekhalot* literature contains passages that envision the coordination of earthly and angelic worship in some kind of shared liturgy. One passage speaks of "surging fires that flicker and emerge from the mouths of the Cherubim and the mouths of the Ofannim and the mouths of the Holy Hayyot who open their mouths to say 'Holy' when Israel are saying 'Holy' before him [referring to the Trisagion of Isa 6:3]."⁴⁰ Another passage instructs that "the ministering angels are not permitted to utter song first on high until Israel open their mouths in song first in the lower world."⁴¹ The overall tenor of the *hekhalot* literature, however, is to conceive the heavenly liturgy without reference to any earthly worship.⁴²

Early Christians, deeply influenced by their Jewish heritage, also thought about the relation between heavenly and earthly worship. It is not clear how early the church began to regard its own worship as a liturgy shared with angels. No first-century Christian author explicitly asserts that Christians, in their earthly gatherings, participate in heavenly worship or that angels are present in Christian liturgy. At most, a few passages suggest connections between Christian believers and the heavenly realm that may have included ideas of participation with angels in worship:

1. In Gal 4:21–31, Paul works out an allegory in which he asserts that the children of promise belong to the "Jerusalem above," but his focus is not worship.

2. In 1 Cor 11:9–10, Paul insists that women must cover their heads in the assembly, adding the following explanation: "For the man was not created because of the woman but the woman because of the man. For this reason a woman is obliged to have authority on her head because of the angels." This may assume the presence of angels in worship, but interpretations vary widely.

3. In Phil 2:10–11, Paul describes how the exalted Christ receives veneration from the whole cosmos: earthly, heavenly, and subterranean knees are to bend at his name. The theology in these verses may be proleptic (see 1 Cor 15:24–28), but the language has a liturgical ring and might have been part of worship in some of the churches of the Pauline mission.⁴³ One can certainly envision Christians uttering such language and thinking of themselves as part of a wider cosmic praise of the exalted Christ. Moreover, the deutero-Pauline letter to the Ephesians locates the Christian community with Christ "in the heavenlies" (Eph 2:6).

4. The Book of Revelation presents a number of vivid heavenly-worship scenes involving angels. In one (Rev 7:9–17), a gathering of saints appears in heaven with the angels in a service of continuous praise. This scene may be a projection of the future or a description

---

³⁹ Translation from Cashdan and Epstein (1980, 182).

⁴⁰ *Hekhalot Rabbati* § 101 in Schäfer (1981), as quoted and translated in Elior (1997, 256; punctuation slightly modified).

⁴¹ *Hekhalot Rabbati* § 788 in Schäfer (1981), as quoted and translated in Elior (1997, 257n 77).

⁴² See Elior (1997, 257).

⁴³ Phil 2:6–11 was first identified as a pre-Pauline hymn by Lohmeyer in the 1920s, and his view eventually won near universal assent. Recently, however, this opinion has been challenged by a number of scholars. See especially Brucker (1997). Even if verses 6–11 are not from an early Christian hymn, they probably reflect the language of Christian worship.

of what the author believes is already in some way a present reality. In any case, the saints of this gathering are not living members of the church but deceased believers who have purified themselves by martyrdom in the "great tribulation" (v. 14).

5. In a context that ends with an admonition not to neglect meeting together, the author of Hebrews urges that "since we, brothers, have boldness to enter the Holies [= the *heavenly* Holy of Holies[44]] by the blood of Jesus ... let us approach with a true heart ..." (Heb 10:19, 22). The language of "approach" and "entry" may have Christian worship in view, but it is also possible that the author is speaking more generally about the attitude and self-understanding that Christians should adopt in their life of faith. Later, the author describes how Christians "have come to Mount Zion and to the city of the living God, the heavenly Jerusalem, and to myriad angels in festal assembly, and to the gathering of the firstborn who are enrolled in heaven ..." (Heb 12:22–23). The language and syntax of this passage are somewhat ambiguous and the purpose of the passage is not to describe Christian liturgy.[45]

The preceding shows that some first-century Christians may have believed that the angels were present with them in worship or that in some way the church joined the worship of heaven. But the evidence is tenuous and ambiguous. The most we can say is that certain texts are suggestive of these ideas and seem to lay a foundation for future thinking along these lines.

Suggestive language also appears in *1 Clement* (early second century), which urges the church to imitate heavenly worship:

For the scripture says, "Myriad upon myriad stood before him and thousands upon thousands were serving him, and they cried out, 'Holy, Holy, Holy, Lord Sabaoth, the whole creation is full of his glory'." Therefore, let us gather together in unity of mind and in (good) conscience, and cry earnestly to him as from one mouth, that we might be partakers of his great and glorious promises. (*1 Clem.* 34.6–7 Ehrman)

These words sound like an explicit comment on the relation between heavenly worship and the liturgy of the church, but the context is not about worship; it concerns service to God in good works (vv. 3–4), imitating angelic service to God through obedient lives. Therefore, the passage does not prove that Roman Christians recited the Trisagion in worship; nor is there any suggestion here that Christian liturgy is attended by angels.

The earliest explicit evidence for the idea that Christian devotion occurs in the company of angels appears in late second-century Egypt. Clement of

---

[44] "Holies" refers to the Holy of Holies or the space just in front outside the curtain (Heb 9:2–3; 9:8, 12, 24–25). The author has in view the Holies of the heavenly temple. He assumes the Jewish tradition that the earthly temple is a copy of the heavenly temple but takes this idea in a novel direction by arguing that worship in the earthly temple is not ultimately efficacious since it is *merely* an imitation of the true reality of heavenly worship, having been established as a shadow of the ultimate liturgical act (Christ's sacrifice) to come (Heb 8:5; 10:1). That sacrifice took place in the heavenly Holy of Holies. For this reason, the earthly temple has representational and instructional value but brings about no final sacrificial cleansing from sin (Heb 10:1–10). The Holies into which Christians enter through Christ is also the heavenly Holy of Holies.

[45] On the uncertainties about how to construe the language and syntax, see Attridge (1989, 374–75).

Alexandria holds that the enlightened one (ὁ γνωστικός) at prayer is in the company of angels: ὁ δὲ καὶ μετ' ἀγγέλων εὔχεται, ὡς ἂν ἤδη καὶ ἰσάγγελος, οὐδὲ ἔξω ποτὲ τῆς ἁγίας φρουρᾶς γίνεται, κἂν μόνος εὔχηται, τὸν τῶν ἁγίων χορὸν συνιστάμενον ἔχει ("What he prays he prays even with the angels, as if he were already their equal, and he is at no time outside their holy keeping. And if he prays alone he has the chorus of the holy ones standing with him") (*Str.* 7.12.78.6 Stählin, Früchtel, and Treu).[46] The angels here may be thought of not as a band of worshipers but simply as protectors, which is what the words οὐδὲ ἔξω ποτὲ τῆς ἁγίας φρουρᾶς suggest. But a liturgical note is struck by the expression "chorus of the holy ones," which is probably to be understood as a choir of angels who add their praise to the prayer of the enlightened human worshiper (see also *Str.* 7.7.49).

In another place, Clement envisions an ideal liturgy on God's heavenly mountain where "the daughters of God ... proclaim the solemn rites of the Word and assemble a modest choral dance" in which "the dancers are the righteous" and "their song is a hymn to the king of all" (*Protr.* 12.119.1–2 Stählin and Treu). In this celebration (the antithesis of the Bacchic rites on which the scene is polemically modeled), "the maidens sing to the lyre, the angels give glory, the prophets speak, and a sound of music goes forth" (ψάλλουσιν αἱ κόραι, δοξάζουσιν ἄγγελοι, προφῆται λαλοῦσιν, ἦχος στέλλεται μουσικῆς) (*Protr.* 12.119.2 Stählin and Treu). Clement goes on to add, "if you will, be initiated yourself and you will dance with angels (χορεύσεις μετ' ἀγγέλων) around the unbegotten and imperishable and only true God, while the Word of God joins in our hymn (συνυμνοῦντος ἡμῖν τοῦ θεοῦ λόγου)" (*Protr.* 12.120.2 Stählin and Treu). This picture is figurative, but it describes an experience of spiritual consummation, some elements of which Clement may have understood in a quasi-literal way. However the angels are to be conceived, the soul of the enlightened one is in their company and the glory of the exalted celebration is participation in a kind of heavenly music and dance that Clement probably understood as real – the rational, supra-sensible music of heaven on which mundane, matter-bound song and dance are based.[47]

In the two passages just discussed, Clement is thinking of the individual's relation to heavenly powers. He probably also believed that when enlightened ones gathered as a group for prayer and song, or to celebrate the Eucharist, angels were present; but he nowhere says so explicitly.

Origen, a third-century Christian teacher also associated with Alexandria, remarks at one point in *Contra Celsum*, "we hymn God and his Only-begotten as do the sun, moon, stars, and the whole heavenly host. For all these being

---

[46] The designation ὁ γνωστικός for the kind of person he is describing (see *Str.* 7.12.78.4) is Clement's word for a believer of true and mature understanding.

[47] See Cosgrove (2006a, 276–81).

a divine choir, together with the righteous among human beings, hymn God who is over all and his Only-begotten" (ὑμνοῦμέν γε θεὸν καὶ τὸν μονογενῆ αὐτοῦ ὡς καὶ ἥλιος καὶ σελήνη καὶ ἄστρα καὶ πᾶσα ἡ οὐρανία στρατιά. ὑμνοῦσι γὰρ πάντες οὗτοι, θεῖος ὄντες χορὸς, μετὰ τῶν ἐν ἀνθρώποις δικαίων τὸν ἐπὶ πᾶσι θεὸν καὶ τὸν μονογενῆ αὐτοῦ) (*Cels.* 8.67 Koetschau). The point of these assertions, which echo Ps 148:3, is to reject claims by Celsus about the relation between polytheism and worship of the supreme God, specifically, the notion that to hymn "the sun and Minerva" redounds to the glory of the supreme deity. Hence, Origen is not describing a liturgical moment in which Christians are united with angels and cosmic elements in joint worship of God.

More suggestive is a passage in *De oratione*, where Origen imagines that "at the gathering of the saints, there is a twofold congregation, one of human beings and one of angels" (*Or.* 31.5; cf. *Or.* 11.5). The context of this statement is a discussion of the benefits for believers in coming together in a place of prayer. When they do so, angels are likely (ὡς εἰκός) with them, along with "the powers" of Christ, saints who have died, and saints still alive (*Or.* 31.5 Koetschau). To show that angels attend Christian prayer, Origen quotes Ps 33:8 (LXX), "The angel of the Lord encircles those who fear him and he rescues them." Then he adds Jacob's words in Gen 48:16 (LXX), which he takes as applying not only to Jacob but to all who rely on God: "The angel rescued me from all evils." Origen interprets this as implying that when the church is gathered, the angel of each believer is present as a protector. The arrival of protecting angels creates the "twofold church, one of human beings and one of angels." In the same place Origen also adduces Tob 12:12, which describes the angel Raphael declaring that when Tobit and Sarah prayed, Raphael himself brought the "memorial" of their prayers before God. Origen takes this to mean that whenever Christians pray, Raphael is ready to assist them. To sum up, in *De oratione* 31 Origen paints a picture of the church gathered in a place for prayer and surrounded by angels who protect them and see to it that their prayers reach heaven. This falls short perhaps of the idea that the angels join in a common *liturgy* with the gathered church on earth, but it comes close.

The Latin version of the *Apostolic Tradition* asserts that midnight is a time of praise for angels and all creation, making it also an appropriate moment for Christian prayer. We have already considered this text in connection with the silence motif. The passage closes with the following words: "all the host of angels serve him at this hour by praising God along with the souls of the righteous" (*omne agmen angelorum ministrat ei in hac <h>ora una cum iustorum animabus laudare deum*) (*Trad. ap.* 79.30–32 // 41.15 Tidner). The idea of angels praising with the church at midnight is also found in the other versions of the *Apostolic Tradition* at this point (in the Sahidic, Arabic, and Ethiopic). This belief persisted into subsequent centuries. Chrysostom, for example, refers to the church praising God with angels in the midnight office (*In 1 Tim.*, *hom.* 14.4; PG 67:576).

A passage in the *Apostolic Constitutions* depicts heavenly powers engaged in ongoing worship and then declares that "Israel" ("the church from the nations") competes in praise with these powers by singing night and day (*Apos. Con.* 7.35.3–4 Funk). This statement probably derives from one of the source documents of the fourth-century *Apostolic Constitutions* and may be part of a reworked Jewish prayer. There is no mention of angels and the church being together in the same place. Instead, separate but corresponding liturgies – one on earth and the other in heaven – are in view.

A number of fourth-century fathers mention angels in connection with Christian worship.[48] In *Mystagogic Catechesis* 5.6, Cyril of Jerusalem describes the eucharistic service as a cosmic liturgy in which "we call to mind the seraphim which Isaiah, in the Holy Spirit, saw around the throne of God [Isaiah 6] ... saying 'Holy, Holy, Holy, Lord Sabaoth'" (*Myst. Cat.* 5.6).[49] Cyril then adds, "Therefore, we say the doxology transmitted to us by the seraphim, that we might become sharers of the hymnody with the heavenly armies (κοινωνοὶ τῆς ὑμνῳδίας ταῖς ὑπερκοσμίοις γενώμεθα στρατιαῖς)" (*Myst. Cat.* 5.6 Piédagnel). In another work, his lenten *Catecheses,* Cyril remarks that the church's singers imitate the angels by hymning God unceasingly (οἱ σπουδαῖοι τῆς ἐκκλησίας ψαλμῳδοί [or ψαλτῳδοί], οἱ τὰς ἀγγελικὰς μιμούμενοι στρατιὰς καὶ πάντοτε τὸν θεὸν ἀνυμνοῦντες) (*Cat.* 13.26 Reischl and Rupp). And in another place he urges the catechumens waiting for the completion of the exorcisms that form part of the baptismal ritual to imagine that they are already in heaven listening to the choir of angels (*Procat.* 15). It is not clear whether Cyril has in mind anything more than that the unceasing praise of God conducted by the seraphim and other heavenly beings is imitated or reinforced by the church when Christians celebrate the Eucharist or carry out other liturgical acts of praise. It would probably go too far to suggest that there is in these texts any clear implication of a *unified and coordinated* liturgy of the church and angels.

Perhaps a unified eucharistic liturgy of church and angels is envisioned by Gregory of Nyssa, who invites catechumens who are about to be baptized "to sing with us what the six-winged seraphs say when they hymn *with* the mature Christians (μετὰ τῶν τελείων Χριστιανῶν ὑμνοῦντα)" (PG 46:421C). In other words, when the church intones the Trisagion at the Eucharist, it sings the

---

[48] On conceptions of angelic presence in Christian worship in fourth-century patristic understanding, see Muehlberger (2008, 103–28). I am grateful to this study for alerting me to a number of the relevant passages.

[49] As the context in *Myst. Cat.* 5.6 shows, this liturgical act is to be imagined as taking place in a cosmic setting of "heaven, earth, sea, sun and moon, stars, all creation, rational and irrational, visible and invisible, angels, archangels, powers, dominions, rulers, authorities, thrones, and the many-faced cherubim."

song of the angels in which it is joined by the seraphim. It is not clear whether the angels are imagined as being present with the church as participants in the Eucharist. Perhaps the thought is simply that the church and the seraphim both sing the Trisagion.

The idea of angels coming down from heaven and joining the church's worship is found explicitly in John Chrysostom. When the words "Let us pray" are uttered, he says, and when the curtain is drawn up, one should know that "the angels descend" (*In Eph. 1, hom.* 3.5).[50] This language recalls the ladder to heaven (Gen 28:12) and the reference to the ladder in the Gospel of John, where Jesus makes a promise to Nathaniel in the second-person plural, indicating that the Johannine community regards these words as a promise for itself. Naturally, the church fathers would have regarded the plural form of the verb in John 1:51 as a prophecy for the church. The gospel passage reads, "You [plural] will see heaven opened and the angels of God ascending and descending upon the Son of Humanity."

The angels imagined by Chrysostom are not ministers of the sacrifice but congregants, since, according to him, it is not angels but Christ's priests who have been given authority "to administer the things of heaven" (*Sac.* 3.5 Malingrey quoting Matt 18:18). As Chrysostom pictures the scene, "The angels surround the priest and the whole sanctuary, and the place around the altar is filled with heavenly powers to honor the one present ["the one lying there": τοῦ κειμένου]" (*Sac.* 6.4.41–43 Malingrey; cf. *In Eph. 4, hom. 14.4*[51]). In other words, the church does not join a heavenly liturgy; *the angels descend to take part in the Christian liturgy*. Chrysostom bolsters his claims about angels at the liturgy by recounting the testimony of a worthy old man, a saint given to visionary experiences, who was favored "to see a crowd of angels ... visible in shining clothes encircling the altar ..." (πλῆθος ἀγγέλων ἰδεῖν ... στολίδας ἀναβεβλημένων λαμπρὰς καὶ τὸ θυσιαστήριον κυκλούντων ...) (*Sac.* 6.4.48–49 Malingrey).

A different picture is painted by Chrysostom's friend, Theodore of Mopsuestia, who also studied at Antioch and became a presbyter there. In the second book of his homilies addressed to baptizands, Theodore envisions the Eucharist as a representation of the past death of Jesus and of a present heavenly liturgy in which believers will one day, through resurrection, participate directly. According to Theodore, angels, who were present at the original

---

[50] ὅταν ἀκούσῃς, Δεηθῶμεν πάντες κοινῇ, ὅταν ἴδῃς ἀνελκόμενα τὰ ἀμφίθυρα, τότε νόμισον διαστέλλεσθαι τὸν οὐρανὸν ἄνωθεν, καὶ κατιέναι τοὺς ἀγγέλους (PG 62:29 [col. 1.38–41]); cf. PG 62:29 [col. 1.19–20]): Σκόπει, παρακαλῶ, τράπεζα πάρεστι βασιλική, ἄγγελοι διακονούμενοι τῇ τραπέζῃ.

[51] "Bear in mind with whom you stand at the time of the mysteries – with the cherubim, with the seraphim" (Ἐννόησον μετὰ τίνων ἕστηκας κατὰ τὸν καιρὸν τῶν μυστηρίων, μετὰ τῶν χερουβὶμ, μετὰ τῶν σεραφίμ [PG 62:104]).

sacrifice (the death of Jesus), minister at the heavenly sacrifice. Meanwhile, on earth, the saints in worship are to imagine that they are in heaven and are to form a mental picture of the heavenly service of which the earthly Eucharist is a representation (*Hom. cat.* 15.20).[52]

The preceding survey shows that P.Oxy. 1786 offers some of the earliest explicit evidence for the idea that angelic powers and Christian believers worship *together in a unified liturgy*. To summarize, the earliest hints along these lines appear in Clement and Origen. A unified earthly and heavenly liturgy is explicitly described in the instructions about midnight worship in the *Apostolic Tradition*, a writing whose contents are a composite of many traditions likely formulated at different times and places from as early as the mid-second century to as late as the mid-fourth century.[53] The idea of angels sharing with the church in a unified liturgy is elaborated by Chrysostom and may have been assumed by other fourth-century Greek fathers in their descriptions of the Eucharist.

The hymn of P.Oxy. 1786 summons the powers to intone a doxology while the church ("we") hymns the Trinity: ὑμνούντων δ'ἡμῶν πατέρα χυἱὸν χἅγιον πνεῦμα πᾶσαι δυνάμεις ἐπιφωνούντων ἀμὴν ἀμὴν κράτος αἶνος ... ("As we hymn Father, Son, and Holy Spirit, let the powers respond, 'Amen, Amen. Strength, praise ...'"). This language does not locate the powers in any particular place, whether on earth with the worshiping saints or in heaven around the throne or a heavenly altar. That is left to the imagination, and not everyone who sang or heard the hymn at Oxyrhynchus (or elsewhere) will have had the same picture in mind.

The word ἐπιφωνέω, used of the angelic doxology, can have the general meaning "say" or "proclaim," but in a liturgical context means to say something *in response*.[54] Some scholars have entertained the possibility that the hymn of P.Oxy. 1786 was sung responsively.[55] There is no reason to think so. Granted, the hymn text of P.Oxy. 1786 describes a responsorial hymnic event: once the stars, rivers, and other natural elements have fallen respectfully still, the community intones its hymn and the angelic powers answer with a doxological re-

---

[52] Mingana (1933, 83); Tonneau and Devreesse (1949, 497 [French translation]).

[53] See the opinion in Bradshaw et al. (2002, 14).

[54] The term is used in this way already in 1 Esdras. When the law was read aloud, "Ezra blessed the Lord God Most High, God of Hosts, Almighty, and all the crowd responded, 'Amen' (ἐπεφώνησεν πᾶν τὸ πλῆθος Ἀμήν)" (1 Esdr 9:46–47). For the use of the word in late antiquity, see *PGL*, s.v. ἐπιφωνέω.

[55] Wagner (1924, 219) suggests that in view of the use of ἐπιφωνέω, the doxology may have been sung as a response by the congregation; he laments that the text does not make this clear. Leclercq (1937, 1480) also suggests that the doxology was sung responsively, perhaps by a choir or the congregation to a soloist. Reinach (1923, 14) entertains the possibility of responsorial performance but thinks it unlikely.

frain. But that is something different from P.Oxy. 1786 itself being performed as a responsorial hymn.

The Doxological Formula (lines 4–5)

The Double Amen (line 4 and line 5)

In the New Testament, a single "amen" closes a number of doxologies and blessings, some of these being interpolations by second-century Christian scribes influenced by established liturgical practice.[56] Similarly, an "amen" was added to the end of the Lord's Prayer in the manuscript tradition of Matt 6:13, no doubt reflecting the liturgical form of the prayer known to the copyist(s). These early uses established the later universal practice of closing a doxology (and other formulas) with "amen."

The double amen appears in the New Testament only as an introductory formula (in statements by Jesus in John[57]). But it is found as a closing formula in the Jewish scriptures. As precedents for its use in P.Oxy. 1786, the most relevant examples are closing double-amen formulas that finish the first, second, and third divisions of the Psalter: Ps 41:13 (40:14 LXX); Ps 72:19 (71:19 LXX); and Ps 89:52 (88:53 LXX). The first of these closings runs as follows: "Blessed be the LORD God of Israel from age to age. Amen and amen (אמן ואמן; γένοιτο γένοιτο in LXX)." The double amen is more frequent in the liturgical fragments from Qumran.[58]

The double amen in P.Oxy. 1786 may be the earliest extant example of the *Christian* use of the double amen as a *liturgical formula*. Our hymnist is almost certainly relying on established Christian liturgical practice, but I have found no other examples in Christian literature from the first through third centuries of the liturgical double amen. A double "so be it" appears in the Syriac *Testamentum Domini* (fourth or fifth century). In addition to saying "amen" (which would have been the transliteration ἀμήν in the original Greek of the *Testamentum*) in response to various lines of the priest's prayer, the people are to say "So be it, so be it" (which would have been γένοιτο γένοιτο) after one of the blessings of the eucharistic benediction (*T. Dom.* 1.23).[59] The *Tes-*

---

[56] "Amen" at the close of doxologies: Rom 16:27 (part of an early interpolated doxology); Phil 4:20; 2 Tim 4:18; Heb 13:21; 1 Pet 5:11; Rev 1:6 and 7:12; at the close of blessings: Rom 16:24 (an early interpolation); Phil 4:23 (in some mss.); 2 Tim 4:22 (in some mss.); Heb 13:25 (in some mss.); 1 Pet 5:14 (in some mss.); Rev 2:21 (some mss.). The textual uncertainty in a number of these cases probably reflects a tendency of copyists to add "amen" where their knowledge of the liturgical tradition suggested it. The probably secondary "amen" in P[46] for Phil 4:23 suggests that the tendency to add "amen" was already a practice of second-century copyists.

[57] John 3:3 and passim. This same introductory usage also appears in *T. Ab.* 20.1–2 (long recension).

[58] Olson (1992, 313).

[59] See Cooper and Maclean (1902, 75).

tamentum reflects tradition, but we do not know how old its double γένοιτο tradition is. In time, a threefold amen appeared. In *De trinitate* Didymus the Blind gives a threefold ἀμήν at the close of a prayer and adds the people's response as a threefold γένοιτο (PG 39:769.10 and 769.12). In the Liturgy of St. Basil, the people say a threefold ἀμήν after words of the eucharistic service (PG 31:1367).

The double amen appears twice in our hymn: once in the opening words of the response of the powers and again at the close of that response. It is natural to interpret the first double amen as an introduction to the doxology, so that both sets of double amen frame it, by analogy with Rev 7:12, where a single amen opens and closes an angelic doxology: ἀμήν· ἡ εὐλογία καὶ ἡ δόξα καὶ ἡ σοφία καὶ ἡ εὐχαριστία καὶ ἡ τιμὴ καὶ ἡ δύναμις καὶ ἡ ἰσχὺς τῷ θεῷ ἡμῶν εἰς τοὺς αἰῶνας τῶν αἰώνων· ἀμήν ("Amen. Blessing and glory and wisdom and thanksgiving and honor and power and strength be to our God for ever and ever. Amen"). This framing (inclusio) strengthens the impression that all the words from the first double amen through the closing are an utterance of the powers. The whole of the doxology, from the first double amen to the end, is a concluding and affirming response of the angels to the church's hymn.

Strength and Praise (line 4)

The pairing of κράτος with αἶνος is unique in surviving ancient Christian doxologies, but neither word is an unfamiliar doxological term. The word κράτος appears in some of the earliest doxologies, and a number of texts use the formula ἡ δόξα καὶ τὸ κράτος (see Rev 1:6; 5:13; 1 Pet 4:11; *T. Ab.* 20:48; *Acts Andr. et Mth.* 33; *Contra Noetum* 18:10).[60] In a non-doxological context, 2 *Clement* speaks of the day when unbelievers will see τὴν δόξαν ... καὶ τὸ κράτος of Jesus (2 *Clem.* 17.5 Ehrman). The pairing ἡ δόξα καὶ τὸ κράτος also shows up in certain manuscripts of a variety of other early Christian writings dated to the second and third centuries (including *Mart. Andr.* 19.3 Prieur; Melito, *Pasch.* 823 Perler; *Acts Paul* 45.6 Lipsius and Bonnet[61]). It appears without the copulative in the fourth-century Christian hymn in P.Ber. 8299 (σοὶ δόξα, κράτος εἰς αἰῶνας in Heitsch no. 45.3). The pairing ἡ δόξα καὶ τὸ κράτος is very frequent in the writings of Origen, Basil, Athanasius, Epiphanius and others. Examples from Egypt are found in a late-third- or early-fourth-century prayer preserved in P.Oxy. 407, in the doxology that closes the *Apology* of Dionysius of Alexandria (PL 5:128, no. 16), and perhaps in a late fourth-century liturgi-

---

[60] The textual tradition for some of these examples shows uncertainty about the definite articles.

[61] The expression in this text is part of a doxology in the longer ending found in some manuscripts of the *Acts of Paul (and Thecla)*.

cal fragment.⁶² The expression κράτος καὶ τιμή appears in *1 Clement*, preceded by δόξα καὶ μεγαλωσύνη (*1 Clem.* 64 Ehrman). In *1 Clem.* 65 we find δόξα, τιμή, κράτος, καὶ μεγαλωσύνη, θρόνος αἰώνιος. These passages display the kind of compounding of ascriptions we see in Rev 5:13: ἡ εὐλογία καὶ ἡ τιμὴ καὶ ἡ δόξα καὶ τὸ κράτος. Clement of Alexandria also writes δόξα τιμὴ κράτος αἰώνιος μεγαλειότης (*Quis* 42.20 Stählin, Früchtel, and Treu). A doxology in a prayer in P.Ber. 13415 (fourth century) is phrased δόξα καὶ τιμὴ καὶ κράτος.⁶³

The word αἶνος is not a common doxological term, but it appears in the traditional blessing recorded by Justin in his description of the Eucharist: αἶνον καὶ δόξαν τῷ πατρὶ τῶν ὅλων κ.τ.λ. (*1 Apol.* 65.3; cf. ἔπαινος in Phil 1:11). Of the ancient Greek doxologies that have come down to us, apparently only the one in P.Oxy. 1786 combines κράτος with αἶνος.

As the preceding suggests, Christian doxologies commonly ascribe *power* and *honor* to God. Various words for power appear, usually δύναμις or κράτος, also βασιλεία and like terms.⁶⁴ Honor is typically expressed with δόξα and τιμή, but also with σέβας, προσκύνησις, and similar words.⁶⁵ Although certain liturgical and literary traditions crystalized to make particular terms and expressions standard, traditions varied from place to place and there also appears to have been considerable flexibility and cross-fertilization. In our hymn, κράτος expresses power and αἶνος expresses honor (along with δόξα, if that term once stood where there is now a lacuna).

Giver of Good Things (line 5)

As noted in chapter two, West has drawn attention to the Classical pedigree of the phrase δωτῆρι μόνῳ πάντων ἀγαθῶν, pointing out that these words are a variation of the epic formula θεοὶ δωτῆρες ἐάων.⁶⁶ Examples are found in Homer (*Od.* 8.325) and Hesiod (*Theog.* 46, 111, 633). Callimachus describes Zeus as δῶτορ ἐάων (*Hymn. Jov.* 90 Asper). A hymn to Telesphorus from the Roman era begins with the words, ὑμνέομέν σε μάκαρ φαεσίμβροτε, δῶτορ ἐάων ("We hymn you, blessed one, bringer of light, giver of good things").⁶⁷

---

⁶² Ghedini (1933, 672).
⁶³ Schermann (1917, 3).
⁶⁴ A variety of terms for power is found in early doxologies. In an early expansion of the ending of the Lord's Prayer, we find ἡ δύναμις (along with ἡ δόξα; see *Did.* 8.2; cf. 10.5 and 9.4). Some versions of the Lord's Prayer add ἡ βασιλεία as the first of this series to make a threefold predication. In a quasi-doxological formula, Rev 5:12 lists δύναμις and ἰσχύς (along with πλοῦτος, σοφία, τιμή, δόξα, and εὐλογία) as perquisites of exaltation that the Lamb is worthy to receive. A doxology in the next verse lists κράτος (along with εὐλογία, τιμή, and δόξα).
⁶⁵ We find ἡ δόξα καὶ τὸ σέβας in *Apos. Con.* 7.38.8 and 8.22.4 (Funk); δόξα τιμὴ καὶ σέβας in 8.7.8. Basil has δόξα κράτος καὶ προσκύνησις (*Hom. dicta tempore*; PG 31:328.42) and δόξα τιμὴ κράτος καὶ μεγαλοπρέπεια (*Serm. de mor. a Sym. Met.*; PG 32:1328.44).
⁶⁶ West (1992a, 50–51).
⁶⁷ Furley and Bremer (2001, 2:236 [Hymn 7.7.2, line 1]).

In the Christian tradition, the concept of God as a giver of good things appears in a wisdom form in the gospel saying, "If you who are evil know how to give good things to your children, how much more will your father in heaven give good things (δώσει ἀγαθὰ) to those who ask him" (Matt 7:11). Paul makes a similar affirmation: "He who did not spare his own son but gave him up for us all, will he not also give us all things (τὰ πάντα ἡμῖν χαρίσεται) with him?" (Rom 8:32). That assurance is eschatological. The idea that God gives more immediate gifts is expressed just before a doxology in Phil 4:19: "God will furnish every need of yours (πληρώσει πᾶσαν χρείαν ὑμῶν)" (cf. θεῷ τῷ παρέχοντι ἡμῖν πάντα in 1 Tim 6:17). Words closer to the traditional Hellenistic formula appear in Clement of Alexandria, who describes God as ὁ τῶν ἀγαθῶν δοτήρ (*Str.* 7.7.43.2 Stählin, Früchtel, and Treu; cf. *Str.* 7.7.36.4), as does Origen (ἀγαθῶν ἐστιν ὁ θεὸς δοτήρ).[68] Eusebius, speaking of the few pagans of old who arrived at knowledge of the one God, says that they perceived "that he alone is God, the savior of all and the sole giver of good things (μόνον ἀγαθῶν δοτῆρα)" (*Praep. ev.* 2.6.12 Mras et al.). In his comments on the Psalms, Eusebius describes God as "lover of humanity and giver of every good thing" (ὁ φιλάνθρωπος καὶ παντὸς ἀγαθοῦ δοτὴρ θεός) (PG 23:645.39–40).[69] In another place he refers to Christ as δοτήρ: "the giver of good things has come to us, God's Christ" (ἡμῖν ἀγαθῶν παρέστη δοτὴρ ὁ Χριστὸς τοῦ θεοῦ) (*Praep. ev.* 3.5.5 Mras et al.). In comments on Ps 118 attributed to Chrysostom, we find "I will praise you, the giver of good things" (αἰνέσω σε τὸν δοτῆρα τῶν ἀγαθῶν) (PG 55:707.12–13).

Concluding Summary

The text of the hymn reflects traditional Christian formulations along with language from the pagan Hellenistic tradition. The form of the Trinitarian praise statement – the names of the persons of the Trinity linked by the copulative without the use of prepositional phrases – is not common in the late-third / early-fourth century, although it is attested in another hymn that dates to perhaps the same time (the vesper hymn quoted by Basil). The concluding doxology contains a Christian conception of God as the sole source of good gifts, and the two double "amens" that enclose this doxology reflect Christian liturgical practice and its Jewish roots. Yet the doxology also uses a term for "giver" (δωτήρ) that derives from pagan descriptions of the gods (Zeus in particular) going back to Homer. This term is also used by Clement of Alexandria and Origen, Christian scholars shaped by Alexandrian culture

---

[68] *Frag. ex comm. in Prov.* (PG 13:28.13–14).
[69] Cf. also, in the same work, PG 23:704.25–26.

and education. The call for nature to fall still is a poetic conceit borrowed from Greek hymnody. The idea of nature's silence – although not the poetic *form* that expresses this idea in Greek hymnody – also appears in descriptions of the church's midnight prayer (in the *Apostolic Tradition*). Our hymn describes a shared liturgy of the church and angels. Two Christian theologians associated with Alexandria (Clement of Alexandria and Origen) taught that angels are present with believers when they pray, and the *Apostolic Tradition* describes the midnight office as a moment of worship in which the church praises God with the angels. By the fourth century, at least one of the eastern fathers (Chrysostom) believed that angels descend to observe with reverent devotion the eucharistic celebrations of the church. Others of that era described Christian worship as an imitation of heavenly worship or perhaps also as part of a unified liturgy of the church and angels.

Our hymn depicts and directs, through the use of imperatives, an act of communal praise. The natural elements are summoned to silence in preparation for the church's offering of praise to the Trinity. The angelic powers are called upon to respond to this praise with amens and a doxology. The call for the natural elements (including stars) to be still and the command that the angelic powers answer with a doxology give the church's praise of the Trinity a cosmic scope. Viewed rhetorically, that cosmic praise is a hymn within the hymn, a hymnic moment that the hymn of P. Oxy. 1786 describes and orchestrates with its imperatives. This rhetorical aspect of the poem is the subject of the next chapter.

CHAPTER FOUR

Formal and Rhetorical Analysis

We are limited in our efforts to analyze the form of the hymn by the fragmentary condition of the papyrus. Nevertheless, the call for cosmic stillness is a clue to the length of the hymn.

By logic and custom, calls for stillness belong to the openings of Greek hymns. In fact, in none of the hymns in which the motif appears is it found anywhere but in the opening. A brief survey of the hymns discussed in chapter three establishes this point.[1] Callimachus' hymn to Apollo starts off with a description of the scene as the god approaches his temple: listeners are summoned to be silent for Apollo's hymn, and the sea falls spontaneously silent. One of Mesomedes' hymns to the Sun (Heitsch no. 2.2) begins with a call for stillness on the part of natural elements. One of the satirical hymns to Gout in Lucian's *Podagra* begins with a call for both the goddess' devotees and the natural world to be still in preparation for her epiphany (*Pod.* 129–33). The gnostic hymn in *Corp. herm.* 13.17–20 opens with a summons to receptive cosmic silence. A hymn preserved in several forms in the magical papyri also begins with a call for the natural world to be silent.[2] Moreover, even in the hymns of Synesius, where the stillness motif appears after many lines, it nonetheless belongs to the hymnic opening. The beginning of Synesius' Hymn 1 consists of 117 lines but takes up only the first 16% of the hymn, which is 734 lines long. The silence motif occurs in this opening at lines 72–85. Synesius' Hymn 2 is shorter (299 lines) but also has a lengthy opening (lines 1–59) in which the silence motif occurs at lines 28–43. Hence, the presence of a call to stillness in the second of the five extant lines of P.Oxy. 1786 suggests that the remains are not the conclusion of a long hymn. The hymn was originally probably not much longer than what we have, consisting perhaps of only the five partially-intact manuscript lines that have come down to us.

---

[1] I include in the following only the hymns that have a *call* for stillness. Two other hymns have the motif but not as a call. The anonymous hymn to Apollo (Heitsch no. 51) opens with an account of the birth of the god and a description of stillness in nature. Limenius' paean to Apollo begins with an invocation of the Muses (section 1 = lines 1–7), followed by a description of cosmic silence and the epiphany of Apollo (section 2 = lines 8–12).

[2] See Preisendanz and Henrichs (1973–1974, 1:40 = *PGM* III.198–205) (// Hymn 5 in 2:241–42); also idem (1973–1974, 2:14–15 = *PGM* VII.320–24).

On the assumption that the hymn consisted of only these five manuscript lines, Pöhlmann devised a possible opening based on considerations of meter and guided by language in Clement of Alexandria and Synesius: Σὲ πάτερ κόσμων, πάτερ αἰώνων, μέλπωμεν ὁμοῦ ("Let us praise you, father of the cosmos, father of ages").³ In content and meter this is a satisfying supplement. Of course, the opening might have been quite different. While the ὁμοῦ, the first decipherable word in line 1, encourages the conjecture that the beginning line summons the community to praise God "together," it is also possible that the ὁμοῦ goes with what follows ("all the eminent ones of God" doing something "together"). Moreover, Clement's expression, μέλπωμεν ὁμοῦ, appears not in the opening of Clement's hymn but near the end (line 59). The same goes for the language taken from Synesius, which is not found in any of the openings of Synesius' hymns but derives from the middle of his first hymn.

Apparently, ms. line 1 made reference to "eminent ones of God." Since the hymn paints a cosmic scene in ms. lines 2 ff., it seems likely that the eminent ones are cosmic powers and hence that a cosmic scene was suggested at the beginning. Perhaps the hymn began with a description of God ruling above the heavens together with the eminent ones. After οὐ τὰν ἠῶ, the hymn is relatively intact to its close and consists of a call to cosmic silence and a summons to angelic powers to intone a doxology while a "we" hymns the Trinity. A closer look at the poetic tradition of ancient Greek hymns sheds further light on the form and rhetoric of the composition.

Genre and Form

According to an ancient definition in Proclus' *Chrestomathy*, the Greeks "called anything composed for the higher beings 'hymns'" (ἐκάλουν ... πάντα τὰ εἰς τοὺς ὑπερόντας γραφόμενα ὕμνους).⁴ Since heroes fell under the category of "higher beings," a hymn could also be defined as "a poem containing praises of gods and heroes with thanksgiving" (ποίημα περιέχον θεῶν ἐγκώμια καὶ ἡρώων μετ' εὐχαριστίας) (Dionysius Thrax, second century B.C.E.).⁵ Poetic praises were also composed to honor mortals, but these were not called hymns.⁶

---

³ Pöhlmann (1970, 106 [apparatus]).

⁴ Proclus in Photius (in Henry [1959–1977, 5:159–60 = Bekker 320a9–10). A Byzantine Greek dictionary says that a hymn is "speech crafted with adoration and prayer in praise to a god" (ὁ μετὰ προσκυνήσεως καὶ εὐχῆς κεκραμένης ἐπαίνῳ λόγος εἰς θεόν) (*Etymologicum graecae linguae Gudianum* Sturz [1818, 540]). The date of the dictionary is uncertain; Marquard Gudius (Gude) (1635–89) was a onetime owner of the manuscript.

⁵ Hilgard (1901, 451).

⁶ The hymn as praise of higher beings is distinguished from poetic praise of mortals such as the *epinikion*. Plato differentiates between the *hymnos* for gods and the *encomion* for worthy human beings (*Rep.* 10.607a Shorey). But the term *encomion* was also applied to praise of the gods.

Among the subcategories of the Greek hymn are the *prosodion* (processional hymn), the *hymnos* sung around the altar, the *paian*, the *dithyrambos* (a type of hymn associated with the cult of Dionysus), the *nomos*, and others.[7] All of these had in common praise of deities, the purpose of which was to secure and maintain divine favor. As one ancient formulation put it: οἱ δὲ πανημέριοι μολπῇ θεὸν ἱλάσκοντο, καλὸν ἀείδοντες παιήονα ("all day long they propitiated the god with song, singing a beautiful paean" (Homer, *Il.* 1.472–73).

The cultic hymn inspired and served as a model for non-cultic hymns, which appear in a variety of contexts and social settings. These include hymns in dramatic, literary, and oratorical contexts; hymns at festivals as part of ceremonial events, competitions, and rhetorical entertainment; and hymns sung at dinner parties of various kinds and in music halls. A religious function is definitional to the cultic hymn but was often present in the performance of hymns in non-cultic settings.

The Greeks knew both the metrical hymn (in hexameters, various lyric meters, elegiacs, and eventually in anapaests) and the prose hymn (a hymn cast in elevated, non-metrical diction). Both could be used for cultic or non-cultic purposes.[8] By the Roman era the heritage of hymns and their uses made for considerable variety. Hence, we should not imagine that Greek-speaking churches who relied on the Greek hymnic tradition inherited a fixed form. Nevertheless, certain hymnic topics and rhetorical devices had become typical. We can distinguish the following most basic aspects of hymnic expression:

Voice. The hymn was usually couched in the voice of the worshiper(s), although some hymns were in the voice of the god. The voice of the worshiper(s) could be cast in the first-person (singular or plural) or the third-person. Combinations of these different voice forms could be used in the same hymn.

Address. The hymn could address the deity directly (using second-person verbs and pronouns) or indirectly (in third-person statements) or could combine both forms of address.

Content and structure. The content of the hymn varied depending on the deity for whom it was composed, but a typical arrangement was an opening (invocation / *epiclēsis*) that named the god, a body (*eulogia*) extolling the god's deeds and benefactions, and a closing prayer (*euchē*).[9] Praise of the deity in the body of the hymn was designed to win divine favor and to lay a foundation for petitions in hymns that closed with a prayer.[10]

---

[7] Proclus remarks that Greeks speak of "hymn of prosodion, hymn of encomium, hymn of paean and the like," but he goes on to say that "the hymn properly speaking was sung to the cithara while standing (around the altar)" (ὁ δὲ κυρίως ὕμνος πρὸς κιθάραν ᾔδετο ἑστώτων) (in Photius; Henry [1959–1977, 5:159–160] = Bekker 320a9–10). On the subject of the Greek hymn and its subtypes, see Furley (1995, 31–32).

[8] Prose hymns survive in inscriptions at religious shrines. See Furley and Bremer (2001, 1:48–49).

[9] On the form of Greek hymns, see Norden's foundational study, *Agnostos Theos*, originally published in 1913 (Norden [1974, 143–77]). For a more recent treatment, see Furley and Bremer (2001, 1:50–64). A discussion of form with detailed references to secondary literature can also be found in Brucker (1997, 38–43).

[10] The frequency with which hymns dwell on the history of the god, narrating the deity's great

P.Oxy. 1786 is a cultic hymn cast in the voice of the worshipers (a hymning "we" as the ὑμνούντων δ' ἡμῶν in line 3 expresses it). The extant lines do not include any direct address to the deity, although a naming of God was likely part of the missing words at the beginning.

The call to silence reflects the Greek hymnic tradition. As noted above, both convention and poetic function (the motif as preparatory) make the opening of the hymn before the body a logical place for it. Hence, it seems likely that the stillness motif in ms. lines 2–3 of P.Oxy. 1786 is part of the hymn's opening. In that case, we have a short hymn containing the following elements:

Beginning lines that include an invocation and something about "the eminent ones of God."

A call for the stars, rivers (and other natural elements) to be still as the church hymns the Trinity and the angelic powers respond with a doxology.

The hymn has no closing prayer. How far does its opening extend? Does it have a distinct body? A closer examination of the structure of Greek hymns can help answer these questions.

The Opening of a Greek Hymn

Basic to any opening is the naming of the deity. This is done as a form of address or through third-person reference. In either case this naming serves as an *epiclēsis*. Other elements which may appear are the use of epithets and titles to describe the god, a reference to the god's abode, a rehearsal of the god's genealogy, mention of companion deities, a description of the approach of the god to the shrine, a call for proper decorum, a reference to the singing of the hymn or an exhortation to sing the hymn, and an invitation to the Muses to join and assist the singer. These traditional elements provide the poet with a variety of ways to shape the proemium.

Depending on the length of the hymn, openings can be very brief or quite elaborate. For example, the opening of a hymn to Telesphorus found in an inscription at Athens is short:

We hymn you, blessed one, light-giver, bestower of necessities,
    image of Paean, illustrious and expert Telesphorus.[11]

By contrast, the opening of Synesius' Hymn 1 is extensive, although it is less than a sixth of this 734-line hymn:

---

deeds, led Ausfeld to term the middle part of the hymn *pars epica* (Ausfeld [1903, 515]). Because the middle section often lays a foundation for a petition, that is, serves as a rhetoric of persuasion, Bremer has suggested calling the middle section "argumentation" (Bremer [1981, 196]).

[11] Furley and Bremer (2001, 2:236 [= Hymn 2]).

Announcement of the hymn(s) that the worshiper is about to offer (1–72)
    Soul summoned to awake and sing
    Description of God and the "place" in God where the hymnist "comes" to sing
    Description of the nature of the song, witnesses to the song, and the pure state of the worshiper
Call for cosmic silence "while these sacred hymns are offered up" (72–85)
Prayer that the demon of matter will be kept away from the hymnist (86–104) and that God's messengers may carry the hymns to God (105–7)
Declaration that the hymnist has been "carried back to the starting-point of sacred poesy" (108–12)
Prayer that God will be good and merciful to the poet as he expresses his song (113–17)

Although many Greek hymns display the tripartite structure of opening (with some combination of its characteristic elements), body (extolling the deeds and benefactions of the god), and closing prayer, not all do. Some hymns lack a closing prayer. Some lack both a closing prayer and a conventional body. The latter look like freestanding openings, composed of an invocation of the god's name(s), application of titles and epithets, and often other elements common to openings. No doubt a hymn of this sort often served as an introduction to a series of songs.

One of the hymns attributed to Mesomedes appears to be of the introductory type. It is simply an invocation of the Muse:

Sing to me, kind Muse,
and begin my song.
Send a breeze from your groves
to stir my mind.[12]

In a longer hymn, lines like these would typically have served as an opening to a body that went on to describe the deeds and virtues of the god. For example, a paean to Apollo begins as follows:

Come here to far-seen [dance-loving] Parnassus
of twin-peaked fame and begin [my] hymns,
Pierian Muses ...[13]

After this opening (which also includes a naming of the god, a description of his birth and his characteristic place of abode, and a request that he come now to his mountain), the paean goes into a narrative about Apollo's great deeds and closes with a prayer. By contrast, the lines from the invocation of the Muse consist of only a single element common to the openings of hymns: a call to the Muses to assist the singer in composing/performing the hymn.

Similar in subject and brevity is Mesomedes' invocation of Calliope and Apollo:

---

[12] Pöhlmann and West (2001, 92–93).
[13] Opening of Limenius' paean to Apollo in Pöhlmann and West (2001, 74–75).

Wise Calliope,
    leader of the delight-making Muses,
and skillful initiator into the mysteries,
    son of Leto, Delian Paean,
favor me with your presence.[14]

Presumably, the invocation of the Muse and the invocation of Calliope and Apollo would have been performed as introductions to a concert of song. As a matter of form, however, they are freestanding hymns.

Another example of a hymn composed solely of elements otherwise associated with hymnic openings is the following prayer to Asclepius found in Athens (as part of the Kassel stone inscription):

Wake up, Savior Asclepius, lord of the people,
kindhearted child of Leto and holy Coronis.
Shed the sleep from your eyelids, listen to the prayers
of your people, who joyfully supplicate
your strength, kindhearted Asclepius, first of all for health.
Wake up and hear our hymn – Iē! Ie! – with joy.[15]

This hymn consists of a naming of the deity through the use of titles and an epithet, reference to the genealogy of the god, and an expanded invocation in which the singers refer to themselves and their hymn. The framing with "Wake up!" addressed to the god, as if the singers had not yet begun to present their petitions to the slumbering deity, also makes the hymn sound like an opening, an invocation. A petition for health is incorporated into this invocation.

Another hymn to Asclepius is also constructed mostly of elements that in other hymns make up the opening:

    Sing, youths, of famous Paean,
    son of Leto, far-shooter,
        – Hear us, Paean!
    who was the father of great delight for mortals
5   by being joined in love with Coronis
    in the land of Phlegyas,
        – Hear us, Paean! Asclepius,
    famed divinity,
        – Hear us, Paean!
10 from whom descended Machaon,
    and Podaleirus and Iaso as well,
        – Hear us, Paean!

---

[14] Pöhlmann and West (2001, 94–95). These lines follow immediately after the invocation of the Muse and may be a continuation of that hymn. If the lines are part of the invocation of the Muse, as a later Byzantine editor who added the titles thought, they increase its length by five lines but do not change its formal character as an invocation that stands on its own as a hymn. On the basis of the page layout and differences in meter and dialect, Pöhlmann and West judge that the lines addressed to Calliope and Apollo are a separate hymn (ibid., 112–13).

[15] Furley and Bremer (2001, 2:234; ET in 1:267).

and his children, beautiful Aegla, Panacea, too,
and Epione, along with glorious,
15   holy Health
     – Hear us, Paean! Asclepius,
     famed divinity,
     – Hear us, Paean!
     I salute you, look mercifully on
20   our broad city.
     – Hear us, Paean!
     Grant that we may enjoy the sun's
     esteemed light accompanied
     by glorious and holy Health,
25   – Oh! Paean, Asclepius,
     famed divinity,
     – Hear us, Paean![16]

Here we have naming of the deity, liturgical instruction to the chorus of young men, description of the deity with epithets and the noting of divine benefactions, mention of the god's genealogy, reference to the god's descendants and a divine associate (Apollo, who is mentioned first perhaps because of his association with the art of music), and an epicletic refrain. The refrain expresses the implicit prayer for divine favor, which is made explicit at the end. One could construe lines 1–9 as a proemium and lines 10–18 as the body of this hymn. Or one could interpret the hymn as an extended epiclesis (lines 1–21) followed by a closing prayer (lines 19–26). The important thing to see is that what dominates the hymn are elements more generally associated with openings. A humorous hymn to Asclepius among the mime poems (*mimiamboi*) of Herodas (no. 4) displays a similar character and structure.[17]

The tripartite hymn form was well established by the Hellenistic period. The preceding examples show that poets in the Roman era (and perhaps also in earlier times) felt free to use elements traditionally associated with the opening of a hymn as components of a freestanding form. Apparently, this is what the composer of P.Oxy. 1786 did. After mentioning the subject of the hymn and perhaps describing some sort of cosmic scene involving certain "eminent ones of God," he added a call for stillness, combining this with a reference to community song and an instruction addressed to the angels. Hence, viewed from the vantage of the Greek hymnic tradition, P.Oxy. 1786 is not analyzable as a tripartite hymn.

Nevertheless, assuming that our hymn opened with some kind of invocation, we might be tempted to interpret it as exhibiting a bipartite form: invocation (opening) followed by praise (the body or *eulogia* section). A musical

---

[16] Powell (1925, 137); Furley and Bremer (2001, 2:161–62).
[17] Furley and Bremer (2001, 2:199; ET in 1:243–44).

feature suggests a division of the hymn into two parts. Nearly-identical cadences are found for the words οὐ τὰν ἠῶ and the closing ἀμὴν ἀμήν. Moreover, the diseme rest after οὐ τὰν ἠῶ and the musical pattern for σιγάτω (a rising large interval) are consistent with the start of a new song section.[18] Hence, the melody perhaps structures the hymn into two halves: 1) from the opening words through οὐ τὰν ἠῶ and 2) from σιγάτω through the end of the hymn. Moreover, the lines from σιγάτω through the concluding "amen" (constituting the second of these two parts) are unified by the use of commands, liturgical instructions to the natural elements and angels.

On the basis of this analysis of the hymn into two parts, we might conclude that the second part is the body. Militating against that inference, however, is the presence of the call for silence in the second half. By convention, a call for silence precedes the body of the hymn. In that case, should we construe the body as the material after the call for stillness, from ὑμνούντων to the end? The body of a Greek hymn often extolls the character and deeds of the deity. If we distinguish the lines after the cosmic stillness motif as the body of P.Oxy. 1786, this body can be fittingly described as *eulogia*. But it is not *eulogia* in narrative form with descriptions of the god's past deeds and benefactions. Nor is it an enumeration of excellences to the deity. Instead, we have a set of liturgical instructions addressed to natural elements and angelic powers. And while liturgical instructions can be found at many points in a hymn, when combined with a call to stillness they suggest the opening of the hymn, the beginning in which the hymn speaks *as if it were only about to begin*. It is this quality of the extant lines that gives the impression that P.Oxy. 1786, as a whole, has the formal character of a hymnic opening.

One might contemplate the possibility that our hymn was designed as an introduction to a liturgy of song, along the lines of the invocation of the Muse and the invocation of Calliope and Apollo as concert introductions. A few ancient Christian texts from the first through the fourth centuries speak in the plural of hymns in worship and also at communal meals, some of which may have entailed liturgical elements.[19] Hence, a time of extended singing is conceivable, particularly in churches that held a common meal with a postprandial symposium. Tertullian, for example, mentions a community dinner where, after eating, washing of hands, and lighting of lamps, church members were invited to come individually to the middle (*in medium*) and sing to God, whether from the holy scriptures or from their own invention (*de scripturis*

---

[18] On the musical framing of the hymn, see chapter five.

[19] Tertullian, *An.* 9.4; *Apol.* 39.18; *Trad. ap.* 25 Botte = 29C Bradshaw et al.; Clement, *Paed.* 2.4.43.3; *Str.* 7.7.49.4. The terms most frequently used are ὕμνος and ψαλμός (and, in the case of Tertullian, their equivalents in Latin transliteration), the term ψαλμός being a general term in Christian usage of the first three centuries for a religious song (a sung hymn) and not a designation meaning a specifically biblical Psalm.

sanctis vel de proprio ingenio) (*Apol.* 39.18 Becker). This sounds quite informal, not the sort of setting in which a planned-out hymnic liturgy took place. Apart from this description in Tertullian, we know almost nothing about the structural organization of music in Christian gatherings, formally liturgical or otherwise, prior to the end of the fourth century.

Nor is it necessary to interpret the introductory form of P.Oxy. 1786 as an indication that it served an introductory function. The introductory elements are internal to the imaginal world of the hymn and need not have external referents. This will become clear in the following discussion.

Deictic Self-Referentiality

In chapter three, we examined the tradition of a call to silence before an offering. Since a hymn was conceived as an offering, some poets incorporated a call to silence into the openings of their hymns. In this way, they introduced into their songs language suggesting preparation to hymn. A similar conceit is the opening invitation to the Muses to inspire the singer, as if the hymn had not yet been composed; or to start the song, as if the song had not yet begun. In these and other ways the poet effects a kind of temporal displacement of the hymn's speaking voice. A closer examination of temporal displacement in hymns will shed light on the poetic rhetoric of P.Oxy. 1786.

When self-references in Greek poetry have to do with the singing of the poem itself and its setting, they are described as deictic, that is, as referring to the here and now of the poem's performance. In a study of this device, Calame defines deixis as "verbal references to the space and time of, as well as the participants in, the act of communication."[20]

An example of a hymn dramatizing its own present moment of performance is a Cretan song to Zeus-Kouros, which paints a picture of the worshiping event of which the hymn is a part. The song invites the god to draw near and enjoy "the music, which we weave for you (τοι κρέκομεν) ... having taken our stand (στάντες) around your well-walled altar."[21] An ancient Christian vesper hymn (some form of the hymn *Phos hilaron*) dramatizes itself in a similar way, although the setting is very different: "Having come (ἐλθόντες) to the setting of the sun and having seen (ἰδόντες) the vesper light, we praise (ὑμνοῦμεν) the

---

[20] Calame (2004, 415). On deixis and self-referentiality, see also the foundational treatments of choral lyric by Henrichs (1994–95, 56–111); idem (1996). See further the articles in *Arethusa* 37 (2004) and also the bibliography included in that volume, which is devoted to the subject of deixis in Greek lyric poetry.

[21] Translation from Furley and Bremer (2001, 1:68; Greek in 2:1–2). Many examples of deictic self-referentiality focused on the present moment of performance are found in the choral-dance hymns of Greek drama.

Father, Son, and Holy Spirit of God."²² The aorist participles tell the narrative that leads to the present act of praise and also suggest the external circumstances of that praise.

More prosaic examples are first-person present-tense verbs that appear at various points in hymns but typically in openings. An example has already been quoted above from the hymn to Telesphorus, which begins, "We hymn you, blessed one ..." (ὑμνέομέν σε μάκαρ).²³ There is also the formula ἄρχομ' ἀείδειν (literally "I begin to sing" but probably meaning simply "I sing"), which appears in the openings of *Homeric Hymns* 2, 11, 13, and 16.

An intriguing aspect of deictic self-referentiality is the freedom with which poems play with the temporal perspective of their own speaking voice. We see this in a variety of poetic forms, including hymns. Greek hymns sometimes speak about themselves *as if* in the middle of their performance; they also speak about themselves *as if* in a time *just before* their performance. In these ways, deictic self-referentiality has the effect of dramatizing the hymn as a liturgical event.

Any discussion of temporal displacement in Greek poetry must touch at least briefly on Pindar's use of future verbs to describe present actions of singing, dancing, and so forth. For example, when Pindar says, "We shall sing of ..." (κελαδησόμεθα) (*Ol.* 10.79 Race), he is not referring to a future song; he is talking about the song he has just begun. Poetic locutions of this sort often have a telltale "now" (νῦν). Various theories have been advanced to explain this and other kinds of Pindaric futures, and we need not be detained by them, except to note the theory of a few scholars that at least in some cases Pindar's futures were designed to function as literal stage directions, intended to coincide with the moment just before the chorus arrived at the place where it was to stand and sing.²⁴ In the words of D'Alessio, Pindar composed certain poems with the aim of making "coding time" coincide with "reception time."²⁵ In that case, there is no intended temporal displacement, so long as the choreography comes off precisely.

It is possible that Pindar's futures, in their original intention (and in original performance), had some special purposes; but on the whole, self-referential futures in poetry belong to a grammar of temporal displacement in which the

---

²² Plank (2002, 37). These words are found in the hymn *Phos hilaron*, which is difficult to date. In any case, the second stanza of *Phos hilaron* probably goes back to at least the third century, since Basil quotes a form of its words as part of a vesper thanksgiving (Basil, *De spir. sanct.* 29.73.37–43 Pruche; PG 29:73). In view of the vesper setting and the connection with *Phos hilaron*, it is very likely that Basil is quoting from a vesper *hymn*, either from the second stanza of *Phos hilaron* itself or from a shorter hymn that was later expanded to make the hymn *Phos hilaron*.
²³ Furley and Bremer (2001, 2:236).
²⁴ Slater (1969, 86–94); Danielwicz (1990, 15–16).
²⁵ D'Alessio (2004, 267–95).

poem dramatizes the present act of its own performance – actual in the case of cultic hymns or only as imagined in the case of literary hymns.[26]

A hymn to Hestia opens with a jussive future, "Let us hymn (ὑμνήσομεν) Hestia, holy queen of sacred things."[27] Furley and Bremer observe that such opening exhortations are so common as to constitute a typical structural element.[28] A model is Terpander's opening formula, "Now let my heart sing of the Marksman [Apollo]" (ἀμφί μοι αὖτις ἄναχθ' Ἑκατήβολον ἀϊδέτω φρήν), which evolved into the verb ἀμφιανακτίζειν ("sing a hymn").[29] A hymn to Asclepius from Erythrai begins by inviting a boys chorus to praise the god: "Sing, youths (ἀείσατε κοῦροι), of famous Paian."[30] A cult hymn composed by Macedonicus and inscribed at the Athenian Asclepion (and dating to some time in the first century B.C.E. to the second century C.E.) includes the following instructions to an Athenian chorus of young men: "Take the suppliant branch in hand (ἐν παλάμηι θέτε), the lovely olive and beautiful shoot of laurel, Athenian youths, Ie, Paian. Youths, let your perfect hymn sing (ἄμεμπτος ὕμνος ἀείδοι) the far-shooting son of Leto" (lines 3–5).[31] In each instruction the hymn seems to call for the start of its own performance, although it is already underway. We hardly notice this temporal oddity in hymns where it is expressed in a single word (such as a lone ὑμνήσομεν); it is more evident when it entails a detailed declaration or directive.

Another common formula in which the hymnic voice is temporally displaced is the rhetorical question, "How shall I (or "we") hymn you?" Sometimes the poet suggests that the god may be too magnificent for mere human praise or that every form of praise has already been rendered, leaving the poet nothing new to say. "How, then, shall I hymn you?" (πῶς τάρ σ' ὑμνήσω), asks the poet in one of the *Homeric Hymns*, "for everywhere, O Phoebus, traditional song has been presented to you" (πάντηι γάρ τοι, Φοῖβε, νομὸς βεβλήαται ὠιδῆς) (*HHApollo* 3.19–20 West). There follows a description of such hymning, after which the poet reiterates the question, "How shall I hymn

---

[26] For example, most recent interpreters believe that Callimachus' "mimetic" hymns – to Apollo, to Demeter, and *Bath of Pallas* – were meant not for performance at a cultic event but for private reading or declamation (Bulloch [1985, 3–13]; Hopkinson [1984, 3–4, 35–39]; Williams [1978, 2–5]). The elements of deictic self-reference in these hymns do not connect in any direct and immediate way with the external world of the performative here-and-now, although they help produce a vivid and realistic imaginal world in which the fictive cultic event takes place. As Hopkinson puts it regarding the hymn to Demeter, "the setting is 'real' in so far as imagination can make it so, but attempts to pinpoint an exact locale only confirm the success of an illusion" (Hopkinson [1984, 3–4]).

[27] Furley and Bremer (2001, 2:38).
[28] Furley and Bremer (2001, 1:51–52).
[29] Furley and Bremer (2001, 1:52n156).
[30] Powell (1925, 136; cf. parallel inscription from Dion, p. 137); Furley and Bremer (2001, 2:163).
[31] Furley and Bremer (2001, 2:229).

you?" and proposes ways of doing so. Although these proposals are presented as *possibilities*, as if they were only being considered, the listing of them is itself the enactment of praise (3.207 ff.). Callimachus' hymn to Zeus begins almost immediately with the question, "How to sing of him? Shall we sing of him as Dictaean or Lycaean? My heart is greatly in doubt, since his descent is disputed" (πῶς καί νιν, Δικταῖον ἀείσομεν ἠὲ Λυκαῖον; ἐν δοιῇ μάλα θυμός, ἐπεὶ γένος ἀμφήριστον) (1.4–5 Asper). The hymn goes on to give the traditions about Zeus' birthplace.

Deliberations about how to sing are a device for introducing narratives about the god. At the same time they also dramatize the act of hymnic composition, as if the poet were still contemplating what to say in a hymn not yet composed or at least not finished – as if the act of singing and the act of composing were one and the same.

Hymns often invite the Muses to inspire, lead, or join the song. Sometimes these invitations are given as if the hymn would commence only once the god appeared. A paean of Limenius (2nd century B.C.E.) opens, "Come to far-seen Parnassus ... and be[gin my] hymns, Pierian Muses" (Ἴτ' ἐπὶ τηλέσκοπον τάνδε Παρ[νασί] ... ὕμνων κα[τάρ]χ[ετε δ' ἐμῶν], Πιερίδες).[32] Likewise, calls for silence imply that the hymnic voice is setting the stage for the performance of the hymn, which is about to begin and must be attended by proper decorum:

Let all heaven keep holy silence;
let earth and sea and winds,
mountains, valley, be silent,
squalls and cries of birds.
For there is about to step forth to us
Phoebus with beautiful unshorn hair.

Pöhlmann and West (2001, 95); Heitsch no. 2.2

In this opening of a hymn to Apollo by Mesomedes, the call for silence dramatizes an (imagined) liturgical event in which worshipers fall silent as the hymn begins and the god draws near.

In Callimachus' hymn to Apollo, the place of the hymn in such an imagined scene is made explicit through deictic self-references:

1 How the laurel branch of Apollo trembles!
2 How the whole shrine trembles! Away, away, whoever is sinful!
3 Phoebus knocks at the doors with his beautiful foot.
...
6 Open you bolts of doors,
7 Open your locks! The god is no longer distant.
8 You young men, get ready for song and dance!
...

---

[32] Pöhlmann and West (2001, 74–75 [with supplements]); Furley and Bremer (2001, 2:92).

16 The shell [lyre] is no longer idle.
17 Keep holy silence, listeners to the song of Apollo.
18 The sea, too, keeps holy silence ...

Callimachus, *Hymn. Apoll.* 1–18 Asper

In the poetic paradox of temporal displacement, this hymn opens by narrating in the present tense (and giving liturgical directions in "real-time" imperatives) the events leading up to its performance.[33]

A moment of deictic self-reference occurs in P.Oxy. 1786 with the genitive-absolute ὑμνούντων δ' ἡμῶν ("as we hymn"). This self-description is connected to a more elaborate deictic scene, one that involves natural elements and heavenly powers in the community's act of worship. Specifically, from σιγάτω through the end of the hymn we have a series of likely four imperatives: σιγάτω in line 2, ἐπιφωνούντων in line 4, and two others that are implied but difficult to reconstruct from the remains.[34] It is natural to interpret these directives as belonging to the same moment. Since the first three exhortations, as preparatory liturgical instructions to the natural elements, belong logically to the moment before the hymn commences, they are an example of temporal displacement. It is not as clear whether πᾶσαι δυνάμεις ἐπιφωνούντων κ.τ.λ. belongs to this same anticipatory moment, since one could construe it as a mid-performance instruction to the angelic powers. This ambiguity is a consequence of the genitive absolute, ὑμνούντων δ' ἡμῶν, which could be construed to mean "when we sing" or "as we now sing."

Deictic Self-Referentiality and the Imaginal World of the Hymn

Recent studies of deixis in Greek poetry have referred to a distinction made by Bühler (in a curious mixture of Latin, Greek, and German) between *demonstratio ad oculos* and *Deixis am Phantasma*. The former refers to what the hearer can perceive in the here and now; the latter appeals to the hearer's imagination, which can embrace anything and everything, including the narration of myth and history.[35] For example, deixis in ordinary conversation may refer to actual persons, things, and actions in the speaker's immediate environment or to persons, things, and actions remembered or imagined. A Roman-era grammarian, made this distinction by speaking of δεῖξις τῆς ὄψεως

---

[33] Similar moment–by–moment self-dramatization is found in a highly self-referential hymn in Aristophanes, *Thesm.* 947–1000.

[34] χ[..]δε[σ]θων and ἐ[κ]λειπ[όντων]. Although uncertainty attaches to these words, the surrounding context (with the two other imperatives and the signs of a cosmic stillness conceit) argues for the assumption that both are imperatives.

[35] See Bühler (1965, 79–82 and 121–40).

(deixis of the eye) and δεῖξις τοῦ νοῦ (deixis of the mind) (Apollonius Dyscolus, *Syntax* 1.96 and 2.11–17).[36]

Those who have examined self-referentiality in ancient Greek poetry have been especially interested in the various moments of deixis that appear in the choral dance hymns of drama. A hymnic burlesque in *Thesmophoriazousai* has Agathon (dressed as a woman) in the role of chorus-leader, leading the chorus and giving instructions to the dancers: "Take up this torch, girls, ... and dance out my cry" (101–104).[37] The deictic references here are in one sense deixis for the eye: this torch, the girls, the taking up, the dancing. But all of these persons, things, and actions are fictional: the torches (if there are torches) are props, the girls who take up the torches and dance are actors playing fictional roles. Hence, the deictic language here is more properly described as deixis of the mind or, better, deixis of the imagination. The staging of the drama realizes what the words of the play propose to the imagination. Hence, even without the staging, the imagination creates a here-and-now picture of the scene.

When a hymn is fictional, its deictic self-referentiality is also fictional. But cult hymns are not fictional. They purport to speak about and to involve the real world of gods and human beings. Moreover, the deictic language of cult hymns often seems to have actual and immediate external referents. When the first performers of the hymn to Zeus-Kouros at Crete stood at the shrine and sang of the musical offering "which we weave for you ... having taken our stand around your well-walled altar," the words had a direct external referent – the music they were making and the wall and altar before their eyes. In the development of the *literary* hymn, by contrast, this interest in the immediate environment of performance faded, and deictic language was not crafted to be situation-specific. At least this is the argument of Calame, who describes a historical shift from the use of externally-referential deixis in cult hymns to immanent deixis in the Alexandrian literary tradition.[38] One of his examples is Callimachus' hymn to Demeter, in which the poet appropriates the voice of the chorus at the end of the hymn, a "self-conscious move," Calame says, "that distances the text from any situational reference."[39] Callimachus' hymns are "literary productions, constituted by *Deixis am Phantasma* even in their deployment of the strategies of *demonstratio ad oculos*."[40]

By immanent deixis or "deixis am Phantasma" Calame means "here-and-now" language whose referents exist only in the hymn itself. They belong exclusively to the imaginal world of the hymn. In the cult hymn, by contrast, deictic language is externally referential.

---

[36] See Calame (2004, 421).
[37] Translation from Furley and Bremer (2001, 1:350; Greek in 2:341).
[38] Calame (2004, 442).
[39] Calame (2004, 441).
[40] Calame (2004, 441).

Calame makes a helpful distinction, but it would be a mistake to think that deictic language in cult hymns refers to the external world in the manner of ordinary conversation, as when someone refers to the book on a table by saying, "Please hand me that book." As a poetic form and a liturgical entity that persists through time and can be used in different contexts, the cult hymn does not have an inherent relation to a particular setting. This is true even of those cult hymns composed originally for a specific setting, since they can be taken into new settings. For example, a hymn inscribed on a stone at Erythrai is preceded by instructions stating that the hymn is to be sung three times around the altar by the one who brings the sacrifice. But the text of the paean (with its references to youths and choral worship) strongly suggests that it was composed originally for performance at a festival with a chorus.[41]

Or consider once more the Cretan hymn to Zeus-Kouros:

Io! most mighty youth,
I salute you son of Cronus
...
Come to Dicta this New Year's day
and take delight in the music,

which we weave for you with harps,
adding the sound of pipes,
which we sing having taken our stand
around your well-walled altar.[42]

In the original performances of this hymn at its intended shrine, the references to the singing, the musical instruments, the wall, and the singers around the altar were instances of deixis with clear external referents, since all these things were physically present for the eyes and ears.[43] But we can contemplate a performance of this hymn with pipes but no harps, in which case the reference to harps is in the hymn, part of the hymn's imaginal world, but has no referent in the performance setting. Likewise, we can contemplate the singing of this hymn on site after a war had destroyed the wall. Singing the hymn at a ruined shrine would have produced a bifocal deixis – an actual "we" now self-consciously aware that they were identifying with an imaginal "we" (the hymn's persona or "implied" worshipers) and that they stood before an imagined wall and altar. History would likely also insinuate itself. *Once* people *did* stand before a "well-walled" altar and not in a ruins. *Now* we (actual singers) sing *as if* we were in their place. Thus, a deictic element intended to make immediate the connection with the exophoric here and now of performance can have an opposite effect in changed circumstances, throwing worshipers back

---

[41] Text in Campbell (1995, 5:348); Furley and Bremer (2001, 1:212–213).
[42] Translation from Furley and Bremer (2001, 1:68).
[43] Excavations of the site in Crete have shown that the precinct was enclosed by a wall, see Furley and Bremer (2001, 2:12 [comment on οὐερκή]).

into the imagination and exposing the fact that there is a formal difference between the imaginal world of the hymn and the external world.

It is important to keep in mind that the differentiation between the imaginal world and the external world of hymns is not a distinction between the imaginary and the real or even between the figurative and the literal. We *imagine* both the real (the awaited loved one who has not yet stepped off the plane) and the unreal (the prancing unicorn in a mythical tale). Moreover, both literal and figurative language are vehicles of the imagination.

In the imaginal world of P.Oxy. 1786, at least four sets of characters appear – the natural elements, a Christian "we," heavenly powers, and the triune God ("Father, Son, and Holy Spirit," "God").[44] The hymn also implies a sequence, a cosmic liturgy in which the elements of nature fall still, the "we" hymns the Trinity, and the angels respond with a doxology. The hymn does not narrate this sequence but instead gives directions for it, issuing liturgical instructions to the participants about their proper deportment and involvement. These instructions do not reflect traditional language from a Christian liturgy. As far as we know, no early Christian liturgy involved a set of instructions of the following form: a liturgist commands that the natural elements be silent while the church sings a hymn to the Trinity and instructs angelic powers to sing a doxology in response to this hymn. This does not mean, however, that early Christians would have regarded the imagined liturgical moment in the hymn as purely fictional. For ancient singers/hearers, picturing the imaginal world of P.Oxy. 1786 would have meant conceiving *themselves* as part of a cosmic liturgy involving nature and angelic beings.

That conception must have varied depending on the worshipers and the time and place of performance. As we saw in chapter three, according to a tradition that goes back to at least the third century, the midnight hour of prayer was conceived as a time when angels worship God together with all creation (*Trad. ap.* 79.27–30 // 41.15 in the Latin, Sahidic, Arabic, and Ethiopic versions). Speaking of prayer, Origen taught that "at the gathering of the saints, there is a twofold congregation, one of human beings and one of angels" (*Or.* 31.5 Koetschau). According to John Chrysostom, when the words "Let us pray" are pronounced and "when the curtain is drawn up," one should know that "the angels descend" (*In Eph.* 1, *hom.* 3.5; PG 62:29 [col. 1.38–41]). Moreover, as Chrysostom pictures the scene, "The angels surround the priest and the whole sanctuary, and the place around the altar is filled with heavenly powers to honor the one lying there [Christ present in the Eucharist]" (*Sac.* 6.4.41–43 Malingrey).

---

[44] "Eminent ones of God" in ms. line 1 may be another name for the "powers" or may refer to a different group of beings.

A Christian magical prayer from Egypt (*Prague* 1), dated to about 300 C.E.,[45] assumes that its own formulation effects the presence of angels. After an invocation addressed to God through Jesus Christ, the formula asks God to send the archangels who serve at the altar in heaven to protect the petitioner. As the petition unfolds, the angel protectors are described as already present, surrounding the one who prays the formula. The implication seems to be that in the moment when the prayer formula is uttered, the angels arrive and are then, as the prayer continues, to be regarded (and spoken of) as present.

The preceding examples show how natural it would have been for early Christians to interpret the language of P.Oxy. 1786 as referring to the exophoric world. But the cosmic stillness motif comes directly from a Greek hymnic tradition where it was not meant to have exophoric referents. Hence, it is possible that some educated Christians – perhaps the composer himself – construed the language of natural elements falling silent and angels singing a doxology in a purely poetic way, that is, as a picture of liturgical activity in the imaginal world but not in the exophoric world. More likely, however, even well-educated and philosophically-minded Christians interpreted the language of this hymnic picture as referring to exophoric reality in a literal or quasi-literal way, rather than regarding it as purely symbolical or only poetic. The direction in which the church was headed in its thinking about angels was toward the increasingly literal, as subsequent centuries show. For example, the *Regula Magistri*, a monastic text composed or edited in the early sixth century, instructs priests to take care how they blow their noses at the altar, lest they dirty one of the angels there (*Reg. mag.* 48.6–9). In the same century, Gregory of Tours advises praying monks to turn to the side if they need to expectorate, lest they spit on the angels gathered in front of them (*Glor. mart.* 75). And closer to the time of our hymn, even Origen, an erudite scholar who was not given to the overly-literal, teaches that angels are really present, even if invisible, when Christians gather for prayer. Those who used the hymn of P.Oxy. 1786 may have differed in how literally they interpreted its language, but common tenets of Christian faith in the third and fourth centuries provided reasons for them to believe that what the hymn describes of a reverent natural world and worshiping angels who join the church in a unified liturgy was in some way a true description of the real and the actual in their own worship.

---

[45] Preisendanz and Henrichs (1973–1974, 2:229–30). The text is in the form of a Christian prayer. Its enunciation of the names of various angels suggests that it belongs to the loose genre of magical formulas for invoking the aid of divine powers.

Chapter Five

Musical Analysis

Musical analysis of P.Oxy. 1786 depends on two basic sources: the body of Greek music theory that has come down to us in musicological treatises and the extant Greek musical scores. Neither source offers a comprehensive picture. Some of the most important treatises are incomplete, and the scores preserve only a tiny fraction of a vast tradition of music, the great majority of which was never memorialized in writing. From the musicological treatises we learn the methods of notation and the nature of scales and intervals, without which the scores would be indecipherable. The theorists, however, never discuss particular compositions. They deal with the general elements of music, not the realization of those elements in particular melodies. Hence, they do not make clear the import of much of what they say for the interpretation of actual pieces of music.

In addition to an absence of ancient musical analyses of individual composers and compositions, there is also the question of how the music of the later scores relates to the older theoretical foundations of Greek music. There is reason to believe that late Hellenistic and Roman-era theorists, who presumably knew the living musical traditions to which the scores of those eras give witness, often preoccupied themselves with musical questions and principles of an earlier time that lacked direct connection with music of their own periods (after 200 B.C.E. or so). One finds this interpretation of the evidence in an introduction to ancient Greek music by Neubecker, who considers it doubtful that musical practice in the late Hellenistic and Roman periods still corresponded to what the older music theorists had established.[1] West also raises questions about whether practicing musicians in the post-Classical era operated with the conception of "modes" (*harmoniai*) found in the theorists.[2]

If there are grounds for caution in relating Greek music theory to the scores, a number of studies suggest that careful efforts to connect theory and practice can pay off. Bélis draws on Greek music theory in discussing each section of

---

[1] Neubecker (1977, 93). A somewhat dissenting view has been registered by Solomon (1984 and 1986). His opinions as they pertain to melodic analysis are taken up below and in the appendix chapter.
[2] West (1992b, 184–89). Some scholars avoid using the word "mode" of ancient Greek music so as to avoid the suggestion that Greek melodies structure their tonality in the fashion of the church modes.

the Delphic paeans inscribed on the wall of the Athenian treasury in Athens (and dating to the second century B.C.E.),[3] as do Chailley and Landels in treating selected scores in their general introductions to ancient Greek music.[4] Solomon presents a painstaking music-theoretical analysis of the Seikilos epitaph, a second-century monument containing a short song.[5] Although one may contest details of these interpretations of the scores, the analyses as a whole leave no doubt that efforts to understand the musical documents can benefit from the light of ancient music theory beyond the mere decipherment of notation.

A Theoretical Introduction

A basic introduction to ancient Greek music theory is necessary before any analysis of P.Oxy. 1786 can be presented.

Several major schools are represented in ancient musicological literature: Pythagorianism, Platonism, Aristotelianism, and Neoplatonism.[6] Roman-era treatises often combine elements from more than one school, but the musicological tradition emanating from the fourth-century theorist Aristoxenus became largely standard in later centuries. This tradition has its limitations for carrying out musical analysis of the scores, but is nonetheless extremely valuable for interpreting them.[7] Its chief extant exponents are Aristoxenus himself and Cleonides. Later theorists also rely on the Aristoxenian tradition in particular areas of music theory, notably Aristides Quintilianus, Bacchius, and Alypius.[8] What follows leans heavily on the Aristoxenian organization of music theory without ignoring insights found in writers who are perhaps less dependent on it.

---

[3] Bélis (1992).

[4] Chailley (1979, 141–83); Landels (1999, 218–63).

[5] Solomon (1986). Brief musical analyses of individual scores are also given by West but using modern musical terms adapted to the character of the ancient music. See West (1992b, 277–326).

[6] Mathiesen (1999, 289).

[7] Solomon (1986, 458), in his analysis of the Seikilos inscription, draws primarily on what he terms the "'standardized' Aristoxenian method."

[8] On Aristides, see Mathiesen (1999, 527–540), who notes that in sections 6–19 of his first book on music Aristides' dependence on the Aristoxenian tradition is especially evident (in dealing with, among other things, intervals, scales, genera, *tonoi*, modulation, melic composition, ethos, and rhythmics). On Bacchius and Alypius, see Mathiesen (1999, 588 and 595).

Scales

The Aristoxenians define scales according to genus (γένος) and compass. Analysis of genus assumes a four-note scale, the tetrachord (διὰ τεσσάρων). The three basic genera of tetrachords are diatonic, enharmonic, and chromatic.[9] The enharmonic and chromatic use microtonal intervals as part of the measurement between tones. The diatonic uses only whole tones and half tones, roughly corresponding to the whole tones and half tones of modern Western scales. The genera also have additional "shadings" (χρόαι or χροίαι), that is, slight modifications of the intervals that define them. By the Roman era, Greek music seems to have become dominated by the diatonic genus, which is the genus of P.Oxy. 1786.[10]

A scale for the Aristoxenians is a consecutive pattern of notes consisting of more than one interval (i.e., a consecutive pattern of more than two notes). Of special importance are scales that span consonant (concordant) intervals. For Greeks these are the perfect fourth (διὰ τεσσάρων), perfect fifth (διὰ πέντε), and octave (διὰ πασῶν). A scale spanning a fourth consists of four notes, the tetrachord mentioned above. A scale spanning a fifth is a pentachord, and so on. The Greeks evidently heard concordant intervals as especially agreeable or beautiful. According to the Aristotelian *Problems*, the octave is the most beautiful of all (*Probl.* 19.35), which suggests that the praise of concordant intervals by theorists may have to do less with intervals *in a melody* (octave leaps being rare) than with theoretical contemplation of intervals composed of simple ratios (calculated as lengths of vibrating strings) and of the resonance heard when two concordant notes are sounded simultaneously.[11]

Greeks derived the notes of scales from the names for the seven strings of the Classical lyre: *nētē* ("bottom"), *paranētē* ("alongside the bottom"), *tritē* (third), *mesē* ("middle"), *lichanos* ("forefinger"), *parhypatē* ("alongside the top"), and *hypatē* ("top"). The lyre was held more or less perpendicular to the body with a slight downward angle, so that the string nearest the body was thought of as the top string. This string was named, accordingly, *hypatē* ("top"), but it produced the lowest note in sound. *Nētē*, the bottom string, was acoustically the highest note.

The seven note names were later expanded to encompass notes above and below, perhaps first on the basis of instruments with more than seven strings but eventually in an abstract way. Theorists worked out scalar systems in an

---

[9] The terms "enharmonic" and "chromatic" do not carry their modern musical senses.

[10] The musical documents of the Roman era suggest that the diatonic had become "as good as universal" (West [1998, 81]). On the marginalization of the enharmonic and chromatic, see West (1992b, 165–66).

[11] "Why is the consonance (συμφωνία) of the octave the most beautiful? Is it because its ratios (λόγοι) are in whole numbers ... ?" (Ps.-Aristotle, *Probl.* 19.35 Hett).

effort to bring various scales into an all-encompassing framework. One framework became dominant, at least among the theorists. It consisted of two grand scales, the Greater and Lesser Perfect Systems, which share the same trunk and branch at a middle point, *mesē* (originally the name of the middle string of the classical lyre).[12] Together the Greater and Lesser Perfect Systems form a unity, the Unmodulating System. The name may express the idea that a melody that moves from the shared trunk into one branch or the other could be thought of not as modulating but as simply using a particular path of a single system;[13] or the idea is that this system is to be differentiated from modulating systems that consist of more than one perfect system (and more than one *mesē*) and hence entail shifts of *tonoi*.[14]

In the Unmodulating System, the note names from the acoustic bottom begin with *proslambanos*, a note "taken additionally." The note names that follow in acoustically ascending order are *hypatē hypatōn* ("high top"), *parhypatē hypatōn* ("alongside high top"), *lichanos hypatōn* ("high *lichanos*"), and *lichanos mesōn* ("middle *lichanos*"). As the names suggest, the model of strings on a lyre still controls the naming, with the "high" notes corresponding to imaginary top strings (strings nearest the body of the performer), which are acoustically the low notes.[15] Moreover, the note names are not absolute pitches but define a series of intervallic relations. As West points out, *paramesē*, for example, is a note above which the intervals ascend S T T (in the diatonic genus) and below which they descend T T T S.[16]

In the Unmodulating System, two conjunct tetrachords stacked on the bottom reach up to a middle note, *mesē*. From that point the system branches to form a conjunct tetrachord with *mesē* in one branch and a disjunct tetrachord above *mesē* in the other branch. The Unmodulating System with its two branches is set forth in Figure 1. From the bottom up, the System branches to the left and right after *mesē* to complete the Greater and Lesser Perfect Systems. As a result of the fact that the Greater Perfect System builds its tetrachord above the split from *paramesē*, while the Lesser Perfect System builds it from *mesē*, the standing notes (in bold) of the two Systems differ above *mesē*.

---

[12] On the development of systems, see West (1992b, 228–33 [cf. 222–23]).

[13] See West (1992b, 223).

[14] See Hagel (2009, 5–6 with n. 23). The use of the term "unmodulating" varied as applied to scale systems. Ptolemy, for instance, referred to the Greater Perfect System as unmodulating in contrast to the Lesser Perfect System (*Harm.* 2.5–6). See also West (1992b, 223n12).

[15] Not only do the note names but their feminine gender shows their relation to the lyre-based way of note naming. But as West (1992b, 222) points out, the masculine note name, *proslambanos*, was invented by someone who was thinking not of a string (χορδή), even an imaginary one, but of a note (φθόγγος).

[16] West (1992b, 222). S = semi-tone (a half-step in a modern tempered scale and roughly that in an ancient Greek scale); T = a tone (a whole step in a modern tempered scale and roughly that in an ancient Greek scale).

Figure 1 The Unmodulating System
(standing notes in large italic type)

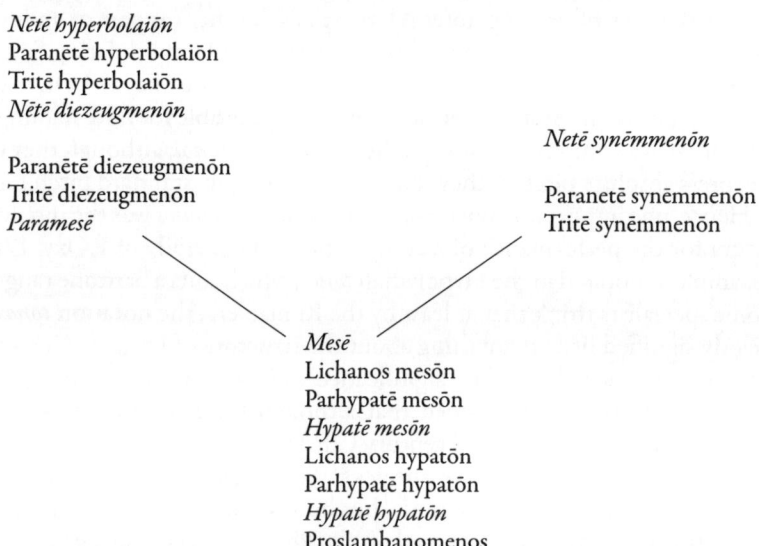

Ancient theorists analyzed the tetrachordal scale into "standing" (ἑστῶτες) notes, sometimes called "fixed" (ἀκίνητοι) notes, and "movable" (κινούμενοι) notes. The standing notes are the first and fourth degrees of the tetrachord (forming a perfect fourth), which modern scholars sometimes refer to as "outer" notes or "frame" notes. The "movable" notes are the "inner" second and third notes, which could be altered to change the genus of the scale (whether diatonic, enharmonic, or chromatic) and the "color" (χρόα) within a particular genus.

A series of two tetrachords that share a note is termed "conjunct." The shared note stands in the middle of a scale formed by the tetrachords, doing double duty as the highest note of the lower tetrachord and the lowest note of the upper tetrachord. Two successive tetrachords forming a scale but not sharing a note are "disjunct." Hence, the two branches of the Unmodulating System are, respectively, scalar paths through disjunct tetrachords and conjunct tetrachords at the middle of the System. The terms *diezeugmenōn* (disjunct) and *synemmenōn* (conjunct) as note-name modifiers in the middle of the System (on the left and right branches, respectively, of Figure 1) express this distinction.

The note names do not discriminate between genera. In using the nomenclature, ancient theorists add qualifiers to the names of movable notes (the two inner notes of the tetrachord) to indicate whether the tetrachord is diatonic, enharmonic, or chromatic. Sometimes they substitute one of these terms for the name of a movable note.[17]

The Unmodulating System can be analogized to the modern *solfeggio* system, that is, a way of naming notes relative to each other (as part of an intervallic series), without reference to absolute pitch. The Unmodulating System could be pitched in various *tonoi*, a term often translated as "keys."[18] Or, to put it a bit differently, the System's terminology was applicable for note naming in whatever *tonos* a composition was pitched. As for the *tonoi*, although they did not express absolute pitches, they did represent roughly standard pitch ranges.[19] Hence, one important consideration in choosing a *tonos* was the intended tessitura for the performance of a composition. The melody of P.Oxy. 1786, for example, is notated in the Hypolydian *tonos*, which suits a baritone range.[20]

Some specialists think that at least by the Roman era, the notation *tonos* of a melody signified little if anything about the structure of its governing scale (that the *tonoi* lacked "modal" significance). Hence, Winnington-Ingram, Solomon, and others have argued that although the *tonos* for the song of Seikilos (a tune from the second century C.E.) is Ionian (Iastian), the melody is based on the Phrygian octave species.[21] West agrees that the *tonos* does not provide a clue to the song's mode, but he also doubts that describing the mode of the Seikilos epitaph as based on the Phrygian octave species is apt or particularly helpful. He prefers to speak of the piece as being in the "G mode," meaning that if one translates the melody's underlying scale into the white keys of the piano (as a convenient reference), its primary note is "G."[22] This tells us not only the intervallic pattern (which one can call "Phrygian") but also the orientation of the melody to that pattern. Hagel also casts doubt on analyzing the Seikilos melody and other compositions of the Roman period according to octave species. He, too, speaks descriptively of modes in terms of intervallic patterns and primary pitches. But he also points out that the G mode, so defined, is typical for the Iastian *tonos* as evidenced by the musical documents,[23] which suggests that *tonoi* did carry some kind of modal quality for ancient musicians.

---

[17] See West (1992b, 222).

[18] West refers to the *tonoi* as "keys," a term that should not be confused with the modern meaning of "key," although it is in some ways analogous.

[19] See the discussion in West (1992b, 273–76).

[20] Today, scholars determine the *tonos* of a notated piece of ancient Greek music by consulting the ancient Alypian notational tables, which set forth the note symbols in their order for each *tonos*. Alypius (fourth or fifth century C.E.) did not invent but only recorded the common notational symbols used by professional musicians.

[21] Winnington-Ingram (1968, 38); Solomon (1986, 461). See also Landels (1999, 253).

[22] West (1992b, 186).

[23] Hagel (2009, 249 and passim); see also his remarks on the Seikilos inscription (2009, 286).

Melodic Hierarchy Among Tones

An appendix chapter on pitch centers in ancient Greek music provides a thorough discussion of the role of orientation notes in Greek melodies and their relation to scalar patterns. The following summarizes the conclusions from that discussion:

1. Ancient Greek melodies establish certain notes as orientation tones, which may be termed their pitch centers. A given melody may have one or more pitch centers.

2. In the Hellenistic era as represented by the Delphic paeans, most but not all pitch centers are standing notes of the *tonos*. Moreover, no non-standing note ever serves as the sole pitch center of a melody of the Delphic paeans. This suggests that the standing notes emphasized in a melody are the governing orientation points. Pitch centers other than standing notes get their melodic meaning from the standing notes, presumably by insinuating a shift away from the primary tonal axis.

3. In the Roman era, pitch centers are standing notes of the *tonos* in some pieces; in other pieces they are not. Even in the few cases where pitch centers are standing notes of the *tonos*, the tetrachordal structure associated with standing notes is not evident. Similarly, the effort to apply the concept of the octave species, understood as a set of disjunct tetrachords, to the Roman-era melodies does not yield uniformly satisfactory results. Using the numeral 1 for the lowest note of a pitch-center nexus, we can describe the forms of pitch-center nexuses in the analyzable compositions as 1–4–5 (in the Berlin paean and P.Oxy. 1786), 1–3–5 (in Mesomedes' hymn to the Sun), 1–4–8 (in the Seikilos inscription), 1–5 (in the invocation of the Muse), 1–(3) (in the invocation of Calliope and Apollo), and 1– (2) or perhaps (1)–4–(5)–(8) (in Mesomedes' hymn to Nemesis). We may reasonably assume and certainly cannot rule out that some ancient Greek melodies were oriented to a single pitch center; two of the extant compositions (invocation of Calliope and Apollo and the hymn to Nemesis) may be interpreted as examples of this.

4. In many but not all melodies, one pitch is emphasized at the beginning and at the end. It seems appropriate to term this note the primary pitch center, whether it is the sole pitch center or one of several pitch centers.

5. At least in the Roman era, the Greek ear was accustomed to hearing a composition end on its sole pitch center or on the lowest note of its pitch-center nexus.

6. Cadences (suggested through musical patterns, notation, or the syntax of the lyrics) may be restful or suspensive. A restful cadence concludes on a note that does not imply a continuation. A suspensive cadence expresses a temporary pause, implying more to come. Candidates for restful cadences

are the pitch centers of the melody, but not all pitch centers are restful. In Hellenistic-era melodies, at least as evidenced by the Delphic paeans, non-standing notes sometimes serve as pitch centers but are not restful. Where a melody has a single pitch center, that note is the natural choice for its final. Where a melody has more than one pitch center operating in the context where the cadence is found, the most restful note is the lowest of these pitch centers. Evidently, restfulness is a function of two factors – the quality of being a pitch center and a pitch center's height relative to the compass of the melody. Lower notes, provided they are pitch centers, carry a greater weight of repose than higher notes. Cadences that end on notes that are not pitch centers are suspensive. At the end of certain internal sections of the Delphic paeans we find standing notes from the upper register of the melody serving as finals. It is not clear whether a cadence that ends on a high pitch center is suspensive or restful. It is perhaps simply a matter of degree on a continuum.

Musical Analysis of P.Oxy. 1786

The Hierarchy of Tones in P.Oxy. 1786

P.Oxy. 1786 uses note symbols belonging to the Hypolydian *tonos*: R Φ C O Ƶ I Z E (*f g a b c d e f′* in the transcription, Figure 2). These notes run through the disjunct branch of the Unmodulating System. If we assume that the hymn is based on an octave species, the pattern of tones and semitones suggested by these notes is Hypolydian: T T T S T T S.

Mountford offers a different interpretation. He regards the melody's bottom note as unimportant. In other words, the bottom note does not receive emphasis and need not be treated as *hypatē*, the first note of the octave species. Hence, Mountford identifies the hymn's governing scale pattern as T T S T T S, which is Hypophrygian (with the highest note unused, at least in the extant remains of the melody). To support his interpretation, Mountford observes that *mesē*, by which he means the fourth step of the octave species, predominates in P.Oxy. 1786 when the octave species is taken as Hypophrygian.[24] Winnington-Ingram also suggests that the octave species of the hymn is Hypophrygian.[25]

Frequency of occurrence (F) and durational value (D)[26] for each tone of the piece are as follows:[27]

---

[24] Mountford (1929, 176).

[25] Winnington-Ingram (1968, 44–45).

[26] D = the combined values of rhythmic length, where a monoseme (short) counts as '1' and divided monosemes count as '.5'.

[27] Note names in parenthesis correspond to the modern transcription used in this book. The transcription in Pöhlmann and West (2001, 191) is also in the same modern "key."

Chapter Five: Musical Analysis   91

E (*f′*)   F3 / D2.5
Z (*e*)   F13 / D16
I (*d*)   F20 / D24
Ƶ (*c*)   F21 / D19
O (*b*)   F14 / D14[28]
C (*a*)   F12 / D13
Φ (*g*)   F20 / D24.5
R (*f*)   F3 / D3.5

This analysis shows that the notes receiving the greatest emphasis are Φ, Ƶ, and I.[29] If we take our cue from Solomon's approach to analyzing melodies and assume what he terms "thetic shift,"[30] we can say that these three notes are the standing tones *hypatē*, *mesē*, and *paramesē* in the Hypophrygian octave species. As neat as this analysis appears, however, it is subject to doubt. The concept of thetic shift is not a firmly established element of ancient Greek music theory, based as it is on only one ancient author (Ptolemy) and on a debatable interpretation of that author.[31]

We can also describe the tune by saying that what has been preserved of the hymn uses an eight-note scale segment (*parhypatē mesōn* to *tritē hyperbolaiōn* in the Hypolydian *tonos*), which may have been longer, seeing as we do not know whether any pitches above or below the extreme ends of this scale segment appeared in the missing part of the hymn. The melody treats the second (Φ), fifth (Ƶ), and sixth (I) steps of this scale segment as pitch centers, giving nearly equal weight to each. Hence, like the Berlin paean (P.Ber. 6870 + 14097 [1–12]), another Roman-era melody (2nd/3rd century), the Christian hymn is oriented to three notes in relations of 1–4–5. We can represent the tonal structure of the piece in scalar terms by putting the pitch centers in large bold type and indicating the intervallic relations beneath as follows:

```
R Φ  C  O  Ƶ  I  Z  E
  T T  T  S  T  T  S
  [    a 4th    ]
  [        a 5th    ]
```

---

[28] If the uncertain reading for the second syllable of πατέρα in line 4 is O, then these counts are F15 / D15.

[29] Of these notes, Φ and I (*g* and *d*) receive appreciably more durational emphasis than Ƶ. But Ƶ has high durational value compared to the other notes in the melody; it has the same frequency value as Φ and I; and it is also prominent at points of structural importance for the melody (see below).

[30] Solomon (1984) suggests that Greeks in the Roman era operated with two ways of naming notes: according to *tonos* and according to octave species. Thetic note naming was according to octave species. Hence, compositions in which the standing notes of the melody's notational *tonos* do not correspond to the standing notes of the octave species that governs the melody are to be interpreted according to the theory of "thetic shift."

[31] See the appendix, "Pitch Centers and Tonal Structure in Ancient Greek Melodies."

Of these notes, Φ is a restful note because it is a pitch center of the melody. The two other pitch centers, Ζ and Ι, may also be restful. But it appears from the scores that the higher the note, relative to the compass of the melody, the less restful it is. The two upper pitch centers belong to the upper half of the melody's compass. They probably have less weight of repose than Φ.

The Φ–Ζ–Ι tonal axis entails a fourth from Φ to Ζ and a fifth from Φ to Ι. At two points in the melody all three notes appear in sequence – Φ Ζ Ι – thus reinforcing these particular notes and the intervals they express (as referenced from Φ) for the structure of the tonal space. Greek music theorists regarded intervals of a fourth and a fifth as consonant (along with the octave). It is not known what musical qualities these intervals carried for the ancient listener or how the listener heard them in comparison to the more frequent intervals of a second and a third or the less frequent intervals of a sixth, seventh, or octave. The most that can be inferred is that the use of fourths and fifths made out of notes that the melody emphasizes helps reinforce the tonal structure of our hymn. We see this at a number of points. After two syntactical breaks marked by musical rests, the melody resumes with Φ Ζ Ι, which marks out a fourth (Φ to Ζ) and the outline of a fifth (the whole pattern from Φ to Ι).[32] The tonal axis Φ–Ζ–Ι is also structurally important in the cadence that concludes the hymn, a cadence that appears in slightly different form just before σιγάτω in line 2. The top and bottom notes of this cadence are Ι and Φ. In each instance of the cadence, Ζ is also emphasized, appearing before and after Ι. This also applies to the anticipation of the final cadence in the pattern for πάντων ἀγαθῶν in line 5.

Figure 2

P. Oxy. 1786

( ) = uncertain reading; [ ] = supplement

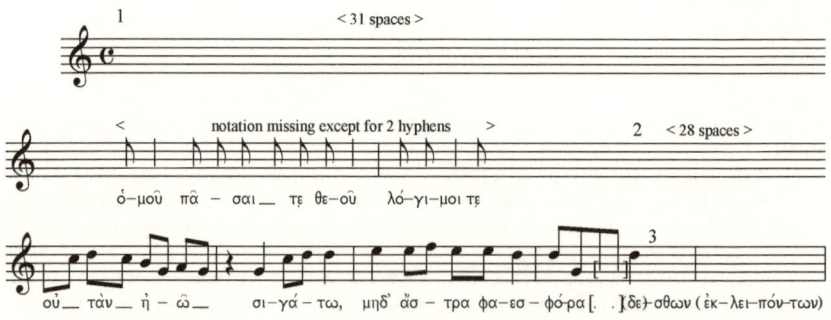

---

[32] These Φ Ζ Ι patterns are in line 2 for σιγάτω and in line 3 for the first two syllables of ὑμνούντων.

The Unfolding of the Melody

The first legible pattern of notes appears with οὐ τὰν ἠῶ in line 2 (Figure 3). Several features support the interpretation of these notes as a cadence. The pattern ends on Φ (*g*), the melody's most restful note, and is followed by a diseme rest. As we have observed, the pattern is a variant of a cadence that also appears at the end of the melody.

Figure 3

The cadence spans the concordant interval of a fifth from Ι (*d*) down to Φ (*g*) and forms a nearly scalar descending line. According to the author of the Ps.-Aristotelian *Problems*, descending notes are particularly satisfying, because a low note sounds "nobler" (γενναιότερον) and "more euphonious" (εὐφωνότερον) after a high note (Pseudo-Aristotle, *Phys. probl.* 19.33 Hett). In the cadence on οὐ τὰν ἠῶ, the pleasure of the descent is also the concordant interval and conclusion on reposeful Φ.

The rest following this cadence forms the first half of an acephalous ("headless") anapest, which is completed in the text by σιγάτω and in the melody by a pattern that echoes in reverse the interval of a fifth by which the preceding cadence is structured. This pattern is made up of the three notes of the hymn's tonal axis – Φ-Ζ-Ι (*g–c–d*) – set forth in ascending order, no doubt to reassert the melody's tonal orientation at the start of a new statement in the hymn (Figure 4).

Figure 4

σι – γά – τω

The notes for σιγάτω are part of a longer musical phrase that takes the melody to the high note of its compass (Figure 5).

Figure 5

σι – γά – τω   μηδ' ἄσ – τρα φα-εσ – φό-ρα

Despite the lacunae, the orientation to I is evident in this musical line. The interval at -φόρα outlines the fifth formed by the two pitch centers I and Φ. The stress on Z (*e*) in the middle of this phrase creates momentum since this note is not a pitch center and belongs to the upper range of the melody.

After a portion of missing papyrus in the first half of line 3, in which only a few letters of words are preserved and no musical notation, we have music for the end of the "call to stillness" (Figure 6).

Figure 6

πο–τα–μῶν__   ρο – θί – ων__   πᾶ – σαι__

There is a degree of symmetry in this melodic structure. The first three notes of the *c d e f'* rise on ποταμῶν are echoed with a melismatic variation that lengthens the melodic pattern rhythmically. Figure 7 illustrates this lengthening by eliminating the second note of each of the last three melisms in order to make the symmetry stand out.

Figure 7

Both halves of this pattern are essentially rising, finishing in the upper part of the register, which creates an expectation of more to follow, just as the words do (the call to silence being introductory). A very different effect would have been achieved had the phrase been brought to an end on Φ (*g*), as the altered version shown in Figure 8 illustrates.

Figure 8

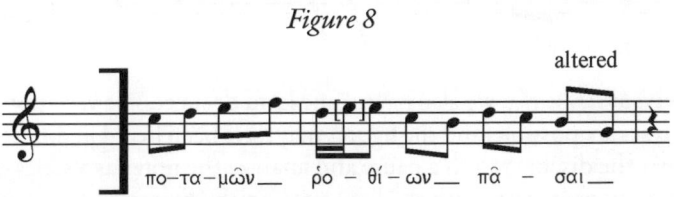

This altered ending is reposeful and makes the line sound static. The pleasing echo (through variation) of the rising line is also lost.

A notable feature of the rhythm in this melodic phrase is the subdivision of time at ῥοθίων ("rushing"). Other examples of subdivided melisms are found elsewhere in the hymn. Here one might suspect a bit of tone painting, since the energy injected by the rhythmic subdivision seems to suit the motion of "rushing" rivers.[33] But the musical figure for ῥοθίων is probably not to be interpreted as mimetic since similar rhythmic figures in the hymn are not applied to energetic images in the text (for χἄγιον in line 4, ἀμήν in lines 4 and 5, and [θεῷ] in line 5).

Following the diseme rest, the melody changes character by using larger intervals for the words ὑμνούντων δ'ἡμῶν ("as we sing"). These figures reemphasize the basic tonality of the melody through an initial restatement of the pitch centers in the sequence Φ Ζ Ι Φ (*g c d g*) and a repetition of Φ (*g*) throughout the line as other notes of the tonal palette are brought in (Figure 9).

Figure 9

As noted above, there is also a distinct echo here of the earlier melodic figure for σιγάτω (see Figure 10).

---

[33] Suggestions of tone painting are found in the Delphic paeans. See West (1992b, 201, 291, 292, and 294).

Figure 10

With ὑμνούντων κ.τ.λ. we also have some kind of successive variation. Different analyses are possible, and the figures may have been heard in different ways. If we hear the diseme rest as a pause and analyze the notes as a series of three-note patterns that starts with the long note on the first syllable of ὑμνούντων, then a dactylic effect emerges that crosses the meter. This is represented by the A brackets in Figure 11. But if we assume that the rhythm of the underlying meter strictly governs the Greek way of hearing these figures, then the long note on the first syllable of ὑμνούντων expresses the rhythm of an acephalous anapaest and serves as a kind of pick-up to anapaestic patterns on -νούντων, δ'ἡμῶν, and πατέρα. This interpretation is represented in Figure 11 by the B brackets. The diseme rest of the acephalous anapaest creates the ambiguity. Hearing it as a silent moment filling the first half of an anapaestic figure leads to one sense of the rhythm; hearing it as an extra-metrical pause before a "dactylic" figure leads to another sense. Of course, one need not choose between these ways of interpreting the structure from a listening standpoint. In music, multiple organizational possibilities can be available to the ear. It should be emphasized, however, that the composer himself intended not an extra-metrical pause but the anapaestic way of hearing the pattern, as the overall anapaestic scheme of the hymn text testifies.

Figure 11

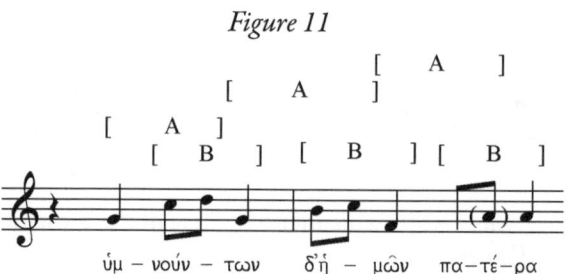

The note Φ (*g*), the bottom note of the tonal axis, is emphasized throughout the melodic line extending from ὑμνούντων to πνεῦμα. It occurs six times in all and gives the line tonal stability until the very end when the melodic phrase soars to Z (*e*) at the close of the Trinitarian praise formula and finishes on this note before another rest. This Z, a high note that is not a pitch center, is not tonally restful. It creates a strong expectation of continuation.

After the rest, the compass of the entire preceding melodic line (Φ – Z, *g – e*) is restated by the opening two notes for the next melodic phrase (Figure 12). These notes form the plunging sixth on πᾶσαι mentioned above. The repeated Φ (*g*) is the anchor of the tonal axis. From Φ the melody works its way up a fifth to I (*d*) by thirds, skipping Z (*c*), the inner member of the tonal axis (unless the missing note was Z).

Figure 12

The melody continues on uninterrupted to Z on the first syllable of ἀμήν. That word suggests a possible conclusion but is in fact the beginning of a doxology. Moreover, Z is not a stable note. Hence, the melody implies more to follow after ἀμήν and moves into a descending pattern that stresses Z (*c*) of the tonal axis (Figure 13).

Figure 13

After some indecipherable and missing notation for the conjectured ἀεὶ καὶ, the melody begins to climb again (Figure 14).

Figure 14

The doxology is built melodically so that the note for the last syllable of μόνῳ implies continuation, just as the sense of the words does (the formula with δωτήρ being incomplete without a noun in the genitive such as ἐάων or, as we have here, ἀγαθῶν). The melodic structure for δωτῆρι μόνῳ is then echoed on πάντων ἀγαθῶν with a variation, which closes on Φ (*g*), thus bringing the pattern to a point of rest. The tonal structure of both patterns echoes the cadence in line 1 before σιγάτω. The near repetition of this same cadence for the final double amen brings the hymn to a close. Thus, the hymn comes to an end with three variations of the cadence first introduced in line 2 (Figure 15).

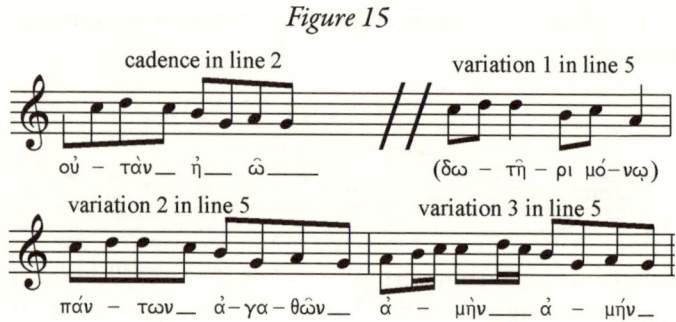

Figure 15

Variation 1 in line 5 is not as similar as the others to the cadence of line 2, but it prepares for the final double cadence by insinuating the notes Ζ Ι Ο C (*c d b a*) in a rising and falling movement that resembles the cadence of line 2 in certain respects. An important difference is that it does not end on the final Φ (*g*) but concludes instead on the forward-implying C (*a*). Variations 2 and 3 (like the cadence in line 2) end with melisms that fall from C to Φ (*a* to *g*), creating a restful close. On first hearing the melody, the listener might expect the hymn to end with πάντων ἀγαθῶν, which is a suitable close in both sense and tonal form. But the ensuing near repetition of the cadence reinforces the sense of finality, and the double amen makes the sense of an ending textually explicit.

Structure and Character of the Melody

A number of ancient writers comment briefly on melodic patterns. Aristides Quintilianus distinguishes different kinds of consecutive (stepwise) movement, which he and other theorists term *agōgē* (ἀγωγή). This concept, according to the straightforward definition of Cleonides, refers to "the course of the melody through consecutive notes" (Cleonides, *Eis. harm.* 29.2–3 Solomon; cf. Aristoxenus, *Harm. stoich.* 1.29.31–33). *Agōgē* takes different forms, which Aristides describes as direct movement (ἀγωγὴ εὐθεῖα), returning movement (ἀγωγὴ ἀνακάμπτουσα), and circular movement (ἀγωγὴ περιφερής) (*Peri mous.* 1.12.8–13 Winnington-Ingram). In modern terminology, direct consecutive movement is "ascending;" returning consecutive movement is "descending."

The metaphor of circular movement implies that the melodic pattern comes "full circle," starting and ending in the same place, but ἀγωγὴ περιφερής applies to a movement that entails a type of modulation. According to Aristides, circular movement proceeds via a modulation of scale form (σύστημα): movement through the disjunct tetrachord and back through the conjunct tetrachord (and perhaps vice versa) (*Peri mous*. 1.12.12–13).³⁴

We are apt to think of direct *agōgē* as ascending, returning as descending, and their combination (including "circular" movement) as forming a melodic arc, because in modern notation, where ascending notes on the staff rise and descending notes fall, the suggested picture is an arc. But Greeks did not use the metaphors of "high" and "low" to describe note range. Instead they spoke of "sharp" (ὀξύς) and "heavy" (βαρύς). Nor did their notational system depict tones in spatial relations. Hence, they did not picture melodic arcs but conceived of notes moving through time according to scalar patterns. For convenience, one can use the modern metaphor of an arc to describe melodic contours in Greek music (including formations of *agōgē*), so long as one bears in mind that this metaphor does not suggest the way Greeks imagined melodic movement.

Melodic movement that proceeds not by steps (consecutively) but by larger intervals (disjunct motion) is called *plokē* (πλοκή), a word that means "weaving" (Cleonides, *Eis. harm.* 29.3–4; Aristides Quintilianus, *Peri mous.* 1.12.14–17). The term *petteia* (πεττεία) is also used to describe compositional technique. Aristides uses this word for a composer's choice of notes, perhaps in the sense of "disposition" of notes, that is, the selection and arrangement of notes to form a melody (*Peri mous.* 1.12.18–21). Cleonides, however, uses the term to mean consecutive repetition of the same note (*Eis. harm.* 29.4–5). When the same note is repeated after a higher note, this is called *eklēmmatismos* (ἐκλημματισμός) in vocal melody and *ekkrousmos* (ἐκκρουσμός) in instrumental melody.³⁵

Definitions of *agōgē*, *petteia* (in Cleonides' usage), *eklēmmatismos / ekkrousmos*, and other melodic figures and devices are descriptive, but without examples in actual melodies and explanatory comment about their significance and use (which the ancient theorists do not offer), their interpretive value for musical analysis is unclear. Some aspects of this terminology, however, may be revealing about Greek music in general. West points out that if descending *agōgē* is a returning movement (ἀγωγὴ ἀνακάμπτουσα), this suggests that Greeks thought of melodies as moving in the ὀξύς direction (what we call "rising") before moving in the βαρύς direction (what we call "falling").³⁶ Of the melody openings preserved by the fragments – openings of both compositions

---

³⁴ Aristides finishes his definition with the words ἢ ἐναντίως, which seem to suggest "vice versa" or "conversely," however that is to be taken.

³⁵ See *Anonymous Bellermanni* 2–10 and 84–93 for this figure and other examples of melodic figures.

³⁶ West (1992b, 192).

and sections of compositions – more begin with a rise than with a descent.[37] The evidence is as follows:[38]

P.Ber. 6870, lines 16–19: repeated note followed by downward opening interval

paean of Athenaeus
    section 3 (end of line 16): upward opening octave leap
    section 4 (beginning of line 25): repeated note followed by upward movement

paean of Limenius
    section 2 (line 8): downward opening interval
    section 3 (line 13): downward opening interval
    section 4 (line 15): upward opening interval
    section 6 (near end of line 21): probably a rising opening interval
    section 7 (middle of line 23): rising opening interval
    section 8 (near beginning of line 26): rising opening interval

Seikilos inscription: rising opening interval
[Mesomedes], invocation of the Muse: rising opening interval

Mesomedes
    invocation of Calliope and Apollo: opening rise through three consecutive notes
    hymn to the Sun: rising opening interval after repeated opening notes
    hymn to Nemesis: falling opening interval; also falling opening interval in companion piece (or coda) at ms. line 16

P.Oslo 1413a lines 15–19, g–m: a pair of downward opening intervals
P.Ber. 6870+14907 1–12 (Berlin paean): opening rise
P.Ber. 6870 13–15 (instrumental piece): opening descent
P.Ber. 6870 20–22 (instrumental piece): opening rise

Of these nineteen openings, twelve are ascents, seven descents, a ratio of 2 to 1. This shows that an opening descent was by no means unusual or odd. At most one can say that there seems to have been a certain preference for starting a melody with an ascent, although this tendency is not strong enough to suggest a compositional convention.

As it happens, there is little sustained *agōgē* in P.Oxy. 1786. We find places where two consecutive notes ascend or descend, but in only three instances do longer forms of direct or returning *agōgē* appear: in two places three descending notes and in one place four notes ascending. There is no circular movement (with modulation of system). No instances of *eklēmmatismos* occur, but in two places there are intercalations with a higher note (a step up). In one or perhaps two places there are also intercalations with both a higher and a lower note between instances of the same note. The melody of the hymn is marked

---

[37] West (1992b, 192–94).
[38] I have not included the instrumental exercises preserved in *Anonymous Bellermanni* 97–104 and 106. They all begin by rising but are patterns, not melodies. I have not included the starts that mark shifts of voice in the sung dialogue of P.Mich. 2958 lines 1–18 since these are probably not to be thought of as the beginnings of new melodies. I have also not included P.Oxy. 3705, four bits of different notation for a line from Menander, which are probably not music. See Pöhlmann and West (2001, 184–85).

Chapter Five: Musical Analysis

by *plokē*. Instances of *petteia* (in the sense of consecutive note repetition) also appear: two notes in a row (13×), three notes in a row (1×), four notes in a row (1×), five notes in a row (1×).[39]

In the cases of two notes in a row, the patterns are often the effect of melisma, the second note of a melism anticipating the note for the next syllable (or the first note of a melism for the next syllable). We might term these "linking" melisms. At points the melody uses linking melisms to climb or descend in a scale-wise fashion. The effect is to produce a rhythm that moves in shorts but a scale structure marked out by the first half of each long. Hence, the scale is perceptually slowed down even though the energy and flow of the rhythm are kept up. A notable example is observed above (see the discussion connected with Figures 6 and 7). Instances of linking melisms can also be found in the musical patterns for σιγάτω, for ἐπιφωνούντων ἀμήν ἀμήν κράτος αἶνος, and for δόξα θεῷ δωτῆρι μόνῳ πάντων ἀγαθῶν ἀμήν ἀμήν. Perhaps the linking melisms give a feeling of greater stability at points in a melody that is almost always moving through short notes.

In some types of music, melisma slows down the articulation of the text in relation to the time. This is a familiar effect in Gregorian chant, where a single syllable may be sung to many notes. But in ancient Greek music, where long syllables generally have the duration of a diseme and short syllables the duration of a monoseme, the temporal relation of syllable to time is generally a constant, whether a syllable is treated melismatically or not. As a consequence of this basic metrical relation of syllables to notes, the use of melism does not slow down the words in relation to time but does inject energy. For example, the words ποταμῶν ῥοθίων are the same in relation to the time whether treated melismatically or not, as Figure 16 shows by setting the original next to an altered form (repeating Figures 6 and 7 and adding the words). But the original has more rhythmic energy.

Figure 16

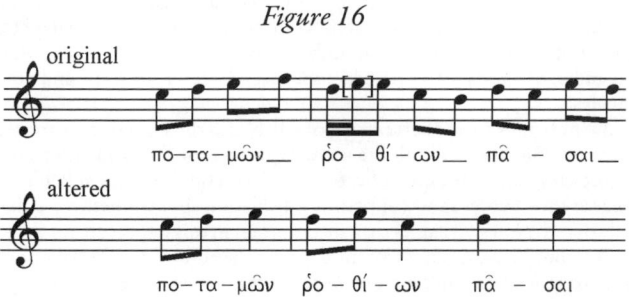

---

[39] If we had the full score and all the missing notes of the extant portions, these numbers would be different but the proportions would likely not change significantly.

We have observed that the tonal axis – Φ–Ζ–Ι (*g–c–d*) – is asserted twice after rests to begin new melodic phrases (and new sense units) within the song (see Figure 10 above). The notes of this axis are also important to the cadences for οὐ τὰν ἠῶ (in line 2) and at the end. One suspects that the lost opening of the hymn also began with an emphasis on these three notes, perhaps even a variant of the rising pattern used for σιγάτω and ὑμνούντων.

Looking at composite intervals,[40] we see that the melody more than once rises from Φ to the upper two notes of its compass: from Φ (*g*) for the first syllable of σιγάτω to the Ζ Ε Ζ (*e f′ e*) figure for ἄστρα in line 2; from Φ on the first syllable of χυιόν to Ζ for the last syllable of χἄγιον, which is repeated, after a melism, for the last syllable of πνεῦμα in line 4; and from the repeated Φ on πᾶσαι to Ζ Ζ Ε for ἀμήν in line 4 . (There may be a similar ascent from Φ to the Ε on the last syllable of ποταμῶν in line 3, but the notes are missing before ποταμῶν.) Hence, the melody moves periodically up from its tonal anchor to peaks that lie outside and above its tonal axis. These rising lines propel the hymn forward before the melody arrives at the tonally stable patterns of line 5.

Degree of Melisma

P.Oxy. 1786 uses a good deal of melisma. It is instructive to compare the percentage of melisma in our hymn with that in other vocal compositions from the Roman era:[41]

P.Oslo 1413 a lines 1–15; b–f [42]
(1st/2nd cent.)   19 %
P.Oslo 1413 a lines 15–19; g–m
frg. a (1st/2nd cent.)   14 %
P.Yale CtYBR inv. 4510 (early 2nd cent.)[43]

---

[40] Composite intervals are intervals not bounded by consecutive notes (i.e., intervals formed of a span of three or more notes). For purposes of melodic analysis, it seems best to use the concept of composite intervals for a span of notes forming an interval marked off by some other feature, such as rests, changes of direction in the melody, etc. The term "composite interval" is found in Cleonides, *Eis. harm* 10.3–10. Cleonides uses the term abstractly and not as a concept of melodic analysis.

[41] The following figures are the percentages of syllables in the score that are treated melismatically. The pieces examined include all the vocal fragments for the Roman period except those that contain just a few notes. The quantifications are based on the scores in Pöhlmann and West (2001), insofar as those scores show (or permit a deduction about) whether a syllable is treated melismatically or not. Notes/syllables that are uncertain in this respect are for the most part left out of the counts, but I have taken into consideration the editors' occasional informed guesses. Others might arrive at slightly different counts, but this will not affect the overall impressions about the use of melisma in the documents.

[42] I have combined the two sets of notation for this song. The damage to the manuscript makes it difficult at points to deduce syllabic and melismatic treatments of syllables.

[43] The original editor (Johnson [2000]) interprets the fragment as containing two songs: col. 1.1–10 + col. 2.1–5 as the first song and col. 2.6–10 as the second song. A coronis marks

col. 1.1–10 + 2.1–5	23 %
col. 2.6–10	2 %
Seikilos epitaph (2nd cent.)	21 %
invoc. of the Muse (2nd cent.)	15 %
invoc. of Calliope and Apollo (2nd cent.)	8 %
hynm to the Sun (2nd cent.)	15 %
hymn(s) to Nemesis (2nd cent.)	2 %
P.Oxy. 2436 col. 2 (2nd cent.)	13 %
P.Mich. 2958 lines 1–18 (2nd cent.)	32 %
P.Mich. 2958 lines 19–26 (2nd cent.)	32 %
P.Oxy. 3704 frg. 1 → (2nd cent.)	3 %
P.Oxy. 3704 frg. 1 ↓ (2nd cent.)	16 %
P.Oxy. 4461 (2nd cent.)	
col. 1.6 + col. 2.1–3	5 %
col. 2.4–7	no melisma
P.Oxy. 4462 frg. 1 (2nd cent.)	22 %
P.Oxy. 4463 (2nd cent.	35 %
P.Louvre E 10534 (2nd cent.)[44]	20 %
P.Oxy. 4464 (2nd/3rd cent.)	15 %
P.Oxy. 4465 (2nd/3rd cent.)	29 %
P.Ber. 6870 + 14097 (1–12) (2nd/3rd cent.)	47 %
P.Oxy. 3161 recto frg. 1 (3rd cent.)	13 %
P.Oxy. 3161 recto frg. 2.1–10 (3rd cent.)	41 %
P.Oxy. 3161 recto frg. 3 (3rd cent.)	13 %
P.Oxy. 3161 recto frg. 4 (3rd cent.)	16 %
P.Oxy. 3161 verso frg. 3 (3rd cent.)	17 %
P.Oxy. 3162 (3rd cent.)	4 %
P.Oxy. 4466 (3rd cent.)	29 %
P.Oxy. 4467 (3rd cent.)	16 %
P.Oxy. 1786 (3rd/4th cent.)	41 %
P.Ms.Schøyen 2260 (3rd/4th cent.)	44 %
P.Oxy. 4710 (3rd/4th cent.)[45]	no melisma

These statistics exhibit great variety in the use of melisma in the second through late-third / early-fourth centuries. Three scores dated to the second century show more than 30 %. Three scores dated to the third century or late-third / early-fourth centuries show more than 40 %. These figures suggest an increasing tendency toward the use of melisma with the passage of time.[46]

---

the beginning of the second song. The two songs may be part of the same larger composition (Pöhlmann and West [2001, 136]).

[44] Bélis (2004) (published subsequent to Pöhlmann and West [2001]).
[45] Yuan (2005) (published subsequent to Pöhlmann and West [2001]).
[46] The Berlin paean (2nd/3rd century and perhaps earlier) has the highest percentage of all (47 %). It is difficult to know just how to regard this fact. The piece's very slow tempo in a spondaic meter gives its melisms a different quality than melisma has in other melodies.

Compared with the Hellenistic and Classical eras, the Roman period as a whole shows much greater use of melisma.

It is unclear what calls forth the use of a melismatic style – or the degree of melismatic treatment. The style seems not to be connected with a particular genre. Of compositions in the 30%+ percent range, two appear to be tragic dialogue (P.Mich. 2958 lines 1–18 and maybe P.Oxy. 4463); another is dramatic verse of some kind (P.Oxy. 3161 recto frg. 2.1–10); one is a paean (P.Ber. 6870 + 14097 [1–12]); and one is a hymn (P.Oxy. 1786). Nor is there an evident pattern in the kinds of words (poetically or grammatically considered) that are treated with melisma.[47]

Repetition and Variation

In 1929 Mountford remarked of the ancient Greek scores that "nothing appears so unsatisfactory as the lack of purely musical structure and form,"[48] at least from a modern Western point of view. "In the music of Western Europe," Mountford observed, "we are accustomed to a musical clarity and orderliness; themes and phrases stated and balanced one with another, repeated, and variously embellished."[49] By contrast, "in Greek music, so far as we can judge, there are no themes and phrases, and no sequences of melody dictated by musical grammar and logic," the closest thing to modern musical structure being "the repetition here and there of a cadence."[50] If musical order is a way of organizing similarity and difference, then Mountford did not find an order he recognized in ancient Greek music. But the approach of our ancient scores to the interaction of similarity and difference is not hidden. It shines through in the predominant forms of Greek melodic construction: in rhythms that express similarity and note choices that add variety. This is quite unlike balancing similarity and difference by treatment of a motif or a theme, understood as a pattern of *pitches and rhythm* that is stated and developed through variation and embellishment.

More recently, in the most comprehensive analysis to date of the nature and form of Greek melodies in the scores, West observes that "Greek melody in general has a sinuous, writhing character."[51] West goes on to note that "there is little repetition of phrases; the composers seem to be always finding new paths through their scales." He suspects, however, that "if we had more extended

---

[47] Ursprung (1923, 112–13) speculated that the melismatic style was an "Oriental" influence on Greek music, seen already in the Song of Seikilos and the Berlin paean. But we have no period scores of "Oriental" music (Jewish music? Syrian?). Nor do ancient writers happen to mention melismatic floridity as a special feature of the music of eastern Mediterranean peoples.
[48] Mountford (1929, 166).
[49] Mountford (1929, 166).
[50] Mountford (1929, 166).
[51] West (1992b, 194).

fragments from the Classical period we should see less of this variety and more that looked formulaic."[52] West's generalizations are accurate and important. Just as important is to see that similarity occurs not only through rare repetition but also through variation, that is, through musical formulations that resemble earlier material. The scores exhibit very little exact repetition (except at a purely rhythmic level) but a good deal of variation.

The following is a list of repetition and variation of musical patterns in the hymn, some of which have been mentioned above:

1. Six notes in line 2 for τὰν ἠῶ are repeated exactly in line 5 for –των ἀγαθῶν. This repetition is part of two back-to-back variations, at the end of the hymn, of the cadential phrase for οὐ τὰν ἠῶ.

2. The musical pattern for σιγάτω (line 2), including the rest, is echoed in a close variation in the pattern for ὑμνούντων (line 3). This echo is also part of a series of sequential variations for ὑμνούντων δ'ἡμῶν πατέρα that can be heard as dactylic rhythmic patterns crossing the underlying meter (crossing the "bar line" so to speak) or as anapaestic rhythms (see the description above in connection with Figure 11).

3. In line 3, there is a threefold sequence of two-note falls on –ων πᾶσαι. A sequence of two-note falls also occurs at ἀμήν κράτος αἶνος, the last of them after a bit of note repetition on κράτος.

The melody of P.Oxy. 1786, perhaps more than any other in the extant scores, gives the impression of being composed to a large extent of loosely-paired patterns, where the second pattern varies the first in obvious or more subtle ways. To speak of antecedent and consequent phrases would suggest a greater degree of precision in definition and correlation of units than is present. Nevertheless, one can find short adjacent note groups that have more to do with each other than with what precedes or follows them.

Sequential melodic repetitions and variations, if not immediately apparent to every listener, would have become recognizable (memorable) through rehearings. We can assume that repetitions of patterns, especially at cadences or points of modulation, would also have been noticeable, particularly after rehearings. It is difficult to know whether patterns that are the same or similar but not adjacent or otherwise near to each other would have made a strong impression. Certain traditions of musical analysis in the twentieth century have taken the view that some musical structures discovered by minute examination of scores are operative for listeners at an unconscious level.[53] Whether or not "unconscious" is a useful or accurate term here, there is the common experience, after multiple hearings of a given piece of music, that our understanding and enjoyment of it are enriched not only by distinct recognition of inner connections but also by a vague sense of many inner associations that we

---

[52] West (1992b, 194).
[53] Cook mentions Keller as a prime exponent of this view but also suspects that Heinrich Schenker thought in similar terms. See Cook (1987, 221).

cannot pinpoint (without analyzing the score) yet experience as contributing to our pleasure in the music.

To understand how repetition and variation function in ancient Greek music, it is helpful to make a comparison with Gregorian chant. Although some chants make important structural use of repetition (strophic forms, for example), most do not. In Crocker's words, "avoidance of obvious, unvaried repetition ... is the most basic, most characteristic feature" and "generates the sense of mystery heard in Gregorian chant."[54] Those who regularly sing or hear Gregorian chant become aware of formulas (or "idioms") common to more than one chant.[55] But repetition of a melism within a chant is difficult to detect merely by hearing; even the repetition of a whole section, as in the Gradual, can be difficult for the ear to detect, Crocker observes.[56] Crocker interprets the significance of the non-repetitive character of Gregorian chant by describing it as "lyric fantasy."[57] From the standpoint of subjective musical experience (and meditative purpose), the important thing is the detail of the moment, not an overall design. Thus, chant is not "narrative" or "dramatic" in form.[58]

Neither Gregorian chant nor ancient Greek music lends itself to those forms of musical analysis that find musical meaning primarily in the relation of parts to a whole, whether by analyzing for "thematic" content or by defining the relation of the music's basic *Ursatz* to its hierarchical structure.[59] An essay on repetition by Chávez illustrates the difficulty of using the "part–whole" model as a way of analyzing and judging ancient Greek music.[60] According to Chávez, the "intrinsic value of each part and the degree of cohesion existing between all the parts are the ultimate measure of the actual merit or artistic value" of a piece of music.[61] One technique of cohesion is repetition (includ-

---

[54] Crocker (2000, 47). Crocker means avoidance of melodic repetition, not rhythmic. In Gregorian melodies, constant melodic variety is expressed through almost unchanging rhythm, suggesting that rhythmic sameness provides ballast for melodic changefulness. Apel also stresses that Gregorian chant is "highly variable and unpredictable, exhibiting a tendency toward constant change of design," the opposite principle, repetition, occurring only occasionally (Apel [1958, 258]).

[55] Crocker (2000, 54).

[56] Crocker (2000, 60).

[57] Crocker (2000, 62).

[58] There are a few famous exceptions, chants that display dramatic ascents or descents, but, contra a previous generation of scholarship, most chants do not display broad melodic arcs as a structural feature. See Crocker (2000, 61–62).

[59] On these approaches to musical analysis, see Kerman (1985, 75–85).

[60] Chávez has a traditional canon of Western music primarily in view, even though he writes as if he were setting forth criteria of musical value applicable to all music (which may be his opinion).

[61] Chávez (1961, 55). This same point is stressed by Cone. Enjoyment of music increases as one is able, through rehearing, to enjoy simultaneously the immediate moment and its relation to the whole (Cone [1968, 96–97]).

ing variation). "Somehow, music that is rich in repetition," Chávez emphasizes, "is also rich in success."[62] He has in mind Beethoven's Ninth Symphony, which exemplifies how repetition through composition in pairs "provides great comfort."[63] For Chávez, repetition is primarily rhythmic; hence rhythmic similarity with melodic variation is the kind of repetition that provides coherence and satisfaction. This type of variation makes for "symmetry," "good balance and proportion," which are "essential ingredients to integrated form," making for a symmetry that we "instinctively enjoy."[64] Ancient Greek music also exhibits rhythmic unity and melodic variety but lacks high concentrations of the kind of melodic repetition that Chávez prizes: a distinctive rhythmic pattern that stands out from its surroundings and is repeated in multiple ways with the same or similar melodic content, so that it makes an unmistakable impression on the listener. This difference is significant because, in Chávez's analytic scheme, repetition is "the only way to solve the contradiction" between similarity and contrast as opposing forces in music.[65] Musical unity is the final achievement of a musical drama of these opposing forces. Cook likewise proposes that two of the most useful questions in musical analysis are "What is the most striking feature of the piece?" and "Does it create a sense of *moving towards some goal*?"[66]

In the ancient Greek musical scores, however, musical unity has a different meaning. Unity is less something to be achieved than something present and taken for granted from the beginning – the unity supplied by rhythmic regularity. That is, rhythmical regularity (as repetition with modest variation) is the background of familiarity against which melodic variety is imposed as foreground. In this respect ancient Greek music is more like Gregorian chant. The immediate musical moment is primary, not connections between parts separated by intervening material. And, as in the case of Gregorian chant, this seems to hold even on rehearings – at least to the extent that performances based on reconstructions of this music give us a sense of how the music was heard.

Despite this similarity with chant, however, there are some important differences. If the detail of the moment is the distinguishing mark of Gregorian chant, Greek music exhibits echoes of momentary detail, sometimes a successive repetition or variation, more often a later echo. Not only that, contrast between similarity and difference does seem to be an important compositional principle. If Greek composers "seem to be always finding

---

[62] Chávez (1961, 66).
[63] Chávez (1961, 66).
[64] Chávez (1961, 77).
[65] Chávez (1961, 83).
[66] Cook (1987, 242 [emphasis added]). See also Cone (1968, 13), who speaks in this way of musical performance: it must be a *dramatic* event.

new paths through their scales" (West), this tendency to avoid sequential melodic similarity is by no means absolute. Some pieces make important use of sequential variation (notably P.Oxy. 1786). Other pieces have a substantial concentration of separated repetition and variation, with the result that certain pattern-types become memorable for the listener, evoking a distinct sense of the recurring, the familiar (particularly in the paean of Limenius, Mesomedes' hymn to the Sun, and P.Ber. 6870 [13–15]). Notable is the use of repetition and variation in cadences to create endings that involve a return to the familiar (the paean of Limenius, Mesomedes' hymn to the Sun, P.Ber. 6870 [13–15], and P.Oxy. 1786). Of these, P.Ber. 6870 (13–15) seems to exhibit the most symmetrical form. This instrumental song, perhaps meant for a dance, may have been composed of opening and closing periods made up of antecedent and consequent phrases, with a middle period of contrasting character. The fragmentary condition of the piece precludes any final judgment. Nevertheless, we are reminded by the singularity of this piece, in comparison to the other extant scores, that our generalizations about ancient Greek melodies must be made cautiously, given the relatively small number of surviving examples.

Melody and Verbal Accent

Specialists in ancient Greek music have long recognized that in some of the extant scores the melody reflects the influence of the verbal accents in various ways.[67] The "rules" of accent / melody relations are abstractions from tendencies observed in the musical documents. These rules, understood as *conventions of composition*, can be summarized as follows.[68]

1. The accent-bearing syllable of a multisyllabic word (two syllables or more) carries a note as high or higher than notes for other syllables in that word. In cases of melisma, the highest note of the melism is what counts for adherence to the rule.

2. The melody often falls after an acute accent; in polysyllabic words (three syllables or more), the melody often rises to and then falls from the acute.

3. The circumflex accent is usually set to a falling figure.

4. After a grave accent, except in cases of a grammatical pause, the melody does not fall again until after the next accent. Successive grave-accented syllables tend to be set to the same note.

---

[67] A correlation of melody and word-accent was first noticed by Crusius (1893, 173) in the Seikilos inscription.

[68] The following formulation of the rules is a summary based on the observations of Winnington-Ingram (1955, 64–73). See also West (1992b, 199). The Delphic paeans from the second century B.C.E. display the most consistent and complex adherence to such conventions and are the primary basis on which Winnington-Ingram worked out the rules. A sophisticated study of these paeans as evidence for the melodic contour of speech in relation to accent can be found in Devine and Stephens (1994, 171–94).

Almost every ancient Greek musical document shows a degree of melody/ accent association as defined by these conventions. It should be evident, however, that some degree of correlation must occur by chance in compositions uninfluenced by the conventions. In the case of P.Oxy. 1786, opinion over the years has been divided as to whether the evidence of correlation with one or more of the conventions suggests design or mere chance. Winnington-Ingram counts 13 of 20 instances of pitch-height accord (rule 1) and sees some tendency for the circumflex accent to be set to a falling melodic pattern. In view of this evidence, he remarks that "it is hard to deny all influence of the accent, which is, however, sacrificed fairly freely to the melodic formula."[69] Mountford takes the same view, as do Abert and, apparently, Dihle, as well as, somewhat noncommittally, Wagner.[70] But Pöhlmann and Reinach find no evidence that the composer paid attention to the pitch-height convention.[71]

Determining whether correlation in a particular song is by design should not rest on impressions of whether breaches of the conventions are "many" or "few," since these terms are relative. Only percentages are meaningful. More important, interpreting percentages requires some prior knowledge about what chance alone would produce. In a study of this question, Meyer (a statistician) and I used computer simulations to model random associations of pitch height and verbal accents as a test of rule 1 for individual songs. The simulations mimicked the melodic characteristics for each melody tested. Detailed explanations of the method of computer simulation and statistical interpretation can be found in the published article that reports the results of this study.[72] For convenience, we term rule 1 the "Pitch Height Rule" and refer to its subject as "PH accord."

A purely logical reflection reveals that three principles of chance accord govern correlations of pitch height and accent: 1) as the proportion of polysyllabic words (and their number of syllables) goes up in comparison to two-syllable words, the likelihood of chance accord goes down; 2) as the note compass (range of intervallic movement) goes up, the likelihood of chance accord goes down; 3) as the repeated-note frequency goes up, the likelihood of chance accord goes up. The computer simulations, which generated 100,000 random matchings for each melody tested, confirm these logical observations.

Two sets of computer simulations were run for P.Oxy. 1786, one using a text-critically secure set of data (based on twenty secure words), the other using a somewhat less secure, expanded set of data (based on the first set and an additional five words – the somewhat doubtful ἠῶ, δόξα, θεῷ, δωτῆρι, and

---

[69] Winnington-Ingram (1955, 71).
[70] Mountford (1929, 165); Abert (1921/22, 528); Dihle (1954, 190); Wagner (1924, 205).
[71] Pöhlmann (1970, 109); Reinach (1922, 19n2).
[72] Cosgrove and Meyer (2006). The following discussion relies on information in this article.

μόνῳ). The secure set shows 13 of 20 correlations (65% accord). The expanded set shows 17 of 25 correlations (68% accord).

Although correlations in the range of about two thirds might strike us as evidence of an influence of the accent on the melody, the simulations raise doubts. If this seems counterintuitive – how can correlations that substantially exceed 50% be random? – two things must be kept in mind. First, the nature of the PH accord rule causes random correlations typically to exceed 50%. Second, chance PH accord distributes in "bell curve" formations, which means that a good deal of chance correlations distribute in decreasing number on either side of the bell curve peak. For example, in a simulation for chance PH accord based on the words and melody movements of P.Oxy. 1786, the peak of the bell curve turned out to be 11 out of 20 accords. That is, the highest purely random frequency of PH accord was 55% accord. This occurred approximately 19% of the time (19,105 in 100,000 chance correlations). PH accord of 12 out of 20 (60% accord) occurred almost 16% of the time (15,734 times in 100,000 simulations). The actual accord for P.Oxy. 1786 – 13 of 20 (65% accord) based on words for which there are no doubts about readings – occurred approximately 10% of the time (10,176 in 100, 000 simulations). These random frequency percentages – 19%, 16%, and 10% – define part of the slope on one side of the bell curve from its peak; there is a similar graded decrease from the peak on the other side.

The metaphor of a bell curve is important here. In the example above, mere chance produces random PH accord of 11 out of 20 about 19% of the time, but also 12 out of 20 about 16% of the time. Given this information, one would not conclude from an actual PH accord of 12 out of 20 in a Greek melody that the degree of accord was by design. Does one additional instance of accord (making for a result that occurred 10% of the time in the simulations) constitute grounds for inferring the operation of design?

When we compare the frequencies of different degrees of chance accord, it becomes clear why a PH accord of 65% in the melody of P.Oxy. 1786, a value that occurs randomly some 10% of the time in the simulations, is not unambiguous evidence of design. A statistician does not consider a given correlation percentage in isolation but regards it in relation to other correlation percentages. A standard way of doing so is to ask how often '≥ x' occurs in chance simulations. This is represented as a p-value. If we let 'x' be '13' out of 20, then the p-value for x is the percentage of random PH accord of 13 *or more* out of 20 in the random simulation. In the simulation just described for P.Oxy. 1786, 13 of 20 occurred about 10% of the time, but the p-value for 13 is 18%.

I have been writing in a way that might suggest that the results from the computer modeling were based on only a single simulation of random correlations. The experiment in fact involved six different simulations – three different simulation methods applied to two different counts of PH accord in the hymn. One count was based on readings of twenty words about which there is no doubt. The other count was based on an expanded set of twenty-five words that included some uncertainty about readings, although three of these less certain readings are highly likely in my view.[73] Each simulation was run to 100,000 random distributions of pitch height to accent. The three different methods of random matching as applied to the two different counts all produced similar results. I have already given an idea of these by summarizing those obtained using the first method. To repeat, simulations (100,000) based on the secure list (twenty words) showed that some 18% of the time as many as 13 or more correlations occurred randomly. The p-value for this frequency is .18 (18%).

P-values are used to summarize the evidence for an *alternative* hypothesis (pattern produced by design) against a *null* hypothesis (pattern produced by chance). A conventional standard of judgment in the field of statistics is that $p < .05$ is grounds for rejecting the null hypothesis. In other words, the null hypothesis is assumed unless the p-value is below five percent. Of course, this is a rule of thumb, not a fixed measure; it is a conservative threshold, marking off a statistical space that is beyond reasonable doubt.[74] It is also a basic principle of statistical interpretation that the p-value is not to be treated as providing evidence of the likelihood of the null hypothesis, only as evidence for an alternative hypothesis. Hence, a p-value of 50% is not to be regarded as stronger evidence in favor of the null hypothesis than a p-value of 10%.

Our null hypothesis was that PH accord in P.Oxy. 1786 resulted from chance correlations and not from design. In order to draw the conclusion that design was operative, the evidence had to be strong enough to overcome the null hypothesis. Using the conventional statistical standard for rejecting a null hypothesis, $p < .05$, there turned out to be no basis for concluding that PH accord in P.Oxy. 1786 was by design. All the p-values obtained through the simulations exceeded the threshold $p < .05$. The results for all six simulations are as follows:

PH accord: 13 of 20 (65%) based on a confident reading comprising the following words: 2 σιγάτω, ἄστρα, φαεσφόρα (non-accord); 3 ποταμῶν, ῥοθίων, πᾶσαι (non-accord), ὑμνούντων, δ'ἡμῶν (non-accord); 4 χυιόν, χάγιον (non-accord), πᾶσαι, ἐπιφωνούντων, ἀμήν, ἀμήν (non-accord), κράτος, αἶνος; 5 πάντων, ἀγαθῶν (non-accord), ἀμήν, ἀμήν (non-accord).

Random frequency percentages for 13 of 20 resulting from the three simulation methods, respectively: 10.2%, 11.4%, 10.1%.

---

[73] I refer to the reading ἠῶ in line 1 (as a discrete word), δωτῆρι in line 5, and μόνῳ in line 5.
[74] The purpose of judging the statistical probability of an outcome can lead to a more restrictive threshold. For example, in cases where human health or life is at stake in the application of statistical measurements, the threshold for rejecting the null hypothesis is usually lowered – made less than .05.

Corresponding *p*-values for 13 of 20 based on the three simulation methods: 18.2 %, 21.7 %, 18.8 %
(The *p*-values do not fall below 5 % until 15 of 20.)

PH accord: 17 of 25 (68 %) based on expanded reading comprising the words above and the following additional likely readings: 2 ἠῶ (non-accord); 5 δόξα, θεῷ, δωτῆρι, μόνῳ

Random frequency percentages for 17 of 25 resulting from the three simulation methods, respectively: 6.1 %, 6.4 %, 5.5 %
Corresponding *p*-values for 17 of 25 based on the three simulation methods: 10.6 %, 11.4 %, 9.5 %
(The *p*-values fall below 5 % with 18 of 25.)

Since the conventional standard for rejecting the null hypothesis – $p < .05$ – is not a bright line but a consensus judgment of statisticians about roughly where to draw a line, the *p*-values for the expanded reading may lead some to conclude that there is sufficient evidence to doubt the null hypothesis in the case of PH accord for P.Oxy. 1786. This doubt may also be encouraged by the observation that a single additional accord (in the expanded reading) would have put the *p*-value below 5 %. Nevertheless, any hypothesis that PH accord is by design in the hymn must overcome the objection that if the composer considered the rule an aesthetic value, it is difficult to explain why he did not hew more closely to it. Some explanation of the rationale for departing from the convention more than a third of the time (32 % of the time according to the expanded reading, 35 % of the time according to the more secure reading) would have to be given.

Before leaving this topic, a few more considerations are in order. First, there is the wider context of the ancient Greek musical tradition in which to regard the evidence. We know that during the Hellenistic age, the PH rule governed composition, at least among some professionals.[75] The convention persisted into the Roman era, but the general degree of conformity seems to have slackened with time. Nevertheless, the fact of the tradition – strong from the Hellenistic era into the first century of the Roman era and to a significant degree into the second century – is a reason for suspecting PH accord for third-century songs where simulations produce *p*-values not much above .05.

The following is a summary of the evidence based on our simulations for eighteen Roman-era melodies whose degree of preservation admits analysis for PH accord. The two songs dating to the first century C.E. both show clear evidence of PH accord by design (the two songs of P.Oslo 1413a). The picture is not as straightforward for the second century. Eight of twelve songs show indubitable evidence of PH accord by design. A question mark stands over P.Oxy. 4463 and *perhaps* over the Seikilos melody and the invocation of

---

[75] The Delphic paeans show PH accord of 97 % (paean of Athenaeus) and 99 % (paean of Limenius). See Cosgrove and Meyer (2006, 68).

the Muse (but evidence of other kinds of melody/accent correlation argues in favor of assuming PH accord by design). P.Oxy. 3704 frg. 1→ shows no marks of design (2 out of 5). Degree of accord diminishes for the songs of the third century, none of which display convincing evidence, as judged by *p*-values, of having been composed with regard for the PH rule: P.Oxy. 3161 recto frg. 1 (*p*-values in the range of .30–.40 for the six simulations); P.Oxy. 3161 recto frgs. 1–4 (taken together on the possibility that all the fragments come from the same song) (*p*-values in the range of .10–.17 for the six simulations); P.Oxy. 3161 verso frg. 3 (*p*-values in the range of about .08–.30 for the six simulations); and P.Oxy. 1786 (*p*-values in the range of about .10–.22 for the six simulations). These statistical results do not prove that accent had no influence on pitch height in the third-century melodies, only that no single piece, taken on its own, displays evidence beyond a reasonable doubt in favor of inferring the operation of the PH rule.

A second consideration has to do with the statistical results as a whole. If we consider all these songs not in individual isolation but as a group, we find a reason for concluding that some influence of the PH rule did affect the composition of the later Roman-era songs. That reason is based on a pattern that emerges when we examine the bell curves for the simulations of all the melodies of the second and third centuries. If most of these songs were not influenced in any way by the PH convention, we would expect that the random frequency percentages for the actual degrees of accord in them would range over both sides of the bell curve, so to speak, the high side and the low side. Instead, we find that in each case (with the exception of P.Oxy. 3704 frg. 1→), the *p*-value attaching to the song's PH accord lies on the side of the bell curve that, sloping away from the peak, moves in the direction of low *p*-values. That is, if the bell-curve diagram reflecting the simulations describes from left to right an increasing percentage of PH accord, in 14 of 15 cases for second- and third-century songs the value for actual accord is found somewhere on the right-hand slope of the bell curve associated with the song.[76] This is difficult to explain unless some tendency to correlate accent and pitch height was in operation. Clearly, the tendency was not rigorous in these third-century songs, which makes it difficult to interpret.

The breaches of PH accord in P.Oxy. 1786 occur with the following words (based on both certain readings and one very likely reading): ἠῶ (line 1);

---

[76] The result is 14 out of 15 if we treat P.Oxy. 3161 recto frg. 1 as a part of a song that does not include the other three fragments on the recto or that does include them. We ran simulations based on both assumptions. The putative exception, where PH accord value probably falls on the other side of the bell curve, is P.Oxy. 3704 frg. 1→ (2 out of 5). This melody is a very small fragment; we did not run simulations for it. It is certain that its 2 of 5 would have fallen on the left-hand side of the bell curve had we done simulations; one more preserved word displaying PH accord would probably have shifted it to the right-hand side of the bell curve.

φαεσφόρα (line 2); πᾶσαι (line 3); δ'ἡμῶν (line 3), χἄγιον (line 4), the second ἀμήν (line 4), ἀγαθῶν (line 5), and the second ἀμήν (line 5). Three of these eight (ἠῶ, ἀγαθῶν, and the last ἀμήν of the song) are part of the cadence pattern that appears in line 1 (just before σιγάτω) and is echoed at the end in three closing variations (see Figure 15 above). Altering the melody to fit the word accents would have spoiled this pleasing musical pattern together with its integrating function (repetition through variation). A similar interest could explain the breach at πᾶσαι (in line 3), where the notes to which this word is sung are part of a varied repetition of the melodic contour that immediately precedes (illustrated by Figures 6 and 7 above). The same goes for δ'ἡμῶν in line 3. It is part of a sequential variation, which was possible only by placing its accented second syllable on a lower note than its first syllable (see Figure 11). More difficult to explain are the breaches for φαεσφόρα, χἄγιον, and the second ἀμήν in line 4. Moreover, we do not know to what extent the composer did or did not feel free to alter the words to suit the pitches of the melody. Was he setting someone else's poem to music or did he compose both words and music? If the latter, he would have felt freedom to adjust the words to the melody; if the former case, perhaps not.

As for conformity to the other three rules of accent / melody correlation,[77] the evidence suggests an inclination to observe no. 2 and perhaps no. 3, but not no. 4. The small sample size is reason for caution in interpreting the evidence. According to rule no. 2, the melody often falls after an acute accent and in words of three or more syllables rises to and then falls from the acute. In the melody of P.Oxy. 1786, we find eight of twelve cases where the melody falls immediately after the acute or at least after a few repeated notes (without first going higher). Four out of five (or five of six) instances of words of three or more syllables[78] show a rise to the acute (and in two cases also a fall from the acute). According to rule no. 3, the circumflex accent is usually set to a falling figure. In P.Oxy. 1786, five out of nine instances of the circumflex show a falling figure. In two cases the syllable is set to a rising figure, and in two cases the syllable carries a single note. If we leave aside the two instances where there is no melisma, five out of seven melismatic figures are falling for syllables that carry a circumflex accent. According to rule no. 4, after a grave accent, except in cases of a grammatical pause, the melody does not fall again until after the next accent. The melody / accent relation conforms to this rule in two of four places in P.Oxy. 1786, which is what mere chance would produce.

---

[77] See the statement of these rules at the beginning of this section.

[78] σιγάτω (rise to the acute), φαεσφόρα (fall to the acute), ῥοθίων (rise to and fall from acute), ὑμνούντων (rise to and fall from acute), ἐπιφωνούντων (rise to the acute). A third three-syllable combination of καί and ἄγιον to form χἄγιον shows a rising and falling melisma *on* the initial, acute-bearing syllable.

One cannot rule out that the accent in everyday speech influenced the composition process in the third century. The general opinion is that by the third century the tonal accent had been eclipsed by a stress accent in everyday speech.[79] Nevertheless, it is possible – perhaps even likely – that the tonal accent persisted to some degree even as the stress accent insinuated itself.[80] If we could examine first-hand the living language, we might discover that a tonal element was operative in ways that shed light on the extant musical compositions.

Use of Typical Melodic Patterns

In making the case that P.Oxy. 1786 belongs squarely in the Greek musical tradition, West has pointed out a number of similarities between its melodic patterns and those found in other pieces of ancient Greek music. He lists notable parallels from P.Ber. 6870+14097 (1–12) and P.Oslo 1413 a, lines 1–15; b–f.[81]

The notes Ƶ Ι Ƶ Ο Φ in the melodic phrase for οὐ τὰν ἠῶ in line 1 of our hymn resemble the intervallic contour of the pattern Ι Ƶ Ι Ƶ C in the melodic phrase for Παιάν ὃς Μούσαις in line 5 of the Berlin paean. The parallel is particularly striking because each pattern uses its melody's pitch centers in the same way (the pitch centers of P.Oxy. 1786 being Φ, Ƶ, and Ι; the pitch centers of the Berlin paean being C, Ι, and Ƶ).[82] A second parallel is Φ Ƶ Ι Ι Ƶ Ƶ Ε Ƶ Ƶ for σιγάτω κ.τ.λ. and C Ι Ƶ Ƶ U A U A A for τὸν Δάλου τέρπει τᾶς in line 2 of the Berlin paean. These patterns display similar contours and also use their melodies' pitch centers in the same way.

The pattern C O Ƶ Ƶ Ι Ƶ O Φ C Φ for the double amen at the close of P.Oxy. 1786 resembles Φ C O Ƶ Φ C Φ for Ἰξείων in line 4 of P.Oslo 1413 a (lines 1–15; b–f). The phrase in P.Oxy. 1786 is structured in terms of its pitch centers. Too much is missing from P.Oslo to fully identify its pitch centers, but it appears that C is its primary tone. Hence, although the two patterns are intervallically similar, it does not appear that they are tonally similar.

One more example of a resemblance between note patterns in P. Oxy. 1786 and another score is the way the melismatic pattern for the syllables of [τo] ξότης in P.Oxy. 4463 resembles the pattern for the syllables for –μῶν ῥοθί in

---

[79] See West (1982, 162–63).

[80] Sampson points out that stress accents in many languages entail high pitch. Hence, the shift to a stress accent in Greek may have included a correlation of accent and high pitch. See Sampson (1985, 107).

[81] West (1992a, 53).

[82] For an analysis of pitch centers for P.Oxy. 1786 and the Berlin paean, see "Tonal Analysis of Individual Scores" at the end of the appendix, "Pitch Centers and Tonal Structure in Ancient Greek Melodies."

P.Oxy. 1786, which suggests the use of a typical melismatic figure in both cases. Similarities are also found between melodic patterns of other musical documents. If we had an abundance of scores, we would likely see more evidence of these resemblances, both intervallically and tonally, as indications of the formulas of composition for given periods.

Performance

Little is known about the performance of Greek music in the Roman era. Besides the notes and rhythm, the scores have no tempo markings and few other performance indicators.

Articulation

Articulation marks are found here and there in the ancient Greek musical documents. The two instrumental pieces in the Berlin papyri – P.Ber. 6870, lines 13–15, and P.Ber. 6870, lines 20–22 – use a sign that probably means "detached" or "semi-detached" (a kind of staccato sign).[83] The *Anonymous Bellermann* uses and gives explanations of indicators for detached, semi-detached, and connected (legato) (*Anon. Bell.* 2, 9–10, 86–92). The connected form of articulation is the Greek "hyphen" (a semicircular sign written beneath the note symbols to connect them). This sign is also frequent in the scores as a way of defining rhythm. Along with the colon and the signs for rhythmic length (diseme, tetraseme), the hyphen is used to group notes together as a way of showing subdivisions of the time. It is likely that the hyphen implies both rhythm and articulation, namely, a melismatic division that is to be sung or played in a legato (connected) style. But its primary meaning must be rhythmic, since it is not used to group notes longer than a monoseme, and it is used to group notes of monoseme value or less only where they form a melism (i.e., when they are all sung to a single syllable). Hence, the use of the hyphen for melisms leaves open the question of how other notes are to be articulated. One could infer from the fact that the instrumental pieces in the Berlin papyrus display a few staccato marks that the rest of the notes are to be articulated in a non-staccato style. But "non-staccato" includes tenuto and legato articulations. One might assume that words, at least, are to be articulated in song the way they are pronounced, unless there is some indication to the contrary. For example, it is hard to imagine that σιγάτω in line 2 of P.Oxy. 1786 was not sung in a legato style. Separating the syllables by stopping the air after iota and alpha (a very odd way to say or sing this word) would almost certainly have called for special articulation marks. But it is also likely that Greeks connected words

---

[83] See Pöhlmann and West (2001, 170–73).

in song where they sometimes made short articulation breaks in speech. For instance, the words χυιόν and χἄγιον may have been separated in speech but connected in singing by keeping the air going as the ending consonant of χυιόν and the initial consonant of χἄγιον were articulated.

The singers on modern recordings of P.Oxy. 1786 take an overall legato approach to articulation, which seems right.

Tessitura

We have a rough idea of tessitura from the notation. The hymn is pitched for a baritone voice. West's investigation of tessitura suggests that the range of the hymn, as notated (R to E), is from about *c#* (second space from the bottom of the bass clef staff) to about *c#ʹ* above middle *c* (C♯3 to C♯4 in the American Standard System).[84] Of course, unless the singers were given a starting note by a fixed pitch instrument (such as an *aulos*) or by a singer with "perfect pitch," the absolute pitch compass will have varied somewhat from one performance to another. A modern transcription that sought to approximate this tessitura as closely as possible would use the bass clef staff and three sharps in the key signature. The transcription in *Documents of Ancient Greek Music* uses the treble clef and an all-naturals key signature. This transcription pitches the piece about an eleventh too high but has two advantages. First, treble clef is the clef most familiar to readers in general. Second, the all-natural key signature reflects the fact that the Hypolydian *tonos* in which the hymn is notated is, in terms of ancient Greek notational systems, a natural key.[85] For these reasons and also for the purpose of facilitating convenient comparison with the transcription in *Documents of Ancient Greek Music,* the transcription provided in Figure 2 (along with excerpted examples) also pitches the melody within the treble clef staff system and uses the natural key signature.

Tempo and Phrasing

Guides to phrasing are rests, the sense of the words, and the nature of the musical patterns. It is left to the performer to decide, on the basis of these features, where to breathe.

If we go by the rests, there is a break before σιγάτω and one before ὑμνούντων. Unless a rest once stood before πατέρα in the damaged part of the papyrus at the beginning of line 4 (which seems unlikely for reasons of meter and space), no rests break the melody from ὑμνούντων in line 3 to πνεῦμα in line 4. Does

---

[84] See the chart in West (1992b, 256) in the light of his conclusion (ibid., 276). Hagel's extensive investigations lead to a similar judgment (Hagel [2009, 71 in the context of 68–95]).
[85] See Hagel (2009, 9).

this mean that all of these words were sung with one breath? That would have been suitable from the standpoint of sense, since these words constitute a unified phrase. Whether they can be sung in a single breath depends on the lung capacity of the singer, the tessitura and volume at which they are sung, and the tempo. Low notes take more air than high notes, loud notes more air than soft notes, and notes sung at a slow tempo more air than notes sung at a faster tempo. In considering the limitations of lung capacity, we have to keep in view that the average Greek man was about 168 cm (= about 5 feet 5 inches).[86] Lung capacity generally correlates to height and age and is maximal in a person's early twenties; then it begins to decrease slowly with age.[87] What a modern European or North American male of 5′10′′ (179 cm) finds comfortable in breath control[88] cannot be assumed for the ancient Greek.

Naturally, one must distinguish in this matter between the professional and the non-professional. Professional Greek singers underwent intensive physical and technical training, which no doubt made them efficient users of their lung capacities. That training would not have increased their actual lung capacities; nor would it have retarded the shrinking of their lung capacities over time. But it likely would have meant that they worked at learning how to breathe maximally. Professional singers and wind-instrument players today also devote practice to maximizing their breathing – how to take a full but relaxed breath – in order to have greater control over their phrasing.[89]

In the following text of the hymn, breaths are marked with ⁹ according to natural syntactical units:[90]

---

[86] See Hagel (2009, 88 [based on research by Poulianos]).

[87] On the physiological question and its relation to the use of the breath in music-making, see the discussion of the work of Jacobs in Frederiksen (1996, 97–134). In the field of wind instruments, Jacobs, tuba player with the Chicago Symphony Orchestra for many years, is the renowned master and pioneer in studies of the use of air in wind instruments. In work that applied the physiology of the lungs and breathing to playing a wind instrument and singing, Jacobs developed methods (and devices) for measuring lung capacity and evolved an approach to breathing that maximizes the use of lung capacity.

[88] "Breath *control*" is a standard term but can be somewhat misleading when applied to length of phrasing. The length of a sung phrase depends on lung capacity (a physiological given for each person) and on the ability to take a full breath while remaining relaxed (a matter of technical training). The rate at which the air is expended (control of the breath) depends in part on tessitura (pitch) but also on musical considerations having to do with vocal quality and volume. The same holds for wind instruments.

[89] Fundamental to well-founded approaches to breath control in singing and wind-instrument playing are 1) that lung capacity is a physiological given that decreases with age and cannot be increased by exercise or other means; 2) that people tend not to use their given lung capacities efficiently and can be trained to do so. See Frederiksen (1996, 89).

[90] The uncertain readings and supplements between φαεσφόρα and ποταμῶν make the phrasing uncertain because we cannot be sure whether we have one verb, making for a very long clause, or two. The gaps at the end after αἶνος pose less uncertainty for phrasing since we have enough to know that the hymn finishes with a doxological ascription to God as the giver of all good things.

σιγάτω, ⁹ μηδ' ἄστρα φαεσφόρα χ[..]δεσθων, ⁹
[ἐκλειπόντων ῥιπαὶ πνοιῶν, ⁹ πηγαὶ] ποταμῶν ῥοθίων πᾶσαι. ⁹
ὑμνούντων δ' ἡμῶν πατέρα χυἱὸν χἅγιον πνεῦμα, ⁹
πᾶσαι δυνάμεις ἐπιφωνούντων ἀμὴν ἀμήν, ⁹
κράτος αἶνος [ἀεὶ καὶ δόξα θεῷ] ⁹ δωτῆρι μόνῳ πάντων ἀγαθῶν, ⁹
ἀμὴν ἀμήν.

Each of these breaths falls in a rest or follows a long note, except two: the breath before the doxological formula (κράτος κ.τ.λ.), which must be "sneaked" after a short note (the second note of a melism), and the breath before δωτῆρι, which follows a subdivided melism. This syntax-based phrasing poses challenges. At a slow tempo (say under 50 diseme beats per minute), it would have been difficult for the ancient Greek male of average lung capacity in the height range of 5′ 3′′ to 5′ 7′′ to sing the clause ὑμνούντων to πνεῦμα in one breath. I think this applies certainly to the typical untrained singer but also to most trained singers.[91] The phrase from πᾶσαι through ἀμὴν ἀμήν would also have been difficult to sing in one breath, and the breath before δωτῆρι is really impossible after the subdivided melism on the last syllable of θεῷ without adding time. It seems likely, then, that the long phrase from ὑμνούντων to πνεῦμα was phrased in at least two units and that the syntax of the doxology was not strictly honored. The following provides more practical breath points:

ὑμνούντων δ' ἡμῶν ⁹ πατέρα χυἱὸν χἅγιον πνεῦμα, ⁹
πᾶσαι δυνάμεις ἐπιφωνούντων ⁹ ἀμὴν ἀμήν, ⁹
κράτος αἶνος [ἀεὶ⁹ καὶ δόξα θεῷ] δωτῆρι μόνῳ ⁹ πάντων ἀγαθῶν, ⁹
ἀμὴν ἀμήν.

Some of these additional breaths follow short notes, which requires that they be taken quickly. A breath might be taken after καί (long note) instead of after ἀεὶ, but that would make an unhappy interruption of the syntax. Nevertheless, this is how an ensemble led by Paniagua phrases this part of the doxology (see below). A breath after ἀεί is preferable from the standpoint of the words. Of course, the fact that we are dealing with a textual supplement at this point means that the best phrasing of the syntax is guesswork.

---

[91] My tests with trained singers suggest that for those whose vital capacity is about 3.5, the slowest tempo at which the clause ὑμνούντων to πνεῦμα can be sung well in a single breath is about 60 diseme beats per minute (at a moderate volume). "Vital capacity" refers to the volume available for exhalation (the lungs have greater volume than vital capacity, but they collapse if deflated below vital capacity). If we let modern measurements be our guide, the average vital capacity at age twenty for an ancient Greek male of average stature (a man standing 168 cm tall or 5 ′5 ′′) would have been 3.9 liters. By age forty it would have dropped to 3.5. This information is based on tables in Frederiksen (1996, 114). Hence, most ancient Greek men would likely have found the range of 50–60 bpm about the slowest they could have sung ὑμνούντων to πνεῦμα in one breath with good sound production.

The demands of phrasing have a bearing on tempo. Even with the breath points suggested above, the hymn would have been difficult to phrase according to sense units below 50 diseme beats per minute (bpm), especially for ancient Greeks, who had lung capacities commensurate with heights in the general range of 5′3′′ (160 cm) to 5′5′′ (165 cm).[92]

We can assume that Greek musicians generally felt that breaths should be taken only at syntactically appropriate points. Greek versification was based on the principle of uninterrupted utterance,[93] and concern for the primacy of the words, one would think, should have produced respect in phrasing for the poetic syntax. But practice no doubt varied. Moreover, we find in some of the musical documents what look like marked pauses (*leimmata*) in the middle of sense units.[94]

It should also be kept in mind that individuals vary greatly in terms of lung capacity, which means that what one ancient professional singer could do with a phrase at 50 beats per minute would have been impossible for another. In the case of choral singing, the limits for slow tempos must have been accommodated to the average lung capacity of the group, with some members sneaking breaths if the tempo was too slow for them. Moreover, singers in a choir also stagger their breathing to preserve phrasing. That is, individual singers breathe at different times so that felicitous syntactical and musical connections can be achieved.

Modern recordings of P.Oxy. 1786 vary in tempo from about 38 diseme beats per minute to about 78. A very slow tempo is taken in a recorded concert performance by Lyravlos, a professional Greek music ensemble led by Stefos.[95] In an exquisite realization at a flexible 38 diseme bpm, the singer breathes very frequently, after almost every word and in the middle of two words – in ἐπιφωνούντων and in δωτῆρι.[96] In answer to my query about the group's phrasing, Stefos replied: "Generally we agree about not taking a breath in the middle of a word; it sounds wrong. But sometimes it can be acceptable for expressive reasons."[97]

---

[92] See the preceding note.

[93] Moreover, sometimes long poetic units were designed to be performed without pause. In private correspondence, Stefan Hagel has drawn my attention to the *pingos* in Greek poetry, a long series of dimeters uttered without a pause.

[94] Diseme *leimmata* that may indicate musical pauses in the middle of sense units: P.Oxy. 3704 Frag. 1 ↓ (in line 4 after ἐ]ξ σκοπέλων; in line 5 after Σικελῶν; in line 6 after πρηστήρ and after ἢ τυφώς); cf. the triseme *leimma* in P.Yale CtYBR inv. 4510 col. i (line 3) and see Pöhlmann and West (2001, 137).

[95] Lyravlos under the direction of Panagiotis Stefos. Recording of P.Oxy. 1786 at http://www.lyravlos.gr/multimedia-en.asp. (c) 2007. Accessed April, 2009.

[96] At only seven points does the singer group more than one word together. Ten words are phrased singly. Two words are phrased in two parts.

[97] Personal communication.

Another slow rendition of P.Oxy. 1786 is a recording made by Ensemble Kérylos under the guidance of Bélis, a specialist in ancient Greek music.[98] The chosen tempo of around 44 diseme bpm requires that the choir (men and women singing in octaves) breathe more frequently than only at the natural syntactical breaks. The breaths taken by the ensemble are indicated below:

σιγάτω, ⁹ μηδ' ἄστρα φαεσφόρα [λαμπέσθων⁹⁹], ⁹

... πηγαὶ] ποταμῶν ῥοθίων πᾶσαι. ⁹

ὑμνούντων δ' ἡμῶν πατέρα ⁹ χυιὸν χἄγιον πνεῦμα, ⁹ [The breath after πατέρα breaks up the Trinitarian formula, although it would preserve the meter at a point where the formula does not permit a perfect anapaestic treatment.[100]]

πᾶσαι δυνάμεις ⁹ ἐπιφωνούντων ⁹ [The breath after δυνάμεις is not necessary as a matter of breath control and separates subject from verb.]

ἀμὴν ἀμὴν κράτος αἶνος ⁹ [ἀεὶ καὶ δόξα θεῷ] δωτῆρι μόνῳ ⁹ πάντων ἀγαθῶν, ⁹ [The breath after αἶνος disturbs the flow of the doxology.]

ἀμὴν ⁹ ἀμήν. [The breath after ἀμὴν is taken in order to set off the final ἀμήν as part of the closing phrasing.]

As the preceding shows, the choice of a very slow tempo resulted in awkward phrasing at two places (after πατέρα in the Trinitarian formula and after αἶνος in the doxology). The other instance of awkward phrasing (after δυνάμεις) was not necessitated by the length of the line and must have been motivated by a musical consideration, perhaps the thought (misguided, I think) that there should be a pause after the long note.

A recording of the hymn by De Organographia, a professional period-instrument ensemble,[101] renders the hymn with two voices (male and female in octaves) at about 52 diseme beats per minute, just a little faster than the tempo adopted by Ensemble Kérylos. Like Ensemble Kérylos, the singers breathe after σιγάτω, [λαμπέσθων[102]], πᾶσαι, πατέρα, πνεῦμα, and μόνῳ. Unlike Ensemble Kérylos, they do not separate δυνάμεις from its verb. In the doxological formula they breathe not after αἶνος but after ἀεί (hence before καί), which makes better sense but still interrupts the doxological formula.

---

[98] Track 15 of *Musiques de l'Antiquité Grecque* by Ensemble Kérylos. Recorded in Paris in 1996. CD K617069.

[99] The ensemble sings the conjecture λαμπέσθων, which has since been excluded. See chapter two.

[100] The final alpha of πατέρα is short when the meter calls for a long. The musical notation indicates a long and thus saves the anapestic meter at a musical level. A breath at this point, if it made space for a monoseme pause, would allow the alpha to be short in a way that preserved the meter. The composer might have indicated a rest as a way of accomplishing this.

[101] Track 17 of *Music of the Ancient Greeks*. Ensemble De Organographia. Recorded in 1995. PRCD1001 (Pandourion).

[102] Ensemble De Organographia based their renditions on the transcriptions in Pöhlmann (1970) and West (1992) and found in West the conjecture λαμπέσθων, first suggested by Del Grande for the damaged word after φαεσφόρα in line 2 but since excluded as a possibility.

A recording with male singers of apparently very average ability was made by Paniagua's Atrium Musicae de Madrid.[103] This group takes a faster tempo than that adopted by De Organographia – about 78 diseme bpm. Despite the brisker tempo, the singers breathe about every two anapaestic metra (just like the singers on the other recordings) and at certain points even more frequently. They also add a full diseme beat of rest after every breath, with the result that every breath brings a pause. The choices about where to breathe coincide at most points with the phrasing by De Organographia. Faced with the two most difficult phrasing challenges – how to treat ὑμνούντων to the end of the Trinitarian formula and how to manage the doxology – the Paniagua ensemble, like De Organographia and Ensemble Kérylos, breaks up the doxology (by breathing before καί), but, unlike De Organographia and Ensemble Kérylos, keeps the Trinitarian formula intact (by breathing after δ'ἡμῶν instead of after πατέρα). The overall musical effect of the group's rendition is choppy because of the added beats of rest. One wonders whether the composer, who marked rests to make the meter work out right, would have been happy with all these extra beats!

Another important consideration that bears on tempo is the ancient view of the appropriate way to sing a religious song. One tradition (which persisted from the Archaic period through the Roman era) used only long syllables (spondaic meter) to express the solemnity and dignity of its subject matter.[104] Consider the following spondaic lines attributed to Terpander: Ζεῦ πάντων ἀρχά, πάντων ἀγήτωρ / Ζεῦ, σοὶ πέμπω ταύταν ὕμνων ἀρχάν.[105] In these decasyllabic cola, every syllable is long, and the lines would have been sung slowly. Examples of the use of spondaic meter in the hymnic literature of the imperial period include the opening lines of one of Mesomedes' hymns to the Sun (Heitsch no. 2.2, lines 1–6), a hymn to Nature by Mesomedes (Heitsch no. 2.4), a hymn to Attis preserved in Hippolytus (Heitsch no. 44.3), and Hymn 3 of the fourth-century Christian Neoplatonist Synesius.

In the case of notated song, not only the use of spondees in the text but also note lengths in the musical symbols are a clue to tempo. One example is preserved in the musical documents. The Berlin paean exhibits a text made up of spondees that are treated in the musical notation predominately with long notes.[106] The rhythm is expressed by groups of two, three, or four long notes in a row followed by a melism. Moreover, some of the long notes are of even greater than diseme value. Of interest is the fact that the meter of the paean

---

[103] *Musique de la Grèce Antique.* Atrium Musicae de Madrid. Recorded in 1979. HMA 1901015 (Harmonia mundi).
[104] See West (1992b, 153 and 155).
[105] In Clement of Alexandria, *Str.* 7.2.88 = Page (1962, no. 698).
[106] Pöhlmann and West (2001, 166–69); West (1992b, 317–18).

can be scanned as "greater anapaests"[107] – that is, the half-time, slow form of anapaests, as distinguished from regular anapaests, which are traditionally associated with a walking tempo.

The use of the term "spondee" to describe pairs of long syllables derives from the traditional religious song – the *spondeion* or libation song – made up of long syllables. The *spondeion* and many traditional paeans composed to honor deities were sung at a slow tempo. But not all paeans were slow, witness the Delphic paeans among the musical scores.[108] Nor were all hymns slow. Choral dance hymns were probably performed at a bright tempo, and we have a hymn to Isis by Mesomedes (2nd century C.E.) composed in the same lively meter (cretic paeonic) as the Delphic paeans. The musical rhythm of an anonymous third-century (C.E.) hymn to Apollo (or perhaps to the Nile River) also suggests energy.[109]

The choral dance hymns that have come down to us were composed for drama, and the hymns to Isis and Apollo mentioned above were likely written for entertainment (in a theater or at a dinner party). Nevertheless, there is good reason to believe that at least some of these non-cultic hymns reflect, at least in basic ways, cultic song forms.[110] As for the Delphic paeans, they were composed for ceremonial use and hence, along with their entertainment value, were meant to honor Apollo. The evidence, taken together, shows that religious devotion did not always restrict itself to very slow songs. Different occasions called for different kinds of song, which varied in tempo.

Clues to the tempo of the hymn of P.Oxy. 1786 are found in its meter and musical rhythm. The anapaestic meter of the hymn is expressed at the level of the text with quite a few spondees (contracted anapaests). The musical rhythm breaks up all of these spondees by treating one or both syllables melismatically. As a result short notes dominate the melody. The relation of poetic rhythm to musical rhythm is shown in the following comparison:

---

[107] See Pöhlmann and West (2001, 169).

[108] The meter of these hymns is paeonic (or cretic-paeonic), a quintuple rhythm associated with lively dance. See West (1992b, 140–41); idem (1982, 145). Ensemble Kérylos (under the guidance Bélis, who has written a highly-regarded monograph on the Delphic paeans) performs the various movements at tempos in the neighborhood of 130–140 monoseme bpm (65–70 diseme bpm). See Tracks 4 and 5 of *Musiques de l'Antiquité Grecque*.

[109] Hymn to Isis (Heitsch no. 2.5); P.Oxy. 4466, a hymn to Apollo (or to the Nile) in Pöhlmann and West (2006, 186–87).

[110] The words and meters of the choral dance hymns found in Greek drama tell us something about the energetic manner in which they were performed. Furley and Bremer think that the choral dance hymns in drama reflect cult song in a general way, although they caution that these hymns should not be treated as examples of cult song since they have been fashioned to serve the dramatic interests of the plays in which they appear. See Furley and Bremer (2001, 1:275–76).

	Scansion of Text[111]	Notated Rhythm
.....]ὁμοῦ	.....] ⌣ _	
πᾶσαι τε θεοῦ	_ _ ⌣⌣ _	
λόγιμοι [...	⌣⌣ _ [	
[3 metra?]		
ο]ὐ τὰν ἠῶ	_ _ _ _	[ ]⌣⌣⌣ ⌣⌣⌣⌣
σιγάτω	(diseme rest) _ _ _	(diseme rest) _ ⌣⌣ _
μηδ' ἄστρα φαεσ–	_ _ ⌣⌣ _	_ ⌣⌣ ⌣⌣ _
φόρα χ[ ]δε[σ]θων	⌣⌣ [ ] _	⌣⌣ [?_] _
[ἐκ]λειπ[όντων]	_ _ _ _	[ ]
ῥ[ιπαὶ πνοιῶν	_ _ _ _	[ ]
πηγαὶ] ποταμῶν	_ _ ⌣⌣ _	[ ] ⌣⌣⌣⌣
ῥοθίων πᾶσαι	⌣⌣ _ _ _	⌣⌣⌣⌣ ⌣⌣⌣⌣
ὑμνούντων	(diseme rest) _ _ _	(diseme rest) _ ⌣⌣ _
δ'ἡμῶν [π]ατέρα	_ _ ⌣⌣ _	⌣⌣ _ ⌣⌣ _
χυιὸν χἄγιον	_ _ ⌣⌣ _	_ ⌣⌣ ⌣⌣⌣⌣
πγεῦμα	_ _ (tetraseme rest?)	⌣⌣ _ (tetraseme rest?)
πᾶσαι δυνάμεις	_ _ ⌣⌣ _	⌣⌣ _ ⌣⌣ _
ἐπιφωνούντων	⌣⌣ _ _ _	⌣⌣ _ ⌣⌣ _
ἀμὴν ἀμήν	⌣_ ⌣_ treated as _ _ _ _	_ ⌣⌣⌣ ⌣⌣⌣⌣
κράτος αἶνος [ἀεὶ	⌣⌣ _ ⌣⌣ _	⌣⌣⌣⌣ ⌣⌣[ ]
καὶ δόξα θεῷ]	_ _ ⌣⌣ _	[ ]⌣⌣⌣ ⌣⌣⌣⌣
δ[ωτ]ῆ[ρι] μόγῳ[ι]	_ _ ⌣⌣ _	⌣⌣ _ ⌣⌣ _
[πάν]των ἀγαθῶν	_ _ ⌣⌣ _	⌣⌣⌣⌣ ⌣⌣⌣⌣
ἀμὴν ἀμήν.	⌣_ ⌣_ treated as _ _ _ _	⌣⌣⌣ ⌣⌣⌣ ⌣⌣⌣⌣

Note: In the representation of musical rhythm, small shorts (⌣⌣) are divided shorts:

In the poetic text there are twenty-two contracted anapaestic feet (spondees) and fifteen uncontracted anapaestic feet. By contrast, if one is permitted to

---

[111] The rules for determining quantity of syllables are summarized in Smyth (1956, 35–36 [§§ 142–48]; see West (1982, 7–18) for a more detailed discussion. Synesius' anapaestic Hymn 1 is a valuable source of comparison for judging the quantities of syllables in our hymn where these are not immediately clear. The first two syllables of σιγάτω, which one might think are short, were in fact long, as an instance of σιγά in Synesius, *Hymn.* 1.82 shows. Likewise, the first syllable of the conjectured ῥιπαί in line 3 is long (see Synesius, *Hymn.* 1.78). Traditional

speak in metrical terms about the melody,[112] there are no "contracted anapaests" (no "spondees") in the musical rhythm unless we include rests as longs. Otherwise every long is adjacent to shorts within the foot. Nor are there any adjacent longs within the metron, that is, through the joining of two anapaestic feet. It is only through the joining of metra that adjacent longs are found – three of them. The musical rhythm helps define the metrical conception.[113] The numerous spondees in the lyrics suggest perhaps that the hymn was meant to be sung slowly. But even at a slow tempo, the musical rhythm, with its many melisms, creates a feeling of constant movement.

Anapaests were traditionally for marching or processing, and in the Classical period are found in music for entrances and exits to and from stage. The walking tempo could be slow or fast – perhaps in the range of 70 to 90 diseme bpm (assuming one step per long). In later times, anapaests were used for other kinds of poems and became common in the Roman era.

Apparently, an anapaestic meter was regarded as suitable for hymns. A number of examples are known to us from the Roman period: a satirical hymn to Gout by Lucian, two hymns to Apollo by Porphyry, and several Christian hymns: P.Oxy. 1786, Clement's hymn at the end of *Paedagogus*, perhaps a fragment of a fourth-century hymn (Heitsch no. 45.3), and the first and second hymns of Synesius.[114] It is not known for certain whether a walking tempo continued to be associated with anapaests when they were pressed into service for other kinds of poetry, but we have seen an instance in the musical documents where "greater anapaests" are notated with tetraseme value in the long position (see above regarding the Berlin paean). This suggests that regular anapaests were not particularly slow (although also not necessarily fast).

The preceding allows us to reach some tentative conclusions about tempo. Considerations of technical execution and phrasing argue for a lower limit not slower than about 50 diseme beats per minute. Below this tempo it would have been difficult for a Greek man of average lung capacity to phrase in a way that

---

Christian language was treated anapaestically despite unsuitable syllable quantities in some places. The first syllable of ἀμήν is short but is treated as long for the sake of the anapaestic scheme, as the musical rhythm makes clear in each occurrence of this word. The same goes for the final syllables of πατέρα and πνεῦμα, which are short but are treated as long. See further below (with n. 113).

[112] It is improper to use technical metrical terms (contracted and uncontracted anapaests, spondees, etc.) to describe musical rhythm, but these terms help me make a comparison here. The quotation marks around the terms are meant to indicate that they are being used in a transferred sense.

[113] Part of the challenge for the composer was that at points traditional Christian language was not amenable to the meter. At these points he used musical rhythm as a remedy. See West (1992a, 48); Reinach (1922, 15–16) ("On peut d'ailleurs admettre, avec Hunt, que le poète s'est permis de temps en temps des vers 'hors cadre', de structure plus ou moins irrégulière, que la distribution des durées musicales ramenait dans le schéma général").

[114] See West (1982, 170–71).

respected the sense units and also made for good sound production. My guess is that most singers of average lung capacity would have sung the hymn with better breath control and phrasing at a tempo well above 50 bpm. The musical notation suggests that the composer was not trying to achieve the ponderous dignity associated with religious offerings such as the *spondeion* or the slow paean. On the other hand, P.Oxy. 1786 is not a dance hymn and was probably intended to be sung at a moderately slow tempo. I suggest a range of 50–70 diseme bpm. If an ancient Christian singer felt that a slower tempo lent the hymn greater dignity and if he regarded this consideration as more important than a natural phrasing of words, he may have preferred a tempo close to 50 bpm or even slower.

Solo or Ensemble?

Wagner believed that the hymn poses technical difficulties to the singer and was meant to be performed by a trained soloist.[115] In fact, apart from the question of where to phrase (for which there are various solutions), the hymn is not technically difficult and could easily have been sung by an untrained soloist with a musical ear, by a non-professional choir, or by a congregation.[116] In favor of a congregational rendition is the first-person plural voice of the song. But this "we" is first of all rhetorical, the "we" of an imagined Christian community, whose voice could have been adopted in performance by a soloist, a choir, or a congregation.

Some scholars have suggested that the hymn was performed responsively, with the doxology at the end serving as the closing response of a choir to a soloist (or of the congregation to a choir).[117] But this conclusion is based on a confusion about the rhetorical nature of the hymn. The hymn describes a cosmic scene in which natural elements of the universe fall still, the congregation hymns the Trinity, and the angelic powers respond with a doxology. In the imaginal world of the hymn, the angelic doxology is a response (expressed by the imperative ἐπιφωνούντων) that occurs *while* the church praises the Trinity – note the present-tense genitive absolute, ὑμνούντων δ'ἡμῶν. Of course, what grammar suggests as simultaneous actions may be meant generally. In the hymnic event there is the church praising the Trinity and powers in heaven

---

[115] Wagner (1924, 212). On this point Wagner was echoing Abert, who also judged that the melody of P.Oxy. 1786 is an advanced form of hymnody not meant for the "poor in spirit" (Abert, [1921/22, 529]). These claims have recently been repeated by Meier (2004, 47).

[116] I have taught the hymn to nonprofessional student choirs at Northern Seminary, Garrett-Evangelical Theological Seminary, and the University of Chicago Divinity School. Some have found the ancient melody somewhat foreign and for that reason a bit challenging at first, which is not a problem ancient singers would have faced. None of the students had any difficulty learning the hymn after a few rehearsals.

[117] Wagner (1924, 219); Leclercq (1937, 1480).

responding with a doxology. The *text* of the church's hymn is not given, only the suggestion that it is addressed to the Trinity; nor is there any precise indication of when the powers are to respond. The laconic description permits a variety of mental pictures. In any case, the dramatization of the hymnic event is in the hymn – within its imaginal world. As we saw in chapter four, this kind of self-referential dramatization is attested in other Greek hymns and does not call for parceling out different lines of the hymn to different singers. Moreover, deictic self-referentiality is a matter not of *identity* between the hymn and its performance but only of dramatic association.

Unison

If sung by more than one person, the rendition would have been in unison, a concept that includes singing in octaves. There is no evidence of vocal polyphony (or paraphony) in the sources, and a comment by the author of the Pseudo-Aristotelian *Problems* makes it clear that when people sang at intervals from each other, it was only in octaves (*Phys. probl.* 19.17–18).

Instrumental Accompaniment

Nothing in the notation indicates instrumental accompaniment, but this in itself tells us little. Only a few of the surviving Greek musical documents containing vocal music include notes for instrumental accompaniment and instrumental interludes.[118] Moreover, not even all those pieces for which there was undoubtably instrumental accompaniment (such as the Delphic paeans and the songs of Mesomedes) include instrumental notation.

The question whether musical instruments were used in early Christian worship has received no definitive answer, although the evidence appears to suggest that at least by the late-second century it was not common. An older scholarly view is that the polemic against musical instruments in the writings of a number of church fathers was directed against the use of instruments in Christian worship. In that case, there must have been an inclination of some congregations to sing to the lyre or the cithara, if not also to the *aulos*.[119] Otherwise the fathers would have had no reason to raise objections. A more recent view, however, is that the patristic polemic against musical instruments has in view not worship services but dinner parties and the theater, which many Christians attended. McKinnon points out that the relevant passages in the writings of the fathers make no explicit mention of the use of instruments in church. He interprets this silence as evidence that Christians were not in the habit of sing-

---

[118] See Pöhlmann and West (2001, 15, 20, 51, 55, 143).
[119] See Stäblein (1955, 1047); Gelineau (1964, 150).

ing to the lyre or other instruments in worship settings and therefore gave no offense to those who associated musical instruments with sensuality.[120]

One writer who urged Christians not to amuse themselves with musical instruments was Clement of Alexandria, but he grudgingly allowed singing to certain stringed instruments: "if you wish to sing to and play the cithara or lyre, this is not a disgrace (μῶμος οὐκ ἔστιν); you would imitate the righteous Hebrew king in his thanksgiving to God" (*Paed.* 2.4.43 Stählin and Treu). The focus of Clement's remarks is probably domestic devotional practices,[121] although what he says would not rule out the use of the lyre or cithara at the common synaxis. The fact that he makes the concession strongly implies that he knew Christians in Alexandria who were accustomed to singing Christian hymns to stringed accompaniment.

As far as the use of a lyre or cithara to accompany the hymn of P.Oxy. 1786, whether in a domestic or ecclesial setting, we have little to go on. In a recent study of ancient Greek string instruments, Hagel concludes that neither the classical cithara nor the tall lyre could have accommodated the full range of the melody of P.Oxy. 1786: "The vocal line ... exceeds the compass of the classical lyre four times (R), and the supposed range of a potential tall lyre thrice (E)."[122] In other words, if the hymn were sung in its notated *tonos*, a string accompaniment could not have performed the lowest note (in the case of the classical cithara) or the highest note (in the case of the tall lyre) of the extant melodic remains. That does not rule out an instrumental accompaniment, but it does suggest that the composer, if he envisioned a string accompaniment, did not have in mind a doubling of the melody at every point. A more heterophonic style of accompaniment may have been used.[123] Or the accompanist may have reinforced some but not all of the melody notes. It is also possible that the hymn was sung without any accompaniment.

The modern recordings of the hymn by Ensemble Kérylos, De Organographia, and Atrium Musicae de Madrid all use accompaniment performed on modern reconstructions of ancient citharas. In the version by De Organographia, the cithara plays the melody throughout in unison with the two voices. The other two renditions use the cithara to outline the melody or to reinforce only certain pitches. The Madrid ensemble adds bells at points.

---

[120] See McKinnon (1965, 69–82).
[121] On the passage and its context, see Cosgrove (2006a, 260–61).
[122] Hagel (2009, 318).
[123] On heterophonic accompaniment in ancient Greek music, see Barker (1995, 41–60); West (1992b, 205–7).

Chapter Six

Social Setting

The site of the ancient city of Oxyrhynchus is a hundred miles south of Cairo and ten miles west of the Nile. Today the place is occupied by the town of el-Behnasa. The scrap of ancient paper that came to be labeled *Papyrus Oxyrhynchus* 1786 was gathered from the rubbish mounds of that site during one of six excavations carried out by Grenfell and Hunt between 1896 and 1907.[1]

Date of the Hymn

Hunt assigned the fragment to the latter part of the third century on the grounds that its handwriting is not as late as the fourth century and that the grain account on the recto appears to date from the first half of the third century (but after the Constitutio Antoniniana of 212 C.E.).[2] Presumably, the papyrus containing the grain account was later placed on the market as used paper, as so many documents were, and its verso ended up being used for our hymn. Eric Turner's study of the time lapse between the use of the recto for an official document and the use of its verso shows that a hundred years was the maximum interval, leaving aside the rare instance; and that "within the 100-year limit, there is a slight balance of probability in favour of re-use within 25 years."[3] Of forty examples where recto and verso contain different documents and both are dated, Turner found twenty-eight instances of re-use within twenty-five years (70 %), eleven cases after twenty-five but within a hundred years (28 %), and one "freak case" of more than two hundred years.[4] In only eight of these forty cases (20 %) did the lapse of time exceed fifty-five years. If we assume Hunt's dating of the grain account (somewhere between 213 and approximately 250) and his judgment that the hand of the hymn dates to the latter part of the third century, and if we also assume that the use of the verso occurred within fifty years of the use of the recto, this gives us a range of roughly 250–300 for the writing down of P.Oxy. 1786.

---

[1] See Parsons (2007, 14–17).
[2] Hunt and Jones (1922, 21).
[3] Turner (1954, 106).
[4] Turner (1954, 103–106).

Certain features of the language and content of the hymn (examined in chapter three) may at first sight suggest a somewhat later date: the precise linguistic form of Trinitarian praise in P.Oxy. 1786, the use of a liturgical double amen, and the idea of an earthly Christian liturgy in which angels participate. The wording of the Trinitarian formula became common only after the great controversies of the mid fourth century, and the double amen as a Christian liturgical formula is otherwise not found until *Testamentum Domini* 1.23. The idea that angels participate in Christian worship is conceivable for the later third century, but the idea of a *shared liturgy* of the church and angels appears explicitly only later (in the *Apostolic Constitutions* and in Chrysostom). Perhaps we should not put too much weight on these considerations in settling on a date, since Basil quotes a traditional vesper formula, which he calls "old," that contains the same wording as the Trinitarian formula in P.Oxy. 1786; the double amen in *Testamentum Domini* probably reflects a liturgical tradition older than the document; Clement of Alexandria placed the enlightened one at prayer in the presence of angels; and Origen taught that the gathered community is attended by a church of angels. Hence, the hymn contains elements that appear in some form already in other Christian writings from the second and third centuries, becoming more pronounced and developed in the fourth century.

Considering together the evidence of handwriting (third century and not early fourth), lapse of time before re-use of a piece of papyrus (probably before 300), and the internal evidence (more closely associated with traditions of the fourth century than the third), we may incline to a date close to the end of the third century.

Oxyrhynchus

When our hymn was set down on papyrus, Oxyrhynchus was the capital of the nineteenth province of Upper Egypt (the Oxyrhynchite nome) and a thriving metropolis of somewhere between 15,000 and 30,000 inhabitants.[5] The ethnic make-up of the city included Egyptians, Greeks, Romans, Jews, and others. The city was named for the *oxyrhynchos* ("sharp-nosed fish"), a creature of the Nile worshiped by people in that part of Egypt.[6]

A wall of a little over three miles (5,298 meters) surrounded a compact town (about 1 and 1/4 miles long and 1/2 mile wide) and provided access

---

[5] On this range in estimates of the population, see n. 22 below.
[6] Plutarch implies that the Oxyrhynchites still venerated the *oxyrhynchos* in his day (*Mor.* 380 B–C).

through five gates.⁷ Within the walls stood some thirty temples, three or four public baths, a gymnasium, a race-course, a theater with a seating capacity for more than 11,000, a city hall, and a military post. The River Tomis (modern Bahr Yusuf) ran along the border of the city. Smaller villages lay in the surrounding rural countryside.⁸

The full honorific title, "the glorious city of the Oxyrhynchites," was expanded around 272 C.E. to "the glorious and most glorious city of the Oxyrhynchites."⁹ This and other bits of evidence suggest a metropolis on the rise in the latter half of the third century.¹⁰ We get glimpses of the lives of the landed elite from commercial documents (including household bills), wills, and letters, such as invitations to dinner parties celebrating *epikrisis* and crowning.¹¹ Little is known about the economic condition of the average person. Many city-dwellers lived in apartment buildings, and houses were sometimes shared by unrelated persons.¹² From time to time food crises occurred, and the ordinary person must have suffered acutely when corn and grain were in short supply. From 268–72 a public dole served some of the inhabitants and was perhaps administered at other times as well.¹³ The ration was not directed to the poor but depended on qualification by ancestry to enter the ranks of metropolites (who enjoyed certain tax reliefs) or by the performance of a liturgy (a public service).¹⁴ Many who received the dole were persons of means.¹⁵ The city council (*gerousia*) provided support for the elderly (perhaps those aged fifty-five and older) at public expense.¹⁶ The lives of slaves depended on the wealth of the households to which they belonged and the character of their masters.¹⁷

---

⁷ See Turner (1952, 81) (referring to Jomard's measurement of the walls and Grenfell's estimate for the width and breadth of the city).

⁸ On the city in Roman times, see Turner (1952); Krüger (1990); Alston (2002).

⁹ See Turner (1952, 78 with n4).

¹⁰ See Parsons (2007, 59). According to a long-held view, third-century Egypt was in economic chaos and decline. See, for example, MacLennan (1935, 23–24, 30, 35–36). It has been argued more recently that this picture is overstated. See Alston (2002, 249–59).

¹¹ See Turner (1952, 84–85); Bagnall (2007, 182–93).

¹² See Bagnall (2007, 185). A seven-story house, apparently a kind of apartment building, is mentioned in P.Oxy. 2719.

¹³ See Sharp (2007, 223–27); Rea (1972, 1–26).

¹⁴ See Rea (1972, 1–5); Sharp (2007, 223–25); Bagnall (2007, 187); Parsons (2007), 107.

¹⁵ See Parsons (2007, 107), who calls the dole "not a charity for the have-nots but a bonus for the haves."

¹⁶ See P.Oxy. 3099: "being now fifty-eight...and having reached the age of those to be maintained at public expense. ..." (*The Oxyrhynchus Papyri* 43 [1975], 31). On the age requirement, see the editor's comment (ibid., 33n7).

¹⁷ In Roman Egypt, one in five households had one or more slaves (Bagnall [2007, 184]). Male slaves were usually manumitted in their early thirties, female slaves usually only after their childbearing years (Bagnall [2007, 191–92]).

The Size of the Christian Population

Speaking of the growth of the numbers of Christians generally in the empire, Stark estimates that the church increased from about two percent of the population in 250 to about ten percent by 300. These estimates tally generally with those of other historians of early Christianity. Moreover, according to Stark, a growth rate of forty percent per decade agrees with growth rates of modern religious movements and explains how the ancient church could have gone from being a very small fraction of the population in the middle of the third century to making up fifty percent or more of the population by the middle of the fourth.[18]

Using Stark's arithmetic and assuming that Oxyrhynchus had a population in the neighborhood of 20,000 in the latter half of the third century,[19] we can calculate the growth in the number of Christians in Oxyrhynchus for the years 250–320: 380 Christians in 250 (about 1.9%), 540 in 260 (2.7%), 760 in 270 (3.8%), 1,080 in 280 (5.4%), 1,500 in 290 (7.5%), 2,100 in 300 (10.5%), 2,940 in 310 (14.7%), and 4,120 in 320 (20.6%).[20] By 350 there would have been some 11,320 Christians in the city (56.6%).

Of course, these numbers provide only a rough guide. The starting percentage derived from Stark for the year 250 may be wide of the mark. Even if the calculated growth curve is reliable as a general estimate for the increase of Christians in the empire, Oxyrhynchus may have had more or less than the average percentage of Christians in 250.[21] Moreover, the population estimate of 20,000 inhabitants for Oxyrhynchus could be off by several thousands,[22] and the growth rate will not have been exactly forty percent per decade.

Using evidence of Christian names in a number of Egyptian papyri and a calculus designed to account for the fact that not all Christians had Christian names, Bagnall estimates that around 10% of the population were Christians in 275 and almost 25% by 300.[23] In a subsequent study, he arrives at lower

---

[18] Stark (1997, 4–21).

[19] Based on the range of estimates by other scholars and his own judgments, Parsons suggests about 20,000 (2007, 47 with n9).

[20] Stark's raw numbers for the year 250 are 1,171,356 Christians out of 60,000,000 people in the empire (about 2%) (Stark [1997, 7]).

[21] There is no reason, however, to think that Oxyrhynchus would have been untypical. It is generally assumed that in the early centuries most of the largest populations of Christians were in the east (Asia Minor, Palestine, Egypt) and in cities. Estimates of numbers of Christians in the population are based to a significant extent on impressions derived from study of these centers of the faith (along with Rome), being gathered primarily from literature emanating from Christians in these areas.

[22] Bowman (2007, 171) suggests 15,000 to 30,000 inhabitants for the city "at its height in (say) the early second century A.D." Alston (2002, 333) settles on about 15,000 for third-century Oxyrhynchus. Fichman (1921, 114–16) suggests 30,000 for Roman-era Oxyrhynchus. Parsons (2007, 47 with n9) suggests about 20,000.

[23] See Bagnall (2003a, 119–20 with graph on p. 124).

numbers: 9.8% to a 11.9% for 278 and 16.8% to 20.4% for 313.²⁴ The growth rate implied by these percentages is much lower than that assumed by Stark, only 15% per decade, but the resultant number of Christians in Oxyrhynchus during the period of 250–300 is higher.

If we assume a stable population of 20,000 for Oxyrhynchus in 250–350 C.E., Bagnall's revised percentages suggest around 2,170 Christians at Oxyrhynchus in 278 and 3,720 in 313 (based on averages of his ranges). Working from the 15% growth rate suggested by his percentages, we arrive at a little more than 1,400 for the year 250 (about 7%) and about 2,900 for 300 (14.5%), compared to 400 (2%) for the year 250 and about 2,000 (10%) for 300 based on Stark's method. The disparate results obtained from Stark's and Bagnall's very different approaches preclude confidence about the percentages. All we can say is that efforts at estimating the Christian population at Oxyrhynchus suggest growth from about 400–1,400 in the year 250 to 2,000–2,900 in the year 300. All the numbers are rough estimates.

By about 300, Oxyrhynchus had at least two *buildings* known as "churches" and probably one or two more. The evidence comes from P.Oxy. 43 verso, a list of the locations of guards about the city.²⁵ The enumeration refers to a guard "in the street by the north church" (ῥύμῃ τῇ βορινῇ ἐκκλησίᾳ) (col. 1, line 10) and one "in the street by the south church" (ῥύμῃ τῇ νοτινῇ ἐκκλησίᾳ) (col. 3, line 19).²⁶ If there were 2,000 or more Christians in Oxyrhynchus at this time, they could not have been accommodated by two church buildings, unless those buildings were very large, which is extremely doubtful for this period of church history. More likely, services were held in other buildings as well, some of which may have been church buildings, others rented or borrowed spaces, along with domestic dwellings of various sizes. Congregations were found in the small villages of the Oxyrhynchite nome as well; some of them Greek-speaking, as a letter in Greek written in 304 by a former reader in the church of Chusis shows.²⁷ By perhaps the middle of the third century, the number of churches in the region was great enough to warrant a bishop of Oxyrhynchus,²⁸ and one served there at least as early as 325.²⁹

---

²⁴ Bagnall (2003b, 249); idem (1995, 85–89).

²⁵ The recto of this document dates to 295, and the original editors judged that the verso, where the streets with churches are named, was written not long after (*The Oxyrhynchus Papyri* 1 [1898]:89).

²⁶ *The Oxyrhynchus Papyri* 1 (1898):96 and 98.

²⁷ This letter, by Aurelius Ammonius, is discussed below.

²⁸ Luijendijk makes a credible case that in the period of roughly 250–275 the Christians of Oxyrhynchus enjoyed the care of a bishop named Sotas (Luijendijk [2008a, 81–151]). If Christians amounted to 7% of 20,000 Oxyrhynchites in 250 (a percentage based on Bagnall's numbers), the bishop would have overseen some fourteen hundred souls, about four hundred if Stark's method of calculation is correct.

²⁹ "Palagius in Oxyrhynchus" in list of bishops made up by Athanasius in 325 in his defense against the Arians (*Apol. sec.* 71.6.12).

Persecution of Christians in Egypt

From the middle of the third century until the peace of Constantine, there were three periods of persecution sanctioned by Roman emperors: 250–251 under Decius,[30] 257–260 under Valerian,[31] and 303–311 under Diocletian and his co-emperors.[32]

The Decian edict regarding worship of the traditional Roman deities was probably not aimed specifically at Christians. Nevertheless, it put them in a difficult predicament by requiring that whole households present themselves before the authorities and that each member carry out the prescribed ritual, upon completion of which the head of the household would receive a notarized certificate of compliance. Nearly fifty certificates have survived from Oxyrhynchus.[33] It is not known whether any of these belonged to Christian families.

The Valerian persecution was directed specifically against Christians. The emperor's first edict of 257 banished prominent clergy to remote places and prohibited Christians from assembling. A second edict in 258 was harsher: confiscation of property from wealthy Christians, who were threatened with execution if they refused to renounce their faith, and immediate punishment of clergy at all levels.[34] The bishop of Alexandria at the time was Dionysius. According to Eusebius' account of Dionysius' own description of what happened to him and others in Alexandria and Egypt,[35] Aemilianus, prefect of Egypt, acted on the emperor's initial edict by seizing and exiling the bishop and a number of priests and deacons who refused to sacrifice to the imperial deities. The exiles were first sent to Cephro outside Alexandria, later to the Mareotian nome, a rough district farther away. In both places Christians went out to assemble with the exiles, and some of the local inhabitants were converted.

The reach of the Valerian persecution into Oxyrhynchus is perhaps attested by P.Oxy. 3119. The fragmentary remains of this missive have been interpreted as referring to the listing of the property of Christians, which was to be con-

---

[30] The generally-accepted dates are 250–51. Already in 249, however, with his accession, Decius promulgated an edict ordering sacrifice to honor the beginning of his new reign and required certificates as proof that one had made sacrifice. This put Christians in a bad way. See Clarke (2002).

[31] Haas (1983, 133–44); Healy (1905).

[32] Odahl (2004, 67–97); Barnes (1981, 20–26).

[33] Parsons (2007, 202).

[34] On the two edicts (or "rescripts") of Valerian, see Haas (1983, 135–36, citing *Acta Proconsularia Sancti Cypriani* 1.1–7); Cyprian, *Ep.* 76–80; Eusebius, *H.E.* 7.11.4–10; and Augustine, *Serm.* 273.7). See also Keresztes (1975, 81–95).

[35] See Eusebius, *H.E.* 7.10.9–11.25, on which the following description of the persecution is based.

fiscated.³⁶ The "seventh year" mentioned in the letter may be the seventh year of Valerian and Gallienus (259/60 C.E.), a time of persecution, but the dating is uncertain.³⁷

By 293, the Roman empire was ruled by four co-emperors of unequal status: Diocletian and Maximian (whom Diocletian had appointed as his junior co-emperor in 285), along with Constantius and Galerius (two more junior Caesars appointed in 293). Each of these men had his own domain and standing army by which to defend his part of the realm.³⁸ The universal Diocletian persecution of Christians began in February 303 following an oracle of Apollo at Didyma.³⁹ The first edict of this persecution called for the destruction of the Christian scriptures and churches. It also imposed penalties on those who refused to renounce their faith: loss of civil rights for those of high status and loss of liberty for ordinary people (Eusebius, *H.E.* 8.2.4–5). Two fires in Rome were blamed on Christians and executions followed. Later edicts required the destruction of church buildings and demanded that church leaders offer sacrifice to the Roman gods on penalty of imprisonment, torture, and death.⁴⁰ Soon the scope was broadened, with letters to various cities and towns directing that all inhabitants be required to sacrifice and offer libations (Eusebius, *Mart. Pal.* 3.1).

A good deal of the non-Christian public frowned on these imperial actions, which may have ameliorated their effects to a degree, depending on the attitudes of local officials and their deference to public opinion. Diocletian's co-emperor Constantius – who ruled over Spain, Gaul, and Britain – was perhaps only a reluctant enforcer of the edicts,⁴¹ and his son Constantine, upon becoming his successor in 306, restored the rights and property of Christians in his domain. According to Eusebius, Galerius, on his deathbed in 311, admitted that the campaign against the church had been a failure and rescinded the edicts (*Vit. Const.* 1.57). In 312, the year of Constantine's defeat of Maxentius at the Milvian Bridge, Maximinus II (Daia), who still ruled parts

---

³⁶ Parsons (2007, 202, cautiously).

³⁷ See the comments by Rea, the original editor of P.Oxy. 3119, in *The Oxyrhynchus Papyri* 43 (1975):77.

³⁸ Lactantius speaks explicitly of a division of the empire into four parts (*Mort.* 7.2). In practical effect the empire was divided into two domains because of the ways pairs of these rulers worked together. See Barnes (1982, 196–97). On the appointment of Maximian, see Barnes (1981, 6 and 287n30 [citing Eutropius, *Breviarum ab urbe condita* 9.20.3 and *Passio Marcelli* 2]).

³⁹ Lactantius, *Mort.* 10.6–12.5; Eusebius, *Vit .Const.* 2.50–51 (where Eusebius has Constantine tell how he recalls the giving of the oracle and the interpretation of the oracle as pointing to Christians as the enemies of Rome). See also Barnes (1981, 21).

⁴⁰ See Barnes (1981, 24).

⁴¹ According to Eusebius, Constantius did not enforce the edicts but was a friend to Christians (*H.E.* 8, appendix in codices A, E, and R). Lactantius paints a different picture. According to him, Constantius permitted churches to be torn down but did not put any Christians to death (Lactantius, *Mort. pers.* 15).

of the east, issued an edict against the Christians (Eusebius, *H.E.* 9.7.2–16). He was defeated by Licinius in 313 and shortly after restored the property and rights of Christians. Maximinus died soon after,⁴² which left Licinius full sway in the east. Licinius, who in 312 joined with Constantine in calling for an end to persecution of Christians (Eusebius, *H.E.* 9.9.12), subsequently turned on the church (Eusebius, *Vit. Const.* 1.49–56).⁴³ Tensions between imperial power and the church did not fully cease in the east until Constantine gained control of the whole empire in 324 after his final victory over Licinius.⁴⁴

There are a few bits of evidence of the Diocletian persecution in Oxyrhynchus and its vicinity. One is a letter from 304 by a man named Aurelius Ammonius, "reader of the former church (ἀναγνωστὴς τῆς ποτε ἐκκλησίας)" of the village of Chusis (near Oxyrhynchus), wrote to the *prutanis* (chief city magistrate) at Oxyrhynchus to swear that all the property of any value belonging to the church – which amounted to some "bronze stuff" – had been handed over to the *logistēs* (accountant) at Oxyrhynchus for shipment to Alexandria.⁴⁵

At Oxyrhynchus there were also a number of martyrs.⁴⁶ A papyrus from the fourth century describes the refusal of the martyr Dioscorus to sacrifice to the gods during the Diocletian persecution (P.Oxy. 3529).⁴⁷ A certain "Paul from the Oxyrhynchite nome," whose property was confiscated and whose person was put under sentence (P.Oxy. 2665), may have been another martyr.⁴⁸ Other Christians – at least in times of less severe persecution – found ways to get around the laws designed to ensnare or disadvantage them. P.Oxy. 2601 deals with a Christian named Copres⁴⁹ who had someone else go to court for him so that he could avoid being compromised by a recent requirement, probably designed to put pressure on Christians, that anyone who appeared in court must sacrifice.⁵⁰ Evidently, at the time he wrote, the authorities were carrying

---

⁴² The death of Maximinus is described as suicide by Lactantius (*Mort.* 49).

⁴³ See Odahl (2004, 150–154).

⁴⁴ On the defeat of Licinius, see Odahl (2004, 159–60).

⁴⁵ P.Oxy. 2673 in *The Oxyrhynchus Papyri* 33 (1968):106–107; Rea (1979, 128, correcting πύλην ["gate"/"door"] to ὕλην ["stuff," "material"]). On this text, see also Luijendijk (2008b, 344–57).

⁴⁶ On traditions about martyrs at Oxyrhynchus, see Timm (1984, 283–85, s.v. al-Bahnasā = Oxyrhynchus).

⁴⁷ There are also later Syriac and Latin manuscripts of the story. The Syriac version dates the interrogation of Dioscorus to 306/7. See *Papyrus Oxyrhynchus* 70 (1983):22.

⁴⁸ P.Oxy. 2665, dated to the time of the Diocletian persecution, is a report of the city registrars in response to a query about the property of a certain Paul, who was sentenced under Satrius Arrianus, governor of Thebaid. The registrars were unable to find any records concerning Paul or his property. The reference to Paul's conviction does not indicate the penalty.

⁴⁹ Copres states that he prays "before the Lord God," and "Lord God" is treated as a nominum sacrum with abbreviation and an overstrike. At the close of the letter, Copres adds "amen" in the form of a cryptogram.

⁵⁰ See the text and discussion of P.Oxy. 2601 in *The Oxyrhynchus Papyri* 31 (1966):167–71; also Luijendijk (2008a, 216–26).

out at least perfunctory enforcement of some decree but had not set in place any comprehensive mechanism for ferreting out Christians. Hence Copres, with due precautions, was able to carry out his business unmolested.

Imperial animosity to the Christian movement raises the question of how openly Christians in Egypt were prepared to practice their faith. It seems clear that in periods of calm, open profession was possible. Around 300, the authorities referred expressly to *churches* in naming guard stations around the city (see above). Perhaps in the period from the end of the Valerian persecution to the beginning of the Diocletian – that is, from 260 to 300 or so – Christians in Egypt lived in relative peace.

The Hymn in an Era of Sporadic Persecutions

What danger might possession of P.Oxy. 1786 have posed to its owner? Although it is hard to imagine that during the Valerian or Diocletian persecutions, a Christian musician would have hired a scribe he did not know to make a copy of a Christian hymn[51] and so risk exposure, there is no reason to think that our musician could not have used a trusted scribe, perhaps a Christian scribe. But a copy of a hymn discovered in a search of homes during the Diocletian campaign would have betrayed its owner as a Christian. The document itself would have been subject to confiscation and destruction, since the imperial orders called for the destruction of Christian writings (no doubt meaning Christian sacred writings in the broad sense and not simply what Christians regarded as "scriptures").[52] The abundance of Christian literature that survives from the second and third centuries shows, however, that the authorities did not manage to confiscate and destroy everything. Moreover, it is not clear to what extent authorities in Oxyrhynchus felt a motivation to be thorough in rooting out Christians and applying the full measure of the law against them. In any case, assuming a dating of P.Oxy. 1786 to the late third century, the score lived through the Diocletian persecution, since it was not destroyed but only eventually discarded; or it had already been thrown out before the persecution commenced.

Whether the musician who owned the copy of P.Oxy. 1786 kept it for a long time or discarded it as soon as he had memorized it,[53] the hymn itself likely had a place in worship during the late third century and perhaps into the fourth. Hence, it is worth contemplating the significance of the hymn text in its political time and place. It appears that from the middle of the third century until Constantine's command over the whole empire in 324, Christians

---

[51] On P.Oxy. 1786 as a copy made by a scribe, see below.

[52] According to Eusebius, the first edict of Diocletian against the Christians called for the "destruction of the scriptures by fire" (*H.E.* 8.2.4).

[53] On the uses of notation in a music culture based primarily on oral transmission, see below.

in Egypt experienced episodic periods of persecution (250–251 under Decius, 257–260 under Valerian, and 303–311 under Diocletian and his co-emperors). Hence, even in the period of relative quiet from 260–303, the church knew that it might become a target and could not help but regard the imperial power as a potentially hostile force. Under these political circumstances, and perhaps in the years of persecution that followed, Christians at Oxyrhynchus sang a hymn in which they imagined all creation falling reverently still for the church's praise of the Trinity, while the true powers of the cosmos, representing God's dominion, answered and affirmed that praise.

Social Status and Property of Christians at Oxyrhynchus

Brown concludes that some churches in the Oxyrhynchite nome must have had considerable wealth since the church at Chusis had "bronze doors valuable enough to be confiscated and transported all the way to Alexandria in 303."[54] Brown is referring to the letter of Aurelius Ammonius (P.Oxy. 2763), mentioned above, and the translation "bronze doors" is based on a reading that has since been corrected to "bronze stuff." The bronze stuff may have been lamps or liturgical vessels, and it is unknown how many the church owned or whether it possessed other valuables that Ammonius does not mention (perhaps things that church members had taken home or sold to protect them from confiscation). The letter details items the authorities had asked about, giving us an idea of the kinds of property they expected to find in the possession of congregations: lands, cattle, buildings, precious metals and money, clothes, and slaves. Officials found considerable wealth at a church in Cirta in Numidia: gold and silver chalices and urns, silver lamps and a silver cooking pot, various bronze candlesticks and lamps, four jars and six barrels, considerable clothing (whether vestments or, more likely, clothing collected to distribute to the poor), and a large codex.[55] Whether churches in Oxyrhynchus possessed similar wealth is uncertain. Nevertheless, it stands to reason that many classes of persons were numbered among the Christians at Oxyrhynchus, including those of the wealthier set, who would have acted as patrons of the congregations.

Christian Literature

Christian documents from Oxyrhynchus reflect a robust interest in Christian literature, comparable to the educated Christian culture known to us from Alexandria. Literary interest finds personal testimony in an early fourth cen-

---

[54] Brown (1978, 58).
[55] *Gesta apud Zenophilum* 2–4, discussed in Luijendijk (2008b, 350–51).

tury letter probably from one Christian to another: "To my dearest lady sister, greetings in the Lord. Lend the Ezra, since I lent you the little Genesis. Farewell in God from us" (P.Oxy. 3465).[56] This correspondence concerns private book exchange and reading. No names or addresses are given, which suggests that the communication was a local letter delivered by a servant.

Among the texts from Oxyrhynchus belonging to Christian circles are copies and fragments of the following: seventeen of the writings that came to make up the New Testament, along with other early Christian writings, including the *Shepherd of Hermas* (seven copies), the *Gospel of Thomas* (three copies), the *Gospel of Mary* (two copies), the *Acts of Peter* (one copy), the *Acts of John* (one copy), the *Acts of Paul* (one copy), the *Didache* (one copy), the *Sophia of Jesus Christ* (one copy), the *Gospel of Peter* (two copies), maybe the *Apocalypse of Peter* (one copy), three unknown gospels / sayings of Jesus (one copy of each), Irenaeus' *Against Heresies*, and a magical text.[57] Most of these copies were made in the third and early-fourth centuries. Copies of parts of the Septuagint and Philo have also been found, some of which probably belonged to Christians. Considering that survival rates for literature in Egypt have been estimated at about 10–20%, the extant remains of Christian literature at Oxyrhynchus indicate a lively interest in books for the sustenance of the faith.

There were significant intellectual and literary connections between Oxyrhynchus and Alexandria.[58] Educated Christians from the two cities knew one another, corresponded, and shared literature with each other.[59] They interested themselves not only in Christian and Jewish literature but also in pagan classical literary works. An early-fourth-century copy of the Epistle to the Hebrews is preserved on the verso of a Latin epitome of Livy (P.Oxy. 657). The owner patched the papyrus before the addition of Hebrews, apparently in order to preserve both writings. The Bodmer Papyri likely come from a Christian school in Panopolis where both Christian works and Greek classics, including the *Iliad* and Menander's comedies, were copied and studied.[60] In Caesarea, Origen taught general education and philosophical subjects along with theology.[61]

The high degree of literary activity attested for Oxyrhynchus as a whole and for the Christian communities there supports both Roberts' conclusion that a

---

[56] Epp gives a very detailed analysis of the letter and argues persuasively that it is between Christians (Epp [2004, 21–35]).

[57] Epp (2004, 12–18). The fragment from Irenaeus and the magical text are listed in van Haelst (1976, nos. 696 and 1076).

[58] See Krüger (1990, 198–204).

[59] On connections between Christians of the two cities in the third century, see Roberts (1979, 24–25); Rubenson (1995, 110).

[60] See Cribiore (2001), 200.

[61] See van den Broek (1996, 203).

Christian scriptorium probably existed in the city[62] and Epp's judgment that literacy rates in the church were probably higher than Gamble's estimate of ten percent or less for Christians generally in the Greco-Roman world.[63] P.Oxy. 1786 attests the activity in the church of at least one professional musician who was musically literate – able to read a score.

Greek Music Culture at Oxyrhynchus

Music was an important part of private and institutional culture at Oxyrhynchus, as it was throughout the ancient Mediterranean world. Musicians could be found at virtually every festive or ceremonial occasion. Surviving contracts and payment accounts for musicians testify to professional musical activity in the city.[64]

Among the musicians who appeared in the various social and religious venues of Oxyrhynchus were highly-trained professionals who understood something of music theory and used musical notation. This is evident from various musical remains from Oxyrhynchus, all of them stemming from the Roman era – from the second century to the end of the third/early fourth centuries. Some of these remains are scores containing what appear to be repertoires of professional singers and citharodes.[65] It was common in Hellenistic and Roman times for musicians to set the lyrics of past poets and dramatists to new melodies, as well as to compose new songs based on well-known dramatic situations. Venues for such music included the dinner party,[66] social events at the gymnasium, concerts or variety shows at the city odeon, and recitals in the home of a patron of the arts. An Oxyrhynchus papyrus from the late-first or early-second century lists forty odes composed by one "Epagathos, the choral piper."[67] To judge from the titles of his songs, they were musical settings of

---

[62] Roberts (1979, 24); also Pearson (2004, 35).

[63] Epp (1997, 15–37).

[64] A number of contracts and related documents from the second and third centuries give a glimpse of professional musical activity. See P.Oxy. 1275 (third-century contract for musicians to perform at a five-day festival at Souis in the Oxyrhynchite nome); P.Oxy. 2721 (contract for pipers [*aulētai*] and a dancing girl to perform at a four-day festival at an Oxyrhynchite village in the early third century); P.Oxy. 519 (second-century payment list for actor, rhapsode, music and dancing at the public games). Similar documents have turned up elsewhere. The editor of P.Oxy. 2721 (Rea in *Oxyrhynchus Papyri* 34 [1968]:115) mentions P.Alex. 6; P.Strasb. 341; and other documents in Vandoni (1964, nos. 14–28). See also Westermann (1932, 16–27 [discussing P.Columb. 441, a contract for *aulos* music at a village festival, and related papyri]). Of the many contracts of this sort that must have been made, only a small percentage survives.

[65] See West (1998, 81 [discussing P.Oxy. 4461–67]).

[66] See Johnson (2000, 57–85).

[67] Cockle (1975). Epagathos was an αὐλητής, a term difficult to translate. His instrument (the αὐλός, often mistranslated "flute") was oboe-like.

lyric portions of dramatic works and newly-composed poems based on familiar dramatic situations.

Musicians trained in the Greek tradition studied with professional music teachers and learned to play one or more of the instruments of the lyre family (since the songs they sang were typically accompanied by a lyre or cithara). Some learned to read musical notation and practiced notated instrumental exercises, a few examples of which have survived.[68] The musician who composed or at least owned P.Oxy. 1786 no doubt came from the professional musical circles of Oxyrhynchus and earned a living teaching and performing songs to the lyre or cithara. In the course of his musical training, he will have been exposed to the works of influential composers.

Musical Scores

One of the influential composers of the second century was a Greek musician from Crete named Mesomedes, court musician of the emperor Hadrian.[69] A number of Mesomedes' compositions have been preserved with musical notation. Although he carried out his professional life in the first half of the second century, his music was still being performed in the fourth century and was evidently well known. The Christian Neoplatonist (and hymn-writer) Synesius quotes some lines from Mesomedes' hymn to Nemesis, which, Synesius says, "we sing to the lyre" (*Ep.* 95).[70] The opening of that hymn is given in Figure 1.

Figure 1

Mesomedes, Hymn to Nemesis, line 1 (*DAGM* No. 28)

Νέ-με-σι πτε-ρό-εσ-σα βί-ου ρο-πά, κυ-αν-ῶ-πι θε-ά, θύ-γα-τερ Δί-κας

Mesomedes wrote compositions of varying length, all in the diatonic genus, with little or no modulation of *tonos* and a sparing use of melisma. Other

---

[68] *Anon. Bell.* 97–101 and 104 (third – fourth century C.E.) are thought to be instrumental exercises. Preserved in three medieval manuscripts, they derive their name in scholarship from the fact that Bellermann, a modern editor, appended them to his compilation of a set of ancient treatises on Greek music. See Pöhlmann and West (2001, 118–19).

[69] For the few bits of information that have been preserved about Mesomedes, see West (1992b, 383–84). West thinks it likely that the composer of P.Oxy. 1786 knew the standard works of Mesomedes (West [1992a, 50]). For the extant compositions of Mesomedes preserved in musical scores, see Pöhlmann and West (2001, 92–115).

[70] Αὕτη μέντοι σαφῶς ἐστι, περὶ ἧς πρὸς λύραν ἄδομεν: λήθουσα δὲ πὰρ πόδα βαίνεις / γαυρούμενον αὐχένα κλίνεις / ὑπὸ πῆχυν ἀεὶ βιοτὰν κρατεῖς. These are lines 9–11 of Mesomedes' hymn to Nemesis, as quoted in Synesius (*Ep.* 95 Garzya).

compositions from the second century through the early fourth (where the record breaks off) display more frequent use of melisma and moments of highly-florid composition. This melismatic style was evidently a new trend in the Roman era, since surviving scores from Hellenistic times show only occasional use of very simple melisma. Typical in the more florid scores of the Roman period is alternation between syllabic and melismatic treatment of the lyrics. This can be illustrated with an excerpt from P.Oxy. 4463 (Fig. 2).

Figure 2

P.Oxy. 4463, lines 5-8 (fragmentary, following the readings of *DAGM* No. 47)

The melismatic pattern for the syllables of [το]ξότης in P.Oxy. 4463 resembles the pattern for the syllables of -μῶν ῥοθί in P.Oxy. 1786 (compare Figs. 3 and 4), which suggests the use of a typical melismatic figure in both cases. This and other comparisons of P.Oxy. 1786 with the surviving scores from Oxyrhynchus show that our hymn fits the Greek music of its time and place.[71]

The Purpose of P.Oxy. 1786 as a Musical Score

To understand the significance of P.Oxy. 1786 in the history of early Christian music, it is useful to begin by asking why the document – the score – was produced. We can approach this question by considering whether P.Oxy. 1786 is the autograph of the composer.

In the ancient world, people who could read and write sometimes acted as their own scribes, writing letters in their own hand or serving as their own copyists. Professional musicians sometimes produced scores as part of their

---

[71] See further chapter five.

composition process[72] and probably copied the scores of other musicians for their own use.

When musical notation and lyrics are in two different hands, this is a sign that a copyist wrote out the text and someone else added the notation, presumably a musician. In such a case, the musician may have been the composer or someone interested in having a copy of the composer's song. We have what looks like an example of this in P.Oxy. 2436. According to the original editors, the text and notation of this score are in two different hands, the words in a fine formal script (with "small well-rounded letters," displaying "easy elegance" and occasional lapses into cursive), the notation in a "much rougher" hand.[73] In this case, we likely see the hand of a professional copyist in the text (lyrics) and the less-skilled hand of a musician in the notation.

It is not clear whether more than one hand was involved in the production of P.Oxy. 1786.[74] The text of the lyrics looks like the work of a practiced copyist. Hunt judged it a somewhat literary hand, noting the clearly-written upright letters with occasional cursive.[75] The symbols of musical notation are also clearly formed, but it is not certain that they are by the same person.

Mistakes in the notation may have bearing on whether we have the composer's autograph, another musician's copy in his own hand, or a copy produced by a paid copyist (with notation written in by the musician or the copyist). A first mistake is an oversight in line 3. Above the syllable ῥο-, the musical notation is incomplete. The double point above ῥο- signals that two or more note symbols are to follow forming a melism, but only one symbol is visible. More mistakes appear in line 4–5, where the arsis pointing is off by one position, from πᾶσαι to the end. As noted in chapter two, Reinach chalked up the problem with the arsis pointing to a copyist's error. Winnington-Ingram agreed and offered an explanation. The copyist, he suggested, mistook a rare tetraseme above the leimma in line 4 of his exemplar for the common diseme, the tetraseme sign being perhaps unfamiliar to him. This led him to write a diseme and add the arsis marks in the wrong places from that point on.

If we accept Winnington-Ingram's explanation, it seems more likely that a copyist made the mistakes in the arsis pointing and notation. In view of West's demonstration of how carefully the composer labored to maintain the metrical scheme by overcoming challenges imposed by traditional Christian

---

[72] It has been suggested that at least one of the surviving ancient Greek scores is just that, an autograph in which the composer edits his composition(s). See Winnington-Ingram (1955, 56–57); also Pöhlmann and West (2001, 128). Mountford (1931, 92) makes a similar suggestion about another musical document.

[73] Turner and Winnington-Ingram (1959, 113).

[74] Hunt (Hunt and Jones [1922, 21]) was uncertain whether the hand that laid out the text also added the notation; Pighi (1941, 192) saw the same hand in both the words and the music.

[75] Hunt and Jones (1922, 21). Hunt notes that the epsilon of πατέρα, for example, is cursive.

language, it is clear that the arsis points and rhythmic signs that help express this metrical scheme would have been very important to him. It is perhaps easier to imagine that a copyist and not the composer wrote out the hymn, mistook a tetraseme rest for a diseme, then sought to correct what he took to be mistaken pointing from there to the end of the hymn.[76]

The purpose in writing out the hymn with musical notation is another consideration pertinent to working out an idea of its history.[77] Very little music was written down in antiquity, and for the most part musical notation was the province of highly-trained professionals.[78] The notated Greek music that survives takes a number of different forms, suggesting a variety of purposes for notation. One kind of musical document is the papyrus score containing some of the repertoire used by a professional musician. In addition to its value for the process of composition, this type of score was likely used for both transmitting music and memorizing it.[79] Naturally, the longer and more complicated a piece, the more helpful it was to have a score as an *aide-memoire*.

Keeping in mind the uses of notation in a society that made and transmitted music primarily through oral means, it is instructive to consider the possible reasons why someone made a score – original or copy – of our hymn.

1. *The composer was from Oxyrhynchus and produced the score as part of his compositional process.* Assuming that the full text of the hymn was only five lines, or not much more, it is very unlikely that a professional musician would have felt the need to write out the notation (or even the hymn text) as he composed it. He would have committed it to memory in the process of composing. Moreover, if he did find it useful to notate the hymn as he

---

[76] In private correspondence, West has communicated to me that he thinks the artifact is probably a copy. He judiciously cautions that one cannot "presuppose the existence of many copies or of wide distribution," and he observes that "we have never yet found more than one copy of the same musical score."

[77] On the origin, history, and uses of Greek musical notation, see West (1992b, 254–76); Pöhlmann (2005, 131–45); idem (1997, 283–89, 417); idem (1994, 23–25, 32); Prauscello (2006).

[78] According to many specialists, musical notation was used primarily by professional musicians as an *aide-memoire* and, with some exceptions, scores were not written and copied for a more general audience. See Barker (1995, 59–60); Comotti (1988), 24; West (1992b, 269–70); Pöhlmann and West (2001, 1). Consistent with this view is the fact that Quintilian, who urges the study of music as essential to the development of the orator (*Inst.* 1.10.1–33), remarks that it is not necessary for the student of oratory to go so far as to learn how to sing from a musical score (*Inst.* 1.12.14). Another indicator is that the texts of classical Greek drama, which included musical elements, were transmitted without musical notation. According to Pöhlmann (1997, 287–88), the musicians connected with performing troupes made use of scores, a separate tradition. It may be that some of the surviving musical documents come from such scores.

[79] Sometimes scores may have been read during performance. Several vases depict musicians singing or playing an instrument in front of a papyrus roll. Pöhlmann (1960, 83–84) argues that the vases show musicians playing from scores. Comotti (1989, 9) registers a caution. Even if the rolls are to be interpreted as containing notation, the settings are not clear (whether performance or practice).

composed it, it is very unlikely that he would have made or left uncorrected the mistakes in arsis pointing and notation, although the possibility of a discarded copy replaced by a more accurate one cannot be ruled out. The evidence of a practiced hand in the writing out of the words also speaks against P.Oxy. 1786 being an artifact of the composing process.

2. *The score was made by the composer in Oxyrhynchus as a way of distributing/teaching the hymn there.* If the composer of P.Oxy. 1786 was from Oxyrhynchus and sang the hymn in one of the churches there, perhaps teaching it to others as well, these activities would not have required a score. He would have taught it to others by singing it to them, not by providing them with notated copies, which only highly-trained professional musicians could read.

3. *A church at Oxyrhynchus paid a scribe and/or musician to make a score of the hymn for the purpose of liturgical preservation.* If we had a papyrus containing a number of hymns along with other liturgical formulae, written on the front (and perhaps also the back) of the papyrus, an archival use would be more plausible. But what we have is a fragment of a hymn written on the back of a grain account. This suggests a musician's personal copy rather than an archival copy.

4. *A Christian musician in Oxyrhynchus wished to make a copy of his hymn for a musician friend from a church in Alexandria or elsewhere.* A notated piece of music would have been a valuable means of passing music from one professional musician to another in circumstances where time or distance made oral transmission difficult or impossible. Our hymn score, written on the back of a grain account that mentions towns in the Oxyrhynchite nome, was almost certainly made in Oxyrhynchus or its vicinity. But if it was produced to be given to a visiting musician or to be sent to a distant musician, it would not have ended up in the dump at Oxyrhynchus, unless the copy we have was discarded, because of its imperfections, and a better copy made to replace it (see above). If a scribe was hired to make the copy and produced a faulty score, one marred by incorrect arsis pointing and other slips, one can imagine that this score was discarded in Oxyrhynchus and a better copy provided to its intended recipient.

5. *A Christian musician from Alexandria or elsewhere visited Oxyrhynchus with a collection of personal scores, including one containing our hymn, and let a copy of that hymn be made for use in the Oxyrhynchite church(es) by a musician in Oxyrhynchus.* A musician passing through Oxyrhynchus who did not have the time or inclination to linger there might have let his score(s) be copied in lieu of trying to teach them to a musician he met there. Under such circumstances, aspects of the copying might have been a bit hurried. If a scribe or the musician who wanted a copy of the music did this work, he could easily have made mistakes. Once the visiting musician was gone, the Oxyrhynchite musician may have used the copy in its uncorrected form to learn the hymn. Or, wishing to have a copy with the correct arsis pointing, he may have used his imperfect copy (our artifact) to make an accurate copy and then discarded the faulty one.

If forced to choose from these five possibilities, I would embrace the last speculation as the best explanation of the fact and features of P.Oxy. 1786. But the truth may lie with one of the other scenarios or with none of them. We certainly cannot settle on the last possibility (or any other) as the most probable. Instead, the group of five possibilities gives us an idea of ways in which the score may have come into existence.

The Performance Setting of P.Oxy. 1786

It has been claimed that the use of the back of a grain account suggests that the composer was too poor to afford decent paper[80] or that the hymn was meant only for private use.[81] The owner of the score may have been poor; most people were. But the use of the back of a grain account does not suggest that the score was for private devotion and not corporate worship. One-sided writing was preferred in fine books,[82] but musical scores were not fine library copies. They were practical documents used by working musicians. A significant number of surviving musical documents on papyri are written on the backs of other documents. Of the thirteen musical fragments (or sets of fragments) from Oxyrhynchus published thus far, four have music on the verso and non-musical writing on the recto.[83]

The hymn's use of Classical imperative endings[84] might suggest an erudite audience for the hymn and not a church setting. But the church in late third-century Egypt was socially mixed and included well-educated persons, who were almost certainly the ones in charge of the liturgy. Moreover, even uneducated people would have had no difficulty understanding the Classical verb forms and would undoubtedly have felt that they lent an aura of dignity to the hymn. We should keep in mind that ancient Greek hymn-texts at shrines were preserved and performed for centuries with little updating of language. For example, a hymn to Zeus from a shrine at Crete (inscribed in the third century C.E.) displays Roman-era chiseling of letters and some late-era orthography but also grammatical forms and vocabulary consistent with a much earlier date of composition (late Classical).[85] Either the Roman-era inscription preserved a much older hymn or a Roman-era composer engaged in some deliberate archaizing in imitation of Classical poetry. In either case, performed in the third century of the Roman era, the hymn would have had the ring of much older poetry. Hence, even those without an education were used to hearing vener-

---

[80] Tripp and Wheeler (1997, 20–24 ["leaves the impression" of poverty]).

[81] Hiley (1993, 487).

[82] Most of the writings on papyrus from Oxyrhynchus are on only one side of the roll. Krüger (1990, 160–61) argues that these one-sided literary texts come from the library of the gymnasium or a library maintained by scholars. Copies with writing on both sides usually belonged to private persons and schools.

[83] P.Oxy. 4466 has a musical text on the verso, Latin words on the recto; P.Oxy. 4467 has a musical text on the verso, part of an unidentified prose work on the recto; P.Oxy 4461 has a musical document written on the back, an agricultural account on the front; P.Oxy. 4465 has music on the recto, a register of names on the verso. Our hymn is on the verso of a grain account.

[84] The hymn uses the Classical 3rd pers. imperative form at least once and probably twice (ἐπιφωνούντων and probably χ[...]δε[σ]θων). It may also use Doric forms. A plausible interpretation of οὐ τὰν ἠῶ in line 2 involves construing τάν as the Doric form of τήν. See the discussion in chapter three.

[85] For the text and a discussion of the language and dating, see Furley and Bremer (2001, 2:4).

able grammatical forms and words in cult hymns. Moreover, Classical word forms and style are found in the writings of Greek-speaking church fathers and would have been familiar to the uneducated church members from sermons, which the illiterate had no difficulty understanding because they heard "high" Greek in other settings as well.[86]

Early Christian literature refers to a variety of settings in which hymns were sung: at the primary eucharistic gatherings (1 Cor 14:26; Col 3:16-20;[87] probably Clement of Alexandria, *Paed.* 3.11.80; a passage in the *Acts of Paul* treating Paul's time in Corinth;[88] Cyril of Jerusalem, *Myst. cat.* 5.6); in household devotion (Tertullian, *Ad uxorum* 2.8.8-9); at common meals that may or may not have included the Eucharist (Clement of Alexandria, *Paed.* 2.4.44; Tertullian, *Apologeticum* 39.16-18);[89] at morning prayer (Codex Alexandrinus labeling the Gloria a "morning hymn"); at vespers (*Testamentum domini* 2.11; also Basil, *De spir. sanct.* 29.73, if he is referring to a hymn) and presumably at other times of prayer. According to Clement of Alexandria, the pious accompanied many of their daily activities with psalms and hymns (*Str.* 7.7.35 and 7.7.49). Since we have no external evidence for the occasion of the hymn of P.Oxy. 1786 and since its text seems suitable for a variety of settings, it is impossible to know whether the hymn was intended for a particular liturgical event and, if so, which event.

This last-mentioned fact has not prevented some scholars from fixing the setting. Wolbergs, for example, has argued that P.Oxy. 1786 was composed for a eucharistic service.[90] In support of this judgment he observes that 1) as a general rule, silence reigned during the *prosphora* (the offering of the bread and wine), which corresponds to the theme of silence in P.Oxy. 1786; 2) angels

---

[86] See Chrestou (2005, 86-87), who notes that "the audiences of John Chrysostom applauded his sermons with clapping, to his great consternation of course, although their linguistic form was quite high [Atticizing]" (ibid., 87).

[87] Assuming that Colossians is deutero-pauline and dates from the late first century, one might question whether the gathering presumed in the letter's remarks about singing was eucharistic. But a late-first-century date for Colossians probably precedes the differentiation between morning Eucharist and non-eucharistic evening agape. See further n. 89 below.

[88] *Acts Paul* no. 9 in Elliott (1993, 383). The narrative about Paul in Corinth derives from P.Heid. 44b-3, 51-52 and P.Hamb. 6-7.

[89] A longstanding scholarly consensus is that by the second century, the Eucharist had been separated from the common meal and had become the central ritual act of a gathering on Sunday morning (and perhaps also on other mornings). According to this interpretation of the evidence, the evening common meal, termed "agape," did not include the Eucharist. Recent challenges to this view make it uncertain that a differentiation between eucharistic synaxis and agape had been established even as late as Tertullian's time. Of course, developments probably varied from place to place. For recent treatments of the subject, see McGowan (1997); idem (2004); Bradshaw (2004, 99-101). By the time of our hymn, however, it is likely that many churches, perhaps most, had made the Sunday morning gathering the occasion for eucharistic celebration and no longer included the Eucharist in their evening suppers.

[90] Wolbergs (1971, 102-4 and 107-11).

were thought to participate in some way in the eucharistic liturgy; and 3) from an early period it was customary to follow the offering with a doxology (and a closing amen). To document these claims, he offers the following evidence:

1. Silence during the *prosphora*

The *Apostolic Constitutions*, dating to the fourth century but preserving earlier traditions, stipulates that the people are to be silent when the elements are offered: "And after the prayer, let some of the deacons devote themselves to the offering of the Eucharist, serving the body of the Lord with reverent fear, and let other deacons observe the people and command them to be silent" (ἡσυχίαν αὐτοῖς ἐμποιείτωσαν) (*Apost. Const.* 2.57.15 Funk).

The Liturgy of Saint James, which dates to the fourth century in some version, contains the following words from the cherubic hymn of the Great Entrance: "Let all mortal flesh be silent (Σιγησάτω πᾶσα σὰρξ βροτεία) and with fear and trembling stand ... for the King of Kings, Christ our God, comes to be sacrificed and to be given unto mortals ..."[91]

A call for silence appears in the opening lines of the eucharistic prayer of the Pontic liturgy as reconstructed by Brightman: Σιωπάσθωσαν ἡλίου ἀνατολαὶ καὶ σελήνης περίοδοι, κράσεις ἀέρων κ.τ.λ.[92]

2. Participation of angels in the liturgy of the Eucharist

The people sing the cherubic hymn of the Great Entrance (Liturgy of St. James; see above) in imaginary communion with the angels or in imitation of the angelic choir.[93]

3. Doxology with amen following the *prosphora*

In Justin Martyr's description of worship at Rome (mid second century), the *prosphora* is followed by a doxology uttered by the presiding minister, who then offers prayers of thanksgiving, and the people answer "amen" (*1 Apol.* 65).

In the account of the celebration of the Eucharist in *Apostolic Constitutions* 8, a doxology closes a long eucharistic prayer by the priest and the people answer "amen" (*Apos. Con.* 8.12.5–51).

This evidence is not conclusive, and some of it is problematic. First, doxologies are not specific to eucharistic prayers. Already in the New Testament, they are used in a variety of contexts that suggest diversity of use in life and worship: after a greeting in Rev 1:5–7; after the mention of God in the prescript of Galatians; in the opening thanksgiving of 1 Timothy (see 1:17); in a final benediction at the end of Hebrews (in 13:21), which belongs to a custom of concluding an address (by letter or sermon) with a doxology (cf. Rom 16:25–27; Phil 4:20; 2 Tim 4:18; 1 Pet 5:11; 2 Pet 3:18). The *Didache* calls for the Lord's Prayer to be recited three times a day in a form that includes a doxology (*Did.* 8:2–3). The Trinitarian doxology preserved in the fourth-century *Apostolic Constitutions* 7.48 belongs to a vesper service. A

---

[91] In Mercier (1946, 176); see the discussion of this text in chapter three.
[92] Brightman (1896, 522 [extracted from *Regulae fusius tractatae*; PG 31:913]).
[93] Wolbergs (1971, 104).

doxology is part of the rite of baptism as depicted in the Syriac *Acts of John* (fourth or fifth century).⁹⁴

Second, of the bits of evidence Wolbergs adduces to show that silence was commanded during the *prosphora*, only the reference in the *Apostolic Constitutions* – a fourth century composition made up of older materials – is relevant. As for the hymn, "Let All Mortal Flesh Keep Silence" (Σιγησάτω πᾶσα σὰρξ βροτεία), it is almost certainly much later than P.Oxy. 1786. "Let All Mortal Flesh" is one version of the cherubic hymn (or one of the various cherubic hymns) of the Liturgy of St. James. That liturgy is usually dated to the fourth century, but according to our only testimony about when the cherubic hymn was included (the eleventh-century church historian Cedrenus), it was the Emperor Justinian, in the late sixth century, who added the hymn and that hymn was probably not "Let All Mortal Flesh."⁹⁵

Moreover, Wolbergs' reliance on Brightman's reconstruction of the ancient Pontic liturgy is unfortunate. In rendering this liturgy, which he assembles from a variety of sources, Brightman draws the words about falling silent from a passage in Basil's *Regulae fusius tractatae* that has nothing to do with liturgical behavior.⁹⁶

Other evidence besides the late cherubic hymn associates angels with the Eucharist. We have seen that at least by the fourth century, Greek-speaking Christians had come to imagine that the eucharistic service was connected with angelic worship: angels participating in the earthly service or Christians imitating a heavenly worship. We examined this evidence from Gregory of Nyssa, Cyril of Jerusalem, and John Chrysostom in chapter three. As suggestive as these fourth-century witnesses are, they are no proof that P.Oxy. 1786 assumes a eucharistic setting since the presence of angels was also associated with Christian prayer and hence with any gathering for a pious purpose.⁹⁷

It is also important to keep in mind that P.Oxy. 1786 projects an imaginal world in which liturgical events are described and commanded. These events have *associations* with actual liturgical practice: hymning (praising) the Trinity, the use of doxologies, the idea that angels attend Christian worship, the notion that in some mysterious way the cosmos honors Christian worship of God. But it is clear from the fact that the language of the silence motif comes from pagan Greek hymnody that the composer did not model the hymn on

---

⁹⁴ Wright (1968, 2:38).
⁹⁵ Georgius Cedrenus in Bekker (1838, 1:685.3–4).
⁹⁶ *Reg. fus. tract.* 2.3 (from the "Longer Rules"). The context in the *Regula* shows that the verb σιωπάσθωσαν should be taken as a passive (see Demosthenes, *Exord*. 21.2) rather than, with Brightman, as a middle; and it should be translated, "Let them not be spoken about" (meaning "Let us pass over in silence"), not "Let them be silent." See the following translations: Wagner (1950, 237) and Clarke (1925, 155).
⁹⁷ See the discussion of this evidence – from Clement of Alexandria and Origen – in chapter three.

instructions given in a particular Christian liturgy. Nor do we have reason to think that the hymn, with its call for silence and instruction to the angels, belonged to a particular moment of preparation in worship analogous to the role of the cherubic hymn at the Great Entrance.

The Greek Musical Tradition among Ancient Christians

The number of scores we possess for ancient Greek music is just a tiny fraction of the ancient Greek scores produced in antiquity. Not only that, the number of scores produced in the ancient world was a small fraction of the Greek music that was composed and performed through the centuries. Given the survival of the fragment P.Oxy. 1786, it is extremely unlikely that it represents the only ancient Christian hymn ever set down in Greek notation, much less the sole instance of an ancient Christian hymn composed in the Greek musical idiom. The surmise that P.Oxy. 1786 is an isolated instance of Greek Christian hymnody[98] implies a chain of highly-unlikely historical circumstances: that despite the prevalence of the Greek musical tradition in the ancient Mediterranean world, only a single hymn was composed in this musical tradition by Christians, that this single hymn just happened to be notated (when most music was not written down) and, having been notated, managed to survive destruction (when the vast majority of papyrus documents from antiquity perished). On the contrary, the fact that we possess the score of an ancient Christian hymn suggests that a tradition of Greek Christian hymnody existed – in Egypt and elsewhere.

We can put the whole matter in perspective by considering that P.Oxy. 1786 is one of just thirteen known musical documents from Oxyrhynchus and one of twenty-seven of all scores on papyrus.[99] If professional Greek musicians became Christians and used their skills in the service of the church, then

---

[98] Hannick (1980, 368).

[99] If we define a musical document as a single piece of papyrus (single sheet from a roll or a codex) that contains parts of one or more musical compositions, then P.Oxy. 1786 is one of thirteen musical documents from Oxyrhynchus (leaving out P.Oxy. 3705, which is probably not a musical document but a demonstration of intonation in the reciting of poetry, and including P.Oxy. 4710, which appeared after the publication of Pöhlmann and West [2001]). If we count all the musical documents on papyrus (not just those from Oxyrhynchus) from the beginning of the second century to the beginning of the fourth, then P.Oxy. 1786 is one out of some twenty-seven (including the recently published P.Louvre E 10534). This number excludes ten items preserved not on papyrus but as part of literary musical traditions (the instrumental exercises of the *Anonymous Bellermanni* and the songs of Mesomedes). These ten items are not counted because they are found in manuscripts of the late middle ages and therefore cannot be included in comparisons of survival on papyrus. We should also keep in mind that pagan musical documents are likely to have enjoyed a higher rate of survival in the second and third centuries because they were not subject to destruction during times of persecution.

during the first few centuries, when the church grew to about 10%–15% of the population by 300, most of that growth in the latter half of the third century, we would expect that the overall production of Christian musical scores would be well under 15% of the total scores produced in Oxyrhynchus. Here it must be kept in mind that the total number of scores from Oxyrhynchus represents the surviving musical production of a relatively stable population over a period of some two hundred years, during which time Christians were growing from a handful of persons to a sizable number but only a modest fraction of the population by the end of the period.[100] Hence, the fact that only one Christian musical document has appeared so far among the Oxyrhynchus papyri does not tell against the reasonable assumption that musicians from the Greek tradition who became Christians composed hymns reflecting that musical tradition. It counts rather in its favor. To discover that the representation of Christian music in the surviving scores from Oxyrhynchus stands at roughly 7.5% confirms what one would naturally suppose – that in a Greek-speaking metropolitan environment, some number of Greek musicians would have been converted to Christian faith and would have used their skills in the service of the church.

It is possible that already in the third century professional musical training was being passed from experienced Christian musicians to novices. It is also possible that some young men from Christian families gained a professional musical education from a non-Christian musician. It is difficult to judge the likeliness of the first possibility – a tradition of professional-level musical training within the church. The second, however, seems unlikely inasmuch as professional training at the feet of a pagan musician would have entailed learning songs that the church regarded as unsuitable (see below). More likely than either of these possibilities is that most Christian musicians of professional caliber were adult converts to the faith who had acquired their musical training before their conversions. The exponential growth of the church through adult conversion would have supplied an increasing number of skilled persons from all walks of life.

Our earlier examination of Greek music culture in the Roman world provides a starting point for imagining professional musicians who joined the Christian faith. Before their conversions, Greek musicians earned a living teaching music and performing the works of Mesomedes and other composers, as well as their own compositions, in the theater, at pagan festivals, and in private venues. Upon becoming Christians, they likely came under pressure

---

[100] The scores from Oxyrhynchus date from the second century to the beginning of the end of the third / beginning of the fourth century. Stark estimates that the church (in the Greco-Roman world) increased from about 2% of the population in 250 to about 10% by 300. Bagnall's estimates imply that Christians increased from about 7% of the population in the year 250 to about 14.5% in 300. See the discussion above regarding the growth of Christianity at Oxyrhynchus.

to give up supporting themselves in these ways. The second-century *Apostolic Tradition* and the third-century *Didascalia* show that at least some influential church authorities frowned on professions that involved the performance of pagan works. As the *Apostolic Tradition* puts it, "if one is an actor or he does performances, either let him cease or be cast out."[101] Moreover, according to the *Didascalia* and the *Apostolic Constitutions*, Christians should not sing pagan songs.[102] From this evidence one can infer that many also objected to the profession of the musician who earned a living from performing and teaching pagan music. But perhaps this condemnation was not universal or could be tempered depending on particular circumstances. The *Apostolic Tradition* shows leniency toward the teacher who, after conversion, continues to earn a living by providing instruction in pagan subjects: "if he teaches young children it is good indeed for him to cease. If he has no trade, then let him be forgiven" (*Trad. ap.* 16.5).[103] Moreover, as Lampe has noted, patristic authors mention Christians engaged in various "forbidden" professions: fabricators of pagan idols (Tertullian, *Idol.* 5 and 7), an astrologer (Tertullian, *Idol.* 9), racing drivers and owners of racing stables (Jerome, *Vit. Hil.* 20), and an acting teacher (Cyprian, *Ep.* 2).[104]

The earliest musical activity in the Egyptian church for which we have record is a report from Dionysius (bishop of Alexandria 248–268) about the "psalmody" (ψαλμῳδία) of a former Egyptian bishop named Nepos (in Eusebius, *H.E.* 7.24.4). The term ψαλμῳδία originally meant singing to a stringed instrument. At some point Greek-speaking Christians began using this word for unaccompanied chanting of the Psalms. It is difficult to determine the sense of the word in Dionysius' story. Two considerations favor thinking of it as a practice of intoning the Psalms (presumably through the use of simple formulas). First, this is a common meaning of the term among fourth-century Christians. Second, the word more naturally suggests a kind of musical activity than a body of musical compositions. If an early Christian bishop in Alexandria made the intoning of Psalms an important part of Christian devotion in his church, this would go a long way toward explaining why biblical psalmody took root early in Egypt, where it became a defining practice of monastic devotion and spread from there to other regions. Nevertheless, against taking the word in Dionysius' report as a reference to intonation of the Psalms is his remark that Nepos' "abundant psalmody" continues to give pleasure to the

---

[101] *Trad. ap.* 16.4 (Sahidic version); translation from Bradshaw et al. (2002, 88); there is no equivalent in the Arabic or Ethiopic. See also Cyprian, *Ep.* 2.

[102] *Didascalia* 1.6.3–5 (Latin version) = *Didascalia* 2 in Connolly, [1929, 12; English translation of Syriac]; *Apos. Con.* 5.10.2.

[103] Translation from Bradshaw et al. (2002, 88 [column translating the Sahidic version; the Arabic and Ethiopic are in substance the same]).

[104] Lampe (2003, 131n10).

faithful (τῆς πολλῆς ψαλμῳδίας, ἣ μέχρι νῦν πολλοὶ τῶν ἀδελφῶν εὐθυμοῦνται) (Dionysius in Eusebius, *H.E.* 7.24.4 Oulton). This shows that not only the memory of his psalmody but the psalmody itself lived on after him, which in turn suggests that the psalmody of Nepos was in fact a body of compositions (perhaps psalm-like in character), not simply a skilled practice of intoning Psalms.[105]

An interesting question is whether Nepos' psalmody involved the use of a stringed instrument to support the voice. According to Dionysius, Nepos rejected allegorical interpretation of scripture (in Eusebius, *H.E.* 7.24.1–3). Hence, he would not have followed those, such as Clement of Alexandria, who gave a spiritual interpretation to most references to musical instruments in the Psalms. Moreover, even Clement grudgingly allowed singing to the cithara and lyre, perhaps in deference to Nepos, who was bishop of Alexandria in Clement's time (*Paed.* 2.4.43.3).[106]

Clement must have known a good deal about musical practices in Greek-speaking churches of Egypt, but his scattered references to music-making tell us more about his beliefs regarding music outside the church than about the kind of music that went on within. His explicit references to Christian song involve several different words: ψάλλειν, ψαλμός, ψαλμῳδία, ὑμνεῖν, ὕμνος, μέλπειν, and ᾠδή. The verb ψάλλειν appears at a number of places in his writings as a word for Christian singing. These include contexts where he speaks of imitating David singing psalms (*Paed.* 2.4.43.3), of singing and giving thanks before meals (*Paed.* 2.4.44.1), of "praising, hymning, blessing, and singing (ψάλλουσα)" (*Str.* 6.14.113.3), of the singing of the sacred chorus on God's mountain (*Protr.* 12.119.2), of hymning that conforms to the singing and psaltery mentioned in the biblical Psalms (*Paed.* 2.4.44.4), of singing when drinking to soothe desire and glorify God (*Str.* 6.11.90.1), of the singing of those addressed rhetorically in the closing lines of the hymn that concludes *Paedagogus* (μέλπωμεν ὁμοῦ ... ψάλλωμεν ὁμοῦ),[107] and (in a quotation from Col 3:16) of the right kind of Christian song at dinner parties (*Paed.* 2.4.43.2). Most of these examples (perhaps all) use the term ψάλλειν in the sense of literal singing. In only a few cases does it perhaps carry its traditional meaning, "sing to a stringed instrument." The examples also show that the word generally means "sing" in Clement and is not a technical term for the singing of Psalms. This is especially clear from the fact that ψάλλειν is not always singing in a morally approved way, for Clement describes Christians "who before hymned immortality [in Christian worship] but in the end sing (ψάλλοντες) wickedly" by participating in pagan musical revelry (*Paed.* 3.11.80.4).

---

[105] So also Kroll (1968, 26 with n4).
[106] On this passage in Clement, see Cosgrove (2006a, 260–61).
[107] Stählin and Treu (1972, 292).

154　　　　　　　　　　　*Chapter Six: Social Setting*

Clement also uses the noun ψαλμός of Christian song but only three times, two of which draw on Paul's language in Col 3:16: "a psalm is a melodious and wise blessing, and the apostle calls a psalm a spiritual song" (*Paed.* 2.4.44.1); "psalms, hymns, and spiritual songs" (Col 3:16 as quoted in *Paed.* 2.4.43.2); and "psalms and hymns before the banquet and before bed" (*Str.* 7.7.49.4). There is also one instance of the word psalmody (ψαλμῳδία): "For if 'you love the Lord your God' and then 'your neighbor', let (your) kindliness be first toward God through thanksgiving and psalmody and second toward your neighbor ... " (*Paed.* 2.4.43.1). Just as the verb ψάλλειν does not refer narrowly to singing biblical Psalms in Clement but means singing in a broad sense, so the cognate nouns ψαλμός and ψαλμῳδία may have general meanings as song and singing.

At the end of Clement's *Paedagogus*, we find the words of a hymn to Christ (*Paed.* 3.12.101). In the manuscript tradition the hymn carries a title (undoubtably secondary), "Hymn of Christ the Savior by the Holy Clement." Like P.Oxy. 1786 it uses an anapaestic meter, which was popular in the second and third centuries. Whether the hymn was sung at gatherings of Clement and his students or in some other worshipful setting is open to debate. Not all hymns of antiquity, not even all poetic ones, were composed for religious use in a cultic or ceremonial context. Some were composed for use in drama; others were meant as freestanding entertainment songs (presumably the hymns of Mesomedes). Hymns also appear embedded in a variety of types of ancient literature, often at the beginning of a work, sometimes in the middle or at the end.[108] Hence, a number of interpreters hold that the hymn that concludes *Paedagogus* is a purely literary entity, not an actual song for liturgical or devotional use.[109]

Admittedly, Clement's hymn serves a literary purpose in its present context, but it is a *second* ending to *Paedagogus*, being preceded by a first ending in the form of a prayer. This suggests that the hymn is not original to *Paedagogus* but was composed independently and added to a later edition of that work.[110] Hence, it seems natural to assume that the hymn originally served some corporate devotional use. Consistent with such a purpose (but not to be taken

---

[108] See Brucker (1997, 46–47 [hymns used as *prooimia* for epic recitals by rhapsodes, the hymnic *prooimion* for Hesiod's *Works and Days*], 212 [a prose hymn to Philosophy in Cicero's *Tusculan Disputations*], 225 [a prose hymn in Philo's *Life of Moses*], and 235–36 [a prose hymn in Epictetus]). Brucker does not mention any examples of hymns coming at the end of a work, but, in addition to Clement's hymn, I note the hymn that closes Methodius' *Symposium* and the one at the end of the *Apocryphon of John*.

[109] See Kroll (1968,12n1); Eisenhofer (1932, 210); Wolbergs (1971, 86).

[110] That the hymn is secondary is suggested by its redundancy after the prayer, a redundancy made all the more awkward by the fact that the introduction to the prayer is repeated in the introduction to the hymn.

as proof of it) are invitations within the hymn to corporate singing: μέλπωμεν ὁμοῦ in line 59 and ψάλλωμεν ὁμοῦ in line 65.¹¹¹

Mohrmann holds out the possibility that the hymn had a place in the Alexandrian liturgy.¹¹² May, judging that the composition is probably too idiosyncratic and complicated for an ordinary liturgical setting, finds more plausible the suggestion (first put forward by Wilamowitz¹¹³) that the piece was sung by the students of the Alexandrian Christian school.¹¹⁴ Observing that critical research no longer allows one to assume that a Christian school existed in Clement's time (as Eusebius claimed), May proposes that Clement might have prepared the hymn for his own group of students, perhaps for use in a domestic setting.¹¹⁵ Students who kept copies of *Paedagogus* probably also passed on the hymn, which was copied in the manuscript tradition at the end of *Paedagogus*.

Although the secondary character of the hymn in its present location argues for a prior use that was likely devotional, there is no way of knowing whether this use was also *musical*. Clement's musical remarks do not support the inference that he had training as a musician.¹¹⁶ Of course, the hymn might have been supplied with a melody by one of his students. Or it was simply recited (perhaps intoned), not sung to a tune.

Clement's hymn and P.Oxy. 1786 are examples of Greek metrical poetry as a form of Christian hymnody. In addition to Clement's hymn, we know of a poem, "Against Marcus," composed in iambic trimeters by a pious elder (in Irenaeus, *Haer.* 1.15.6). Hippolytus quotes a hymn (or hymns) of the Naassenes under the title "Nomos," which, except for the first line, is in anapaests (*Ref.* 5.10.2ff).¹¹⁷ He also quotes lines from "Theros," a Valentinian hymn in dactylic tetrameters (*Ref.* 6.37.1). A poem among the Jewish and Christian body of poems known as the *Sibyllene Oracles* (no. 8) might be classified as a Christ hymn. The oracle, dating to about 175 C.E., contains a judgment poem in hexameters (lines 218–50) based on an acrostic: ΙΗΣΟΥΣ ΧΡΕΙΣΤΟΣ ΘΕΟΥ ΥΙΟΣ ΣΩΤΗΡ ΣΤΑΥΡΟΣ ("JESUS CHRIST SON OF GOD SAVIOR CROSS"). A hymn to Christ in dactylic hexameters preserved as

---

¹¹¹ Cf. μέλπωμεν ἁπλῶς (or πέμπωμεν ἁπλῶς) in line 59.
¹¹² Mohrmann (1957, 267).
¹¹³ Wilamowitz-Möllendorff (1912, 267) ("das Schulgebet, das sie sangen, hat Clemens am Schlusse [des *Paedagogus*] beigefügt").
¹¹⁴ May (1983, 264).
¹¹⁵ May (1983, 264). In *Paed.* 2.4.44.1 Clement speaks of praising and singing to the Creator at mealtime; in *Str.* 7.7.49.4 he endorses singing psalms and hymns at the Christian banquet (see also *Str.* 6.11.90.1).
¹¹⁶ On Clement's musical understanding, see Cosgrove (2006a).
¹¹⁷ Hippolytus also quotes hymns to Attis (*Ref.* 5.9.8 and 5.9.9) that seem to be associated with the Naasenes, but it is unclear whether they composed these hymns and used them in worship.

Sibylline Oracle 6 dates to the second or third century.[118] A fragment of a hymn to Christ in paroemiacs survives from the fourth century (P.Ber. 8299),[119] as do a number of hymns by Gregory of Nazianzus,[120] along with Apollinaris' metrical paraphrase of the Psalms.[121] From the early fifth century come the metrical hymns of Synesius.

The tradition of Greek metrical poetry also appears in other learned expressions of Christian piety. According to Sozomen, Apollinaris paraphrased the Old Testament (and not only the Psalms) using various traditional Greek meters (Sozomen, *H.E.* 5.18). Around 500, Nonnus of Panopolis, who perhaps eventually converted to Christianity (although this is not certain), paraphrased the Gospel of John in dactylic hexameters.

From the second through the fifth centuries, Christians with a Hellenistic education and a poetic bent composed hymns and other spiritual works in Greek meter. Some of the shorter and more accessible hymns of this sort were undoubtedly sung in devotional settings of various kinds, including worship. By the fourth century, hymns were being edged out of the liturgy by a rage for Psalm-singing and in some circles fell into disfavor due to concerns that nonbiblical hymns were seductive vehicles for heresy.[122] One would like to know more of the history of the use of metrical Greek hymns in Christian worship and other forms of devotion during these centuries, but the historical record is spare. P.Oxy. 1786 gives us an idea of what at least one of them sounded like.

---

[118] Lactantius quotes the hymn in a work dated to around 311 (*Inst.* 14.15–22).

[119] Heitsch, no. 45.3. On the meter, see West (1982, 171).

[120] Most of the hymns of Gregory of Nazianzus belong to a transitional form of poetry in which "the poet appears to have a definite quantitative scheme in view but offends against it" (West [1982, 164]). A few of the poems attributed to Gregory belong to the accent-based type of meter.

[121] PG 33:1313–1538.

[122] *Didascalia* 1.6.3–5 rejects pagan poetry and endorses the singing of the Psalms but does not mention Christian hymns (Latin version) = *Didascalia* 2 (Syriac version) in Connolly, [1929, 12; English translation of Syriac]). This may reflect a suspicion about hymns. Concern about the propagation of heresy through hymns was made official at the Council of Laodicea (c. 360–390). Canon 59 prohibits the chanting of "private psalms" in church (οὐ δεῖ ἰδιωτικοὺς ψαλμοὺς λέγεσθαι ἐν τῇ ἐκκλησίᾳ in Joannou [1962, 154]). Perhaps in this century, so-called biblical canticles were being identified and intoned. By the fifth century these odes would form a group of biblical songs placed as a collection after the Psalms in Codex Alexandrinus.

Appendix

Pitch Centers and Tonal Structure in Ancient Greek Melodies

It has been common to reserve the term "tonality" for the harmonic structures of the major-minor system of Western music, whose origins are said to date from around 1600.[1] In an effort at a basic definition, Réti, writing in the 1950s, distinguished between "harmonic" tonality and "melodic" tonality, associating the latter with Jewish and Gregorian chant, as well as other types of Eastern music. Réti argued that in melodic tonality a melody line is to be interpreted as a musical unity through its orientation to a basic note, which he termed its "tonic."[2] A number of years later, Hoppin proposed that we define tonality in early music (music before the Renaissance) as "the organization of a series of tones around one tone that constitutes a tonal center."[3] Thomson has recently insisted that a pervasive feature of human music-making in all times is the orientation of melodies to pitch centers, including melodies belonging to music based on traditional Western harmony.[4]

The notion of a pitch center perhaps evokes an image of a single tone around which other tones "orbit," but the concept need not be used in this way. A melody can have more than one pitch center, and two or more pitch centers can operate not only successively but simultaneously. One advantage of the term "pitch center" is that it provides an alternative to the term "tonic," which can be misleading when applied to monophonic music.

---

[1] Hyer (2001, 583–84). More recently, musicologists have stressed greater continuity between the harmonic system of "common practice" going back to the seventeenth century and the music that preceded it, challenging sharp distinctions between the "linear harmony" of "modal" music and the "vertical harmony" of "tonal music." See Norton (1984, 133–35 and passim).

[2] Réti (1958, 25–26).

[3] Hoppin (1966, 25).

[4] Thomson (1999); idem (2006). Chapters ten and eleven of *Tonality in Music* (Thomson [1999]) discuss the use of pitch centers in various kinds of music from around the world, including melodies based on Western harmony.

Pitch Centers in Monophonic Music

Pitch centers play a role in traditional monophonic[5] music from around the world. A series of examples can serve as illustrations. Maori chants revolve around a single reciting pitch called *oro*.[6] Archaic Lapp chants exhibit an embroidered reciting tone.[7] The music of the Venda people of South Africa is organized around a chief tone termed *phala*; a tone above *phala* is called *thakhula*, the "lifter," a kind of leading tone "because it leads the melody back down onto the chief tone."[8] The traditional melodies of Malaysia tend to be oriented to a single pitch center, which may be the first, second, third, fourth, fifth, sixth or last degree of the scale from which the melody is formed.[9] In Nagauta, the primary form of traditional Japanese Kabuki music, the melody is usually oriented to two pitch centers, one primary and the other secondary, standing a fourth or a fifth apart.[10] Nagauta melodies tend to begin by orienting themselves to these pitch centers, move away from them, and eventually return to them at the end of the song.

The preceding observations are not meant to suggest that there is a single universal kind of pitch center, only that it is common for people widely separated by time, space, and culture to construct their melodies in somewhat similar ways. One of those ways is the organization of the notes of a melody in a hierarchy so that certain tones serve as orientation points for other tones. The nature of this orientation and the way it is achieved in melody vary from one musical tradition to the next.

Pitch Centers in Ancient Greek Melodies

The concept of a pitch center does not correspond to any ancient Greek musicological *term*, a fact that could reflect an absence in ancient Greek musical experience of the operation of pitch centers in melodies. It is more

---

[5] I use the term "monophonic" of music in which a single line of melody or chant is primary. Usually, monophony is also defined negatively as a melody that is not structured through harmony (a homophonic texture) or polyphony (a group of melodic lines). Monophony often involves accompaniment, which can take forms such as a drone, a unison reinforcement of the melody, or a contrasting line that produces a heterophonic texture. Clearly, there is no sharp line between this kind of heterophony (achieved through accompaniment) and polyphony. But the concept of polyphony usually includes the assumption that the multiple lines are equally important and independent. In monophonic music with a heterophonic texture, a single melody line is primary; the accompaniment is subordinate.

[6] Malm (1996, 26).
[7] Sachs (1965, 168).
[8] Blacking (1973, 85).
[9] Matusky and Tan (2004, 25, 46, 54, 62, and passim).
[10] See Keister (2004, 107–8).

likely, however, that ancient theorists did not develop the concept of a pitch center because certain aspects of the nature of melodies, as a class and in the individual instance, did not present questions of intellectual interest to them. In support of this interpretation is the absence of analysis of individual pieces of music in the ancient Greek musical handbooks and the paucity of comment by the theorists about how melodies unfold. Bélis suggests that the lack of attention in the handbooks to melodic composition owes to the opinion that μελοποιία (melodic composition) is a technical, not a scientific, matter.[11] Solomon likewise observes that ancient Greek music theory tends to be "peripatetic," focused on definition and theory rather than on practical application, even though theory has practical implications.[12] In any case, the theorists comment only briefly on aspects of melodic composition, making no references to any individual pieces of music.[13]

Standing (Frame) Notes

Although the handbooks do not analyze individual melodies for pitch centers, they do analyze scales in ways that indirectly suggest the operation of orientation notes in melodies. Of particular importance is the distinction between "standing" (ἑστῶτες) notes, sometimes called "fixed" (ἀκίνητοι) notes, and "movable" (κινούμενοι) notes.

Standing notes are the first and fourth degrees of the tetrachord, which the ancient theorists regard as the basic scalar building block. Modern scholars sometimes refer to these as the "outer" or "frame" notes to indicate that they are the anchor points that frame the tetrachord. The movable notes are the "inner" second and third notes, which can be altered to change the genus of the scale. In the case of disjunct tetrachords forming an octave scale, the first, fourth, fifth, and eighth degrees of the scale are all standing notes and mark out the concordant (consonant) intervals of a fourth, fifth, and octave.

The distinction between standing tones and movable tones appears to entail the idea that the frame notes of the tetrachord have special importance because they define the basic concordant interval of a fourth. Hence, Solomon interprets frame notes as bearers of melodic emphasis, and he describes other notes as "filler" or "ornament."[14] Landels also regards the standing notes as the

---

[11] Bélis (1992, 32).
[12] Solomon (1986, 456–57). See also Mathiesen (1999, 288–89).
[13] See the summary in Bélis (1992, 32–33). The closest thing to analysis of an individual score / melody is a passage in a famous book on literary composition in which the author seeks to show that there is no agreement between melody and verbal accent in a lyric dialogue from Euripides' *Orestes* (Dionysius of Halicarnassus, *Comp.* 63–64). See Pöhlmann and West (2001, 10–11).
[14] Solomon (1986, 461, 463–64).

most important tones in a melody. In this vein, he thinks of movable notes as passing tones that lead to standing tones.[15]

The reason the standing notes are not movable is that altering them would destroy the integrity of the fourth. Since musicians made melodies that used fixed outer notes and movable inner notes, ancient theorists who speak of the consonance of the fourth are only explaining what people already heard in music: a musically desirable quality of the interval of the fourth, which musicians did not disturb (by augmenting or diminishing it by microtones or semitones) in fashioning their tunes.

It is a short step from this insight into how Greeks heard frame notes in a melody to the concept of pitch centers, especially if the scores show that melodies emphasize and return to frame notes. But it is important to keep in mind something that Winnington-Ingram pointed out more than seventy years ago. In the ancient musical scores, tetrachordal melodic structure seems operative in the Hellenistic-era melodies (notably in the Delphic paeans) but is not a pervasive feature of the Roman-era melodies.[16]

The Role of Mesē

It is possible that in discussing the role of *mesē* (μέση), the author of the *Aristotelian Problems* assumes the concept of a pitch center. He asks why, once an instrument has been tuned, an alteration of the tuning of *mesē* causes not only *mesē* to sound unpleasant and out of tune but the rest of the notes as well; yet when any note other than *mesē* is put out of tune, it alone sounds bad. His answer is as follows: "All good melodies make frequent use of *mesē*, and all good composers recur frequently to *mesē* and quickly return to it if they depart from it; but they do not treat any other note in this way" (Ps.-Aristotle, *Phys. probl.* 19.20 Hett). In another place the author of the *Problems* calls *mesē* the "leader" (ἡγεμών) (*Phys. probl.* 19.33 Hett).

Winnington-Ingram observes that the remarks in the *Problems* about *mesē* have occasioned a good deal of scholarly debate about whether *mesē* is a kind of tonic.[17] This debate seems to have been especially lively in the older scholarship to which Winnington-Ingram (writing in the 1930s) refers. Winnington-Ingram himself occasionally uses the word "tonic" of *mesē* in his analyses of individual scores. The meaning he attaches to the term is briefly given in his description of "mode," which he defines as "essentially a question of the internal relationship of notes within a scale, especially of the predominance of one of them over the others as a tonic."[18] Barker counsels caution. He grants that

---

[15] Landels (1999, 230).
[16] See Winnington-Ingram (1968, 45–46).
[17] Winnington-Ingram (1968, 6).
[18] Winnington-Ingram (1968, 2).

mesē was in some way basic in Greek melodies, but urges that the term "tonic" be used guardedly if at all to characterize *mesē*. The most that can be said is that cithara players tuned *mesē* first and that "a melody was felt somehow to revolve around that degree of the scale."[19] Even this may be saying too much, as we will see from the ancient scores.

In fact, it is not clear what the author of the *Problems* means by *mesē* – the string called *mesē*, a note lying a fourth from the bottom in the scale on which a melody is based, or the central note of the Unmodulating System. Winnington-Ingram thinks that in other contexts where the *Problems* speaks of *mesē*, the author means the central note of the Unmodulating System.[20] If so, the recurrence of melodies to *mesē* could be due to practices of composers in the Classical and Hellenistic eras. Specifically, it is possible that composers of those times typically chose a *tonos* whose middle double octave provided the governing scale of their melodies, so that standing notes of the *tonos* served as melodic orientation points. In that case, *mesē*, lying at the center of the Unmodulating System, might have served as a pitch center for tetrachordally-structured music. Nevertheless, *mesē* is not always the most dominant note in the melodies of the Hellenistic-era Delphic paeans, although it does enjoy special importance in most of them.

A different view of the *Problems* is taken by Hagel, who contends that the author does not have the Unmodulating System in mind but is focused on the lyre, specifically the octave of the lyre that was studied in music education.[21] Hagel makes a convincing argument that when the author speaks of *mesē* as a reference point, he means the *string* called *mesē*, which the lyre player tuned first.[22] In that case, the conception of *mesē* in the *Problems* assumes that lyre tuning involves an octave divided into a fourth and a fifth, for this is the only way in which it makes sense to speak of *mesē* as a tuning reference-point. Most melodies, when performed with such a tuning, would naturally recur frequently to *mesē* because a note in the middle of the scale stands a better chance of being sounded than other notes do. This is especially the case since much of Greek music moves mostly in small steps, so that passing in this way from the lower to higher notes and vice versa would often bring the melody through *mesē*. This explanation does not rule out the possibility that the term

---

[19] Barker (1984, 195n39).
[20] *Mesē* as the central note of the Unmodulating System is technically termed "dynamic" *mesē* and distinguished by some from "thetic" *mesē* as the fourth step of an octave species. On this distinction, see below. Winnington-Ingram doubts that the author of the *Problems* knew the distinction between thetic and dynamic. He believes that the author operates with a single understanding of *mesē* as the central note of the Unmodulating System. See Winnington-Ingram (1968, 6–7).
[21] Hagel (2009, 138 [see also 135 and the wider context]).
[22] Hagel (2009, 135–42 [with detailed discussion of all the relevant evidence]).

mesē was also used to refer to a note as an orientation point or pitch center in melody, but the language of the *Problems* does not require that inference.

Dynamic (Functional) and Thetic (Positional) Note Naming

In the second century C.E., Claudius Ptolemy made a distinction between naming notes "according to their function" (κατὰ δύναμιν) and "according to their position" (κατὰ θέσιν) (Ptolemy, *Harm.* 2.5 Düring).[23] These expressions are often transliterated as "dynamic" and "thetic." They can also be translated more exactly as "functional" and "positional," but the words "dynamic" and "thetic" remind us of the underlying Greek terms.

One interpretation of the distinction sees "dynamic" as having to do with the role of a note in a *tonos* and "thetic" as concerning a note's place in an octave species.[24] Accordingly, dynamic *mesē* is the note at the middle of a *tonos*, where it branches into its conjunct and disjunct tetrachords. In a "thetic" sense *mesē* is the fourth note from the bottom in any octave species. This interpretation has led some interpreters to see the thetic sense of the note names as expressing the tonal structure of an octave species and therefore of melodies, particularly melodies from the Roman era whose tonal structures do not appear to depend on the notation *tonos* in which they are written (the dynamic sense of their notes).

One recent advocate of the view that thetic note naming is a key to understanding Roman-era tonality is Solomon. Solomon interprets the thetic meaning as the role of a note in a scale governing a melody, and he refers to moving from note naming (and tonal structure) by *tonos* to note naming (and tonal structure) by octave species as "thetic shift."[25] Using the melody of the Seikilos inscription for illustration, Solomon argues that although the melodic emphases in the Seikilos tune do not correspond to standing notes of the notation *tonos* in which the song is written (the Ionian *tonos*), they do correspond to the standing notes of the Phrygian octave species when the notes are defined thetically.[26] According to this view, one interprets the first, fourth, fifth, and eighth degrees of the octave species as *hypatē, mesē, paramesē,* and *nētē,* which are standing-notes of the two disjunct tetrachords that make up the octave scale. It turns out, Solomon says, that these scale-steps bear the melodic emphases in the Seikilos melody.

---

[23] A passage in the musical treatise known as *Anonymous Bellermanni* also uses these terms, although it is not clear whether the author means the same thing as Ptolemy (*Anon. Bell.* 21–23).

[24] Winnington-Ingram (1968, 6 and 64–65); Solomon (1986, 461 and 470); Landels (1999, 96); Barker (1989, 315–16n3).

[25] See Solomon (1984, 250–51).

[26] Solomon (1986, 461). See also Duysinx (1981, 307–10 [on the Seikilos epitaph]).

An attractive feature of Solomon's theory of a historical shift from dynamic- to thetic-based tonality is that it provides a way of discovering a basic continuity through an apparent change in the ways Greeks built their melodies. As mentioned above, in our best-preserved documents from the Hellenistic era – the Delphic paeans by Athenaeus and Limenius – melodic emphases correspond to standing notes of the *tonos* in which the melody is notated, implying a correlation between standing notes (defined "dynamically") and the orientation notes of a melody.[27] But in the Seikilos melody and other tunes of the Roman era, this correlation breaks down. Solomon concludes that what guides the composer's decisions about melodic emphases in these Roman-era melodies is not the *tonos* in which he chooses to notate the piece but the octave species conceived as organized by tetrachordal frame notes.

It is important to reiterate that when Ptolemy made the distinction between dynamic and thetic *mesē*, he was speaking of lyre-based music. The term from which we derive the adjective "thetic" is θέσις, which in lyre-based music means position and suggests the location of a string. Hence, according to positional note naming, *mesē* is the fourth note / string from the bottom of a tuned lyre. Ptolemy transferred the familiar idea of strings, physically positioned in a scalar order, to an abstract conception of an eight-tone scale (octave species), which he doubled to make a two-octave system. According to Ptolemy, when notes are named thetically, it is for the purpose of speaking of them as being higher or lower, and when they are named dynamically it is to specify them in relation to something (presumably their function in a *tonos*) (*Harm.* 2.5 Düring).[28] It is dubious to infer from Ptolemy's distinction between dynamic and thetic note naming that the thetic naming assumes the tetrachordal organization of melodies (which may have dominated music in pre-Roman times) and that this tetrachordal organization was enshrined in the octave species, so that choice of *tonos* in Roman-era melodies was largely a matter of register, while the tonal hierarchy of melodies was determined by the standing notes defining the disjunct tetrachords of an octave species. To judge from the extant scores, Roman-era melodies were not oriented generally to tetrachordal structural patterns.[29]

---

[27] This observation is made by Winnington-Ingram (1968, 33–38 and 45).

[28] The idea that "position" is a way of speaking about higher or lower is a lyre-based idea, where strings are positioned in a scalar sequence. See also West: "In the theorists' writings, Hypatē and the other names are almost always used in a dynamic sense, while lyre-players may have continued to use them in the thetic sense, i.e., Hypatē = 'my bottom note', irrespective of the sequence of intervals separating it from my top note" (1992b, 221n10).

[29] See Winnington-Ingram (1968, 45–46). In their discussions of individual scores in *Documents of Ancient Greek Music*, Pöhlmann and West observe places that reflect traditional Greek conceptions of the tetrachord and other old scales mentioned by theorists, and they identify the *tonos* (or in some cases the *tonoi*) for each melody. They do not, however, interpret any of the melodies in terms of the Aristoxenian concept of the octave species. In other words, they

Applications of Greek Music Theory to the Surviving Musical Documents

At a number of points in the preceding, reference has been made to evidence from the ancient Greek scores. Naturally, the student of ancient Greek music theory wants to see how theory illumines the scores and vice versa. Efforts in this direction have often met with frustration. Much of modern scholarship has concluded that ancient Greek music theory contributes disappointingly to our efforts at musical analysis of individual scores.[30] Solomon seeks to show that this judgment is overly negative by offering a detailed analysis of the Seikilos inscription as proof that the categories of ancient Greek music theory fit and illumine at least this one musical artifact. The implication is that other scores are susceptible to similar theoretical analyses.

One aspect of Solomon's study of the Seikilos melody is especially relevant to the question of tonality. As we have seen, Solomon argues that when one uses thetic nomenclature as a way of referring to notes *in an octave species*, the melodic emphases of the Seikilos melody turn out to be standing notes of the Phrygian octave species: *hypatē*, *mesē*, and *nētē* of the Phrygian octave species.[31] It appears, however, that the theory of "thetic-shift" does not succeed generally with the Roman-era melodies. In a classic study of "mode" in ancient Greek music, Winnington-Ingram tested the possibilities for identifying an octave species for the Roman-era melodies known to him in 1936 by looking for a pattern of tones and semitones arranged so that the fourth note of the scale (thetic *mesē*) could be construed as the tonal center of the melody. His conclusion was that only some of the melodies can be analyzed according to the concept of an octave species with thetic *mesē* as tonal center and that even these present anomalies for this analytic framework.[32]

If the Roman-era melodies do not lend themselves to neat interpretation according to the theory of "thetic shift" from *tonos* to octave species, it is equally true that in these melodies the notation *tonos* does not provide the organization of the melody according to its standing tones. Winnington-Ingram is emphatic that the scores as a whole "lend no countenance to the idea that Mese

---

do not use Greek music theory to carry out what has traditionally been called "modal" analysis of the scores. Nor do they use the distinction between "dynamic" and "thetic" note naming to interpret the scores.

[30] See Solomon's reference to studies that express this opinion (1986, 455).

[31] Solomon (1986, 461 with n14, 470). Other specialists have also described the Seikilos melody as Phrygian-based but without injecting the concept of standing notes into the octave species as a basis for analyzing melodies for melodic emphases on the first, fourth, fifth, and eighth degrees of an octave species. See Winnington-Ingram (1968, 38); Landels (1999, 253); Mathiesen (1999, 150).

[32] Winnington-Ingram (1968, 45–46).

(κατὰ δύναμιν) served as a general tonic in all modes: if that were ever so it was not at the time most of these melodies were composed."[33]

Like Winnington-Ingram, West also argues that the Roman-era melodies are not easily assimilated to what ancient Greek theory lays down – whether one looks to standing notes of the notation *tonos* or the traditional *harmoniai* or the octave species.[34] He therefore adopts a "modal" approach worked out inductively from examination of the scores. He looks for a manifest pitch center in the melody, then determines the diatonic intervals up and down from that center. Translating this into the white keys of the piano, he identifies the governing scales of various melodies as "G" mode or "E" mode, etc. Hence, although the scale of Seikilos corresponds to the Phrygian octave species, West contends that it is more accurate to say that the Seikilos melody is in the "G" mode:

> We can say that it displays the D or Phrygian octave-species, but as regards mode, we must say that it is in the G mode, and be resigned to knowing no Greek label that will express this. By the G mode we mean the mode in which the successive scale degrees from the tonic [pitch center] upwards are T T S T ... and downwards T S T T ...[35]

A significant judgment in West's view of the relation between theory and Roman-era melodies is that the concept of the octave species, if applied to the scores on the assumption that the fourth degree of the scale (*mesē*) is an orientation pitch, does not suit many of the melodies. Hence, identifying an octave species for a melody tells us little. "Only when we determine how the pattern of tones and semitones relates to the tonic will we know something about the modality of the piece."[36] By "tonic," West means a pitch center.[37] Hence, his concept of "mode" is a scalar pattern of intervals in relation to a pitch center, which may or may not be the fourth degree of the scale used by the piece. For example, Mesomedes' hymn to the Sun is notated in the Lydian *tonos* and its scale (eight notes) corresponds to the Lydian octave species, but its tonic, West says, is the third degree of this scale, which means that the hymn to the Sun is in the E mode.[38]

Comparing West to Winnington-Ingram, we see certain similarities along with differences. Winnington-Ingram reaches the following conclusions about the Roman-era fragments he examined:[39]

---

[33] Winnington-Ingram (1968, 46).
[34] See West (1992b, 184–89 [discussing mode in the post-Classical era]).
[35] West (1992b, 186). T = tone; S = semitone.
[36] West (1992b, 186).
[37] Winnington-Ingram also uses the term "tonic" in a similar way in his discussions of scores (1968, 30–47).
[38] West (1992b, 186–87).
[39] Winnington-Ingram (1968, 45–46) (my summary of his conclusions).

1. The Seikilos inscription, Mesomedes' hymn to Nemesis, and the Berlin paean present melodies based on the Phrygian octave species and are oriented to a tonic that is thetic *mesē* in that octave species. But the octave analyzes into a fourth (*hypatē* to *mesē*) and a fifth (*hypatē* to *paramesē*), not two consecutive tetrachords joined disjunctively. This suggests that the old tetrachordal orientation of the music has given way to approaches in which other intervals play a greater structural role.

2. The invocation of the Muse, the invocation of Calliope and Apollo, and the hymn to the Sun are oriented to (thetic) *hypatē mesōn*. Some importance is given to *mesē* and *paramesē*. The basic tonal orientation is the fifth from *hypatē* to *mesē*, which reinforces the impression that the Roman-era music is not bound to tetrachordal structures. The hymn to the Muse has a Dorian coloring. The invocation of Calliope and Apollo and the hymn to the Sun operate in the Mixolydian octave species.[40]

3. The Christian hymn seems to be based on the Hypophrygian octave species with dynamic *lichanos mesōn* (which is *hypatē* in the octave species) as final and possible tonic, although other notes could be the tonic.

4. A scrap of music from the *Anonymous Bellermanni* may use the Lydian octave species composed of a fourth and a conjunct fifth.

5. Overall, there is a feeling of triads in the Roman-era melodies, which distinguishes them from the tetrachordal style of the Delphic paeans.

West, in his analysis of the individual scores,[41] drops almost all reference to octave species and proceeds descriptively, observing tonal emphasis, the recurrent use of certain intervals, and shifts of focus. Like Winnington-Ingram, he marks places where it is not fourths that structure the melody but fifths and thirds. He refers at points to "the tonic" of a melody but also finds multiple tonal foci in some pieces, using the words "tonic," "tonal center," and "tonal focus" more or less interchangeably. In some places, however, he speaks of subordination among pitch foci: "secondary foci," a "primary tonic" and a "secondary tonic," the "dominant," a "rival harmonic axis" followed by a return to the "tonic."[42] These concepts do not correspond to established terms of ancient Greek music theory.[43] Having no available ancient terms of analysis for relations between tones in a melody, West uses modern terms. One should not interpret his application of these words as implying an importation into Greek music of the theoretical concepts carried by some of them ("tonic,"

---

[40] In his summary, Winnington-Ingram states that the hymns to the Muse and to the Sun are in the Mixolydian octave species (1968, 45), but in his prior discussion he distinguishes the hymn to the Muse as two songs – invocation of the Muse, which has a "Dorian flavour," and a second part (which is today referred to as the invocation of Calliope and Apollo) based on the Mixolydian octave species (ibid., 42).

[41] West (1992b, 277–326).

[42] West (1992b): "secondary foci" (308 and 319), "primary tonic" and "secondary tonic" (318), "dominant" (289), "rival harmonic axis" and return to "the tonic" (303).

[43] It has been argued that when the author of the Aristotelian *Problems* describes *mesē* as "leader" (ἡγεμών) (*Phys. probl.* 19.33 Hett), this term means "tonic" of some sort; but this is doubtful (see above).

"dominant," "rival harmonic axis") in other musical contexts (e.g., in the study of Gregorian chant and in modern music theory).

Melodic Emphasis

In the preceding discussion we considered the possibility that tonal *systems* – whether *tonoi* or octave species as tonal systems[44] – impart importance to particular tones as orientation points for listeners. Perhaps tonal systems are the grammar of music that every listener has internalized, even if only theorists and a few professionals possess analytic categories for explaining them. We have reason to believe that at least in the Hellenistic era, the tetrachordal structures of the *tonos* imparted some kind of tonal orientation to the listener, but the ancient theoretical literature does not discuss the listener's experience of tonal organization in a melody. Moreover, in the Roman era, music no longer appears to be governed in the same way as before by the notation *tonos*, a circumstance that has given rise to the suggestion that perhaps the octave species imparts tonality to melodies in Roman times.

The basis for the preceding judgments is a close examination of the scores to determine how pitch centers operated. That examination, to be presented below, assumes that pitch centers are emphasized in a melody so that they stand out for listeners as orientation points. A remark by Aristoxenus can help us think about the ways in which melodies make certain tones central for the listener. Aristoxenus observes that "comprehension of music comes from two things: perception and memory; for it is necessary to perceive what is coming into being and to remember what has come into being; there is no other way to follow what is in music" (*Harm. stoich.* 2.38.32–39.3 Rios). One way to discover melodic emphasis is to consider how melodies make certain tones *memorable*. Remembering comprehends the relationship between successive tones. Remembering is also the means by which we judge whether a given tone is "emphasized," imbued with a quality of memorability that makes it more prominent than other tones.[45]

---

[44] To these we might also add the *harmoniai* as these were understood in the Classical or Archaic periods as song types with their own tonal characteristics. But as far as tonal organization through pitch centers goes, our knowledge of the old *harmoniai* is sketchier than our understanding of later Greek music.

[45] Memorability of tones is not memorability of single notes, if by single notes we mean individual instances of sound in a melody, e.g., an 'F#' in bar 13. A melody may cause the tone 'F#' to stick in my mind without my being able to recall, at the end of the piece, the precise places where 'F#' occurs.

The most important factors in melodic accentuation of tones are frequency, duration, and successive repetition:[46]

Frequency[47] can take the form of concentration (frequency in a particular part of a melody) and distribution throughout a melody. Octave equivalency reinforces frequency. That is, a frequent tone is made even more memorable by additional instances of its upper or lower octave. Not surprisingly, Greeks regarded tones an octave apart as equivalent in some way.[48]

Successive repetition is a special kind of concentration. Cleonides calls it *petteia* (πεττεία) (*Eis. harm.* 29.4–5 Solomon).[49]

Duration refers to the length of notes. Cleonides speaks of lengthening of note as *tonē* (τονή) (*Eis. harm.* 29.5–7 Solomon).

In approaching the question of how ancient Greek melodies establish pitch centers by making certain tones memorable, we must also keep in mind that melodies can use pitch centers in different ways. Our earlier discussion of pitch centers in a variety of musical cultures pointed this out. A melody

---

[46] In a 1926 study of factors of accentuation in melodies, Ortmann identified the following means by which melodies make certain tones stand out for consciousness: beginning and ending, highest and lowest, repetition, changes in pitch direction, and degrees of association and contrast through interval magnitude (Ortmann [1926]). More recently, Thomson, drawing attention to Ortmann's largely forgotten work, has singled out some of the same features as imparting salience to certain pitches of a melody: beginnings and endings, rhythmic accentuation, high frequency of occurrence (which is a matter of both number of instances and duration), prominence through "contoural locus" (highest or lowest, pivotal), and "prominence of a simple harmonic relationship (8^{ve}, 5th, 4th)" (Thomson [2006, 90]). Speaking of Greek melodies, Winnington-Ingram listed the following criteria for identifying the "tonic": "frequent recurrence, its appearance in a prominent position as the first note or the last, the delaying of its expected occurrence by some kind of embellishment" (Winnington-Ingram [1968, 2]). I use only frequency, successive repetition, and duration as criteria for identifying tones emphasized in a melody. Experiments in various aspects of acoustic psychology suggest that other factors besides these may play a role in making tones memorable. But scientific studies in music perception have not made memorability of tones a primary focus, and the studies that bear directly or indirectly on the subject do not present uniform results. Moreover, no convincing proof has been made that other factors are as influential as frequency, duration, and successive repetition. For a summary of research in acoustic psychology on melodic emphasis, see Huron and Royal (1996).

[47] Bélis takes account of frequency in counting the number of times a tone is sounded in each section of the Delphic paeans. See her charts for each section of each hymn showing the number of times each tone is sung (Bélis [1992, 62, 68, 75, etc.].). These observations become a basis for theoretical interpretation in her study.

[48] The author of the Aristotelian *Problems* asks, "Why do people not sing in correspondence (ἀντίφωνα) at the fifth? Is it because the concordant note (ἡ σύμφωνος) is not the same (ἡ αὐτὴ) in this consonance (τῇ συμφωνίᾳ), as it is in the octave?" (Ps.-Aristotle, *Phys. probl.* 19.17 Hett; English translation from Barker [1984, 194]). The author of the *Problems* also discusses the tendency of people to mistake octaves for unison (*Phys. probl.* 19.18). Moreover, Ptolemy considers pitches an octave apart to be homophones (*Harm.* 1.15), that is, "functionally identical" as Mathiesen puts it (1999, 440). Also suggestive is Ptolemy's observation that *tonoi* an octave apart use the same scalar pattern of intervals and are, therefore, the same *tonos* (*Harm.* 2.8), *tonos* being his term for what others call an octave species.

[49] Other ancient theorists use the term *petteia* for something like disposition of notes (so Aristides Quintilianus, *Peri mous.* 1.12).

can emphasize one pitch center throughout with relatively even distribution, perhaps even beginning and ending on that note. It can also establish a pitch center, then move to a different pitch emphasis, sometimes without returning to the original pitch center. In some music, however, a return is regarded as musically satisfying (e.g., in Japanese Nagauta). Melodies can also operate with multiple pitch centers simultaneously. If the standing notes of ancient Greek *tonoi* were at some point treated as orientation points in melody, then melodies could move from one to the other of these frame notes as part of an overall reinforcement of the basic tonality. In that case, a shift of emphasis from one to another frame note would have provided variety but also a sense of tonal stability. Moreover, movement to sustained emphasis on one or more *non-standing* notes would have created a sense of tonal instability and the expectation of a return to emphasis on tonally stable notes.

The different possibilities and various gradations of tonal play range from the obvious to the subtle. From our distant cultural vantage and with only a modest collection of ancient scores to examine, we cannot hope to discover the whole range of tonal play as it was experienced by ancient listeners. Nevertheless, we can develop a basic understanding of how pitch centers operated in the music represented by the scores, including an idea of differences between the use of pitch centers in the Hellenistic music of the Delphic paeans and how pitch centers functioned in the later music of the Roman era.

Analysis of Greek Melodies for Pitch Centers and Tonal Organization

Analyses of individual scores are presented at the end of this appendix. The following is a summary and interpretation of results based on those analyses.

Not all the scores admit interpretation for pitch emphases. Some are too fragmentary. I have focused primarily on the Delphic paeans, the Seikilos inscription, the hymn to the Muse, the compositions of Mesomedes, the Berlin paean, and the Christian hymn.

Identification of Pitch Centers and Their Intervallic Relations

The results from analysis of the scores show that emphasized notes of ancient Greek melodies tend to be oriented to each other in relationships of fourths and fifths. But the significance of this varies. In particular, it appears that the melodies of the multi-sectioned Delphic paeans, composed in the Hellenistic era, are structured tetrachordally and emphasize to a large extent the frame notes of the *tonoi* in which they are notated. In other words, *tonos* structure seems to govern melodic structure in the paeans. A different picture emerges from the Roman-era melodies, where tetrachordal structure does not seem to be pervasive.

The Delphic paeans are the only substantially-preserved compositions from the Hellenistic era.[50] *Mesē* of the *tonos* is an emphasized note in about half the analyzable sections of these hymns: sections 1 and 2 of the paean of Athenaeus and sections 1, 4, 7?, and 10 of the paean of Limenius. In perhaps as many as four, *mesē* is the primary pitch center (in section 1 of the paean of Athenaeus, probably in section 4 of the paean of Limenius, and perhaps also in sections 1 and 7 of the paean of Limenius). Other pitch centers are also standing notes of the *tonos* in which the melodies to which they belong are notated. The overall results for other standing notes are as follows (an asterisk indicating that a note is the primary or sole pitch center):

nētē diezeugmenōn:
 the paean of Athenaeus, sections 1, 3*, and probably 5
 the paean of Limenius: sections 2, 3*, 5*, 6*, and 8*?

paramesē:
 the paean of Athenaeus: section 2
 the paean of Limenius: section 1 and perhaps section 7

hypatē mesōn:
 the paean of Athenaeus: section 2*, perhaps section 7

The correlation of emphasized notes with standing notes suggests that in the Hellenistic era standing notes of the notation *tonos*, including *mesē*, tended to serve as orientation notes in the melody. However, a number of non-standing notes also appear to serve as pitch centers in the paeans.

The use of non-standing notes deserves additional examination. It stands to reason that in some melodies, emphasis on a non-standing note through frequency of occurrence may be simply a function of its use as a passing tone on the way to a standing note. But how often does this account for the emphasis? In the case of Θ (*tritē diezeugmenōn*) in section 1 of the paean of Athenaeus, some instances might be interpreted as passing tones, but there is also a clear use of the note to structure the melody – e.g., in the stretch from ὅς through the first two syllables of πετέρας in lines 4 and 5, where Θ is not only frequent but is emphasized through successive repetition and in one instance through duration. The exharmonic O of section 2 is also a pitch center and not a passing tone. By contrast, the frequency of *tritē hyperbolaiōn* and *paranētē diezeugmenōn* in section 3 is reasonably interpreted as a result of their use as passing tones on the way to *nētē diezeugmenōn*, the dominant note.

---

[50] The remains of the other pre-Roman-era scores are too fragmentary to admit analysis for pitch emphases.

Likewise, in the case of *paranētē diezeugmenōn* in section 3, this non-standing note appears always to be part of a stepwise movement leading back to *nētē diezeugmenōn*. In the paean of Limenius, section 1, however, nothing about the use of *tritē diezeugmenōn* suggests that it is a passing tone. It is difficult to interpret the use of *paranētē diezeugmenōn* in section 5, but it seems to have some role as a tonal center. *Tritē hyperbolaiōn* in section 8 functions as a tonal center, not a passing tone. *Parhypatē mesōn* in section 10 sometimes leads to *mesē* (the most emphatic tone of the melody) but not always. And the melody ends on *parhypatē mesōn*.

To summarize the preceding analysis, non-standing notes serve as pitch centers in the following sections of the Delphic paeans:

the paean of Athenaeus: *tritē diezeugmenōn* in section 1, an exharmonic note (O) in section 2

the paean of Limenius: *tritē diezeugmenōn* in section 1, perhaps *paranētē diezeugmenōn* in section 5, perhaps the F at the end of section 7, *tritē hyperbolaiōn* in section 8, probably *parhypatē mesōn* in section 10

Significantly, in none of the sections of the Delphic paeans does a non-standing note serve as the sole pitch center of a melody. This suggests that the standing notes emphasized in the melodies are the governing orientation points. Pitch centers other than standing notes get their melodic meaning from the standing notes, evidently by insinuating a shift away from the primary tonal axis.

Seven melodies from the Roman era are analyzable for melodic emphasis: the Seikilos inscription, the hymn to the Muse, three melodies attributed to Mesomedes, the Berlin paean (P.Ber. 6870 + 14097 [1–12]), and the Christian hymn (P.Oxy. 1786).[51] In a number of these, no correlation is found between the standing notes of the notation *tonos* and the notes emphasized by the melody. It appears that in Roman times, a notation *tonos* was often chosen for purposes having to do solely with range of the voice or perhaps even as a matter of habit or fondness for particular *tonoi*. The theory that the Roman-era melodies can be interpreted by applying the category of the octave species is not supported by the evidence. It seems to work with the Seikilos inscription, which uses an eight-note scale corresponding to the Phrygian octave species, emphasizes the fourth and eighth degrees of that scale, and ends on the first degree. This melody, however, is notated a fourth below the Phrygian octave species as given by Ptolemy.[52] Moreover, not all the Roman-era melodies exhibit eight-note scales. The Berlin paean, for example, uses nine

---

[51] One of the Oslo fragments might be included (P.Oslo 1413a lines 1–15 + b–f). It appears that C is its primary pitch center, at least in the last half of the song, but too many long stretches of the composition are missing to permit an overall analysis.

[52] This point is made by Hagel (2009, 311) against the assumption that the tune is to be analyzed as based on the Phrygian octave species.

notes. Hence, analyzing it for its octave species offers the possibility of Lydian or Phrygian, depending on which note we take as the starting note. And in the case of P.Oxy. 1786, which exhibits an eight-note scale, the Hypolydian is the prima facie possibility, but some interpreters suggest that its first note is unimportant and that therefore its second lowest note should be treated as the first note of its operative octave species (in which case the top note of the species does not appear). This alternative interpretation lets one assimilate the notes of the melody to the Hypophrygian octave species.[53]

The tonal significance of the concept of an octave species depends on how we understand its structure. If we treat the fourth step of the octave species as a structurally significant note (whether or not we call this note "thetic *mesē*"), this provides one way of interpreting melodies in terms of the octave species. The results of analysis based on this approach are as follows:

the invocation of the Muse: does not emphasize the fourth note of the octave species that best fits it, Dorian. The Dorian octave species also does not explain the melody's use of the note N. The note receiving greatest emphasis is *mesē* of the *tonos* (Lydian).

the invocation of Calliope and Apollo: emphasizes the fourth note of its octave species, if that octave species is interpreted as Mixolydian (using the lowest note of the song's nine-note scale as the start of the octave species). But this leaves one note unaccounted for – the anomalous N.

the hymn to the Sun: does not emphasize the fourth note of the octave species, Lydian, that conforms to its scale.

the hymn to Nemesis: if the octave species is construed as Hypophrygian (taking the second-lowest note as the first note of the scale), the fourth note is the most emphatic; but this interpretation does not explain the lowest note, R, whose presence makes for a nine-note scale.

the Berlin paean (P.Ber. 6870 + 14097 [1–12]): if the octave species is interpreted as Phrygian (taking the second-lowest note as the first note of the scale), then the note receiving the greatest emphasis is the fourth note of the species. If the first note is taken as the starting point, the octave species is Lydian and the fourth note is not emphasized.

P.Oxy. 1786: if the octave species is interpreted as Hypophrygian (taking the second-lowest note as the first note of the scale), then the fourth note of the piece is one of three most emphasized (all receiving about equal emphasis). But if one treats the eight-note scale of the piece as its octave species, then it is Hypolydian and the fourth note is not emphasized.

In view of this evidence, it seems doubtful that the concept of the "octave species" provides the key to the tonality of Roman-era melodies.

Another way to analyze the melodies is to consider intervallic relations between the most important notes (judged by frequency, duration, and placement). We can refer to the lowest of these notes as 1 (whatever scale step it happens to be) and describe the relations from that point. We can use the note names for the white keys of the piano as a standard frame of reference for de-

---

[53] See Mountford (1929, 176–78); Winnington-Ingram (1968, 44 and 45).

Appendix: Pitch Centers and Tonal Structure in Ancient Greek Melodies 173

fining the place of the notes of the intervallic nexus in the intervallic sequence of the scale on which the melody is based. Using this method of analysis, we discover the following intervallic relations of pitch centers (parentheses indicating secondary emphasis):

1–4–5 Two melodies display this pitch-center nexus.

In the Berlin paean, the chief notes are C, I, and Z, which define relations of a fourth (C and I) and a fifth (C and Z) within a nine-note scale. The nexus C– I –Z corresponds to *d–g–a* in a white-key scale from *c* to *d* '.

In P.Oxy. 1786 the notes receiving the greatest emphasis are Φ, Ƶ, and I, which also define relations of a fourth (Φ and Ƶ) and a fifth (Φ and I) within an eight-note scale. The nexus Φ–Ƶ–I corresponds to *g–c–d* in a white-key scale running from *f* to *f* '.

1–3–5 In the hymn to the Sun, the most emphasized note is M, which the melody accentuates in the middle. The melody emphasizes C at the beginning and end. The movement through pitch centers includes emphasis on triadic relations, and the overall tonal nexus appears to be 1–3–5, C–M–Z, which corresponds to *e–g–b* in a white-key scale from *c* to *c* '.

1–4–8 In the Seikilos inscription, the notes most emphasized are C and Z, which stand a fifth apart. The final, ꓶ, is not emphasized but, significantly, is a fourth below C. The note ꓶ is also entailed as a pitch center through octave equivalency with Z. Hence, one can interpret the Seikilos melody as implying a tonality of a conjunct fourth and fifth (ꓶ to C and C to Z). Looked at in this way, its basic intervallic nexus is 1–4–8 within an eight-note scale. This ꓶ–C–Z nexus corresponds to *d–g–d* ' in a white-key scale from *d* to *d* '.

1–5 In the invocation of the Muse, greatest accentuation is given to Z; the melody begins and ends on C, a fifth below Z, and is based on an eight-note scale that spans a seventh and contains an anomalous note (N). The nexus C–Z corresponds to *g–d* in a white-key scale from *d* to *c*, in which step 5 is the exharmonic note *g#* (N).

1–(3) In the invocation of Calliope and Apollo, one tone, C, the fourth step of the tune's ten-note scale, predominates (with exharmonic note N as scale-step 7). A secondary emphasis falls on M, a third above C. The nexus C–(M) corresponds to *e–(g)* in a white-key scale from *b* to *c* ' with exharmonic note *g#*.

1–(2) The hymn to Nemesis is structured in terms of various fourths and fifths with M (fifth degree of the nine-note scale) as the recurring and dominant pitch center of the tune as a whole. The note I (a step above M) also receives significant emphasis but is not nearly as central as M. The nexus M–(I) corresponds to *g–(a)* in a white-key scale from *c* to *d* '. If we include two other notes (U and Φ), which can be treated as secondary foci if we take them together in view of their octave equivalency, we can interpret the pitch-center nexus as (1)–4–(5)–(8) (with M now as 4).

Melodic Movement Through Pitch Centers

In some melodies there is a movement from an opening pitch focus (or pitch foci) to one or more other pitch foci, usually with a return to the opening pitch focus:

paean of Athenaeus, section 1: M → (M) / U / Θ → M. The pitch foci in the middle include standing notes M (*mesē*) and U (*nētē diezeugmenōn*), and non-standing note Θ (*tritē diezeugmenōn*).

perhaps paean of Limenius, section 1: < / ⊏ → ⊔ → < / ⊏. This is very tentative given the fragmentary nature of the remains. < and ⊏ are *mesē* and *paramesē*; ⊔ is *tritē diezeugmenōn*.

Seikilos epitaph: Z → Z / C → C

invocation of Calliope and Apollo: C → M → C

hymn to the Sun: C → M / Z / C → M / Z → C

In some melodies either a single note or a group (pair or trio) of notes remains the focus throughout:

paean of Limenius, section 3: focus throughout on ⊏ and < (= *nētē diezeugmenōn* and *paranētē diezeugmenōn*).

the hymn to Nemesis: M (*mesē*) is the pitch focus throughout. The hymn exhibits alternating shifts away from and back to M.

P.Oxy. 1786. Pitch emphases fall on Φ, Ƶ, and I throughout.

In some melodies the poor state of preservation permits identification of a primary emphasis or several emphases but precludes any judgment about whether there are shifts to other note emphases: paean of Athenaeus, section 3 (greatest emphasis is on U, the standing note *nētē diezeugmenōn*); paean of Limenius, section 4 (primary emphasis is on C, *mesē*); paean of Limenius, section 6 (greatest emphasis is on ⊏, the standing note *nētē diezeugmenōn*); paean of Limenius, section 10 (the most emphatic notes are <, *mesē*, and ∪, the non-standing note *parhypatē mesōn*); P.Ber. 6870 + 14097 (1–12) (pitch emphases are on I, Z, and C).

In section 2 of the paean of Athenaeus, the melody establishes an emphasis on standing notes, later begins to emphasize a tonally exharmonic note, and ends by emphasizing a standing note along with the exharmonic note, with the latter as final: Γ / U → M / O = *mesē* / *paramesē* → *hypatē mesōn* / exharmonic note. The note O stands outside the notation *tonos*. The emphasis on it creates tonal ambiguity at the end of the section.

Finals

Classical and Hellenistic Eras

No surviving composition from the pre-Roman eras preserves its ultimate final, but finals are intact for two internal melodies of a fourth-century Medea tragedy (P.Louvre E 10534) and for several internal sections of the second-century Delphic paeans:

mesē as final in the two melodies of P.Louvre E 10534

hypatē or *hypatē mesōn* as finals for section 1 of the paean of Athenaeus and sections 5 and 6 of the paean of Limenius

nētē diezeugmenōn as finals for sections 2 and 3 of the paean of Limenius

exharmonic note O as final for section 2 of the paean of Athenaeus

the non-standing note F in the Lydian *tonos* (which is the standing note *mesē* if there is a modulation into Hypophrygian) as final for section 7 of the paean of Limenius[54]

The final for each of the melodies of P.Louvre E 10534 is a frame note (*mesē*) of its apparent *tonos* (Ionian / Iastian).[55] With one or two exceptions, the internal finals of the Delphic paeans are frame notes of the *tonoi* in which their melodies are notated. The internal finals *hypatē* and *nētē diezeugmenōn* stand an octave apart and thus share octave equivalency. It is difficult to know whether *nētē diezeugmenōn*, when used as a section final, created an expectation in listeners that the composition was likely to continue. As we will see below, the evidence from the Roman-era melodies suggests that an orientation note belonging to the upper range of a melody's note compass was probably heard as non-conclusive. If this was also true in the Hellenistic era, *nētē diezeugmenōn* at section close would have implied more to come. This interpretation supports Chailley's description of the final of the second section of the paean of Limenius as "suspensive."[56] Along with *hypatē*, presumably *mesē* had a conclusive sense when used as a final, and it may have been so used at one or more section ends for which notation is lacking. One would guess that each internal section except for the very last could end on a restful *or* a forward-implying note. Unfortunately, we do not have the ultimate final for either paean.

Roman Era

Finals are preserved for at least seven compositions from the Roman period: the Seikilos epitaph, the invocation of the Muse, the invocation of Calliope and Apollo, the hymn to the Sun, P.Oslo 1413a lines 1–15 + b–f, the Berlin paean (P.Berlin 6870 + 14097 [1–12]), and the Christian hymn (P.Oxy. 1786). If we treat the first part of the hymn to Nemesis as a separate composition, we have eight pieces with extant finals. Seven of these melodies are analyzable for pitch-center nexus. The relationship of finals to the pitch centers of these songs is as follows:

---

[54] In the Lydian *tonos* the final F is *lichanos hypatōn* (sometimes referred to as *hyperhypatē*, the string "above *hypatē*," which in terms of pitch is a tone lower than *hypatē*). According to Chailley (1979, 165) and Bélis (1992, 117–18), the melody modulates from Lydian into Hypophrygian and continues in that *tonos* to the end, in which case section 7 closes on *mesē*.

[55] See Bélis (2004, 1318–19).

[56] Chailley (1979, 160); see also Bélis (1992, 97).

the 1–4–5 pitch-center nexus of the Berlin paean and P.Oxy. 1786: in both cases the final is on 1 of the nexus.

the 1–3–5 pitch-center nexus of the hymn to the Sun: the final is on 1 of the nexus.

the 1–4–8 pitch-center nexus of the Seikilos inscription: the final is on 1 of the nexus.

the 1–5 pitch-center nexus of the invocation of the Muse: the final is on 1 of the nexus.

the 1–(3) pitch-center nexus of invocation of Calliope and Apollo: the final is on 1 of the nexus.

the 1–(2) pitch-center nexus of the hymn to Nemesis: the final (of the first part, excepting what may be a coda) is on 1 of this nexus. An alternate interpretation is (1)–4–(5)–(8), with 4 as final.

In each case except the alternative interpretation of the hymn to Nemesis, the final is the lowest note of the pitch-center nexus.

The Aristotelian *Problems* may shed light on composition finals. Seeking to explain why descending melodies are more harmonious than ascending ones, the author of the *Problems* suggests that it is perhaps because low notes sound more noble and euphonous after high ones (Ps.-Aristotle, *Phys. probl.* 19.33). Among the features widely shared by the world's many musical dialects, Nettl includes the tendency to descend at the close of a musical statement.[57] Apparently, in many musical cultures this has been felt to have a conclusive quality. When it comes to ancient Greek music, the evidence of the scores suggests that what qualifies a note as a suitable composition final is both relative position in the range of a melody's compass (on the lower rather than the higher side) and identity as part of the nexus of a melody's pitch centers. A note that is low but does not belong to the melody's pitch-center nexus is not a suitable final. It seems a reasonable inference that an ancient Greek would have heard such a note as unstable, implying continuation rather than conclusion.

Starting Notes

Classical and Hellenistic Eras

The starting notes for the two melodies of P.Louvre E 10534 are not intact, but we do have starting notes for seven sections of the Delphic paeans. In each case, despite some ambiguities, the starting note is a standing note of the *tonos*:

the paean of Athenaeus, section 3: *hypatē*

the paean of Limenius
    sections 2 and 4: *mesē*
    section 3: *nētē diezeugmenōn*
    section 6: *hypatē*
    section 7: *mesē*, *hypatē mesōn*, or *paramesē* (the *tonos* being ambiguous)
    section 8: *nētē diezeugmenōn* or more likely *hypatē*

---

[57] Nettl (1983, 39–40).

Roman Era

Starting notes are intact for nine melodies of the Roman era:

the Seikilos inscription: starts on 4 of its 1–4–8 tonal nexus.
the hymn to the Muse: starts (and ends) on 1 of the 1–5 tonal nexus of the melody.
the invocation of Calliope and Apollo: starts (and ends) on 1 of its 1(–3) pitch-center nexus.
the hymn to the Sun: starts (and ends) on 1 of its 1–3–5 pitch-center nexus.
the hymn to Nemesis: starts on 2 of its 1(–2) pitch-center nexus.
the Berlin paean (P.Berlin 6870 + 14097 [1–12]): starts a step below 1 of its 1–4–5 pitch-center nexus (the first note apparently serving as a "pick-up" note, since the melody then moves directly to 1).
P.Oslo 1413a lines 15–19 + g–m: starting note intact but poor preservation of the tune frustrates interpretation.
P.Ber. 6870 (13–15): starting note is emphasized in the first melodic phrase and serves as the final of the first cadence. Too little of the melody is preserved to make its melodic emphases clear. At most there is a strong impression that the starting note is a pitch center.
P.Ber. 6870 [20–22]): poor preservation makes it unclear what role the starting note plays in the piece as a whole.

The evidence of starting notes suggests a tendency to begin on a note that the piece will go on to emphasize or on a note that leads immediately to an emphasized note.

Temporal Priority and Finality

What comes first influences how we hear what follows, and in music governed by pitch centers the ear naturally seeks to orient itself to a tone (or set of tones). This consideration supports Butler's observation that "any tone will suffice as a perceptual anchor – or tonal center – until a better candidate defeats it."[58] Butler's remark rightly highlights the temporal unfolding of a melody as a crucial factor in establishing tonal orientation, although he seems to make the unwarranted assumption that a melody must orient itself to only one pitch center at a time. In fact, while some ancient Greek melodies display sequential movement from one pitch center to another, in others a number of notes receive emphasis together. In other words, a melody can stress notes of a pitch-center nexus in stages or together in combinations. The listener listens for orientation points right from the start. In this way the beginning has a special power to shape how the tonality of the piece is heard.

In the case of Greek vocal melodies, before the first notes of the song were heard, there was usually an instrumental introduction. No doubt one function of this introduction was to make the tonal organization of the melody appar-

---

[58] Butler (1989, 238).

ent. Hence, in the case of the first section of the paean of Limenius, the instrumental introduction likely prepared the listener to interpret Ц, which the melody emphasizes at the beginning of the singing, as a note from which the melody must inevitably move away (it happens to be a non-standing note).[59] In the same way, tonally and rhythmically, an instrumental introduction could have helped the listener interpret Φ as a pick-up note leading to a pitch center in the opening of P.Ber. 6870 + 14097 (1–12).

Opening notes forming consonant intervals – fourths, fifths, and octaves – probably gave a strong orienting signal. For example, the invocation of the Muse and the Seikilos epitaph each begin with a rising fifth, and both notes turn out to be important in the melody as it unfolds. Section 8 of the paean of Limenius begins with an octave leap up to its most emphasized note: Γ ⊏. This leap (as well as the alternative possibility ⊏ ⊏) orients the ear to ⊏.

Sometimes there is a significant correlation between the opening note or interval and the final or closing interval. For example, the invocation of the Muse, the invocation of Calliope and Apollo, and the hymn to the Sun begin and end on the same note. The beginning and ending notes of section 6 of the paean of Limenius stand an octave apart. The opening fifth (C to Z) and the closing outline of a fourth (C to X to ⌐) of the epitaph of Seikilos mirror each other, suggesting the structural pitch-relation 1–4–8.

Temporal finality plays a different role than temporal priority. How we hear what comes last is influenced by what precedes. Nevertheless, finals impart information about tonal structure. A final is a note on which a melody can come to rest. In some kinds of music (aleatory, for example), any note can be a final, but ancient Greek music appears to be more regulated when it comes to finals. With one exception, the finals of the melodies of the Delphic paeans are all standing notes of the notation *tonos*, notes the melody has also emphasized. The exception is an exharmonic note at the close of section 2 of the paean of Athenaeus, a note previously emphasized in the melody but lying outside the notation *tonos*. The preserved finals of the Delphic paeans belong to internal sections; we do not have the ultimate finals of these compositions. With one exception, the finals of Roman-era melodies whose degree of preservation admits tonal analysis are notes emphasized in the melody. The exception is the final of the Seikilos inscription. That final has been interpreted as having importance thanks to an implicit tetrachordal structure of the scale on which the melody is based, one interpretation being that the melody is founded on two disjunct tetrachords forming the Phrygian octave species. Whether or not it is correct to analyze the Seikilos melody using the concept of the Phrygian

---

[59] The first note of the song is missing but was probably a standing note, which would also have provided an orientation. On the idea that a non-standing note is a note from which the melody must inevitably move away, even if the non-standing note serves as a pitch center, see the discussion of finals above.

octave species, the status of the final as 1 of a 1–4–8 pitch-center nexus and the fact that it is an octave equivalent of 8 strongly suggest that a tonal relation between the final and these other notes made it a suitable ending note. Taking the extant finals as a whole provides a basis for concluding that a composer tended to choose as final one of the lower pitch centers of the melody or a lower octave of one of them.

Cadences

Ancient theorists do not speak of cadences, but it has become common to use this term for places in Greek music where the melody comes to momentary or final closure as a matter of melodic and / or textual phrasing. Cadences can be suggested by one or more of the following: a musical pattern (e.g., a rising and falling pattern such as we see at certain points in the Delphic paeans), a feature of the notation (e.g., a note-length symbol indicating something like a fermata), the organization of the rhythm / meter, and the syntax of the lyrics.

Given what we have seen of finals, internal cadences ending on a note that would also qualify as a composition final (sole pitch center or lowest note of the governing pitch-center nexus) must have been heard as restful. Cadences ending on other notes, perhaps even on pitch centers above the middle range of the scalar ambit, would have implied continuation and may be described as suspensive. Presumably, a cadence finishing on an upper note of a melody's pitch-center nexus was felt as less suspensive than one finishing on a note lying *outside* the pitch-center nexus.

In some pieces, restful internal cadences are combined with suspensive cadences. For example, the invocation of the Muse displays four lines, each a metrical unit. The end-note of each of the first three lines is stressed by its position and by successive repetition, and the last note of the fourth line has its own special emphasis as the final of the tune. In terms of the 1–5 pitch-center nexus of the piece, these end-notes are 1 → 3 → 4 → 1; that is, the first line ends on the melody's lower pitch center (restful), the two internal lines conclude on non-pitch-centers (suspensive), and the last line ends on the tune's lower pitch center (restful) as composition final. The three main cadences in section 2 of the paean of Athenaeus also show a combination of restful and suspensive cadences. The vocal text contains a long sentence and two shorter ones. The musical patterns at the ends of these sentences are similar rising and falling musical phrases, reinforcing their cadential quality. The end-notes of these cadences are an exharmonic note (O), *hypatē* (M), and the exharmonic note again to close the section. The middle cadence is restful, the first and third suspensive; and the final of the third section also creates tonal ambiguity, strengthening the sense that the composition must continue.

Conclusions

From the preceding analysis of the scores, the following conclusions may be distilled:

1. Ancient Greek melodies establish certain notes as orientation tones, which may be termed their pitch centers. A given melody may have one or more pitch centers.

2. In the Hellenistic era as represented by the Delphic paeans, most but not all pitch centers are standing notes of the *tonos*. Moreover, no non-standing note ever serves as the sole pitch center of a melody of the Delphic paeans. This suggests that the standing notes emphasized in a melody are the governing orientation points. Pitch centers other than standing notes get their melodic meaning from the standing notes, presumably by insinuating a shift away from the primary tonal axis.

3. In the Roman era, pitch centers are standing notes of the *tonos* in some pieces; in other pieces they are not. Even in the few cases where pitch centers are standing notes of the *tonos*, the tetrachordal structure associated with standing notes is not evident. Similarly, the effort to apply the concept of the octave species, understood as a set of disjunct tetrachords, to the Roman-era melodies does not yield uniformly satisfactory results. Using the numeral 1 for the lowest note of a pitch-center nexus, we can describe the forms of pitch-center organizations in the analyzable compositions as 1–4–5 (in the Berlin paean and P.Oxy. 1786), 1–3–5 (in Mesomedes' hymn to the Sun), 1–4–8 (in the Seikilos inscription), 1–5 (in the invocation of the Muse), 1–(3) (in the invocation of Calliope and Apollo), and 1– (2) or perhaps (1)–4–(5)–(8) (in Mesomedes' hymn to Nemesis). We may reasonably assume and certainly cannot rule out that some ancient Greek melodies were oriented to a single pitch center; two of the extant compositions (invocation of Calliope and Apollo and the hymn to Nemesis) may be interpreted as examples of this.

4. In many but not all melodies, one pitch is emphasized at the beginning and at the end. It seems appropriate to term this note the primary pitch center, whether it is the sole pitch center or one of several pitch centers.

5. At least in the Roman era, the Greek ear was accustomed to hearing a composition end on its sole pitch center or on the lowest note of its pitch-center nexus.

6. Cadences (suggested through musical patterns, notation, or the syntax of the lyrics) may be restful or suspensive. A restful cadence concludes on a note that does not imply a continuation. A suspensive cadence expresses a temporary pause, implying more to come. Candidates for restful cadences are the pitch centers of the melody, but not all pitch centers are restful. In Hellenistic-era melodies, at least as evidenced by the Delphic paeans, non-standing notes sometimes serve as pitch centers but are not restful. Where a

melody has a single pitch center, that note is the natural choice for its final. Where a melody has more than one pitch center operating in the context where the cadence is found, the most restful note is the lowest of these pitch centers. Evidently, restfulness is a function of two factors – the quality of being a pitch center and a pitch center's height relative to the compass of the melody. Lower notes, provided they are pitch centers, carry a greater weight of repose than higher notes. Cadences that end on notes that are not pitch centers are suspensive. At the end of certain internal sections of the Delphic paeans we find standing notes from the upper register of the melody serving as finals. It is not clear whether a cadence that ends on a high pitch center is suspensive or restful. It is perhaps simply a matter of degree on a continuum.

Tonal Analysis of Individual Scores

Much of the information in the preceding discussions derives from the following analyses, which apply the three basic criteria of melodic accentuation to extant ancient Greek melodies as a means of identifying their pitch centers. Account is also taken of the way in which tones made memorable in these ways are used to structure the melody.

In the analyses of individual scores, frequency counts (F), duration values (D), and successive repetition (R) for a given note are indicated together, separated by slashes. For example, if a note occurs 28 times, the sum of its duration values is 35, and it is repeated 4 times in a row at one point and 3 times at another point, we can represent this as F28/D35/R4,3. References to manuscript lines and musical "bars" follow the transcriptions in Pöhlmann and West (2001) (= *DAGM*). In cases where I refer to analyses by modern scholars who use modern note names from their transcriptions of the Greek scores, I have translated these names back into their original Greek notation symbols.

Paean of Athenaeus remains of 5 sections: Delphi inv. 517, 526, 494, 499

DAGM #20 (second century B.C.E.)

Section 1 (lines 1–8). Noted in the Phrygian *tonos*, the section's most prominent note is M (F28/D35), which is *mesē* in that *tonos*. Emphasis values for this note distribute as follows: F13/D19 in bars 1–11, F6/D6 in bars 12 to 24 (where the melody moves away from an emphasis on *mesē* as it explores the lower and higher regions of the pitch palette), F9/D10/R5,3 in bars 25 to 28 (the end) (where successive repetition helps re-establish the emphasis on M). In the middle part of the melody, U (*nētē diezeugmenōn*) is a prominent note (F9/D14); it is also a standing note. Another prominent note in the middle part is Θ (F11/D12 in bars 12–24), which is a non-standing note, *tritē diezeugmenōn*. Octave equivalency reinforces the focus on U and Θ in the middle part through the notes Φ and F.[60] Section 1 ends a fourth below *mesē* on an emphatic Φ (*hypatē mesōn*), sounded three times. A rough mapping of shifts in pitch emphasis is as follows: M → (M) / U / Θ → M = *mesē* → (*mesē*) / *nētē diezeug.* / *tritē diezeug.* → *mesē*. In this representation, the enclosing of *mesē* in parenthesis for the middle section indicates that it is not emphasized but does continue to appear after being emphasized at the beginning of the melody.

Section 2 (lines 9–16, except for last two notes of 16). The predominant *tonos* is Hyperphrygian chromatic. But in the middle of line 13 there is a modulation briefly into Phrygian diatonic, or at least a use of notes that briefly echo the Phrygian *tonos* of section 1.[61] The Hyperphrygian scale segments in which the piece mostly moves are the pair of disjunctive tetrachords from *hypatē mesōn* to *nētē diezeugmenōn*, with the top two notes unused by the melody; the chromatic K appears in the lower tetrachord: M ∧ K Γ and U ⋔ [followed by unused notes of the upper tetrachord].

The vocal text of the section contains a long sentence and two shorter ones. The melody tends to move a bit more in the upper range of its scale for the first sentence, a bit more in the lower for the two shorter ones. Hence, without meaning to suggest any sharp division, I will refer to the A and B parts of the melody.

The note receiving the greatest emphasis is M (F23/D30), which is *hypatē mesōn* in the Hyperphrygian *tonos*. This note is distributed throughout the B part of the melody. The first extant note of the melody is Γ (the opening notes are missing), which is *mesē* in the Hyperphrygian *tonos*. The tune recurs to this note throughout the section (F15/D21), but its concentration is greatest in the A part of the melody (F12/D17). Another note receives almost as much emphasis as Γ in the A part, namely, U (F11/D14), which is *paramesē*, the lower standing note of the disjunct tetrachord above *mesē* in the Hyperphrygian. This note occurs only in the A part and mostly in the first part of A.

In the B part of the melody, there is a prominent use of O (F9/D13), a note lying a half tone below M and outside the notation key. This emphasis on O

---

[60] West regards M as a "tonic" and U as a "dominant" (West [1992b, 289]). Winnington-Ingram also sees M (*mesē*) as the "tonic" and U (*nētē diezeugmenōn*) as a note receiving special emphasis (Winnington-Ingram [1968, 34]). Similarly, Thomson concludes that M and U ('b' and 'f#' in the transcription of Reinach on which he relies) are tonal centers (Thomson [1999, 198]).

[61] At the beginning of line 11, which is part of an emphatically Hyperphrygian chromatic stretch, there is a note (I) from the Phrygian *tonos*, but it would be misleading to speak of a modulation here. It is simply an echo of the *tonos* of section 1. Later, in line 13, the use of I and Θ in a few bars suggests a brief modulation into (or a stronger echo of) the Phrygian.

already begins at the end of the A part with a melodic arc that rises from O and falls back to O on the word ἀνακίδναται at the end of line 13. In the B part of the melody O is stressed almost as much as M (*hypatē*) (F11/D15), and the section closes with a dual focus on M and O. The last bit of melody is a melodic arc on the final word (ἀναμέλπεται), which runs from O up to Λ and back down to O, using M as a passing tone. The pattern is similar to the one for ἀνακίδναται. Overall, one gets the impression that ἀνακίδναται signals a shift of tonal focus to O, the pitch center for the melody through the close of the section. The scales of the Phrygian family of *tonoi* do not contain O, which is found only in the Aeolian and Ionian *tonoi*. But the O cannot be explained on the theory of a modulation into one of these *tonos* families because neither contains the notation symbols found in lines 14–16: Υ O M Λ K Γ. Other interpreters have explained the O as a product of the composer's delight in chromaticism: moving by half tones in the sequence O M Λ K.[62] Winnington-Ingram observes that O is used in section 2 not merely as a passing tone ("a leading note to Hypatē") but like a standing note.[63] The chromatic play with O found earlier in the section becomes a vehicle for creating a new tonal sense at the end. While three semi-tones in a row do not establish a new *tonos*, the orientation to O as a pitch emphasis in the last two lines suggests some kind of tonal change, perhaps a deliberate tonal ambiguity that heightens the hearer's desire for continuation. We can represent the pitch center shifts as follows: Γ / U → M / O, which is *mesē / paramesē → hypatē /* exharmonic note.

Section 3 (last two notes of line 16–line through line 24, missing notation at the end).[64] This section is in Phrygian diatonic with modulation of genus into the chromatic. The section begins with an octave leap from Φ to U, which takes the melody into the range in which it mostly travels. Greatest emphasis in the section is given to U (F21/D28), the standing note *nētē diezeugmenōn* in the Phrygian *tonos*. After U the most frequent notes are ⋔ (F14/D19) and Γ (F17/D23), which are non-standing notes above and below U (*tritē hyperbolaiōn* and *paranētē diezeugmenōn*). The frequency of these two notes apparently owes to their use in stepwise approaches to U in a melody that moves more often stepwise than not. The section is too fragmentary to make any certain judgments about whether it ever shifts away from a predominant pitch focus on U. The equivalent of three "bars" of notation is missing at the

---

[62] Winnington-Ingram (1968, 34–35); Bélis (1992, 67); Landels (1999, 230); Pöhlmann and West (2001, 73); Hagel (2009, 288).
[63] Winnington-Ingram (1968, 35). As he puts it, the note O "has importance in its own right and receives the final (and one other) cadence."
[64] Bélis (1992, 71, 75) takes the last two notes of line 16 through line 26 as section 3 ("Strophe III"). Her counts are therefore different from those given below but are nonetheless proportional to mine.

end. But the general impression from what we have is that U is the sole pitch center.

Section 4 (lines 25 through the beginning of 27). The *tonos* appears to be Phrygian chromatic. The first note is missing, after which an opening pattern moves up from a repeated U (*nētē diezeugmenōn*) stepwise through the chromatic pyknon and then back down to U, which is again emphasized, this time through note lengthening (*tonē*). Otherwise, too much is missing to admit analysis for pitch emphases. The closing bars are entirely lost.

Section 5 (most of line 27 through line 33). The *tonos* appears to be Phrygian. The opening note and the last several bars are missing, along with other notes. The fragmentary character of the melody precludes analysis for pitch emphases, although there is a prominence of *nētē diezeugmenōn* in lines 27 and 28.

Paean of Limenius remains of 10 sections: Delphi inv. 489, 1461, 1591, 209, 212, 226, 225, 224, 215, 214

DAGM #21 (second century B.C.E.)

Section 1 (lines 1–7). The *tonos* is Lydian. The first and last notes are missing. Three notes appear with nearly equal frequency: ⊏ (F19/D27), which is *paramesē* in the *tonos*; Ц (F18/D28), which is *tritē diezeugmenōn*, a nonstanding note; and < (F18/D22), which is *mesē*. No other notes in the piece are nearly as frequent. *Mesē*, although not the most emphasized note, occurs with even distribution throughout the piece. The last note is missing. *Hypatē mesōn* is sounded three times for the first three syllables of the final four-syllable word. The movement of pitch emphases is perhaps as follows: < / ⊏ → Ц → < / ⊏, which is *mesē / paramesē* → *tritē diezeugmenōn* → *mesē / paramesē*. This schematization is very tentative, given the fragmentary preservation.

Section 2 (lines 8–12). The *tonos* for this section is Hypolydian. The most emphasized notes are < Ц and ⊏, in that order. However, nearly a third of the section is missing, making it impossible to judge which note was most prominent. The section ends on ⊏, which is *nētē diezeugmenōn* in the *tonos*.

Section 3 (lines 13–14). This section, like section 2, is in the Hypolydian *tonos*. Note emphases are as follows: ⊏ (F10/D14 reinforced by octave equivalency through a repeated Γ) and < (F8/D12). Section 3 emphasizes ⊏ throughout, which is *nētē diezeugmenōn* in the Hypolydian *tonos*. The melody starts and ends with this note and regularly returns to it. It also recurs to < (*paranētē diezeugmenōn*, a non-standing note). Nothing in the extant notation, which is mostly intact, suggests a movement away from the one to the other of these pitch centers.

Section 4 (lines 15 through most of 17). This section has many missing notes, especially at the end. The *tonos* is Lydian, and the melody moves through the conjunct chromatic. The opening note, C, which is *mesē*, is well distributed and most frequent.

Section 5 (end of line 17 through most of line 21). The opening bar is lost and there are quite a few missing notes; the ending is intact. The *tonos* is Hypolydian, and the diatonic melody uses the disjunct tetrachord. Chief note emphases are as follows: ⊏ = *nētē diezeugmenōn* (F14/D18), reinforced through octave equivalency by Γ = *hypatē* (F2/D4); < = *paranētē diezeugmenōn* (F13/D18); Ш = *tritē hyperbolaiōn* (F11/D15), reinforced by octave equivalency through L = *parhypatē* (F2/D3); and ⨆ = *tritē diezeugmenōn* (F9/D12). The section ends with an emphatic repetition of ⊏ (3 times) followed by a plunge to a final Γ (*hypatē*) an octave below. As the preceding shows, a standing note (*nētē diezeugmenōn*) receives the most accentuation but <, a non-standing note (*paranētē diezeugmenōn*), is not far behind. It is possible to interpret the frequency of < as a function of its use as a passing tone on the way to *nētē diezeugmenōn* (see in particular the note sequence for δεξάμενος ἀμβρόταν in line 18); but in at least one place the melody seems to focus on < (at the beginning of line 19). Nearly a quarter of the notes are missing, which could make a significant difference in the interpretation of note emphases and functions.

Section 6 (end of line 21 through middle of line 23). As in section 5, the *tonos* is Hypolydian; the melody is diatonic and uses the disjunct tetrachord. About a third of this short section is missing, but one note stands out by emphasis: ⊏, the standing tone *nētē diezeugmenōn* (F11/D14), which is reinforced by octave equivalency through Γ (*hypatē*) (F4/D6), the next most emphatic note, and also by successive repetition (R2, R3, R2).

Section 7 (middle of line 23 to the first notes of line 26). About a third of this section is missing, which may be one reason why its *tonos* is unclear. Efforts at interpretation focus on the following tetrachord: C ∪ ⊃ <. This tetrachord is conjunct Hypolydian, with C as *mesē*. It is also Lydian conjunct chromatic with C as *hypatē mesōn*. The note ⊏, which appears once, is part of the Hypolydian conjunct and the Lydian disjunct. In a brief comment, Pöhlmann and West interpret the section as moving in the chromatic Lydian.[65] The tetrachord C ∪ ⊃ < is also found in the Hypophrygian *tonos* (chromatic), where C is *paramesē*, the lower standing note of the disjunct tetrachord. Hence, Chailley and Bélis settle on Hypophrygian for the *tonos*.[66] Hagel sees a modulation into Hypophrygian, then back to Lydian with the emphatic double "Quintsprung" of C ⊏ C for πλεξάμενος in line 24.[67] In any case, despite ambiguity about the *tonos*, the note receiving the most emphasis,

---

[65] Pöhlmann and West (2001, 85).
[66] Chailley (1979, 165) and Bélis (1992, 117–18) interpret the *tonos* as Hypophrygian.
[67] Hagel (2000, 98).

186   *Appendix: Pitch Centers and Tonal Structure in Ancient Greek Melodies*

C, is a standing note: it is *mesē* (in Hypolydian), *hypatē mesōn* (in Lydian), *paramesē* (in Hypophrygian). The section begins on C but ends on F, which is not a standing note in the Lydian or Hypolydian *tonoi* but is one (*mesē*) in the Hypophrygian *tonos*.

Section 8 (*most of line 26 through line 30*). This heavily damaged section is in the Hypolydian *tonos*, diatonic and disjunct. A third of the section is missing, including the last three "bars." The opening is likely an octave leap from *hypatē* to *nētē diezeugmenōn* (Γ ⊏).[68] The two most emphasized notes are ⊏, the standing note *nētē diezeugmenōn* (F12/D17), which is reinforced by octave equivalency through Γ (F2/D4), and ⊔, a non-standing note, *tritē hyperbolaiōn* (F13/D17).

Section 9 (*lines 31–33*). Too little is preserved to support confident judgments about pitch emphases.

Section 10 (*lines 34 to 40*). This section is also in the Lydian *tonos*. The most emphatic notes are *mesē*, < (F19/D32), and the non-standing note *parhypatē mesōn*, ∪ (F14/D22).

The Seikilos Inscription

DAGM #23 (second century C.E.)

This short song is fully intact. Its notes form a scale that spans an octave (⊓ X Φ C O K I Z) and corresponds to the Phrygian octave species (T S T T T S T). The song is notated in the Ionian (Iastian) *tonos*.[69] The Phrygian octave species provides a better interpretive lens than the *tonos* for analyzing the hierarchical relations of notes.[70] If we use the *tonos* as a guide to identifying standing notes, then X is *hypatē mesōn*, O is *mesē*, and K is *paramesē*. But the melody does not emphasize these notes. The two notes receiving greatest accentuation in the melody are C (*lichanos mesōn*) and Z (*paranētē diezeugmenōn*), both non-standing notes in the *tonos*.[71] In the Phrygian octave species, however, C is so-called thetic *mesē* and Z is *nētē diezeugmenōn*, the outer frame note of the

---

[68] The stone reads ⊏ ⊏. This is interpreted as an error for Γ ⊏ by Reinach (1909–1913, 165) and Bélis (1992, 113). The reason for suspecting an error is that the Delphic paeans do not otherwise repeat note symbols for successive repetition, but let repetition be implied according to the syllables of the words.

[69] Winnington-Ingram (1968, 38); Mountford (1929, 170 [Ionian "key" and Phrygian "mode"]); Solomon (1986, 470); Landels (1999, 253). Mathiesen observes that the notes of the song correspond to what Ptolemy called the Phrygian *tonos*, which was his way of talking about octave species (1999, 150, 465). Hagel (2009, 311) doubts this interpretation, pointing out that the melody is notated a fourth below the Phrygian octave species as given by Ptolemy.

[70] See Solomon (1986, 461 with n14, 470); Landels (1999, 253).

[71] In a somewhat curious analysis, Chailley (1979, 167) suggests that the tune's chief tones – all non-standing notes in the Ionian *tonos* – can be interpreted as related to the standing tones of that *tonos* because they are adjacent to them.

upper, disjunct tetrachord. This correspondence between standing notes of the Phrygian octave species and the notes emphasized in the Seikilos melody appears to support the conclusion that the Phrygian octave species governs the tonal organization of the melody. But if we press this analysis, we discover that the tetrachordal intervals of *hypatē* to *mesē* and *paramesē* to *nētē diezeugmenōn* do not figure as structural elements. The only significant tetrachordal moment comes at the end with the drop from *mesē* to *hypatē*. Otherwise it is fifths and thirds that play the chief organizational roles.

In the unfolding of the melody, there is a gradual shift from more emphasis on Z at first to more emphasis on C at the end. Of these two notes, the greatest overall emphasis is given to C (F8/D11 for C; F6/D9 for Z). Leaving aside the question whether we should interpret the piece through the lens of an octave species to which abstract "thetic" scale-steps are assigned, we have an eight-tone scale with emphases on steps 4 (C) and 8 (Z). The movement through pitch emphases appears to be 8 (Z) → 8(Z)/4(C) → 4(C). The piece ends on 1 (⅂). Using West's way of analyzing for "mode," we should say that the melody is in the "G mode" because the scale-steps up from its tonal center (C) are T T S T and down from this center are T S T T.[72] We can refine this further by describing the tonality of the Seikilos melody as the pattern T S T T T S T oriented to the scale-steps 4 and 8 – and to scale step 1 as well if the final is accorded special structural significance. The fact that the final lies a fourth below its first pitch center and enjoys octave equivalency with the tune's second pitch center suggests that it is a restful note in this melody.[73]

Invocation of the Muse

DAGM #24 (second century C.E.)

Traditionally attributed to Mesomedes, this piece is notated in the Lydian *tonos* (diatonic, disjunct), with one anomalous note, N, that does not belong to the *tonos*. Reinach suggests that the composer imported it to serve as a leading tone to M. This interpretation has been generally accepted.[74] In that case the scale used by the song is Φ C P M N I Z E (in the *DAGM* transcription: *g a b♭ c c♯ d e f*). The tune starts and ends on C (F5/D7/R2), which is the standing note *hypatē mesōn* in the Lydian *tonos*. Greatest accentuation is given to Z (F7/D10/R2,3), which is the standing note *paramesē*. Hagel points out that if we analyze thetically, using the strings of the lyre as an interpretive

---

[72] So West (1992b, 301 with 186).
[73] Chailley claims that the piece is deliberately structured without tonal resolution, ending as it does on the note below *hypatē* in the Ionian *tonos*; and he analogizes this to unresolved appoggiaturas in Western classical music (Chailley [1979, 167]). I find this very doubtful.
[74] Reinach (1896, 18); Winnington-Ingram (1968, 41); Baud-Bovy (1984, 259–60).

framework (which is what Ptolemy means by "thetic"), these two notes are the strings *hypatē* and *paramesē*. They establish the basic tonality of the melody.[75] The same interval (the same notes as well, which means the same lyre tuning of this fifth) opens the Seikilos melody, although the scalar structure of that melody is different.

Like the Delphic paeans but unlike most other pieces of the Roman era, this song emphasizes standing notes of the *tonos* in which it is notated. The tune has been described as exhibiting a Dorian flavor[76] because the intervals down from *mesē* are T T S and the intervals up from *mesē* are T S.[77] That said, it does not appear that the melody is organized tetrachordally. Line 1 consists of a rising opening fifth, followed by a plunging sixth, then a rising second that brings the phrase back to its opening note. Line 2 suffers from missing notation. It ends with a fourth composed of *lichanos hypatōn* to *lichanos mesōn*. Line 3 proceeds from *paramesē* to *mesē* by way of a rise and a descent to the exharmonic N. The closing line is melismatic and can be epitomized as a third from *lichanos mesōn* to *paramesē*, followed by a movement down to *mesē* but through N, then a plunge of a fifth to *lichanos hypatōn*, followed by an ascending scale to *lichanos mesōn* (which marks out a fourth but not a fourth composed of frame notes), then a drop of a fourth back down to *lichanos hypatōn*, the latter note leading to the final, *hypatē mesōn*. Hence, the two intervals of a fourth (one with an intervening note) are built from *lichanos hypatōn* and *lichanos mesōn*, both non-standing notes, and in each case prepare for a return to *hypatē mesōn*. This suggests that although the most memorable tones of the piece are standing notes of the Lydian *tonos*, the melody is not organized on the basis of the tetrachordal structure of the *tonos*.

Using numbers to define the intervallic relations between the pitch centers, we can describe the pitch-center nexus as 1–5. These are steps 2 and 6 of the scale used by the melody (Φ C P M N I Z E).

Invocation of Calliope and Apollo

DAGM #25 (second century C.E.)

This short song by Mesomedes is fully intact. The notation *tonos* is Lydian diatonic (using the disjunct tetrachord), the same as the invocation of the Muse.[78] The notes in scalar order are ⌐R Φ C P M N I Z E (in the *DAGM* transcription: $e f g a b^b c c^{\#} d e' f'$). Again, N is an anomalous note in the Lyd-

---

[75] See Hagel (2009, 312).
[76] See Winnington-Ingram (1968, 42); cf. Solomon (1984, 251).
[77] The Lydian *tonos* inscribes a Dorian octave species from *hypatē* to *nētē diezeugmenōn*.
[78] In the manuscript tradition, these lines have no separate title and have been interpreted by some as a second half of the invocation of the Muse.

ian *tonos*. It occurs only once and could be an error for M.⁷⁹ The song starts and ends on C, which receives the greatest emphasis (F12/D18/R5,2). C is the non-standing note *parhypatē mesōn* in the Lydian *tonos*. Dynamic *mesē* (I) plays only a minor role in the hymn. A different picture emerges if we interpret the melody as governed by an octave species, the Mixolydian scale, with N as an accidental and E as a ninth (S T T S T T T). In that case, C is the fourth note of this scale, so-called thetic *mesē*, the primary tone in the tune. Landels offers a different interpretation. He finds a pair of conjunct tetrachords, as well as a third (and incomplete) upper tetrachord: ⅂ R Φ C + C P M I + Z E [ ].⁸⁰ But tetrachordal intervals are not a significant feature of the piece.

West describes C as the "tonic" but sees a shift of tonic to R (which lies a third below C) in the second hexameter, with a return at the very end to a focus on C.⁸¹ Since R (F2/D4) is scarcely emphasized, the fact that it begins a scalar run at the start of the second hexameter is probably not sufficient to qualify it as a secondary pitch focus.⁸² But West is right to observe that after establishing C as pitch center in the first hexameter, the melody drifts away from it, only to return at the end. A secondary pitch emphasis falls on M, a third above C. The pitch-emphasis movement is roughly C → M → C (1 → 3 → 1). The tonal structure of the song is the intervallic pattern S T T S T T T oriented to the fourth step of a nine-note scale with the sixth step receiving secondary emphasis. We can indicate the secondary status of M by placing it in parenthesis in representing the pitch-center nexus: 1–(3).

Hymn to the Sun

DAGM #27 (second century C.E.)

This hymn by Mesomedes is pitched in the diatonic Lydian and uses the disjunct tetrachord. Three of the four most emphatic notes are standing notes in the disjunct scale segment of the Lydian *tonos*: C (*hypatē mesōn*) (F32/D45/R4,6), I (*mesē*) (F37/D49), and Z (*paramesē*) (F30/D48). But the most emphasized note is a non-standing note, M (*lichanos mesōn*) (F61/D86/R4,5,3,2,3,2,3,2,2). The highest concentration of this note is in the middle of the piece. It is not emphasized at the beginning or the end, where the melody in both places hammers at *hypatē mesōn* (C). That note is also first and final. *Mesē* is evenly distributed but not dominant in any stretch of the melody.

---

[79] So Winnington-Ingram (1968, 42); Landels (1999, 255, 290n35).
[80] Landels (1999, 255).
[81] West (1992b, 304).
[82] Hagel (2009, 313) also doubts that there is any clear "secondary tonal center."

In terms of the Lydian *tonos*, the pitch-emphasis flow develops as follows: *hypatē mesōn* → *lichanos mesōn* / *hypatē mesōn* / *paramesē* → *lichanos mesōn* / *paramesē* → *hypatē mesōn*. The use of *lichanos mesōn* in relation to *hypatē mesōn* and *paramesē* produces intervals of progressive thirds at points, lending the melody what Winnington-Ingram has termed a "triadic" tonal quality.[83]

A different interpretation is suggested if we look for an octave species in the diatonic scale suggested by the notes of the piece. These notes form the Lydian octave species: R Φ C P M I Z E. So-called "thetic" *mesē* in this scale is P, which is not emphasized in the hymn, but *paramesē*, M, is the dominant note in the piece. Nevertheless, if we follow this line of interpretation, the other emphasized notes are not frame notes of tetrachords making up the octave species.

West interprets C as the tonal center, observing that there is also emphasis on Z and M. He does not assign a "mode" to the piece, but his approach to modality suggests the "E mode." This assumes a single tonal center, however, when we have an eight-note scale exhibiting a particular pitch-center pattern in which scale-steps 3, 5, and 7 are emphasized, along with less accentuation on (but even distribution of) step 6. Treating scale-step 3 as '1' of the pitch-center nexus, we have 1–3–(4?)–5.

The tune is structured through fourths but also through thirds and fifths (some of the fifths being made out of two thirds). However, in only one place does the tetrachord from (dynamic) *hypatē* to *mesē* appear (in the opening phrase), and the tetrachord from *paramesē* to *nētē diezeugmenōn* is not used (the upper range of the melody extends no further than *tritē diezeugmenōn*). This means that the tetrachordal structure of the Lydian *tonos* does not govern the melody.

If we look at movement through pitch centers, a triadic orientation emerges involving combinations of 1, 3, and 5. A rough and over-simplified diagram of movement through pitch emphases might be as follows: C → M/C/Z → M/Z → C (1 → 3/1/5 → 3/5 → 1). It is M, throughout the main body of the piece, that produces these triadic tonal emphases by its relation to C a third below and Z a third above. Hence, although there is emphasis on I through even distribution, this tone never becomes a pitch focus. It is therefore best to define the overall tonal nexus as 1–3–5.

---

[83] Winnington-Ingram (1968, 43 [commenting on the hymn to Nemesis] and 46 [remarking on a tendency in the Roman-era melodies generally]).

Hymn(s) to Nemesis

DAGM #28 (second century C.E.)

This music by Mesomedes is either two hymns or one hymn with a coda. The second hymn / coda is a shorter melody (lines 16–20) and lacks almost all of its last line. The first, longer melody (lines 1–15) is missing a few notes. Since there is nothing about the second melody to suggest that it differs in musical character from the first, I will focus on the first, which is longer and substantially intact. The melody of lines 1–15 is notated in the diatonic Lydian using notes of the conjunct and disjunct tetrachords: R Φ C P M I Z E U. The most emphatic note is M (F46/D73/R3,2,8,6,2,3), which is diatonic *lichanos mesōn* in the Lydian *tonos*, a non-standing note. The next most frequent note (I) occurs 21 times.

M is established at the beginning and reinforced periodically throughout. The piece begins on I and moves directly to a thrice-repeated M. In fact, six of eleven notes in the first line (rhythmically an *apokraton*) are M. In what is preserved of the melody as a whole, M occurs 46 times with a duration value of 73, reflective of how often it is held for 2 and sometimes 3 beats. It is emphasized through successive repetition in 6 of 15 lines – in one line with 6 iterations in a row, in another with 8! The melody also ends on M and keeps coming back to M, which is the most regularly recurring end-note of metrical lines. Hence, although there is movement around the scale and various notes are accentuated at one point or the other, the overall tonal emphasis is on M. If we use metrical line ends as a guide to shifting tonal emphasis, we see a movement away from and back to M, which can be diagramed roughly as follows: M → M → U → M → Φ → [ ] → I → M → Φ → M → I → M → I → P → M. These line-end notes feature the primary pitch center in a regularly-recurring way. The other line-end notes are perhaps all secondary pitch centers: I (F21/D30/R2,2) is a line-end note three times; Φ (F12/D13) and U (F10/D15/R4,3), which share octave equivalency, account for three line-end notes. The note P (F15/D20)[84] occurs once at line end; it becomes a pitch focus, if at all, only briefly in line 11.

Almost every line of the melody moves over the compass of a fourth or a fifth (10 of 14 lines[85]), and the comparisons below show that these fourths and fifths are oriented to notes that are also most prominent by frequency and duration, namely M and I, one or the other of which is part of nearly every fourth or fifth. These two notes, as the primary and secondary pitch centers,

---

[84] The counts for P are based on the transcription in Greek notational characters in Pöhlmann and West (*DAGM*, 100), which has ΦPP in line 10, following ms. N; but the facing modern transcription (*DAGM*, 101) treats this as Φ R R, following West (1992, 11), who emended the text based on considerations of melody / accent accord.

[85] The melody has fifteen lines, but line 6 lacks its end-note.

form a 1–(2) pitch-center nexus (with M as 1). If we include Φ and U together as lesser pitch-center foci, then we have a (1)–4–(5)–(8) nexus (with M as 4).[86] If we want to include P, then (1)–(3)–4–(5)–(8). These different ways of expressing the foci reflect the basic fact that the piece revolves emphatically around M and moves away from M always only briefly to emphasize this or that other note. With the exception of I, these secondary pitch foci are very subordinate.

The intervals of fourths and fifths in the melody are as follows:

without intervening notes:

fifths with M and U in lines 3, 4, and 12
perhaps a fifth with Φ and I in line 7
fourths with I and C in lines 1 and 7
fourths with Φ and M in lines 2, 5, 12 (2×), and 13
fourth with I and U in line 4

with intervening notes:

fifths with M and U in lines 4 and 8
perhaps the fifth with Φ and I in line 7, followed by 2 fifths with Φ and I in line 7
fourths with I and C in lines 7, 11, and 13
fourth with Φ and M in line 9
possible fourth with I and U in line 8
fourth with R and P in line 11
fourths with M and E in line 12 (2×), 14, and 15

The incomplete second song or coda of this hymn is similar in character to lines 1–15. Every extant line end finishes with M, the dominant note of lines 1–15.

P. Ber. 6870 + 14097 (1–12)

DAGM #50 (second–third century C.E.)

This paean, contained with other partially-preserved pieces of music in Berlin papyrus 6870 (recently enlarged slightly by the addition of a small fragment – 14097), shows significant preservation, but there are quite a few

---

[86] This way of interpreting the pitch-center nexus lends some support to the conclusion that the melody is based on an octave species, the Hypophrygian (T T S T T S T). This interpretation requires treating the rare R as an incidental note. The governing scale is then not nine notes (R Φ C P M I Z E U, etc.) but eight: Φ C P M I Z E U. According to this construal, the most emphatic note (M) corresponds to so-called "thetic" *mesē* of the octave species, the next most emphatic note (I) to *paramesē*. In a diatonic Hypophrygian octave from Φ to U, the two tetrachords are Φ to M and I to U, a scheme that corresponds to the (1)–4–(5)–(8) pitch-center nexus, assuming that this is the best way to interpret emphasis based on frequency, duration, distribution, and notes at line ends. Nevertheless, although the melody displays a tetrachordal orientation at points to Φ to M and I to U, this orientation does not predominate.

Appendix: Pitch Centers and Tonal Structure in Ancient Greek Melodies   193

lacunae. Notated in the diatonic Hyperionian (Hyperiastian) *tonos*, it uses the disjunct tetrachord: Φ C O Ƶ I Z A U Θ. The notes receiving the greatest accentuation over the course of the melody are I (F22/D41), Z (F19/D34), and C (F11/D32); C is also the final. Of these three notes, only Z is a standing note in the Hyperionian *tonos*. If we analyze by looking for an octave species, the nine notes used by the paean (which form the intervallic series T T S T T T S T) can be interpreted as encompassing the Lydian octave species, with an additional note above, or the Phrygian, with an additional note below.[87] In favor of Phrygian is the fact that in this octave species the principal notes of the paean are the standing notes *hypatē* (C), *mesē* (I), and *paramesē* (Z).[88] These notes also figure prominently at (extant) line ends, 6 out of 9 of which mark syntactical pauses. In three instances the last note of a period is C, and its rhythmic placement in each case suggests that it is lengthened in time value, which lends it greater emphasis. Moreover, C stands at the end of each of the two main sections: the first ending with Εὐ[ρώ]τα at the beginning of ms. line 5 which concludes the fifth catalectic period; and the second ending with [καρ]ποί at the turn from ms. line 11 to ms. line 12, which is the close of the final catalectic period. The extant ending notes of the other catalectic periods, varying in time value, are I (one instance, long), Z (two instances, one short and the other long), and Φ (three instances, all short). Hence, according to this interpretation, the paean puts greatest emphasis on "thetic" *mesē*, accentuates *paramesē* and *hypatē* as well, and ends on *hypatē*.

Given the uncertainty about thetic nomenclature as a way of interpreting the octave species, we can also analyze the tune descriptively by saying that it uses a nine-note scale and treats the fifth and sixth steps of this scale as pitch centers. A third note, the second note of the scale, serves as the final and also receives emphasis in the tune. Hence, the two main pitch centers stand in relations of a fourth and a fifth to this other pitch center, which is also the final.

West does not assign a modal name to the paean, perhaps because he finds two "tonics" in it, C and Z (*g* and *d* in his transcription). He refers to C as the "primary tonic" and to Z as a "secondary tonic."[89] As we have seen, however, the notes receiving the greatest accentuation through frequency and duration are not C and Z but I and Z. West's choice of C and Z as "tonics" is based on the observation that these notes dominate line ends.[90] This argument plausibly assumes that line-end finishes are particularly emphatic forms of recurrence to a tone. The presence of C at the two main end points and the lengthen-

---

[87] See Winnington-Ingram (1968, 39); Mountford (1929, 172–73).
[88] Mountford (1929, 172–73 [using the term Phrygian "mode"]). Winnington-Ingram also judges in the end that the melody of this paean is based on the Phrygian octave species (1968, 45).
[89] West (1992b, 318).
[90] West (1992b, 318).

ing (*tonē*) of C at those points perhaps lends this note greater importance as an orientation tone than is suggested by its frequency and duration alone. Winnington-Ingram's interpretation of the line ends (and no doubt also what he sees as overall emphases) leads him to propose that I is the tonic and shares "modal importance" with C.[91]

Hagel analyzes the piece from the standpoint of cithara tuning, observing that the most frequent notes – I and Z followed by C – are the strings *mesē*, *paramesē*, and *hypatē*, a classical tuning (the *hypertropa*).[92] He also observes "resonant leaps between *hypatē* and *mesē*, *hypatē* and *paramesē*, *paramesē* and *nētē*."[93]

We can describe the pitch-center nexus as 1–4–5. Missing notation in the papyrus frustrates any attempt to diagram the tonal flow.

P.Oxy. 1786

DAGM #59 (late third century C.E.)

The Christian hymn is incomplete, but the manuscript preserves several lines, including the ending. The melody uses note symbols belonging to the Hypolydian *tonos*: R Φ C O Z I Z E. Defining its octave species according to the pattern of intervals from its lowest to its highest note suggests Hypolydian: T T T S T T S. Mountford offers a different interpretation. He regards the melody's bottom note as unimportant, since it occurs rarely and only as a passing tone. Identifying Z as *mesē* because of its frequency in the piece and Φ as *hypatē* of the governing scale, he interprets the melody's "mode" as Hypophrygian (i.e., T T S T T S, with the highest note unused).[94] Winnington-Ingram makes a similar observation about the lowest note, also suggesting that the octave species of the hymn is Hypophrygian rather than Hypolydian.[95]

Leaving aside the question of octave species, which may not be apposite, we observe that the notes most emphasized through frequency and duration are Φ (F20/D24.5), Z (F21/D19), and I (F20/D24). These notes form a 1–4–5 nexus. In addition to prominence through frequency and duration, this 1–4–5 nexus is also the basis for important moments of melodic structuring. Twice we have a fourth after a rest as the start of a new melodic phrase. Each of these fourths is composed of 1 and 4 of the 1–4–5 nexus. The piece ends on 1 of the nexus.

---

[91] Winnington-Ingram (1968, 39 [his 'd' = I; his 'A' = C]).
[92] Hagel (2009, 334, 127–28).
[93] Hagel (2009, 334).
[94] Mountford (1929, 176–78).
[95] Winnington-Ingram (1968, 44 and 45).

Discography

Music of the Ancient Greeks. 1995. De Organographia. Gayle Neuman, Philip Neuman, and William Gavin. PRCD1001 (Pandourion).
Musique de la Grèce Antique. 1979. Atrium Musicae de Madrid under the direction of Gregorio Paniagua. HMA 1901015 (Harmonia mundi).
Musiques de l'Antiquité Grecque. 1996. Ensemble Kérylos under the direction of Annie Bélis. CD K617069.

Works Cited

Ancient Christian and Byzantine Literature

Acts of Andrew

Prieur, Jean-Marc, ed. 1989. *Acta Andreae*. CCSA 6. Turnhout: Brepols.

Acts of John in Syriac: see *Syriac Acts of John*

Acts of Paul (including *Acts of Paul and Thecla*)

Lipsius, Richard A., and Maximilian Bonnet, eds. 1972. *Acta Petri, Acta Pauli, Acta Petri et Pauli, Acta Pauli et Theclae, Acta Thaddaei*. 3 vols. AAA 1. Hildesheim and New York: Georg Olms [reprint of 1891–1903 edition].

Elliott, J. K., ed. 1993. *The New Testament Apocrypha: A Collection of Apocryphal Christian Literature in an English Translation*. Oxford: Clarendon Press.

Acts of Thomas

Bonnet, Maximilian, ed. 1959. *Acta Philippi et Acta Thomas; accedunt Acta Barnabae*. AAA 2. Hildesheim: Georg Olms.

Apostolic Constitutions

Funk, Franz Xaver, ed. 1905. *Didascalia et Constitutiones apostolorum*. 2 vols. Paderborn: F. Schoeningh.

Apostolic Fathers

Ehrman, Bart D., ed. and trans. 2003. *The Apostolic Fathers*. 2 vols. LCL 24 and 25. Cambridge, Mass. and London: Harvard University Press.

Lightfoot, J. B., ed. 1973. *S. Ignatuis, S. Polycarp*. Part II, vol. 3 of *The Apostolic Fathers*. Hildesheim and New York: Georg Olms [reprint of 1889 London edition].

Apostolic Tradition

Botte, Bernard, ed. and trans. 1968. *La Tradition apostolique: d'après les anciennes versions*. 2nd ed. SC 11. Paris: Éditions du Cerf.

Tidner, Erik, ed. 1963. *Didascaliae apostolorum; Canonum ecclesiasticorum; Traditionis apostolicae versiones Latinae*. TUGAL 75. Berlin: Akademie-Verlag.

Duensing, Hugo, ed. and trans. 1946. *Der aethiopische Text der Kirchenordnung des Hippolyt*. AKWG, 3rd series, no. 32. Göttingen: Vandenhoeck & Ruprecht.

Basil of Caesarea

Clarke, W. K. L., trans. 1925. *The Ascetic Works of Saint Basil*. London: SPCK.
Pruche, Benoit, ed. 1968. *Basile de Césarée: Sur le Saint Esprit*, 2nd ed. SC 17. Paris: Éditions du Cerf.
Wagner, M. M., trans. 1950. *Saint Basil: Ascetical Works*. FC 9. New York: Fathers of the Church.

Cedrenus

Bekker, Immanuel, ed. 1838. *Georgius Cedrenus: Historiarum compendium*. 2 vols. Bonn: Weber.

Clement of Alexandria

Sagnard, François, ed. 1970. *Clément d'Alexandrie: Extraits de Théodote*. 2nd ed. SC 23. Paris: Éditions du Cerf.
Stählin, Otto, and Ursula Treu, eds. 1972. *Clemens Alexandrinus: Protrepticus und Paedagogus*, 3rd ed. GCS 12. Berlin: Akademie-Verlag.
Stählin, Otto, and Ludwig Früchtel, eds. 1960. *Clemens Alexandrinus: Stromata Buch I–VI*, 3rd ed. GCS 15. Berlin: Akademie-Verlag.
Stählin, Otto, Ludwig Früchtel, and Ursula Treu, eds. 1970. *Clemens Alexandrinus: Stromata Buch VII and VIII; Excerpta ex Theodoto; Eclogae propheticae; Quis dives salvetur; Fragmenta*. 2nd ed. GCS 17. Berlin: Akademie-Verlag.

Cyril of Jerusalem

Piédagnel, Auguste, ed. 1988. *Catéchèses Mystagogiques*. SC 126. Paris: Éditions du Cerf.
Reischl, W. C., and Joseph Rupp, eds. 1967. *Cyrilli Hierosolymarum archiepiscopi opera quae supersunt omnia*. 2 vols. Hildesheim: Georg Olms [reprint of 1848 and 1860 editions].
Yarnold, Edward, trans. 2000. *Cyril of Jerusalem*. London and New York: Routledge.

Didascalia

Connolly, H., trans. 1929. *Didascalia Apostolorum*. Oxford: Clarendon Press.
Funk, Franz Xaver, ed. 1905. *Didascalia et Constitutiones apostolorum*. 2 vols. Paderborn: F. Schoeningh.

Ephraem Syrus

Phrantzolas, Konstantinos G., ed. 1988–1998. Οσίου Εφρίμ τοῦ Σύρου ἔργα [*Hosiou Ephraim tou Syrou Erga*]. 7 vols. Thessalonica: To Perivoli tes Panagias.

Eusebius

Bardy, Gustave, ed. 1958. *Eusèbe de Césarée: Histoire ecclésiastique livres VIII–X et Les martyrs en Palestine*. SC 55. Paris: Éditions du Cerf.
Praeparatio evangelica. Mras, Karl et al., eds. 1982–1983. *Die Praeparatio Evangelica*, 2nd ed. 2 vols. GCS 8/1–2. Berlin: Akademie Verlag.

Historia ecclesiastica. Oulton, J. E. L., ed. and trans. 2000–2001. *Eusebius: Ecclesiastical History.* 2 vols. LCL 153 and 265. Cambridge, Mass. and London: Harvard University [reprint of 1931–1932 edition].

Hippolytus

Marcovich, Miroslav, ed. 1986. *Hippolytus: Refutatio omnium haeresium.* PTS 25. Berlin and New York: Walter de Bruyter.

John Chrysostom

Malingrey, A.-A., ed. and trans. 1980. *Sur le Sacerdoce (Dialogue et Homélie).* SC 272. Paris: Éditions du Cerf.

Justin Martyr

Munier, Charles, ed. 2006. *Justin. Apologie pour les Chrétiens: introduction, texte critique, traduction, et notes.* SC 507. Paris: Éditions du Cerf.

Liturgy of St. James

Mercier, B.-Ch., ed. 1946. *La liturgie de saint Jacques: édition critique du texte grec avec traduction latine.* PO 26/2. Paris: Firmin-Didot.

Martyrdom of Andrew [part of Acts of Andrew]

Melito of Sardis

Perler, Otto, ed. 1966. *Méliton de Sardes: Sur la Pâque et Fragments.* SC 123. Paris: Les Éditions du Cerf.

Origen

Koetschau, Paul, ed. 1899. *Origenes Werke.* Vol. 1: *Die Schrift vom Martyrium*; *Buch I–IV Gegen Celsus.* Vol. 2: *Buch V–III Gegen Celsus*; *Die Schrift vom Gebet.* GCS 2 and 3. Leipzig: Hinrichs.

Photius

Henry, René, ed. 1959–1977. *Bibliothèque.* 8 vols. Paris: Les Belles Lettres.

Serapion of Thmuis (Serapion liturgy)

Funk, Franz Xaver, ed. 1905. *Testimonia et scripturae propinquae.* Vol. 2 of *Didascalia et constitutiones apostolorum*, ed. F. X. Funk. Paderborn: F. Schoeningh.

Sibyllene Oracles: See under Jewish literature

Synesius of Cyrene

Garzya, Antonio, ed. and trans. 1979. *Synesii Cyrenensis: Epistolae.* SGL. Rome: Typus Officinae Polygraphicae.

Gruber, Joachim, and Hans Strohm, eds. and trans. 1991. *Synesios von Kyrene: Hymnen, eingeleitet, übersetzt und kommentiert*. Heidelberg: Carl Winter.

Syriac Acts of John

Wright, William, ed. and trans. 1968. *Apocryphal Acts of the Apostles*, Vol. 1: *The Syriac Texts*. Vol. 2: *The English Translations*. Amsterdam: Philo Press.

Tertullian

Becker, Carl, ed. 1962. *Apologeticum / Verteidigung des Christentums: lateinisch und deutsch*. 2nd ed. Munich: Kösel-Verlag.

Testament of Our Lord (*Testamentum domini nostri*)

Cooper, James, and Arthur Frances Maclean, trans. 1902. *The Testament of Our Lord*. ANCL. Edinburgh: T. & T. Clark.

Theodore of Mopsuestia

Mingana, Alphonses, trans. 1933. *Commentary of Theodore of Mopsuestia on the Lord's Prayer and on the Sacraments of Baptism and the Eucharist*. WS 6. Cambridge, Mass.: W. Heffer & Sons.

Tonneau, Raymond, and Robert Devreese, trans. 1949. *Les Homélies catéchétiques de Théodore de Mopsueste: Reproduction phototypique de Ms. Mingana Syr. 561*. Vatican City: Biblioteca Apostolica Vaticana.

Ancient Jewish Literature

Babylonian Talmud

Cashdan, Eli, trans., and Isidore Epstein, ed. 1980. *Hullin*, rev. New York: Soncino.

Dead Sea Scrolls

Martínez, Florentino García, and Eibert J. C. Tigchelaar, eds. and trans. 1997–1998. *The Dead Sea Scrolls Study Edition*. 2 vols. Leiden: Brill. Grand Rapids: Eerdmans.

Hekhalot Literature

Schäfer, Peter, ed. 1981. *Synopse zur Hekhalot-Literatur*, with Margarete Schlüter and Hans Georg von Mutius. TSAJ 2. Tübingen: J. C. B. Mohr (Paul Siebeck).

Old Testament Pseudepigrapha

Charlesworth, James. H., ed. 1983–1985. *The Old Testament Pseudepigrapha*. 2 vols. Garden City: Doubleday.

Other Literature of the Greco-Roman World

Anonymous Bellermann

Najock, Dietmar, ed. 1975. *Anonyma de musica scripta Bellermanniana*. Leipzig: Teubner.

Aeschylus

Smyth, H. W., ed. and trans. 1922. *Suppliant Maidens, Persians, Prometheus, Seven against Thebes*. Vol. 1 of *Aeschylus*, ed. and trans. H. W. Smyth. Cambridge, Mass.: Harvard University Press.

Appian

Gabba, Emilio, A. G. Roos, Paul Viereck et al., eds. 1962–1986. *Appiani historia Romana*. 2 vols. Leipzig: Teubner.

Aristides Quintilianus

Winnington-Ingram, R. P., ed. 1963. *Aristidis Quintiliani De musica libri tres*. Leipzig: Teubner.

Aristophanes

Henderson, Jeffrey, ed. and trans. 1998–2000. *Aristophanes*. 3 vols. LCL 178, 488, and 179. Cambridge, Mass.: Harvard University Press.

[Pseudo-]Aristotle

Hett, W. S., ed. and trans. 1953. *Aristotle: Problems, Books 1–21*, rev. ed. LCL 316. Cambridge, Mass.: Harvard University Press. London: William Heinemann.

Aristoxenus

Harmonikōn stoicheiōn [*Harmonic Elements*]. Rios, Rosetta da, ed. 1954. *Aristoxeni Elementa harmonica*. SGL. Rome: Typus Publicae Officinae Polygraphicae.

Callimachus

Asper, Marcus, ed. and trans. 2004. *Kallimachos: Werke, griechisch und deutsch*. Darmstadt: Wissenschaftliche Buchgesellschaft.

Cleonides

Solomon, Jon, ed. and trans. 1980. "Cleonides: ΕΙΣΑΓΩΓΗ ΑΡΜΟΝΙΚΗ: Critical Edition, Translation, and Commentary." Ph.D. diss.; University of North Carolina.

Euripides

Diggle, James, ed. 1981–1994. *Euripidis Fabulae*. 3 vols. Oxford and New York: Clarendon.
Kovacs, David, ed. and trans. 2002. *Euripides: Bacchae, Iphigenia at Aulis, Rhesus*. LCL 495. Cambridge, Mass.: Harvard University Press.

Homer

Murray, A. T., ed. and trans. 1999. *Homer: Iliad*, rev. W. F. Wyatt. 2 vols. LCL 170 and 171. Cambridge, Mass.: Harvard University Press.

Homeric Hymns

West, Martin L., ed. and trans. 2003. *Homeric Hymns, Homeric Apocrypha, Lives of Homer*. LCL 496. Cambridge, Mass.: Harvard University Press.

Julius Pollux

Bethe, Erich, ed. 1998. *Pollucis Onomasticon*. 3 vols. LG 9. Leipzig: Teubner.

Lucian

MacLeod, M. D., ed. and trans. 2001. *Lucian*. Vol. 8 of *Lucian*, ed. and trans. A. M. Harmon, K. Kilburn, and M. D. MacLeod. LCL 432. Cambridge, Mass.: Harvard University Press [reprint of 1967 edition].

Pindar

Race, William H., ed. and trans. 1997. *Pindar: Olympian Odes, Pythian Odes*. Cambridge, Mass.: Harvard University Press.

Plato

Shorey, Paul, ed. and trans. 1980. *Plato: The Republic*. 2 vols. LCL 237 and 276. Cambridge, Mass.: Harvard University Press [reprint of 1930–1935 edition].

Plutarch

Babbitt, Frank Cole et al, eds. and trans. 1927 –1969. *Plutarch's Moralia*. 15 vols. LCL. Cambridge, Mass.: Harvard University Press.

Proclus

Chrestomathia. In Photius (see Ancient Christian and Byzantine Literature)

Ptolemy

Düring, Ingemar, ed. 1980. *Die Harmonielehre des Klaudios Ptolemaios, Porphyrios Kommentar zur Harmonielehre des Ptolemaios*, 2nd ed. New York: Garland [reprint of 1930 edition].

Sophocles

Lloyd-Jones, H., ed and trans. 1994. *Sophocles: Antigone, The Women of Trachis, Philoctetes, Oedipus at Colonus*. Cambridge, Mass.: Harvard University Press.

Theocritus

Beckby, Hermann, ed. 1975. *Die griechischen Bukoliker: Theokrit, Moschos, Bion*. BKP 49. Meisenheim am Glan: Anton Hahn.

Other Literature

Abert, Hermann. 1921/22. Ein neuentdeckter früchristlicher Hymnus mit antiken Musiknoten. *Zeitschrift für Musikwissenschaft* 4:524–29.
—. 1926. Das älteste Denkmal der christlichen Kirchenmusik. *Die Antike* 2:282–90.
Alston, Richard. 2002. *The City in Roman and Byzantine Egypt*. London and New York: Routledge.
Apel, Willi. 1958. *Gregorian Chant*. Bloomington: Indiana University Press.
Attridge, Harold. 1989. *The Epistle to the Hebrews*. Hermeneia. Philadelphia: Fortress Press.
Ausfeld, Karl. 1903. *De Graecorum precationibus quaestiones*. Leipzig: Teubner [reprinted from *Jahrbücher für classische Philologie* with original pagination].
Bagnall, Roger. S. 1995. *Reading Papyri: Writing Ancient History*. London and New York: Routledge.
—. 2003a. Religious Conversion and Onomastic Change in Early Byzantine Egypt. Pages 105–23 in Roger S. Bagnall, *Later Roman Egypt: Society, Religion, Economy and Administration*. Aldershot, Hampshire, Great Britain. Burlington, Vt.: Ashgate / Variorum [reprinted from *Bulletin of the American Society of Papyrologists* 19 (1982):105–23].
—. 2003b. Conversion and Onomastics: A Reply. Pages 243–50 in Roger S. Bagnall, *Later Roman Egypt: Society, Religion, Economy and Administration*. Aldershot, Hampshire, Great Britain. Burlington, Vt.: Ashgate / Variorum [reprinted from *Zeitschrift für Papyrologie und Epigraphik* 69 (1987):243–50].
—. 2007. Family and Society in Roman Oxyrhynchus. Pages 182–93 in *Oxyrhynchus: A City and Its Texts*. Edited by A. K. Bowman et al. GRM 93. London: Egypt Exploration Society.
Barker, Andrew. 1984. *Greek Musical Writings I: Harmonic and Acoustic Theory*. CRLM. Cambridge, Mass.: Cambridge University Press.
—. 1989. *Greek Musical Writings II: The Musician and His Art*. CRLM. Cambridge, Mass.: Cambridge University Press.
—. 1995. Heterophonia and Poikilia: Accompaniments to Greek Melody. Pages 41–60 in *Mousike: metrica, ritmica e musica greca in memoria di Giovanni Comotti*, Edited by Bruno Gentili and Franca Perusio. Pisa: Istituti editoriali e poligrafici internazionali.
Barnes, Timothy D. 1981. *Constantine and Eusebius*. Cambridge, Mass.: Harvard University Press.
—. 1982. *The New Empire of Diocletian and Constantine*. Cambridge, Mass. and London: Harvard University Press.
Baud-Bovy, Samuel. 1984. Chanson populaire de la Grèce antique [corrigenda]. *Revue de musicologie* 70:259–60.
Bélis, Annie. 1992. *Les deux Hymnes à Apollon: Étude épigraphique et musicale*. CID 3. Paris: Boccard.
—. 2004. Un papyrus musical inédit au Louvre. *Comptes rendu de l'académie des inscriptions et belles-lettres* 148:1305–29.
Blacking, John. 1973. *How Musical Is Man?* Seattle and London: University of Washington Press.
Bowman, Alan K. 2007. Roman Oxyrhynchus: City and People. Pages 171–81 in *Oxyrhynchus: A City and Its Texts*. Edited by A. K. Bowman et al. GRM 93. London: Egypt Exploration Society.
Bradshaw, Paul. 2004. *Eucharistic Origins*. Oxford: Oxford University Press.

Bradshaw, Paul F., Maxwell E. Johnson, and L. Edward Phillips. 2002. *The Apostolic Tradition: A Commentary.* Edited by Harold W. Attridge. Hermeneia. Minneapolis: Fortress Press.
Bremer, Jan Maarten. 1981. Greek Hymns. Pages 193–215 in *Faith, Hope, and Worship: Aspects of Religious Mentality in the Ancient World.* Edited by H. S. Versnel. Leiden: E. J. Brill.
Brightman, Frank E. 1896. *Eastern Liturgies.* Vol. 1 of *Liturgies Eastern and Western.* Oxford: Clarendon.
Brown, Peter. 1978. *The Making of Late Antiquity.* Cambridge, Mass.: Harvard University Press.
Brucker, Ralph. 1997. *'Christushymnen' oder 'epideiktische Passagen'? Studien zum Stilwechsel im Neuen Testament und seiner Umwelt.* FRLANT 176. Göttingen: Vandenhoeck & Ruprecht.
Bühler, Karl. 1965. *Sprachtheorie: Die Darstellungsfunktion der Sprache.* Stuttgart: Fischer [reprint of 1934 edition].
Bulloch, A. W. 1985. *Callimachus: The Fifth Hymn.* CCTC 26. Cambridge, Mass.: Cambridge University Press.
Butler, David. 1989. Describing the Perception of Tonality in Music: A Critique of the Tonal Hierarchy Theory and a Proposal for a Theory of Intervallic Rivalry. *Music Perception* 6:219–42.
Calame, Claude. 2004. Deictic Ambiguity and Auto-Referentiality: Some Examples from Greek Poets. *Arethusa* 37:415–43.
Campbell, David A., ed. and trans. 1993. *The New School of Poetry and Anonymous Songs and Hymns.* Vol. 5 of *Greek Lyric.* LCL 144. Cambridge, Mass. and London: Harvard University Press.
Chailley, Jacques. 1979. *La musique grecque antique.* Paris: Les Belles Lettres.
Chávez, Carlos. 1961. *Musical Thought.* Cambridge, Mass.: Harvard University Press.
Chrestou, Panagiotes K. 2005. *Greek Orthodox Patrology: An Introduction to the Study of the Church Fathers.* Rollinsford, N.H.: Orthodox Research Institute.
Clarke, Graeme. 2002. [Review of Reinhard Selinger, *The Mid-Third Century Persecutions of Decius and Valerian.*] *Bryn Mawr Classical Review* 2002.10.22 at http://bmcr.brynmawr.edu/2002/2002-10-22.html (accessed October, 2008).
Cockle, W. E. H. 1975. The Odes of Epagathus the Choral Flautist: Some Documentary Evidence for Dramatic Representation in Roman Egypt. Pages 59–65 in *Proceedings of the XIV International Congress of Papyrologists, Oxford, 24–31 July 1974.* London: Egypt Exploration Society.
Comotti, Giovanni.1988. I problemi dei valori ritmici nell' interpretazione dei testi musicali della Grecia antica. Pages 17–25 in *La musica in Grecia: Storia e Società.* Edited by Andrew Barker, Bruno Gentili, and Roberto Pretagostini. Roma-Bari: Laterza.
—. 1989. *Music in Greek and Roman Culture.* Translated by Rosaria Munson. Baltimore: Johns Hopkins University Press. Revised edition of *La musica nella cultura greca e romana.* Torino: Edizioni di Torino.
Cone, Edward T. 1968. *Musical Form and Musical Performance.* New York: W. W. Norton.
Cook, Nicholas. 1987. *A Guide to Musical Analysis.* New York: G. Braziller.
Cosgrove, Charles H. 2006a. Clement of Alexandria and Early Christian Music. *Early Christian Studies* 14:255–82.
—. 2006b. The Earliest Christian Hymn with Musical Notation: A Critical History of Interpretation of P. Oxy. 1786. *Ephemerides Liturgicae* 120/3:257–77.

Cosgrove, Charles H., and Mary C. Meyer. 2006. Melody and Word Accent Relationships in Ancient Greek Musical Documents: The Pitch Height Rule. *Journal of Hellenic Studies* 126:66–81.

Cribiore, Raffaella. 2001. *Gymnastics of the Mind: Greek Education in Hellenistic and Roman Egypt*. Princeton: Princeton University Press.

Crocker, Richard L. 2000. *An Introduction to Gregorian Chant*. New Haven and London: Yale University Press.

Crönert, Wilhelm. 1922. [Review of *P. Oxy*. 15, 1922.] *Literarisches Zentralblatt* 73:398–400, 424–27.

Crusius, Otto. 1893. Zu neuentdeckten antiken Musikresten. *Philologus* 52:160–200.

D'Alessio, Giovan Battista. 2004. Past Future and Future Past: Temporal Deixis in Greek Archaic Lyric. *Arethusa* 37:267–95.

Danielwicz, Jerzy. 1990. Deixis in Greek Choral Lyric. Pages 7–17 in *Quaderni Urbinati di Cultura Classica* 34 N.S.

Del Grande, Carlo. 1923. Inno cristiano antico. *Rivista Indo-Greca Italica di Filologia, Lingua, Antichità* 7:11–17.

–. 1931. Intorno ai papiri musicali scoperti in Egitto. *Chronique d'Égypte* 6:441–55.

–. 1960. La metrica greca. Pages 133–513 in vol. 5 of *Enciclopedia classica*, sect. II, fasc. 2. Edited by G. Battista Pighi et al. Turin: Società editrice internazionale.

Denniston, J. D. 1954. *The Greek Particles*, 2nd ed. Oxford: Clarendon Press.

Devine, Andrew M., and Laurence D. Stephens. 1994. *The Prosody of Greek Speech*. Oxford: Oxford University Press.

Dihle, Albrecht. 1954. Die Anfänge der griechischen akzentuierenden Verskunst. *Hermes* 82:181–99.

Düring, Ingemar. 1980. *Ptolemaios und Porphyrios über die Musik*. New York: Garland [reprint of 1934 edition].

Duysinx, François. 1981. Accents, mélodie et modalité dans la musique antique. *L'antiquité classique* 38:306–17.

Eisenhofer, Ludwig. 1932. *Allgemeine Liturgik*. Vol. 1 of *Handbuch der katholischen Liturgik*. Freiburg: Herder.

Elior, Rachel. 1986–1987. Schäfer's *Synopse zur Hekhalot-Literatur*. *Jewish Quarterly Review* 77:213–17.

–. 1997. From Earthly Temple to Heavenly Shrines: Prayer and Sacred Song in the Hekhalot Literature and Its Relation to Temple Traditions. *Jewish Studies Quarterly* 4:217–67.

Eliott, J. K., ed. 1993. *The New Testament Apocrypha: A Collection of Apocryphal Christian Literature in an English Translation*. Oxford: Clarendon Press.

Epp, Eldon J. 1997. The Codex and Literacy in Early Christianity at Oxyrhynchus: Issues Raised by Harry Y. Gamble's *Books and Readers in the Early Church*. *Critical Review of Books in Religion* 10:15–37.

–. 2004. The Oxyrhynchus New Testament Papyri: "Not without Honor Except in Their Hometown." *Journal of Biblical Literature* 123:5–55.

Fichman, I. F. 1921. Die Bevölkerungszahl von Oxyrhynchos in byzantischer Zeit. *Archiv für Papyrusforschung* 21:111–20.

Fiensy, David A. 1985. *Prayers Alleged to Be Jewish: An Examination of the Constitutiones Apostolorum*. BJS 65. Chico, Calif.: Scholars Press.

Frederiksen, Brian. 1996. *Arnold Jacobs: Song and Wind*. Edited by John Taylor. n.p.: WindSong Press.

Furley, William D. 1995. Praise and Persuasion in Greek Hymns. *Journal of Hellenic Studies* 115:29–46.
Furley, William D., and Jan Maarten Bremer. 2001. *Greek Hymns: Selected Cult Songs from the Archaic to the Hellenistic Period*. Vol. 1: *Texts in Translation*. Vol. 2: *Greek Texts and Commentary*. STAC 9 and 10. Tübingen: Mohr Siebeck.
Gastoué, Amédée. 1921/22. Une hymne inédite, notée, des premiers chrétiens. *Le Tribune de Saint-Gervais* 23:229–34.
Gelineau, Joseph. 1964. *Voices and Instruments in Christian Worship: Principles, Laws, Applications*. Translated by Clifford Howell. Collegeville: Liturgical Press.
Ghedini, Guiseppe. 1933. Frammenti liturgici in un papiro milanese. *Aegyptus* 13:667–73.
Graves, Raphael. 1997. The Anaphora of the Eighth Book of the Apostolic Constitutions. Pages 173–94 of *Essays on Early Eastern Eucharistic Prayers*, ed. Paul F. Bradshaw. Collegeville: Liturgical Press.
Grese, William C. 1979. *Corpus Hermeticum XIII and Early Christian Literature*. SCHNT. Leiden: E. J. Brill.
Haas, Christopher J. 1983. Imperial Religious Policy and Valerian's Persecution of the Church, A.D. 257–260. *Church History* 52:133–44.
Hagel, Stefan. 2000. *Modulation in altgriechischer Musik*. QSMAG 38. Frankfurt am Main: Peter Lang.
–. 2009. *Ancient Greek Music: A New Technical History*. Cambridge, Mass.: Cambridge University Press.
Hannick, Christian. 1980. Christian Church, music of the early (§ 5 Oxyrhynchus Papyrus 1786). Pages 363–71 in vol. 4 of *The New Grove Dictionary of Music and Musicians*. Edited by Stanley Sadie. London: Macmillan.
Healy, Patrick J. 1905. *The Valerian Persecution: A Study of the Relations between Church and State in the Third Century A.D.* Boston and New York: Houghton, Mifflin and Company.
Heitsch, Ernst. 1960. Drei Helioshymnen. *Hermes* 88:139–58.
–, ed. 1961. *Die griechischen Dichterfragmente der römischen Kaiserzeit*. Göttingen: Vandenhoeck & Ruprecht.
Henrichs, Albert. 1994–1995. "Why Should I Dance?" Choral Self-Referentiality in Greek Tragedy. *Arion* (3rd Series) 3:56–111.
–. 1996. *Warum soll ich tanzen? Dionysisches im Chor der griechischen Tragödie*. LT 4. Stuttgart: Teubner.
Hiley, David. 1993. *Western Plainchant: A Handbook*. Oxford: Clarendon.
Hilgard, Alfred, ed. 1901. *Scholia in Dionysii Thracis Artem grammaticam*. GG 3. Leipzig: Teubner.
Holleman, A. W. J. 1972. The Oxyrhynchus Papyrus 1786 and the Relationship between Ancient Greek and Early Christian Music. *Vigiliae Christianae* 26:1–17.
Hopkinson, Neil. 1984. *Callimachus: Hymn to Demeter*. Cambridge, Mass.: Cambridge University Press.
Hoppin, Richard H. 1966. Tonal Organizations in Music before the Renaissance. Pages 25–37 in *Paul A. Pisk: Essays in His Honor*. Edited by John Glowacki. Austin: University of Texas Press.
Hunt, Arthur S., and Stuart Jones. 1922. Christian Hymn with Musical Notation. *The Oxyrhynchus Papyri* 15:21–25.
Huron, David, and Matthew Royal. 1996. What Is Melodic Accent? Converging Evidence from Musical Practice. *Music Perception* 13:489–516.

Hyer, Bryan. 2001. Tonality. Pages 583–94 in vol. 25 of *The New Grove Dictionary of Music and Musicians*, 2nd ed. Edited by Stanley Sadie. London: Macmillan.

Jammers, Ewald. 1962. *Musik im Byzanz, im päpstlichen Rom und im Frankreich*. Heidelberg: Carl Winter / Universitätsverlag.

Jeffery, Peter. 1982. An Early Cantatorium Fragment Related to MS Laon 239. *Scriptorium* 36:245–52.

Joannou, P.-P., ed. 1962. *Les canones des Synodes Particuliers*. Vol. 1, part 2 of *Discipline générale antique*. FPCRCDCO 9. Grottaferrata (Rome): Tipografia Italo-Orientale 'S. Nilo'.

Johner, Dominikus. 1923. Die älteste entzifferte christliche Melodie. *Benediktinische Monatschrift* 5:148–54.

Johnson, William A. 2000. Musical Evenings in the Early Empire: New Evidence from a Greek Papyrus with Musical Notation. *Journal of Hellenic Studies* 120:57–85.

Keister, Jay. 2004. *Shaped by Japanese Music: Kikuoka Hiroaki and Nagauta Shamisen in Tokyo*. New York: Routledge.

Keresztes, Paul. 1975. Two Edicts of the Emperor Valerian. *Vigiliae Christianae* 29:81–95.

Kerman, Joseph. 1985. *Contemplating Music: Challenges to Musicology*. Cambridge, Mass.: Harvard University Press.

Kroll, Josef. 1968. *Die christliche Hymnodik bis zu Klemens von Alexandrien*, 2nd ed. Darmstadt: Wissenschaftlich Buchgesellschaft [reprint of 1921/22 edition].

Krüger, Julian. 1990. *Oxyrhynchos in der Kaiserzeit: Studien zur Topographie und Literaturrezeption*. EH 3/441. Frankfurt am Main: Peter Lang.

Lampe, G. W. H. 1961. *A Patristic Greek Lexicon*. Oxford and New York: Clarendon.

Lampe, Peter. 2003. *From Paul to Valentinus: Christians at Rome in the First Two Centuries*. Translated by Michael Steinhauser. Edited by Marshall D. Johnson. Minneapolis: Fortress Press.

Landels, John G. 1999. *Music in Ancient Greece and Rome*. London and New York: Routledge.

Lattke, Michael. 1991. *Hymnus. Materialien zu einer Geschichte der antiken Hymnologie*. Freiburg: Universitätsverlag. Göttingen: Vandenhoeck & Ruprecht.

Leclercq, Jean. 1937. Papyrus. Pages 1370–1519 in vol. 30/1 of *Dictionnaire d'archéologie chrétienne et de liturgie*. Edited by Fernand Cabrol and Henri Leclercq. Paris: Librairie Letouzey et Ané.

Luijendijk, AnneMarie. 2008a. *Greetings in the Lord: Early Christians and the Oxyrhynchus Papyri*. HTS 60. Cambridge, Mass.: Harvard University Press.

–. 2008b. Papyri from the Great Persecution: Roman and Christian Perspectives. *Journal of Early Christian Studies* 16:341–70.

McKinnon, James. 1965. The Meaning of the Patristic Polemic against Musical Instruments. *Current Musicology* 1:69–82.

–. 1987. *Music in Early Christian Literature*. Cambridge, Mass.: Cambridge University Press.

–. 2001. Christian Church, music of the early. Pages 795–807 in vol. 5 of *The New Grove Dictionary of Music and Musicians*, 2nd ed. Edited by Stanley Sadie and John Tyrrell. New York: Grove.

MacLennan, Hugh. 1935. *Oxyrhynchus: An Economic and Social Study*. Princeton: Princeton University.

McGowan, Andrew. 1997. Naming the Feast: The *Agape* and the Diversity of Early Christian Meals. *Studia Patristica* 30 (1997):314–18.

–. 2004. Rethinking Agape and Eucharist. *Studia Liturgica* 34:165–76.
Malm, William P. 1996. *Music Cultures of the Pacific, the Near East, and Asia*, 3rd ed. Upper Saddle River: Prentice-Hall.
Mathiesen, Thomas. 1999. *Apollo's Lyre: Greek Music and Greek Music Theory in Antiquity and the Middle Ages*. PCHMTL 2. Lincoln and London: University of Nebraska Press.
Matusky, Patricia, and Sooi Beng Tan. 2004. *The Music of Malaysia: The Classical, Folk and Syncretic Traditions*. Hants, England: Aldershot. Burlington, Vt: Ashgate.
May, Gerhard. 1983. Der Christushymnus des Clemens von Alexandrien. Pages 260–65 in *Historische Präsentation*. Vol. 1 of *Liturgie und Dichtung: ein interdisziplinäres Kompendium*. Edited by H. Becker and R. Kaczynski. St. Ottilien: EOS.
Meier, Siegfried. 2004. *Psalmen, Lobgesänge und geistliche Lieder: Studien zur musikalischen Exegese und biblischen Grundlegung evangelischer Kirchenmusik*. Kontexte 36. Frankfort am Main: Peter Lang.
Mohrmann, Christine. 1957. Altchristliche Dichtung. Cols. 267–68 in vol. 1 of *Religion in Geschichte und Gegenwart*, 3rd ed. Tübingen: J. C. B. Mohr.
Mountford, J. F. 1929. Greek Music in the Papyri and Inscriptions. Pages 146–83 in *New Chapters in the History of Greek Literature*. Second Series. Edited by J. U. Powell and E. A. Barber. Oxford: Clarendon Press.
–. 1931. A New Fragment of Greek Music in Cairo. *Journal of Hellenic Studies* 51:91–100.
Muehlberger, Ellen. 2008. Angels in the Religious Imagination of Late Antiquity. Ph.D. dissertation. Indiana University.
Münscher, Karl. 1952. Zum christlichen Dreifaltigkeitshymnus aus Oxyrhynchos. *Philologus* 80:209–13.
Nettl, Bruno. 1983. *The Study of Ethnomusicology*. Urbana: University of Illinois Press.
Neubecker, Annemarie. 1977. *Altgriechische Musik: eine Einführung*. Darmstadt: Wissenschaftliche Buchgesellschaft.
Newsom, Carol A. 1997. Songs of the Sabbath Sacrifice. Pages 28–32 in *Prayer from Alexander to Constantine: A Critical Anthology*. Edited by Mark C. Kiley. London and New York: Routledge.
Norden, Eduard. 1974. *Agnostos Theos: Untersuchungen zur Formgeschichte religiöser Rede*. Stuttgart: Teubner [reprint of 1913 edition].
Norton, Richard. 1984. *Tonality in Western Culture: A Critical and Historical Perspective*. University Park and London: University of Pennsylvania Press.
Odahl, Charles Matson. 2004. *Constantine and the Christian Empire*. New York: Routledge.
Olson, Dennis T. 1992. Daily and Festival Prayers at Qumran. Pages 301–16 in *The Bible and the Dead Sea Scrolls: The Princeton Symposium on the Dead Sea Scrolls*. Edited by James H. Charlesworth. New York: Doubleday.
Ortmann, Otto. 1926. *On the Melodic Relativity of Tones*. PRM 35/1. Princeton and Albany: The Psychological Review Company.
Page, Denys, ed. 1962. *Poetae Melici Graeci*. Oxford: Clarendon Press.
Parrot, Douglas M., ed. 1991. *Nag Hammadi Codices, III, 3–4 and V,1 with Papyrus Berolinensis 85023 and Oxyrhynchus Papyrus 1081*. Leiden: E. J. Brill.
Parsons, Peter. 2007. *City of the Sharp-Nosed Fish: Greek Lives in Roman Egypt*. London: Weidenfeld and Nicolson.
Pearson, Birger A. 1997. *The Emergence of the Christian Religion: Essays on Early Christianity*. Harrisburg: Trinity Press International.

—. 2004. *Gnosticism and Christianity in Roman and Coptic Egypt.* New York and London: T. & T. Clark.
Pfordresher, Peter Q. 2003. The Role of Melodic and Rhythmic Accents in Musical Structure. *Music Perception* 20:431–64.
Pighi, Giovanni Battista. 1941. Ricerche sulla notazione ritmica greca: L'inno cristiano del POxy 1786. *Aegyptus* 21:189–220.
Plank, Peter. 2002. *ΦΩΣ ΙΛΑΡΟΝ: Christushymnus und Lichtdanksagung der frühen Christenheit.* SAK 20. Bonn: Borengässer.
Pöhlmann, Egert. 1960. *Griechische Musikfragmente: ein Weg zur altgriechischen Musik.* Nuremberg: Hans Carl.
—. 1970. *Denkmäler altgriechischer Musik: Sammlung, Übertragung und Erläuterung aller Fragmente und Fälschungen.* Nuremberg: Hans Carl.
—. 1994. *Altertum.* Vol. 1 of idem, *Einführung in die Überlieferungsgeschichte und in die Textkritik der antiken Literatur.* Darmstadt: Wissenschaftliche Buchgesellschaft.
—. 1997. Notation, II. Antike. Pages 283–89, 417 in vol. 7 of *Die Musik in Geschichte und Gegenwart*, 2nd ed. Edited by F. Blume and L. Finscher. Kassel: Bärenreiter. Stuttgart: Metzler.
—. 2005. Dramatische Texte in den Fragmenten antiker Musik. Pages 131–45 in *Ancient Greek Music in Performance: Symposion Wien 29. Sept.–1. Okt. 2003.* Edited by Stefan Hagel and Christine Harrauer WS 30. Vienna: Verlag der Österreichischen Akademie der Wissenschaften.
Pöhlmann, Egert, and Martin. L. West, eds. 2001. *Documents of Ancient Greek Music: The Extant Melodies and Fragments.* Oxford: Clarendon Press.
Porter, Wendy J. 2000. Misguided Missals: Is Early Christian Music Jewish or Is It Graeco-Roman? Pages 202–27 in *Christian-Jewish Relations through the Centuries.* Edited by Stanley E. Porter and Brook W. R. Pearson. Sheffield: Sheffield Academic Press.
—. 2002. The Composer of Sacred Music as an Interpreter of the Bible. Pages 126–53 in *Borders, Boundaries, and the Bible.* Edited by Martin O'Kane. Sheffield: Sheffield Academic Press.
Powell, John U., ed. 1925. *Collectanea Alexandrina: reliquiae minores poetarum graecorum aetatis Ptolemaicae 323–146 A.C., epicorum, elegiacorum, lyricorum, ethicorum.* Oxford: Oxford University Press.
Prauscello, Lucia. 2006. *Singing Alexandria: Music Between Practice and Textual Tradition.* MS 274. Leiden and Boston: E. J. Brill.
Preisendanz, Karl, and Albert Henrichs, eds. 1973–1974. *Papyri Graecae Magicae: die griechischen Zauberpapyri*, 2nd ed. 2 vols. SWC. Stuttgart: Teubner.
Quasten, Johannes. 1983. *Music and Worship in Pagan and Christian Antiquity.* Translated by Boniface Ramsey. Washington D.C.: National Association of Pastoral Musicians. Translation of *Musik und Gesang in den Kulten der heidnischen Antike und christlichen Frühzeit.* 2nd ed. Munster: Aschendorff, 1973.
—. 1964. *The Beginnings of Christian Literature.* Vol. 1 of idem, *Patrology.* Utrecht–Antwerp: Spectrum.
Rea, John R. 1972. Public Documents: The Corn Dole in Oxyrhynchus, and Kindred Documents. *The Oxyrhynchus Papyri* 40:1–26.
—. 1979. P. Oxy. XXXIII 2673.22 ΠΥΛΗΝ to ΥΛΗΝ. *Zeitschrift für Papyrologie und Epigraphik* 35:128.
Reinach, Théodore. 1896. L'hymne à la Muse. *Revue des Études Grecques* 9:1–22.
—. 1909–1913. Hymnes avec notes musicales. *Fouilles de Delphes* 3:147–69.

–. 1922. Un ancêtre de la Musique d'Église. *La Revue Musicale* 3:8–25.
–. 1926. *La Musique Grecque*. Paris: Payot.
Réti, Rudolph. 1958. *Tonality, Atonality, Pantonality: A Study of Some Trends in Twentieth Century Music*. New York: Macmillan.
Roberts, Colin H. 1979. *Manuscript, Society, and Belief in Early Christian Egypt*. London and New York: Oxford University Press.
Rubenson, Samuel. 1995. *The Letters of St. Antony: Monasticism and the Making of a Saint*. SAC. Minneapolis: Fortress Press.
Sachs, Curt. 1965. *The Wellsprings of Music*. Edited by Jaap Kunst. New York and Toronto: McGraw-Hill.
Sampson, Geoffrey. 1985. *Writing Systems: A Linguistic Introduction*. Stanford: Stanford University Press.
Schermann, Theodor. 1917. *Frühchristliche Vorbereitungsgebete zur Taufe (Papyr. Berol. 13415)*. MBPF 3. Munich: C. H. Beck / Oskar Beck.
Sharp, Michael. 2007. The Food Supply. Pages 218–30 in *Oxyrhynchus: A City and Its Texts*. Edited by A. K. Bowman et al. GRM 93. London: Egypt Exploration Society.
Simon, Erika. 1986. *Augustus: Kunst und Leben in Rom um die Zeitenwende*. Munich: Hirmer.
Slater, W. J. 1969. Futures in Pindar. *Classical Quarterly* 19:86–94.
Smyth, Herbert Weir. 1956. *Greek Grammar*. Revised by Gordon M. Messing. Cambridge, Mass.: Harvard University Press.
Solomon, Jon. 1984. Towards a History of Tonoi. *The Journal of Musicology* 3:242–51.
–. 1986. The Seikilos Inscription: A Theoretical Analysis. *The American Journal of Philology* 107:455–79.
Stäblein, Bruno. 1955. Frühchristliche Musik. Pages 1037–56 in vol. 4 of *Die Musik in Geschichte und Gegenwart*. Edited by F. Blume. Kassel and Basel: Bärenreiter-Verlag.
Stark, Rodney S. 1997. *The Rise of Christianity: How the Obscure, Marginal Jesus Movement Became the Dominant Religious Force in the Western World in a Few Centuries*. San Francisco: HarperSanFrancisco.
Sturz, Friedrich Wilhelm., ed. 1818. *Etymologicum graecae linguae Gudianum*. Leipzig: Weigel.
Terzaghi, Nicola. 1963. Sul Poxy 1786. Pages 669–75 in *Studia Græca et Latina (1901–1956) con presentazione di Francesco della Corte*. Torino: Bottega d'Erasmo [originally published in Nicola Terzaghi, *Raccolta di scritti in onore di Giacomo Lumbrosa (1844–1926)* (Milan: Aegyptus, 1925)].
Thomassen, Joseph M. 1982. Melodic Accent: Experiments and a Tentative Model. *Journal of the Acoustic Society of America* 71:1596–1605.
Thomson, William. 1999. *Tonality in Music: A General Theory*. San Marino: Everett Books.
–. 2006. Pitch Frames as Melodic Archetypes. *Empirical Musicology Review* 1:85–102.
Timm, Stefan. 1984. *Das christlich-koptische Ägypten in arabischer Zeit*, part 1. Wiesbaden: Ludwig Reichert.
Tripp, David H., and Peter Wheeler. 1989. Die älteste christliche Hymne mit Noten – als Thema eines Seminarvorhabens in Liturgiewissenschaft. *Jahrbuch für Liturgik und Hymnologie* 32:94–104.
–. 1997. The Oldest Christian Hymn with Music: Its Use as a Seminary Project in Liturgical Studies. *The Hymn* 48/2: 20–24.
Turner, E. G. 1952. Roman Oxyrhynchus. *The Journal of Egyptian Archaeology* 38:78–93.
–. 1954. Recto and Verso. *The Journal of Egyptian Archeology* 40:102–6.

Turner, E. G., and R. P. Winnington-Ingram. 1959. Monody with Musical Notation. *The Oxyrhynchus Papyri* 25:113–19.

Ursprung, Otto. 1923. Der Hymnus aus Oxyrhonchos, Das älteste Denkmal christlicher (Kirchen–?) Musik. *Société union musicologique* 3:105–32.

—. 1926. Der Hymnus aus Oxyrhynchos (Ende des III. Jahrh.: ägyptischer Papyrusfund) im Rahmen unserer Kirchenmusikalischen Frühzeit. *Theologie und Glaube* 18:387–419.

Usher, M. D. 1995. The Sixth Sibyllene Oracle as a Literary Hymn. *Greek, Roman, and Byzantine Studies* 36:25–49.

van den Broek, Roelof. 1996. *Studies in Gnosticism and Alexandrian Christianity*. Leiden: E. J. Brill.

van Haelst, Joseph. 1976. *Catalogue des papyrus littéraires juifs et chrétiens*. Paris: Sorbonne.

Vandoni, Mariangela. 1964. *Feste pubbliche e private*. Milan: Istituto Editoriale Cisalpino.

Vivell, P. C. 1911. Direkte Entwicklung des römischen Kirchengesanges aus der vorchristlichen Musik. *Kirchenmusikalisches Jahrbuch* 24:2–54.

Vos, Piet G., and Jim M. Troost. 1989. Ascending and Descending Melodic Intervals: Statistical Findings and Their Perceptual Relevance. *Music Perception* 6:383–96.

Wagner, M. M., trans. 1950. *Saint Basil: Ascetical Works*. FC 9. New York: Fathers of the Church.

Wagner, Rudolf. 1924. Der Oxyrhynchos-Notenpapyrus. *Philologus* 79:201–22.

Wellesz, Egon J. 1945. The Earliest Example of Christian Hymnody. *Classical Quarterly* 39:34–45.

—. 1961. *A History of Byzantine Music and Hymnography*, 2nd ed. Oxford: Clarendon Press.

Werner, Eric. 1947. The Conflict between Hellenism and Judaism in the Music of the Early Church. *Hebrew Union College Annual* 20:407–70.

—. 1959. *The Sacred Bridge: The Interdependence of Liturgy and Music in Synagogue and Church during the First Millennium*. London: Dennis Dobson. New York: Columbia University Press.

Wessely, Charles, ed. 1906–1924. *Les plus anciens monuments du Christianisme écrtits sur papyrus*. 2 vols. PO 4/2 and 18/3. Paris: Firmin-Didot.

West, Martin L. 1982. *Greek Metre*. Oxford: Clarendon Press.

—. 1992a. Analecta Musica. *Zeitschrift für Papyrologie und Epigraphik* 92:1–54.

—. 1992b. *Ancient Greek Music*. Oxford: Clarendon Press.

—. 1998. Texts with Musical Notation. *The Oxyrhynchus Papyri* 65:81–102.

Westermann, W. L. 1932. Entertainment in the Villages of Graeco-Roman Egypt. *The Journal of Egyptian Archeology* 18:16–27.

Westermeyer, Paul. 1998. *Te Deum: The Church and Music*. Minneapolis: Fortress Press.

Wilamowitz-Möllendorff, Ulrich von. 1912. Die griechische Literatur des Altertums. Pages 3–238 in Ulrich von Wilamowitz-Möllendorff et al., *Die griechische und lateinische Literatur und Sprache*, 3rd ed. Leipzig and Berlin: Teubner.

—. 1922. Die neuen Texte aus Oxyrhynchos. *Deutsche Literaturzeitung* 43:313–17.

Williams, Frederick. 1978. *Callimachus: Hymn to Apollo*. Oxford: Clarendon.

Winnington-Ingram, R. P. 1954. Greek music, ancient. Pages 770–82 in vol. 3 of *Grove's Dictionary of Music and Musicians*, 5th ed. Edited by E. Blom. New York: Macmillan.

—. 1955. II. The Music. In Eitrem, S. Leiv Admundsen, and R. P. Winnington-Ingram, Fragments of Unknown Greek Tragic Texts, *Symbolae Osloenses* 31:29–87.

—. 1958. Ancient Greek Music: 1932–1957. *Lustrum* 3:5–58.

—. 1968. *Mode in Ancient Greek Music*. Amsterdam: Adolf M. Hakkert [reprint of 1936 edition].

Wolbergs, Thielko. 1971. *Psalmen und Hymnen der Gnosis und des frühen Christentums.* Vol. 1 of *Griechische religiöse Gedichte der ersten nachchristlichen Jahrhunderte.* BKP 40. Meisenheim am Glan: Anton Hain.

Wolfson, Elliot R. 2004. Seven Mysteries of Knowledge: Qumran E/Sotericism Recovered. Pages 177–213 in *The Idea of Biblical Interpretation: Essays in Honor of James L. Kugel.* Edited by Hindy Najman and Judith H. Newman. Leiden and Boston: Brill.

Yuan, J. 2005. Fragment with Musical Notation. *The Oxyrhynchus Papyri* 69:45–46.

Index of Subjects and Names

For ancient authors, see also Index of Ancient Texts; for modern authors, see also Index of Modern Authors

accents (relation to melody) 4, 108–15
accentuation / emphasis (melodic) 167–69
Aemilianus 134
agape (meal) 3
Alexandria 134, 136, 139
Alypius 28–29, 84
amen-Jubilations 4
Anonymous Bellermanni 28, 34, 166
Apollonaris 156
Apostolic Constitutions 38, 130
Aristides Quintilianus 28, 84
Aristoxenus 84
arsis (and arsis points) 3, 34–35
Athenaeus, paean of 170
Atrium Musicae de Madrid 128
Aurelius Ammonius 136, 138

Bacchius 84
Berlin paean 115, 166
Boethius 28
Byzantine music 6

Cephro 134
certificate of sacrifice 134, 136
chant
– liturgical 3, 152
– Byzantine 7–8
– Gregorian 7–8, 106–107, 157
– Japanese 158, 169
– Lapp 158
– Malaysian 158
– Maori 158
– Venda 158
cherubic hymn 149–50
cithara 141, 153

Clement of Alexandria , hymn of 16, 66, 125, 130, 154–55
Cleonides 84
Constantine 134–36
Constantius 135
Copres 136
Council of Laodicea 156 (Canon 59)

Decius 134, 138
deixis 73–81
Delphic paeans 12, 30, 89–90, 95, 112, 123, 161, 163, 166, 169–70
Diocletian 134–36, 137–38
Dionysius of Alexandria 134, 152
Dorian 166, 172, 188

Ensemble Kérylos 121, 128
Ensemble De Organographia 121, 128
Epagathos 140
Eucharist / eucharistic service 147–48

Galerius 135
Gallienus 135
Gaudentius 28
Gloria Patri (Lesser Doxology) 49
Gregorian chant 106–107
Gregory of Nazianzus 30, 156
Greek music 2–3, 6, 8–9, 12, 83–90
– accents (melody and verbal accents) 108–115
– accentuation (melodic emphasis) 168–69
– *agōgē* 98–100
– Athenaeus, paean of (tonal analysis of) 170–71, 174–76, 178–79, 181–84

- Berlin paean (tonal analysis of)
  171–73, 176–78, 180, 192–94
- cadence(s) 89–90, 179–80
- Christian tradition of 150–56
- composite intervals 102
- concordant intervals 85, 160
- conjunct tetrachord (defined) 87
- Delphic paeans (tonal analysis of)
  170–71, 174–76, 178–86, 188
- dynamic (functional) note naming
  161–63
- disjunct tetrachord 87
- *ekkrousmos* 99
- *eklēmmatismos* 99
- finals 175–81
- functional note naming –
  see "dynamic note naming"
- genus 85, 87, 141
- Greater Perfect System 86
- *harmoniai* 83, 164, 167
- Hyperionian (Hyperiastian) *tonos* 193
- Hyperphrygian *tonos* 182
- Hypolydian octave species 172, 194
- Hypolydian *tonos* 184–86, 194
- Hypophrygian octave species 166, 172, 192, 194
- Hypophrygian *tonos* 175, 185–86
- Ionian (Iastian) *tonos* 162, 175, 186
- key (see also *tonos*) 28
- Lesser Perfect System 86
- Limenius, paean of (tonal analysis of)
  170–71, 174–76, 178, 184–86
- Lydian octave species 165, 172, 193
- Lydian *tonos* 165, 175, 184, 186–91
- melodic emphasis 168–69
- *mesē* 86–87, 160–62, 164–65, 170, 182, 184–86, 189, 192
- Mesomedes 141
- invoc. of Calliope and Apollo (tonal analysis of) 171–73, 176–78, 180, 188–89
- hymn to Nemesis (tonal analysis of)
  171–73, 177, 180, 191–92
- hymn to the Sun (tonal analysis of)
  171–73, 177, 180, 189–90
- Mesomedes (?), invoc. of the Muse
  (tonal analysis of) 171–73, 176–80, 187–88

- mode(s) 83, 88, 164–65, 187, 190, 193–94
- modulation 98–99
- movable notes 87, 159–60
- musicians 140–42, 151–52
- Mixolydian octave species 166, 172, 189
- notation 28–31, 141
- note names 85
- octave equivalency 168, 187
- octave species 89, 162–66, 171–72, 178–79, 185–87, 189, 190
- openings of melodies 100–101
- P.Ber. 6870, lines 1–12 (see Berlin paean)
- P.Ber. 6870, lines 13–15 (tonal analysis of) 177
- P.Ber. 6870, lines 20–22 (tonal analysis of) 177
- P.Louvre E 10534 (tonal analysis of) 175
- P.Oslo 1413 a, lines 15–19; g–m (tonal analysis of) 177
- P.Oxy. 1786 (see independent entry)
- *petteia* 99, 168
- Phrygian octave species 162, 164–66, 171–72, 178–79, 186–87, 193
- Phrygian *tonos* 181–84
- pitch center(s) 89–90, 158–63, 165
- *plokē* 99
- positional note naming –
  see "thetic note naming"
- recordings of (modern) –
  see also Discography
- repetition and variation 104–108
- scales 85–88
- Seikilos, epitaph of (tonal analysis of)
  162, 166, 171, 173, 175–78, 186–88
- scores 141–42 (found at Oxyrhynchus), 144 and 146 (purpose of), 150–51 (survival of)
- *spondeion* 123
- standing (fixed) notes 87, 159–60
- starting notes 177
- tetrachord/tetrachordal 86–88, 159–60, 162–63, 165–67, 169–70, 178, 180, 182, 185, 187–89, 191, 192

Index of Subjects and Names

- thetic note naming 161–63, 187–89, 192
- "thetic shift" 162, 164
- theory 83–90, 164–65
- tonal analysis of individual Greek musical scores 181–94
- tonal organization of melodies 177–79
- tonality 158–81
- *tonē* 168, 194
- tonic 160, 165, 166, 189, 193
- *tonos* (*tonoi*) 88, 141, 162–64, 169–71, 180–94
- Unmodulating System 86–87, 161

Grenfell, B. 129, 131

Hesiod, *Opera et dies* (*Works and Days*) 154
hymns, Christian 155–56

Jacobs, A. 118
Jewish music 2, 5–6
John Chrysostom 130
Jomard, E. 131

"Let All Mortal Flesh Keep Silence" 46, 149
Liturgy of Saint James 148
Licinius 136
Limenius, paean of 170
Lucian 125 (hymn to Gout)
Lyravlos 120
lyre
- use by Christians 153
- lyre-based music 141, 161, 163, 188

Mareotian nome 134
Martianus Capella 28
martyrs at Oxyrhynchus 136
Maxentius 135
Maximian 135
Maximinus II (Daia) 135
melisms / melisma 4, 7, 102–104, 141–42
memorability (of tones in music) 167–69
Mesomedes 141, 151
- hymn to Nemesis 166
- hymn to the Sun 166
- invocation of Calliope and Apollo 166
- invocation of the Muse 166

metrical poetry, Christian 155–56
Milvian Bridge 135

Nepos 152–53
Nonnus of Panopolis 156

Origen 81, 130, 139
"Oriental" music 5–7
Oxyrhynchus 129,
- Christians at 132–33, 134–38
- Christian literature at 139
- churches 133, 137–39
- music culture at 140–42
- population 132–33

Papyrus Oxyrhynchus 1786
- accents (melody and verbal accents) 108–15
- angels / powers 37–38, 49–59, 62
- arsis pointing 34–35
- cadence(s) 93, 98
- copy or autograph 142–45
- date 11, 129–30
- deixis 73–81
- doxology 59–62
- form 65–73
- Greek music and 2–3, 6, 8–12, 83–128
- handwriting in 143
- history of interpretation 1–12
- the hymn in time of persecution 137–38
- imaginal world 77–81, 149
- interpretation of text 37–63
- liturgical chant and 3, 7–8
- melisms / melisma 4, 7, 101–104
- meter 1, 4–8, 11, 123–26, 124–25
- melodic patterns 115–16
- melody, nature of 98–102
- musical analysis of 83–128,
- notation 6–7, 9, 28–34, 123–26, 143–44
- octave species 166, 171–72, 193
- performance of 5, 116–128, 146–50
- physical aspects of fragment 13–14
- purpose of 142–45
- recordings of (modern) 121–22, 128
- repetition and variation 104–108

- rhetorical aspects 73–82
- rhythm 35–36, 96, 124–25
- scale 90–91
- self-referentiality 77–81
- silence motif 2, 10, 19–20, 38–47, 62, 138
- survival of 150–51
- text (establishment of) 16–28
- tonal analysis 171–73, 176, 194
- tonal axis 91–92
- transcription 14–16, 92–93 (in modern staff notation)

Panopolis 139
Paul (from the Oxyrhynchite nome) 136
persecution (Roman) 134–38
Phos hilaron 48–49, 73–74
pitch centers 157–81
Porphyry 125
Psalms 152–54
psalmody 6, 152–53
prosphora 147–48
Ptolemy 91, 162–63, 188

Quintilian 144

Satrius Arrianus 136
Seikilos epitaph 4
self-referentiality (poetic) 73–81
silence (ritual gesture and motif) 2, 10, 19–20, 38–47, 149
Songs of the Sabbath Sacrifice 51
Stefos, P. 120
Synesius 1, 66, 141, 156
Syrian music 5–6

Terpander 75
tonality 157–81
tonic 157, 160, 166
Thebaid 136
Trinity 47–49, 130

Valerian 134–35, 137–38
vesper hymn 48–49

Index of Modern Authors

Abert, H. 2, 5, 109, 126
Alston, R. 131–132
Apel, W. 106
Asper, M. 61, 76–77
Attridge, H. 53
Ausfeld, K. 68

Bagnall, R. S. 131–133, 151
Barker, A. VI, 128, 144, 160–162, 168
Barnes, T. D. 134–135
Baud-Bovy, S. 187
Becker, H. 73
Bekker, I. 149
Bélis, A. 12, 83–84, 103, 121, 159, 168, 175, 183, 185–186
Bethe, E. 38, 40
Blacking, J. 158
Bonnet, M. 60
Bowman, A. K.
Bradshaw, P. F. 46, 58, 147, 152
Bremer, J. M. 39, 61, 67–68, 73–74, 78–79, 123, 146
Brightman, F. E. 148–149
Brown, P. 138
Brucker, R. 52, 67, 154
Bühler, K. 77
Bulloch, A. 75
Butler, D. 177

Calame, C. 73, 78–79
Campbell, D. A. 79
Cashdan, E. 52
Chailley, J. 84, 175, 185–187
Charlesworth, J. H. 50
Chávez, C. 106–107
Chrestou, P. K. 147
Clarke, G. 134, 149
Cockle, W. E. H. 140

Coles, R. A. 14
Colomo, D. VI, 14
Comotti, G. 144
Cone, E. T. 106–107
Connolly, H. 152, 156
Cook, N. 105, 107
Cooper, J. 59
Cosgrove, C. H. 4, 54, 109, 112, 128, 153, 155
Cribiore, R. 139
Crönert, W. 1
Crocker, R. L. 7, 106
Crusius, O. 108

D'Alessio, G. B. 74
Danielwicz, J. 74
Del Grande 1, 10, 21, 24, 39, 45
Denniston, J. D. 19
Devine, A. M. 108
Devreese, R. 58
Diggle, J. 40
Dihle, A. 6, 16, 109
Düring, I. 162–163
Duysinx, F. 162

Ehrman, B. D. 53, 60–61
Eisenhofer, L. 154
Elior, R. 44, 52
Elliott, J. K. 147
Epp, E. J. 139–140
Epstein, I. 52

Fichman, I. F. 132
Fiensy, D. A. 50
Frederiksen, B. 118–119
Früchtel, L. 27, 54, 61–62
Funk, F. X. 46, 48, 50, 56, 61, 148
Furley, W. D. 39, 61, 67, 73–74, 78–79, 123, 146

Garzya, A. 141
Gelineau, J. 127
Ghedini, G. 61
Graves, R. 50
Gruber, J. 20, 26 42–43

Haas, C. J. 134
Hagel, S. VI, 86, 88, 117–118, 120,
    128, 161, 171, 183, 185–186,
    188–189, 194
Hannick, Ch. 10, 150
Healy, P. J. 134
Heitsch, E. 41–42, 76, 125
Henderson, J. 19, 40–41
Henrichs, A. 43, 60, 65, 73, 81
Hett, W. S. 93, 160, 168
Hiley, D. 146
Hilgard, A. 66
Holleman, A. W. J. 8–9
Hopkinson, N. 75
Hoppin, R. H. 157
Huron, D. 168
Hunt, A. S. 1, 6, 13, 15–17, 19, 21, 26,
    32–33, 39, 129, 143
Hyer, B. 157

Jammers, E. 6
Jeffery, P. 11
Joannou, P.-P. 156
Johnson, W. A. 102, 140
Jones, S. 1, 13, 15, 17, 19, 21, 27, 32, 34,
    39, 129, 143

Keister, J. 158
Keresztes, P. 134
Kerman, J. 106
Koetschau, P. 55, 80
Kovacs, D. 40–41
Kroll, J. 153–154
Krüger, J. 131, 139, 146

Lampe, G. W. H. 152
Landels, J. G. VI, 84, 88, 159–160, 162,
    164, 183, 186, 189
Leclercq, J. 58, 126
Lightfoot, J. B. 17
Lipsius, R. A. 60
Lobel, E. 14

Lohmeyer, E. 52
Luijendijk, A.-M. 133, 136, 138

Maclean, A. F. 59
MacLennan, H. 131
MacLeod, M. D. 42
Malingrey, A.-A. 57, 80
Malm, W. P. 158
Mathiesen, T. 28, 84, 159, 164, 186
Martinez, D. VI,
Martínez, F. G. 51
Matusky, P. 158
May, G. 155
McGowan, A. 147
McKinnon, J. 6, 11, 127–128
Meier, S. 7, 19, 21, 126
Mercier, B.-Ch. 148
Meyer, M. C. 4, 109, 112
Mingana, A. 58
Mohrmann, C. 155
Mountford, J. F. V, 6, 90, 104, 109, 143,
    172, 186, 193–194
Mras, K. 62
Muehlberger, E. 56
Münscher, K. 6, 16
Murray, A. T. 39

Nettl, B. 176
Neubecker, A. 83
Newsom, C. A. 51
Norden, E. 67
Norton, R. 157

Odahl, C. M. 134, 136
Olson, D. T. 59
Ortmann, O. 168

Pearson, B. A. 140
Parsons, P. VI, 14, 129, 131–132,
    134–135
Perler, O. 60
Pighi, G. B. 6, 10, 13, 15–17, 21, 23–24,
    27–28, 37, 39, 46, 143
Plank, P. 74
Pöhlmann, E. 6, 9–12, 14–15,
    17–19, 21–22, 25, 27, 31, 34, 39,
    66, 69–70, 76, 100, 102–103,
    109, 116, 120–123, 127, 141,

143–144, 150, 159, 163, 181, 183, 185, 191
Porter, W. J. 11
Pruscello, L. 144
Preisendanz, K. 43, 65, 81
Prieur, J.-M. 60
Pruche, B. 48

Quasten, J. 10

Race, W. H. 74
Rea, J. R. 131, 135–136, 140
Reinach, T. 2, 15, 18, 24, 27, 34, 39, 58, 109, 125, 143, 182, 186–187
Reischl, W. C. 56
Réti, R. 157
Rios, R. 167
Roberts, C. H. 139–140
Royal, M. 168
Rubenson, S. 139
Rupp, J. 56

Sachs, C. 158
Sagnard, F. 38
Sampson, G. 115
Schäfer, P. 44
Schermann, T. 61
Sharp, M. 131
Simon, E. 40
Slater, W. J. 74
Smyth, H. W. 20, 124
Solomon, J. 84, 88, 91, 98, 159, 162, 164, 168, 186, 188
Stäblein, B. 3, 127
Stählin, O. 27, 49, 54, 61–62, 128, 153
Stark, R. S. 132–133, 151
Strohm, H. 20, 26, 42–43

Tan, S. B. 158
Terzaghi, N. 1, 6, 10, 16, 37, 39

Thomson, W. 157, 168, 182
Tidner, E. 46, 55
Tigchelaar, E. J. C. 51
Timm, S. 136
Tonneau, R. 58
Treu, U. 27, 49, 54, 61–62, 128, 153
Tripp, D. H. 7, 146
Turner, E. G. 129, 131, 143

Ursprung, O. 3–5, 39, 104

van den Broek, R. 139
van Haelst, J. 139

Wagner, M. M. 149
Wagner, R. 6, 14–15, 17–18, 21–22, 24, 31–34, 39, 45, 58, 109, 126
Wellesz, E. J. 6–8, 11
West, M. L. VI, 4, 6–7, 10–12, 14, 16–19, 21–22, 25, 27–31, 34, 39, 41, 61, 69–70, 75–76, 83, 85–86, 88, 95, 99–100, 102–105, 108, 115–117, 120–125, 127–128, 140–141, 143–144, 150, 156, 159, 163, 165–166, 181–183, 185, 187, 189–191, 193
Westermann, W. L. 140
Wheeler, P. 7, 146
Wilamowitz-Möllendorff, U. 1, 155
Williams, F. 75
Winnington-Ingram, R. P. 8–9, 18, 34–35, 88, 90, 98, 108–109, 143, 160–166, 168, 172, 182–183, 186–190, 193–194
Wolbergs, T. 7–8, 10, 19, 37–39, 147–149, 154
Wolfson, E. R. 51
Wright, W. 149

Yuan, J. 103
Youtie, H. C. 14

Index of Ancient Texts
(see also Subject and Name Index)

(a) Bible

Genesis	
28:12	57

Job	
38:7	50

Psalms	
19	39
23:10 LXX	50
33:8 LXX	55
41:13 (40:14 LXX)	59
47	39
69	39
72:19 (71:19)	59
96	39
148	39
148:2 LXX	50
148:3 LXX	50
148:3	55

Isaiah	
6:3	52

Daniel	
3:61 LXX	50

Habakkuk	
2:20	44

Zechariah	
2:13 (2:17)	44

1 Esdras	
9:46–47	58

Tobit	
12:12	55

Baruch	
3:34 LXX	50

Matthew	
7:11	27, 62

John	
1:51	56
3:3	59

Romans	
8:1	19
8:32	27, 62
12:1	38
16:24	59
16:25–27	148
16:27	59

1 Corinthians	
11:9–10	52
14:15	5
14:26	147
15:24–28	52

Galatians	
4:21–31	52

Philippians	
1:1	61
2:6–11	52
2:10	49
2:10–11	52

4:19	62	10:1	53
4:20	59, 148	10:1–10	53
4:23	59	10:19	53
		10:22	53
Ephesians		12:22–23	53
2:6	52	13:21	59, 148
5:18–19	5	13:25	59
Colossians		1 Peter	
3:16	5, 153	3:22	50
3:16–20	147	4:11	60
		5:11	59, 148
1 Timothy		5:14	59
1:17	148		
4:18	59	2 Peter	
6:17	27, 62	3:18	148
2 Timothy		Revelation	
4:18	148	1:5–7	148
4:22	59	1:6	59–60
		2:21	59
Hebrews		5:12	61
8:5	53	5:13	60–61
9:2–3	53	7:9–17	52
9:8	53	7:12	59–60
9:12	53	7:14	53
9:24–25	53		

(b) Ancient Christian and Byzantine Literature

Acts of Andrew and Matthias		7.38.8	61
33	60	7.43.3	47, 49
		7.48	148
Acts of Paul (including *Acts of Paul and Thecla*)		7.48.3	48
		8.12.5–51	148
45.6	60	8.12.50	48–49
		8.13.10	48
Acts of Thomas		8.15.9	48–49
170.28	49	8.22.4	61
Apostolic Constitutions		The Apostolic Fathers	
	49		
2.57.15	46, 148	*1 Clement*	
5.10.2	152	34.3–4	53
7–8	50	34.6–7	53
7.35.4	50	64	61
7.35.3–4	56	65	61

2 Clement
17.5 60

Didache 49
8.2–3 148

Ignatius

To the Trallians
5 17

Martyrdom of Polycarp
14.1 50

Shepherd of Hermas

Similitudes
59.4 [V.6.4] 38
83.2 [IX.6.2] 38
89.8 [IX.12.8] 38

Apostolic Tradition 45, 63
16.4 152
16.5 152
29C (Bradshaw et al.)
 = 25 (Botte) 72
29.26–32
 (//41.15) 45–46
79.27–30
 (//41.15) 80
79.30–32 (//41.5) 55

Athanasius

Apologia secunda
71.6.12 133

Augustine

Sermo
273.7 134

Basil of Caesarea

De Spiritu Sancto
27.68.25–27 48
29.73 147
29.73.37–43 74
29.73.39–41 48
29.73.42–43 48

Homilia dicta tempore
PG 31:328.42 61

Regulae fusius tractatae
2.3 149

Clement of Alexandria

Excerpta ex Theodoto
1.12.2 38

Paedagogus
2.4.43 72, 128, 153–54
2.4.44 147, 153–55
3.11.80 147, 153
3.12.101 154
3.101.2 49

Protrepticus
12.119.1–2 54
12.119.2 153

Quis dives salvetur
42.20 61

Stromateis (Stromata)
6.11.90.1 153, 155
6.14.113.3 153
7.2.88 122
7.7.43.2 27, 62
7.7.35 147
7.7.35.4 62
7.7.49 147, 155
7.7.49.4 72, 154
7.7.49 54
7.12.78.4 54
7.12.78.6 54

Cyprian

Acta Proconsularia Sancti Cypriani
1.1–7 134

Epistulae
2 152
76–80 134

Index of Ancient Texts

Cyril of Jerusalem

Catecheses
13.26   56

Mystagogic Catechesis
5.6   56, 147

Procatechesis
15   56

Dionysius of Alexandria

Apologia
PL 5:128, no. 16   60

Didascalia Apostolorum
1.6.3–5   152, 156

Eusebius

Commentaria in Psalmos
PG 23:645.39–40   62
PG 23:704.25–26   62

Historia ecclesiastica
7.10.9–11.25   134
7.11.4–10   134
7.24.1–3   153
7.24.4   152–53
8   135
8.2.4   137
8.2.4–5   135
9.7.2–16   136
9.9.12   136

De martyribus palaestinae
3.1   135

Praeparatio evangelica
3.5.5   62
2.6.12   62

Vita Constantini
1.49–56   136
1.57   135
2.50–51   135

Gregory of Tours

De gloria martyrum
75   81

Hippolytus

Refutatio omnium haeresium
5.9.8–9   155
5.10.2 ff.   155
6.37.1   155

Traditio apostolica (see *Apostolic Tradition*)

[Pseuodo-]Hippolytus

Contra Noetum
18.10   60

Jerome

Vita Hilarionis
20   152

John Chrysostom

De sacerdotio
3.5   57
6.4.41–43   57, 80
6.4.48–49   57

In Eph. 1
hom. 3.5   57, 80

In Eph. 4
hom. 14.4   57

In 1 Tim.
hom. 14.4   56

In Psalm. 118
PG 55:707.12–13   62

Irenaeus

Adversus haereses
1.15.6   155

Contra Celsum
8.67 55

Justin Martyr

Apologia i
65 148
65.3 61

Dialogus cum Tryphone
8.2 61
9.4 61
10.5 61
36.4–5 50
85.6 50

Lactantius

Divinarum instituti
14.15–22 156

De mortibus persecutorum
7.2 135
10.6–12.5 135
15 135
49 136

Martyrdom of Andrew
[part of *Acts of Andrew*]
19.3 60

Melito of Sardis

Peri Pascha
82.3 60

Origen

De Oratione
11.5 55
31.5 55, 80

Fragmenta ex commentariis in Proverbia
PG 13.28.13–14 62

Philostorgius

Historia ecclesiastica
3.13 48

Photius

Bibliotheca
apud Proclus,
Chrestomathy
320a9–10 (Bekker) 66–67

Regula Magistri
48.6–9 81

Serapion of Thmuis

Sacramentarium Serapionis
10 38

Sozomen

Historia ecclesiastica
3.20.8 48
5.18 155

Synesius of Cyrene

Epistulae
95 141

Hymni
1 and 2 65
1.1–117 68
1.72–85 10, 23, 42
1.78 124
1.78–80 20
1.82 124
1.266–67 16
1.345 18
2.5 18
2.26–43 10
2.28–43 23, 43
3 122
3.21 18
5.6 18

Tertullian

Ad uxorum 2.8.8–9 147

De anima
9.4 72

Apologeticum
39.16–18	147
39.18	72–73

De idolatria
5	152
7	152
9	152

Testamentum domini nostri
1.23	59, 130
2.11	147

Theodore of Mopsuestia

Homiliae catecheticae
15.20	58

Theodoret

Historia ecclesiastica
2.19	48

(c) Ancient Jewish Literature

Babylonian Talmud

Hullin
91b	52

Dead Sea Scrolls
1QS XI, 8	51
1QSa [1Q28a] II, 8–9	51
4Q403 frg. 1, I, 30–46	51

Hekhalot Literature (*Hekhalot Rabbati*)
§ 101 (Schäfer)	52
§ 173 (Schäfer)	44
§ 788 (Schäfer)	52

Old Testament Pseudepigrapha

Jubilees
2:18	51
8:19	51
30:14	51
31:14	51

Sibylline Oracles
8	155

Testaments of the Twelve Patriarchs
T. Abraham
14.9	49
14.12	50
20.1–2	59
20.48	60

Philo

Confusio linguarum
171	50

(d) Other Literature of the Greco-Roman World

Anonymous Bellermanni
2	116
2–10	99
9–10	116
21–23	162
84–93	99
86–92	116
97–101	141
97–104	100
104	141

Appian

Libica (in *Historia romana*)
385.1	19

Apollonius Syscolus

Syntax
1–2	125
1.96	78
2.11–17	78

Aristides Quintilianus

De musica (*Peri mousikē*)
1.6–19	84
1.12	168
1.12.8–13	98
1.12.12–13	98
1.12.14–17	99

Aristophanes

Acharnenses
237–38	40

Aves
377–78	41
723–24	41

Thesmophoriazusae
39–48	39
101–04	78
295–96	39

Pax
433–34	40

[Pseudo-]Aristotle

Problemata physica
19.17–18	127, 168
19.20	160
19.33	93, 160, 166, 176
19.35	85

Aristoxenus

Elementa harmonica (*Harmonikōn stoicheiōn*)
1.29–33	98
2.38.32–39.3	167

Callimachus

Hymnus in Apollinem
	42–43, 65

Hymnus in Demeter
	75, 78

Hymnus in Jovem
90	61

Demosthenes

Exordia
21.2	149

Cleonides

Harmonica introductio (*Eisagogē harmonikē*)
29.2–3	98–99
29.4–5	99, 168
29.5–7	168

Corpus hermeticum
13.17–20	43, 65

Dionysius of Halicarnassus

De compositione verborum
63.4	159

Dionysus Thrax
451 (Hilgard)	66

Euripides

Bacchae
69–70	40
1084–85	41

Hecuba
529–33	40

Hercules furens
694	39

Index of Ancient Texts

Iphigenia aulidensis
1564 — 40

Hesiod

Theogonia
46 — 61
111 — 61
633 — 61

Homer

Iliad
1.472–73 — 67
9.171 — 39
19.255–56 — 39

Odyssea
8.325 — 61

Homeric Hymns

HHApollo
3.19–20 — 75–76
3.207 ff. — 75–76

Horace

Carmina 3.1.2 — 40

Julius Pollux

Onomasticon
1.176 — 38
4.91 — 40
4.94 — 40

Lucian

Podagra
126–33 — 42
129–33 — 65

Pindar

Dithyrambi
P.Oxy. 1604, 2.10 — 22

Olympionicae
9.2 — 22
10.79 — 74

Pythionicae
4.179 — 22
10.35 — 39

Plato

Leges
801a1 — 39

Respublica
10.607 — 66

Plutarch

Moralia
378D — 40
380B–C — 130

Ptolemy

Harmonica
1.5 — 168
2.5 — 162–63
2.5–6 — 86
2.8 — 168

Tetrabiblos
1.6 (§ 20) — 17

Quintilian

Institutio oratoria
1.12.14 — 144

Sophocles

Oedipus coloneus
1623 — 19

Theocritus

Idyll
2.33–34 — 43

(e) Collections

Furley and Bremer, *Greek Hymns*

1.1 (hymn to Zeus-Kouros at Crete) 73, 78–79
2.3 (hymn to Hestia) 75
6.1.1 (paean to Asclepius at Erythrai) 70–71, 75, 79
6.6 (Herodas, hymn to Asclepius) 71
7.5 (Macedonicus, hymn to Apollo) 75
7.6 (hymn to Asclepius on Kassel stone) 70
7.7.2 (hymn to Telesphorus) 61, 68, 74

Heitsch, *Die griechischen Dichterfragmente der römischen Kaiserzeit*

2.2 (Mesomedes, hymn to the Sun) 20, 42, 65, 122
2.4 (Mesomedes, hymn to Nature) 122
2.5 (Mesomedes, hymn to Isis) 123
44.3 (hymn to Attis) 122
45.3 (Chr. hymn) 125, 156
51 (hymn to Apollo) 41, 65

Pöhlmann and West, *Documents of Ancient Greek Music* (see also Papyri)

Copenhagen inv. 14897 (epitaph of Seikilos) 84, 88–89, 100, 103, 162, 166, 171, 173, 175–78, 186–88
Delphic paeans 170–71, 174–76, 178–81, 181–86, 188
Delph. inv. 489 et al. (paean of Limenius) 41, 43, 65, 69, 100, 170–71, 174–76, 178, 184–86
– Delph. inv. 517 et al. (paean of Athenaeus) 100, 170–71, 174–76, 178–79, 181–84
Mesomedes
– invocation of Calliope and Apollo 70, 89, 100, 103, 171–73, 176–78, 180, 188–89
– invocation of the Muse 69, 89, 100, 103, 171–73, 176–80, 187–88
– hymn to Nemesis 18, 89, 100, 103, 171–73, 177, 180, 191–92
– hymn to the Sun 89, 100, 103, 171–73, 177, 180, 189–90

(f) Papyri

P.Alex. 6	140	P.Columb. 441	140
P.Ashm. inv. 89b / 29–32	29	PGM III.198–205	43, 65
		VII.320–24	43, 65
P.Ber. 6870 + 14097, lines 1–12 (Berlin paean)	4, 7, 89, 91, 100, 103–4, 108, 115, 171–73, 176–78, 180, 192–94	P.Hamb. 6–7	147
		P.Heid. 44b–3	147
		51–52	147
6870, lines 13–15	100, 116, 177	P.Louvre E 10534	12, 103, 150, 174–75, 176
6870, lines 20–22	100, 116, 177		
8299	60, 156		
13415	61	P.Mich. inv. 1250	29

Index of Ancient Texts

2958, lines 1–18	100, 104	verso frg. 3	103
2958, lines 19–26	103	3162	29, 103
		3465	139
P.Ms.Shøyen 2260	29, 103	3529	136
		3704 frg. 1↓	18, 120
P.Oslo 1413 a	112	3704 frg. 1→	113
P.Oslo 1413 a,		3705	29, 150
lines 1–15;b–f	18, 100, 102, 115, 171	4461	146
P.Oslo 1413 a,		col. 1.6 + 2.1–3	103
lines 15–19;		col. 2.4–7	103
g–m frg. a	102, 177	4462 frg. 1	103
		4463	103–04, 142
P.Oxy.		4464	103
43 verso	133	4465	103, 146
407	60	4466	29, 103, 123, 146
519	140	4467	29, 103, 146
657	139	4710	12, 29, 103, 150
1275	140		
1786	passim	P.Strasb. 341	140
2436	143		
2436 col. 2	103	P.Vienna G 2315	29
2601	136		
2665	136	P.Yale CtYBR	
2673	136	inv. 4510	18
2721	140	col. 1.3	120
3074 frg. 1↓	103	col. 1.1–10 +2.1–5	103
3074 frg. 1→	103	col. 2.1–6	103
3099	131		
3119	134–35	*Prague* 1 81	
3161	29		
recto frg. 1	103, 113	Wessely inv.	
recto frg. 2.1–10	103–04	no. 19898 recto	47
recto frg. 3	103		
recto frg. 4	103		

Index of Greek Words
(selected)

ᾄδω 67, 75, 141
ἀείδω 76
ἀήρ 25, 41
ἀγαθός 15, 36–37, 61–62, 93, 97–98, 101, 104, 111, 114, 119
ἀγγελικός 17, 56
ἄγγελος 46, 50, 54, 57
ἅγιος 15, 26, 32, 35, 37, 48, 49, 54, 58, 93, 95, 111, 114, 117, 119, 121, 124
ἀγωγή 98
αἰθήρ 20, 25, 41–42
αἴθρη 41
αἰνέω 48, 62
αἰνός 15, 26–27, 36–37, 48–49, 58, 61, 93, 97, 101, 104, 111, 119, 121, 124
ἀίω 42
αἰών 47–48, 60
αἰώνιος 61
ἀμήν 15, 26, 32, 36–37, 47–48, 58, 60, 72, 93, 95, 97–98, 101–02, 104, 111, 114, 119, 121, 124
ἀμφιανακτίζω 75
ἀναγνωστής 136
ἄνεμος 24–25
ἀντίφωνος 168
ἀνυμνέω 56
ἀοιδή 42
ἀπολείπω 15, 23–25
ἀρχάγγελος 17
ἀρχή 16
ἄστρον 2, 15, 18, 20, 22, 32, 35, 37–39, 50, 55, 92, 94, 111, 119, 121, 124

βαρύς 99
βασιλεύς 15, 27
βασιλεία 61

γᾶ 25, 41
γένος 85

δείλη 15
δεῖξις 77–78
δεσπότις 17
δόξα 15, 26–27, 36–37, 47–48, 60–61, 93, 97, 101, 109, 119, 121, 124
δοξάζω 54
δοξαλογία 48
δούλη 17
δύναμις 15, 17, 26, 36–37, 46, 49–50, 58, 60, 77, 93, 97, 119, 121, 124, 162, 165
δωτήρ (δοτήρ) 15, 26–27, 36–37, 61–62, 93, 97, 98, 101, 109, 111, 119, 121, 124

ἐγκώμιον 66
ἐκκλησία 136, 156
ἐκκρουσμός 99
ἐκλείπω 15, 21, 23, 35, 37, 77, 92, 119, 121, 124
ἐκληματισμός 99
ἐπιφωνέω 15, 22, 26, 32, 36–37, 45, 47, 58, 77, 93, 97, 101, 111, 114, 119, 121, 124, 126, 146
ἐπουράνιος 15
εὐλογία 60–61
εὐφημέω 20, 39–40, 42
εὐφημία 19, 39–40
εὔφημος 40
εὐφωνότερος 93
εὐχαριστία 48, 60
εὐχή 66
εὔχομαι 54

ἡγεμών 160, 166
ἥλιος 55

Index of Greek Words

ἡσυχία 40, 46, 148
ἦχος (ἠχή) 54
ἠχώ 24
ἠώς (ἀώς) 15, 18, 19, 35, 37–38, 66, 72, 92–93, 98, 102, 104, 109, 113, 115, 124

θέσις 162–63
θεός 15, 16, 26–27, 34–37, 48, 55, 60, 62, 66, 92–93, 95, 97, 101, 109, 119, 121, 124, 155
θυσιαστήριον 57

Ἰησοῦς 155
ἵστημι 41
ἰσχύς 60

κελαδέω 23
κηρύσσω 40
κιθάρα 67
κορυφή 15, 24
κοῦρος 75
κόσμος 15, 16
κράτος 15, 26, 36–37, 58, 60–61, 93, 97, 101, 111, 104, 119, 121, 124
κροῦσις 28
κῦμα 41
λαμπρός 57
λάμπω 21, 121
λατρεία 38
λείβω 24
λεῖμμα 30, 34
λείπω 21
λέξις 28
λόγικος 39, 124
λόγιμος 15, 16, 22, 35, 37–38, 92
λύρος 141

μεγαλειότης 61
μεγαλοπρέπεια 61
μέλπω 15, 16, 66, 153, 155
μεσή 160
μηδέ 10, 15, 19–20, 22, 24, 32, 35, 37, 39, 94, 119, 121, 124
μολπή 67
μόνος 15, 26–27, 36–37, 49, 61, 97–98, 101, 109, 119, 121, 124
μουσική 54

νήνεμος 41–42
νοερός 37–38
νόμος 75
νύξ 15, 18

ὁμοῦ 15, 16, 35, 37, 66, 92, 124, 153, 155
ὀξύς 99
ὅρος 15, 24
οὐρανία 55
οὐράνιος 41
οὐράνος 57

πᾶς 15, 16, 23, 24–26, 34–37, 40, 46, 49, 61–62, 92–95, 97, 102, 111, 114, 119, 121, 124
πατήρ 15, 16, 26, 32, 35, 37, 48–49, 58, 61, 91, 93, 95–96, 104, 117, 119, 121, 124
πεττεία 99, 168
πηγή (παγά) 15, 23, 25, 35, 37, 119, 121, 124
πλοκή 99
πνεῦμα 6, 15, 26, 32, 36–38, 47–49, 58, 93, 95–96, 119, 121, 124
πνοή (πνοιά) 15, 23, 25, 35, 37, 93, 119, 121, 124
ποίημα 66
πόντος 25, 42
προσκύνησις 61, 66
ποταμός 2, 13, 15, 20, 23–26, 32, 35, 37, 93–95, 101–02, 111, 119, 121, 124
προχοή 20, 23, 25–26
πρυτανεῖον 15

ῥιπή 15, 23, 25–26, 35, 37, 93, 119, 121, 124
ῥόθιος 2, 13, 15, 20, 23–26, 32, 35, 37, 93–95, 101, 111, 114, 119, 121, 124

σέβας 61
σελήνη 55
σεραφίμ 57
σημεῖον 28
σιγάω 2, 6, 10, 15, 18–20, 24, 35, 37, 39–40, 42, 45–46, 92, 94–96, 98, 101–02, 104, 111, 114–17, 119, 121, 124, 148–49
σιγή 19, 39

σιωπή 19
σοφία 60
σπονδή 40
σταυρός 155
στιγμή 30, 32, 34
στρατιά 17, 55–56
στρατός 40
σύμφωνος 168
συμφωνία 168
σύστημα 99
σωτήρ 155

τάξις 17
τιμή 48, 60–61
τόνος 28
τονή 168
τράπεζα 57
τρόπος 28

υἱός 15, 26, 35, 37, 48–49, 58, 93, 95, 102, 111, 117, 119, 121, 124
ὑμνέω (see also ἀνυμνέω) 15, 19, 26, 35, 37, 47, 55, 58, 61, 68, 72–75, 93, 95–96, 102, 104, 111, 117, 121, 124, 126, 153
ὕμνος 66–67, 72, 75–77, 122, 153
ὑμνῳδία 56

ὑποκηρύσσω 40
ὑψηλός 15, 24
φαεσφόρος 2, 15, 18, 20, 24, 35, 37–38, 92, 94, 111, 114, 119, 121, 124
φαίνω 46
φθόγγος 85
φιλάνθρωπος 62
φόβος 46

χάζω 22–23
χερουβίμ 57
χλάδω 22–23
χορδή 85
χορεύω 54
χορός 55
Χριστός 155
χρόα (χροιά) 85

ψάλλω 54, 153, 155
ψαλμός 72, 153–54, 156
ψαλμῳδία 152–54
ψαλμῳδός 56
ψαλτῳδός 56

ᾠδή 75, 153
ὠκεανός 15, 24

Studien und Texte zu Antike und Christentum
Studies and Texts in Antiquity and Christianity

Editors:
CHRISTOPH MARKSCHIES (Berlin)
MARTIN WALLRAFF (Basel)
CHRISTIAN WILDBERG (Princeton)

Aland, Barbara / Hahn, Johannes / Ronning, Christian (Ed.): Literarische Konstituierung von Identifikationsfiguren in der Antike. 2003. *Volume 16.*
Albrecht, Michael: see *Hirsch-Luipold, Rainer*
Behrmann, Ingrid: see *Breytenbach, Cilliers*
Betz, Hans Dieter: The „Mithras Liturgy". 2003. *Volume 18.*
Bracht Katharina: Vollkommenheit und Vollendung. 1999. *Volume 2.*
Bremer, Jan Maarten: see *Furley, William D.*
Brent, Allen: Ignatius of Antioch and the Second Sophistic. 2006. *Volume 36.*
Breytenbach, Cilliers / Behrmann, Ingrid (Ed.): Frühchristliches Thessaloniki. 2007. *Volume 44.*
Bumazhnov, Dmitrij: Der Mensch als Gottes Bild im christlichen Ägypten. 2005. *Volume 34.*
– : Visio mystica im Spannungsfeld frühchristlicher Überlieferungen. 2009. *Volume 52.*
– / *Seeliger, Hans Reinhard* (Ed.): Syrien im 1.–7. Jahrhundert nach Christus. 2011. *Volume 62.*
Burgsmüller, Anne: Die Askeseschrift des Pseudo-Basilius. 2005. *Volume 28.*
Cancik, Hubert / Schäfer, Alfred / Spickermann, Wolfgang (Ed.): Zentralität und Religion. 2006. *Volume 39.*
Conring, Barbara: Hieronymus als Briefschreiber. 2001. *Volume 8.*
Cook, John Granger: The Interpretation of the New Testament in Greco-Roman Paganism. 2000. *Volume 3.*
– : The Interpretation of the Old Testament in Greco-Roman Paganism. 2004. *Volume 23.*
Cosgrove, Charles H.: An Ancient Christian Hymn with Musical Notation. 2011. *Volume 65.*
Cristea, Hans-Joachim: Schenute von Atripe: Contra Origenistas. 2010. *Volume 60.*
Dörnemann, Michael: Krankheit und Heilung in der Theologie der frühen Kirchenväter. 2003. *Volume 20.*
Egelhaaf-Gaiser, Ulrike / Schäfer, Alfred (Ed.): Religiöse Vereine in der römischen Antike. 2002. *Volume 13.*
Elliott, Mark W.: The Song of Songs and Christology in the Early Church. 2000. *Volume 7.*
Förster, Hans: Die Anfänge von Weihnachten und Epiphanias. 2007. *Volume 46.*
– : Die Feier der Geburt Christi in der Alten Kirche. 2000. *Volume 4.*
Frateantonio, Christa: Religiöse Autonomie der Stadt im Imperium Romanum. 2003. *Volume 19.*
Furley, William D. / Bremer, Jan Maarten: Greek Hymns I. 2001. *Volume 9.*
– : Greek Hymns II. 2001. *Volume 10.*
Gemeinhardt, Peter: Das lateinische Christentum und die antike pagane Bildung. 2007. *Volume 41.*

Gleede, Benjamin: Platon und Aristoteles in der Kosmologie des Proklos. 2009. *Volume 54.*
Görgemanns, Herwig: see *Hirsch-Luipold, Rainer*
Greschat, Katharina: Die Moralia in Job Gregors des Großen. 2005. *Volume 31.*
Gutsfeld, Andreas / Koch, Dietrich-Alex (Ed.): Vereine, Synagogen und Gemeinden im kaiserzeitlichen Kleinasien. 2006. *Volume 25.*
Hahn, Johannes: see *Aland, Barbara*
Hartmann, Götz: Selbststigmatisierung und Charisma christlicher Heiliger der Spätantike. 2006. *Volume 38.*
Henner, Jutta: Fragmenta Liturgica Coptica. 2000. *Volume 5.*
Henze, Matthias: The Syriac Apocalypse of Daniel. 2001. *Volume 11.*
Heyden, Katharina: Die „Erzählung des Aphroditian". 2009. *Volume 53.*
Hirsch-Luipold, Rainer: Plutarchs Denken in Bildern. 2002. *Volume 14.*
– / Görgemanns, Herwig / Albrecht, Michael von (Hg.): Religiöse Philosophie und philosophische Religion der frühen Kaiserzeit. *Ratio Religionis Studien I.* 2009. *Volume 51.*
Horn, Cornelia / Phenix, Robert R. (Ed.): Children in Late Ancient Christianity. 2009. *Volume 58.*
Die ikonoklastische Synode von Hiereia 754. Einleitung, Text, Übersetzung und Kommentar ihres Horos, besorgt von *Torsten Krannich, Christoph Schubert* und *Claudia Sode,* nebst einem Beitrag zur *Epistula ad Constantiam* des Eusebius von Cäsarea von *Annette von Stockhausen.* 2002. *Volume 15.*
Jenott, Lance: The Gospel of Judas: Coptic Text, Translation, and Historical Interpretation of ‚the Betrayer's Gospel'. 2011. *Volume 64.*
Kany, Roland: Augustins Trinitätsdenken. 2007. *Volume 22.*
Kisić, Rade: Patria Caelestis. 2011. *Volume 61.*
Koch, Dietrich-Alex: see *Gutsfeld, Andreas*
Köckert, Charlotte: Christliche Kosmologie und kaiserzeitliche Philosophie. 2009. *Volume 56.*
Krannich, Torsten: Von Leporius bis zu Leo dem Großen. 2005. *Volume 32.*
– : see *Die ikonoklastische Synode von Hiereia 754.*
Leuenberger-Wenger, Sandra: Ethik und christliche Identität bei Gregor von Nyssa. 2008. *Volume 49.*
Lubomierski, Nina: Die Vita Sinuthii. 2007. *Volume 45.*
Maas, Michael: Exegesis and Empire in the Early Byzantine Mediterranean. 2003. *Volume 17.*
Mastrocinque, Attilio: From Jewish Magic to Gnosticism. 2005. *Volume 24.*
Moschos, Dimitrios: Eschatologie im ägyptischen Mönchtum. 2010. *Volume 59.*
Müller, Andreas: Das Konzept des geistlichen Gehorsams bei Johannes Sinaites. 2006. *Volume 37.*
Müller, Barbara: Führung im Denken und Handeln Gregors des Grossen. 2009. *Volume 57.*
Mutschler, Bernhard: Irenäus als johanneischer Theologe. 2004. *Volume 21.*
Phenix, Robert: Rhetoric and Interpretation in Fifth Century Syriac Literature. 2008. *Volume 50.*
– : see *Horn, Cornelia*
Reutter, Ursula: Damasus, Bischof von Rom (366–384). 2009. *Volume 55.*
Ronning, Christian: Herrscherpanegyrik unter Trajan und Konstantin. 2007. *Volume 42.*
–: see *Aland, Barbara*
Rüpke, Jörg (Ed.): Festrituale in der römischen Kaiserzeit. 2008. *Volume 48.*
–: Gruppenreligionen im römischen Reich. 2007. *Volume 43.*

Studies und Texts in Antiquity and Christianity

Samellas, Antigone: Death in the Eastern Mediterranean (50–600 A.D.). 2002. Volume 12.
Schäfer, Alfred: see *Cancik, Hubert*
–: see *Egelhaaf-Gaiser, Ulrike*
Schulze, Christian: Medizin und Christentum in Spätantike und frühem Mittelalter. 2005. Volume 27.
Schurig, Sebastian: Die Theologie des Kreuzes beim frühen Cyrill von Alexandria. 2005. Volume 29.
Schubert, Christoph: see Die *ikonoklastische Synode von Hiereia 754.*
Seeliger, Hans Reinhard: see *Bumazhnov, Dmitrij*
Sode, Claudia: see Die *ikonoklastische Synode von Hiereia 754.oklastische*
Spickermann, Wolfgang: see *Cancik, Hubert*
Steimle, Christopher: Religion im römischen Thessaloniki. 2008. *Volume 47.*
Stockhausen, Annette von: see Die *ikonoklastische Synode von Hiereia 754.*
Thom, Johan C.: Cleanthes' Hymn to Zeus. 2005. *Volume 33.*
Tiersch, Claudia: Johannes Chrysostomus in Konstantinopel (398–404). 2002. *Volume 6.*
Tloka, Jutta: Griechische Christen – Christliche Griechen. 2005. *Band 30.*
Der Tractatus Tripartus aus Nag Hammadi Codex I (Codex Jung).
    Neu übersetzt von Peter Nagel. 1998. *Volume 1.*
Tuschling, R.M.M.: Angels and Orthodoxy. 2007. *Volume 40.*
Zuntz, Günther: Griechische philosophische Hymnen. 2005. *Volume 35.*

For a complete catalogue please write to the publisher
Mohr Siebeck • P.O. Box 2030 • D–72010 Tübingen/Germany
Up-to-date information on the internet at www.mohr.de